YOUNG ACTIVISTS

GAEL GRAHAM

YOUNG ACTIVISTS

AMERICAN HIGH SCHOOL STUDENTS IN THE

AGE OF PROTEST

FOREWORD BY
TODD GITLIN

NORTHERN

ILLINOIS

UNIVERSITY

PRESS

DeKalb

© 2006 by Northern Illinois University Press

Published by the Northern Illinois University Press, DeKalb, Illinois   60115

Manufactured in the United States using acid-free paper

All Rights Reserved

Design by Julia Fauci

Library of Congress Cataloging-in-Publication Data

Graham, Gael, 1958–

Young activists: american high school students in the age of protest / Gael Graham; foreword by Todd Gitlin.—1st ed.

p. cm.

Includes bibliographical references and index.

ISBN-13: 978-0-87580-351-7 (clothbound: alk. paper)

ISBN-10: 0-87580-351-2 (clothbound: alk. paper)

1. High school students—United States—Political activity. 2. Student movements—United States—History—20th century. 3. Student strikes—United States—History—20th century. I. Title.

LA229.G65 2005

373.1'81'0973—dc22

2005020678

TO MY PARENTS, FOR EVERYTHING.

CONTENTS

FOREWORD

In countries that can afford them, high schools are everywhere, but American high school is a particular promise—and ordeal. Some of the time, Americans believe in universality, and so we graduate more than 85 percent of teenagers, placing us in the top ranks of industrialized nations. (The United States got there first.) High schools incubate the sum of American values: consummate dullness, sweet community, moral learning, moral squalor, intelligence, stupidity, authority earned and unearned. Often they are not sure whether to infantilize their charges or to pander to them. In the end, they do both, because America wants both.

American high schools are America writ small because the country has made a promise of democratic access to all. Actually, that promise is a compound of three promises. There is a promise that, because all are entitled to citizenship, regardless of the vagaries of their positions at birth, all must be educated to do their duty as citizens—and also to avail themselves of their citizenly rights. There is a promise of knowledge and know-how—familiarity with methods and facts that entitle the graduate to partake of the collective inheritance of traditions of reason, history, and a range of skills that are, in turn, useful for self-improvement as well as self-government. There is also a promise of knowledge and experience that are convertible into the currency of upward mobility, or employment at least. The knowledge in question here is trade knowledge, and the experience is not only book learning but also teamwork, discipline, and a certain respect for authority.

In other words, high school is one central place where America's ambitions collide. It collects, channels, and confuses all the energies of the society. It is a place of meritocracy and a place of libido. It is a place for finding oneself and a place for losing oneself. It is a place of sobriety and a place of consumerism. It is a place of intellect—budding intellect, anyway—and a place of consummate anti-intellectualism. In these ways and others, it is a place where the larger society's choices about what is worth investing in and what is worth knowing work themselves out concretely for better and worse.

It is no surprise, then, that in the late 1960s and early 1970s American high schools found themselves caught in eddies of conflict. Much of their authority was arbitrary, and administrators were taken aback that anyone should think to object. Energies were coming unstuck, and every attempt to bottle them up only made the energies fiercer. Every value fought over in the larger society—all the rebellions and counter-rebellions—poured into these institutions, which suddenly seemed to have been designed to thwart precisely the energies that now turned against the institutions themselves. The rules of high school itself came under fire—dress codes, appearance rules, censorship, curriculum, discipline. Race, war, sex, and customs all became inflammable materials. Because America prided itself on the energies of the young without making a valued place for those energies, the wider revolts were primarily youth revolts. Once the older brothers, sisters, cousins, friends, and heroes of high school students had been aroused, how could the schools themselves have been exempted from the larger currents?

The questions that high school rebels raised again and again, in a thousand arenas and styles, came down to questions of the rights and limits of authority. Students asked, Whose school is this? as others asked, Whose country is it and who decides? These are perennial questions deep in the American grain, going back to the Puritan emigration, the slave revolts, and the American Revolution itself. Sometimes these questions go into abeyance, and sometimes they erupt. The 1960s were a series of eruptions, and it is to the credit of America's larger traditions that they produced as much constructive reform as they did—reform that even now has not been repealed.

One of the merits of Gael Graham's thorough, lucid book is to make plain just how various and complicated were America's high school upheavals. There were revolts about hair length and skirt length. There were revolts against censorship in the name of the First Amendment. There were even objections to the ways in which schools "track" students into distinctive social class layers. The most intractable collisions, not surprisingly, had to do with the unending wounds of race and racism. Fewer uprisings, she points out, had to do with the national convulsions over the Vietnam War, women's rights, and national politics generally than with race and rules of decorum.

Rules in general lost credibility partly because the rules of race were being torn asunder in the society at large. If the rules of race—that is, the rules and laws of segregation—were being challenged, and immense pent-up democratic energies were being unleashed, what rules could not be questioned and what subterranean streams could not surface? Eventually— to overgeneralize—the clamor was for the great democratic ideals of freedom and participation. Such clamors are always untidy. Diffuse hungers, not always capable of satisfaction, assert their claims. A certain wildness blows through institutions that become stodgy and complacent, and fail to justify the demands they make on their constituents for obedience and order. But it was not an easy time even to be a just authority. Just authorities too like their authority.

The high school student movements, as Graham writes, were galvanized by grievances but confused about what, if they had their way, would replace the authority of the authorities. Such confusion extended beyond the high schools. Overall, the sixties movements were unsure about the limits of their claims. Repelled by injustices, they were not sure how to rise beyond rebellion. What power should they demand, and for which purposes? Sometimes a haze of vague demands ran into a surge of reactive bluster. Authorities did not see why they should have to justify themselves at all, while advertisers and politicians alike encouraged the collective hunger of a generation: they wanted it all, and they wanted it now. The movements' leadership often carried the burden of utopian longings for which they barely had names, let alone practical schemes. In facing demands for student rights in particular, as Graham says, the authorities were caught amid large confusions as to the meaning and prerogatives of childhood. These confusions persist.

Graham's account astutely pays attention to the variety of responses— their range and ambiguities—that the revolts evoked from school administrators and other authorities. Fortunately, the reformers learned to improvise. Over time, police crackdowns became less popular and reasonable reforms more prevalent. The result is a legacy of student rights that, for all the entanglements and inadequacies they sometimes entail, remain a contribution to America's democratic culture. We are a better country for these revolts. In her subtle appreciation of the upheaval and its consequences, Gael Graham fills a hole in our understanding of a tumultuous time whose tumult is still reverberating.

—Todd Gitlin, Columbia University

ACKNOWLEDGMENTS

I am grateful to the many people who have helped make this book possible. To all of you who responded to my letter asking for memories, I enjoyed our brief correspondences and hope this book answers the need that several of you mentioned for your historical experience to be recognized. I apologize if, in the retelling, any of your stories were distorted. My colleague and friend Scott Philyaw encouraged me to think that I had a real topic and helped me hone my arguments and sharpen my writing. Dr. William Tuttle graciously responded to my inquiries about how to get started with this kind of research and shared his list of newspapers. I appreciate the newspaper editors who published my letters. A special thanks to Sue O'Brien of the *Denver Post*, who turned my letter and some of the responses into a feature article. Jennifer Mc-Kee, a student and a friend, contributed her memories and her enthusiasm for the project and helped look over an early draft. Graduate students Nancy Furry, Heather Murray, Guillermo Cervantes, Heather Cyre, and Susan Moody gave invaluable assistance. The Graduate School at Western Carolina University provided financial support for my mailings, and friends and colleagues gave me encouragement and advice. The Western Carolina History Colloquium provided a supportive atmosphere in which to try out ideas. Members of the staff at Hunter Library were very helpful in tracking down obscure bits of information and hard-to-find publications. A special thanks to Melody Herr and the editors at Northern Illinois University Press. I thank my father for his legal expertise and both of my parents for listening to me sort through various issues as the book took shape. Finally, I thank my daughters, Rose-Helen and Kendra, for daily asking, "Did you do research today?" and for cheering when I said yes.

YOUNG ACTIVISTS

INTRODUCTION

THE DIVERSE ORIGINS OF STUDENT ACTIVISM AND DISSENT

When President Richard Nixon announced in May 1970 that he had sent American troops into Cambodia, a storm of protest erupted in the United States. More than a million students boycotted classes, and hastily planned rallies were held in a number of cities. One hundred thousand marchers converged on Washington, D.C. Protests at Kent State and Jackson State Universities left six students dead, fueling still more protests. Less dramatically but no less passionately, a sixth-grade girl in Los Angeles desecrated an American flag. Unlike the other public protests, no one witnessed her ceremony of grief, rage, and disillusionment. She had bought the flag with her allowance, and for three years had flown it proudly on every patriotic holiday. Now, heartsick over Nixon's expansion of the Vietnam War, she took scissors, cut it to bits, and threw the scraps away. Burning the flag would have been more satisfying, but, because she was only twelve, her parents strictly forbade her to play with matches.[1]

I was that girl. My path from flag-flying patriot to bitter critic of the government's foreign policy was hardly unique. Indeed, much of the anti-American rhetoric that characterized young, radical Americans in the late 1960s stemmed more from their outraged love of country and the belief that some of its fundamental ideals were being violated than from a desire to grab the limelight or shock their elders. Inflammatory politics divided Americans in the 1960s and early 1970s. For every person like me, who rejected Nixon's policy of broadening a war he had promised to end, others were infuriated by antiwar protests and believed that citizens ought to support the president. This anecdote illustrates the extreme volatility of political and cultural life in that era; even children took sides, and symbolic acts like destroying American flags, flying Viet Cong, Black Power, or Confederate flags, growing long hair, flashing a "peace sign," or raising a clenched fist plainly showed one's position. Friendships foundered if classmates held opposing views. As a fourth-grader, I knew how all my friends' parents voted in the 1968 presidential election and felt deeply invested in the outcome. In 1968, too, my elementary school, Westwood School, in Los Angeles, was "integrated" by a solitary black boy in my grade, which evoked much earnest discussion among ten-year-olds on the playground. During the same school year when I cut up my flag, I petitioned my principal to permit girls to wear pants to school. In junior high (1970–1973), I wore a black armband on several occasions for reasons I can no longer recall and furtively read copies of the *Red Tide,* an underground newspaper published by students at neighboring University High School. Being caught with an underground paper meant automatic suspension, but it was worth the risk to read articles on such sexy and taboo topics as abortion, the Viet Cong, and communism. At a slumber party in 1972, rather than holding a séance or freezing each other's bras, my friends and I spent the night drafting a letter to President Nixon, asking him to end the war in Vietnam.

Several years ago, I recalled the precocious political awareness of elementary and junior high school children in that era and began to wonder how much more awareness and activism there might have been in American high schools. College and university activism is well known, but what of the slightly younger high school crowd? The civil rights movement and desegregation affected some colleges, but far more high school students confronted mandatory integration. How did black and white students respond? What impact did the appearance of black students have on classes, extracurricular events, and social life? Similarly, although a minority of college students—themselves relatively buffered from the threat of the draft—opposed the Vietnam War, what were the attitudes on high school campuses? College men, by remaining in school where student deferments sheltered them, had already "voted" on the war; they might support it rhetorically, but they simultaneously evaded or at least deferred its claims on them. High school boys, in contrast, had yet to decide where they stood. How important was the war in their lives? Did they experience conflicts between duty and conscience? Was the war much discussed in classrooms, halls, and locker rooms? Finally, while college students resented the in loco parentis stance of university officials and for the most part successfully shook it off, how did high school students react to the reality of parental control and more stringent limits on their liberties imposed by school authorities? Did the antiauthoritarian strains of the era extend to their level?

For the last question, the answer was unambiguously yes. Student activism, although forgotten or minimized today, seriously disrupted many American high schools. Beginning somewhat later than college activism, high school activism peaked between 1968 and 1973, when the college movement was already ebbing. One widely cited 1969 survey published by the National Association of Secondary School Principals reported unrest in 59 percent of responding high schools and 56 percent of junior high schools. More astonishingly, more than half of the rural schools had experienced disruptions. The House Subcommittee on General Education conducted a national survey of all twenty-nine thousand public and private schools in 1968, finding disturbances in 18 percent; the following year, the number soared to 40 percent. Researchers emphasized that they tabulated instances of significant, disruptive, and collective student action, not individual disciplinary problems. Because there were many more high schools than there were colleges and universities, these findings indicate a startling degree of turbulence. In addition to general unrest, more than two dozen schools reported bombings and attempted bombings in 1969 alone. These figures may appear exaggerated, but in fact they probably underestimate the actual degree of disruption, because researchers typically either polled school officials, many of whom did not respond or downplayed events at their school, or counted newspaper stories about high school unrest. Nor is it always clear what was being counted. The terms "unrest" and "protest" suggest both mindless mayhem and purposeful student actions: both are accurate. Some schools essentially experienced race riots—violence devoid of specific political content other than racial hatred. In other cases, student disruptions aimed at obtaining well-articulated demands.[2]

Confirming the widespread occurrence of high school activism and dissidence raises a number of questions. What caused these students to protest? What forms did their activism take? Did they merely mimic college activists? How did school officials, parents, local communities, and government respond to high school dissent?

Every issue that concerned college students engaged some high school students as well. Racial integration, for example, was particularly divisive. School districts and local administrators mandated desegregation, often under compulsion from federal courts, but those in the schools, including students, carried it out and contested the nitty-gritty details. Black, Latino, and white students jostled each other in the halls, bathrooms, and cafeterias, and they fought bitterly over ownership of and access to social space at dances, athletic events, pep rallies, and student clubs. Seemingly trivial issues such as the selection of cheerleaders or homecoming court members sparked furious explosions because many whites believed that compulsory integration required only chilly toleration of the newcomers' presence; they did not intend to incorporate minority students into the fabric of school life, let alone reweave that fabric into a new pattern. But as Black and Brown Power ideologies surged into public high schools in the late

1960s, students of color seized the initiative, hacking out their own racialized spaces through demands for representation among teachers and administrators, a restructured curricula that would celebrate their history and culture, and even the spice of their own food in the cafeteria. Taking to the streets, both Latino and African-American students counted on the support of older community members in their battles with white students and officials. Ironically, many whites objected to separatist school organizations although they had not previously protested all-white school activities or clubs.

If protests against dress codes caused less violence than race relations, they did outnumber racial confrontations. Regulations about hair length and style for boys, skirt length or pants for girls, shirts tucked in or pulled out, armbands, and political buttons prompted fiery debates in schools and communities. Students were by no means united in opposing dress and hair codes. Some student councils drew up codes that embodied the official view that neat attire promoted good attitudes, academic achievement, and school pride. Other students, particularly athletes, acted as unofficial enforcers for dress codes, especially strictures against long hair for boys. Although some students resisted dress codes as individuals or sued their schools, others protested collectively. Punishments for dress code violations and principals' vetoes of more lenient codes passed by student councils in turn led to new debates about student power and the effectiveness of student governance.

Similarly, the blossoming of unofficial underground newspapers and battles over censorship of school newspapers raised questions about the rights of high school students. Here, too, surprising numbers of students filed lawsuits, in a period when the courts vigilantly protected and expanded First Amendment rights. For other students, disputes over both fashions and substantive rights exposed the arbitrary power of school officials and the powerlessness of students. This insight propelled them to wage war over more fundamental issues such as the proper relationship between students and educators, and many students demanded that officials accept them as partners in education.

Those who attacked the status quo in the 1960s did not propose novelty for its own sake; in most cases, they called attention to the gap between rhetoric and reality. African-Americans and Latinos exposed white hypocrisy in publicly affirming a creed of equality while maintaining racial apartheid and discrimination; the Kinsey report showed how little official morality meant behind closed doors, and antiwar protesters emphasized both how poorly the term "free Vietnam" fit the unpopular, repressive government of the South and how the American manner of waging war undercut the values the war was intended to protect. Similarly, high school students perceived multiple divergences between rhetoric and reality, both in society and within the high schools themselves. Some argued, in fact, that the flaws in American society were the flaws in its high schools writ large.

Beyond questioning the status quo and exposing some of the lies Americans told themselves, activists in the 1960s—including high school students—challenged public and private authorities. Although adolescents typically challenge authority, this is usually fought out between individual youths and the authorities in their lives. What is noteworthy in the 1960s is that high school students organized, laid out their reasons for opposing the rules that bound them, using both the language of rights and revolution, and suggested alternative ways of running schools and society. Most collective efforts centered on a single high school, but students in a number of cities created citywide high school student organizations, and several groups attempted (briefly) to create a national high school news network in the late 1960s.

As was the case with many other groups in the 1960s, the term "participation" sums up the overarching demand of activist high school students in this era. African-American and other minority students wanted to participate fully in school and society; they also wanted their contributions and heritage recognized and valued. Even when they rejected participation in white-dominated school and society, they demanded the right to create alternative spaces of their own. Participation also meant having a hand in running the schools. Most student activists of all races accepted the necessity of formal education. They were not seeking to outlaw school itself, but they objected to the absence of any student voice in determining what they should learn, how they should learn it, what rules they should follow, and what consequences there should be for failure to comply.

When high school students analyzed their schools in terms of power relations, they often perceived links between high school politics and the wider society. These students wanted debates about the war in Vietnam, civil rights, Black Power, dissident politics, and, to a lesser extent, feminism and environmentalism brought into the schools, both in the classroom and through outside speakers and student clubs. Although they often couched their demands in terms of balancing the conservative agendas of school officials, these students were unambiguously and self-consciously left wing, calling themselves "liberals" or "radicals."

Just as many southern whites believed that "their Negroes" had been content under Jim Crow law before civil rights "outsiders" came to town, many adults insisted that without outside agitation high school activism would not have developed. The temper of the times greatly influenced high school activists, providing them with a language to speak, methods to borrow, and evidence that agitation worked. In these ways, we can see that high school activism did not occur in a historical vacuum, for all of the social and political movements of the era fed each other, contributing to the heady sense of possibility that many activists felt.

The influence of college activism is more difficult to gauge. Extensive media coverage guaranteed that most high school students knew about events taking place on the campuses. Some doubtless had friends or siblings in college. Moreover, beginning in 1969 the best-known college activist group, Students for a Democratic Society (SDS), actively recruited high school students and established a number of high school SDS chapters. But as SDS degenerated into the Weather Underground in the late 1960s, plans to re-cruit younger students as revolutionaries came to naught. The latter re-sented college students trying to tell them what to do and rebuffed organiz-ers who seemed out of touch with their needs.

High school activists did resemble college activists in some ways: they were a minority, they were among the brightest and most articulate stu-dents, they tended to share rather than oppose the political beliefs of their parents, whose support they generally enjoyed, and most—though not all—tried working first through "proper channels." Other students were not activists in any sustained sense but could be mobilized to protest specific, usually local, grievances. This latter group cut across student types in terms of race, class, and academic achievement.[3]

Despite their similarities, high school student activists were neither pawns nor mere imitators of older dissidents. They generally maintained their distance from college activists. Moreover, activists were often awak-ened in high school, contradicting the belief that influence flowed from older to younger students. In one attempt to predict future college unrest, three professors polled incoming college freshmen from 1966 to 1969 and tracked those who had participated in high school protests. They found that in 1969, as part of a rising curve, about 12 percent had protested U.S. military policy, 20 percent had demanded changes in race relations, and more than 45 percent had challenged high school rules. But researchers ig-nored the implications of this for *high schools,* concentrating instead on how many of these students might become protesters in *college.* Here is a clear instance of high school students potentially bringing their activism to college, rather than the dynamic working the other way.[4] Similarly, one teacher revealed in a 1983 interview that her activism originated during her high school days in the 1960s, when she had lobbied Congress to support school desegregation. After she started college, she found it a "very easy transition" to organize full-time for SDS.[5]

School and government officials and educational experts disagreed on how to handle high school unrest. Many school officials treated dissident students as discipline problems, whereas outside authorities—who did not have to deal with these students on a daily basis—counseled concessions to student demands. Even when these experts advised against concessions, they proposed the creation of a mechanism through which students could express their grievances. While some high school principals and school board mem-bers drew up plans calling for police intervention, professional educational journals recommended setting up student advisory groups and appointing ombudsmen to keep open communications between students and the admin-istration. Educational experts also supported demands for a more up-to-date curriculum, more choice of electives, and greater variety in teaching methods.

High school dissidence in the late 1960s and early 1970s was thus a widespread, highly visible, and much-discussed problem. Adults even feared that it might ultimately prove more disruptive than college demonstrations. At the beginning of the 1970–1971 school year, for example, the superintendent of schools in El Paso, Texas, dramatically warned officials to brace themselves for more "student strikes and demonstrations than ever before in history."[6]

The 1960s, in both popular memory and documented history, were years of trials and painful change for many Americans. By mid-decade, no traditional authority stood unshaken; tremblors and devastating shifts occurred along every major fault line in American society. Race relations, gender roles, and sexual mores underwent fundamental changes. Concepts of citizenship, authority, and freedom in a national-security state were—at least briefly—unsettled. In this context—and in the midst of political assassinations, the impending failure of American policy in Vietnam, and the rage and violence (both rhetorical and real) emanating from numerous groups within the United States, it would be surprising if at least some high school students had not taken notice. The degree to which these students influenced events, as opposed to merely reacting to them, is impossible to gauge. Youthful courage or bravado may inspire adults to take actions they otherwise might not take. We know that a number of government officials' children opposed the policies their parents promulgated. Perhaps these parents simply dismissed their children's ideas, but some may have listened and acted differently because of what they heard.[7]

Historians are just now beginning to investigate childhood as a phenomenon that is both a biological life stage and a socially constructed category. As a social construct, childhood is historically specific and takes different shapes in varying times, places, and cultures. Only in the early twentieth century, for example, were the teen years marked as a special subset of childhood, and strenuous efforts made to segregate teenagers from both younger children and the adult world. In this book, I examine the consequences of age segregation in public high schools during an era of extraordinarily rapid social change. I argue that the internal workings of the high schools, in conjunction with external social movements and improved communications, created the conditions under which teenagers could critically examine their own place in society. Although they had not been consulted about the laws and customs that defined their status, high school students now demanded the right to be heard. Their activism constituted an unprecedented and self-conscious effort to redefine their status and roles. Few sought full adulthood, but at the least they wanted to shed some of the limitations of childhood and gain greater control over their lives.

This was, then, a rights revolution, not that different—at least on the surface—from other rights revolutions simultaneously under way. The high school rights movement was national in scope, although not centrally organized. It was weaker in small-town and rural America than it was in urban and suburban areas, and weaker in southern and southwestern states. Because media coverage focused on college activism, fewer high school students knew about their peers' dissent in the rest of the country. These limitations notwithstanding, perceiving themselves as a social group whose rights had been violated enabled high school students to forge a collective identity and work together—locally rather than nationally—to achieve their goals. Ultimately, they succeeded in expanding their rights and in persuading adults to listen to their views. Many schools did enact changes to accommodate students' demands.

The rights revolution, however, represented only one part of the high school experience in the 1960s and early 1970s. What their common identity as students knit together often came unraveled as students embraced other, conflicting identities along the axes of race, ideology, and lifestyle. Psychologists assert that identity formation is the principal task of adolescents, but teenagers in the 1960s found this complicated. For one thing, by the late 1960s the postwar narrative of nationhood was fraying, replaced ultimately by multiple narratives from different perspectives. Out of this babel of voices, how were young Americans to create a stable identity? At the same time that identity fragmented in the larger society, it also became increasingly politicized. Every choice came burdened with immediate consequences for high school students, defining one's circle of friends, relationships with school officials, and connections to society as a whole.

Thus, the rights and identity revolutions undercut each other within the high schools. Insofar as students identified themselves as blacks or radicals, they found allies outside the schools even as they simultaneously cut ties within. When they highlighted their status as students they built a united front and articulated a common program, but one that outsiders often deemed trivial. Questions the nation asked itself reverberated in its high schools: How can a commitment to equality be squared with (racial, ethnic, gender) difference? What are the responsibilities of the group toward the individual, and the individual toward the group? What are the merits of unity versus pluralism?

Americans answered none of these questions definitively in the 1960s and 1970s, but they did agree on the urgency of addressing them—for adults. Ascribing status based on gender, race, or ethnicity mattered, because most people assumed that these categories were both immutable and relatively straightforward—that is, we can tell who belongs in which group. Age-based status, on the other hand, appeared less urgent because it changed from day to day. If high school students lacked certain rights, in a few years they would gain them, so why fuss about it? Their status was temporary; their role was to prepare themselves for adult lives; they should enjoy their freedom from real responsibilities without seeking premature adulthood. Paradoxically, a burgeoning youth culture valorized youthfulness as a time of sexual power, consumption, and pleasure just as some youths hungered for something more.

In challenging their status as children, high school students assaulted a social boundary that appeared entirely natural to adults. But they did not seek to have that line eradicated, for most students conceded to adults a status separate from and superior to their own. What they wanted was a greater voice in determining where and how that line would be drawn. Activist students implicitly understood that setting adulthood at age twenty-one or eighteen was an arbitrary social fiction, but they never could articulate a compelling argument for lowering it to sixteen or twelve or eight and a half. What they lacked, in essence, was a coherent critique of childhood as a social category. Where other activists succeeded in defining race and gender as "suspect categories," childhood remained a salient classification. Where other rights movements triumphed nationally, high school activists, with some notable exceptions, by and large won local and piecemeal victories.

This is not to suggest that the high school movements emerged and then vanished, like so much foam atop the more significant waves of the times. On the contrary, public high schools on the whole became more democratic, more sensitive to racial and ethnic differences, more open to divergent viewpoints, and more sensitive to students' needs. High school students of the 1960s established themselves as legal citizens, albeit junior citizens, with rights that school officials could not abridge. In so doing, they laid down tracks that today's students still follow. They also challenged the purposes and content of education, forcing a dialogue about both.

Organized topically rather than chronologically, this book begins with a the historical background, so that readers will understand the educational, social, and demographic trends that shaped the high schools in the 1960s. The next two chapters focus on race and race relations, the most explosive issue of the era, particularly in schools that transformed from predominately white to predominately black, as whites fled integrated neighborhoods and schools. Disruptions, however, occurred even in schools where no more than 10 percent of the students were black, if this percentage reflected an altered racial composition. The second chapter discusses integration, and the third black student activism and the Black and Brown Power movements. In these chapters, I look at how black, Latino, and white students acted to create racialized identities.

The two chapters that follow concern students' rights and student power. "Students' rights" refers to the efforts to clarify which constitutional rights applied to high school students. Many claimed First Amendment rights in the matters of speech, writing, assembly, and dress or hairstyles. The majority of activists focused on these issues, because they had the most direct bearing on their lives and because these issues proved less divisive than others, since all students—black and white, moderate and radical—were subject to the same rules and restrictions. Adults outside the schools also often supported students' rights. It is worth noting that the "outside agitator" with the greatest impact on high school activism was not SDS but the American Civil Liberties Union (ACLU) and its state chapters and that it was often *students* or their parents who contacted the ACLU, not the other way around.

Student power is closely linked to student rights; however, although students argued that their rights derived from their citizenship, the student power movement edged into somewhat different territory. Here students spoke less as citizens of the American nation than as coequal partners in education. They demanded a voice in shaping the curriculum, establishing and enforcing school rules, evaluating their teachers, and even playing a role in the hiring and firing of school personnel.

The last chapter on activism explores issues that engaged the smallest numbers of high school students: national politics, the Vietnam War, and the feminist movement. It would seem logical that the draft, at least, would have greatly concerned high school boys, but available evidence does not support this contention. Although the Vietnam War was often central to those students who called themselves "radicals" or "revolutionaries," to many others the war was off the edge of their personal radar screens. Unless the war truly came home to them in the form of a body bag with a friend inside, most high school students found the war impossibly remote. Young men thus faced the draft alone. The students who did oppose the war were the most likely to reach out to SDS or college activists for help or advice.

The book's final chapter probes the adult response to high school unrest. School administrators, school boards and trustees, university-based experts, government officials, judges, and social commentators all offered ideas about what the disturbances meant and how they should be handled. These individuals were generally split into "hawks" (to use the contemporary categorization for one's stance on the Vietnam War), who took a hard-line, call-the-cops, expel-them-all approach, and "doves," who sympathized with many of the students' complaints and recommended accommodation to student demands.

This book emphasizes student political activism, leaving out those elements of the counterculture—sex, drugs, rock music—that did not enter into this activism. I focus primarily on student activists on the left, simply because conservative high school students left much less of a historical record. White high school students who opposed desegregation, for example, tended to operate in mobs rather than through organized groups. Even when they did form groups, the members were often nameless or worked in the dark, like SPONGE (the Society for the Prevention of Niggers Getting Everything), a possibly fictional entity that made a brief but disruptive appearance at Cubberly High School in Palo Alto, California. Despite their names, organizations like Young Americans for Freedom or Young Republicans have not shown up on high school campuses in my research. One writer for the *New York Times* claimed that high school Democrat, Republican, and conservative groups were just as active as the more radical minority. If this was true, they did not rock the boat enough to leave a traceable wake.[8] Students who opposed the activism of those on the left apparently did so in random and episodic ways; they were usually not organized. Only a few of the people who contacted me to relate their high school memories were conservative, and they were not activists. Whereas today the term "activist" applies both to those on the left and right, in the high schools of the late 1960s and early 1970s, the activists were nearly all on the left.[9]

Most of my source material comes from contemporary commentators, who confirm the left leanings of high school activists. Professional journals such as the *High School Journal, American Education, Senior Scholastic, Phi Delta Kappan, School and Society, School Management, Nation's Schools,* and *School Review* have been invaluable for giving the administrators' and educators' points of view, as have the dozens of books written in the late 1960s and early 1970s about American schools. Popular magazines and national newspapers show both the concern and condescension with which most Americans regarded high school activism.

It has been more difficult to recapture the voices of the students themselves, but some of the journals interviewed students or permitted them to submit articles. Two young teachers, Marc Libarle and Tom Seligson, took sabbaticals and interviewed a half dozen self-proclaimed "high school revolutionaries" in 1969–1970. John Birmingham, editor of a high school underground newspaper, wrote a book about the underground scene and included articles from a number of high school undergrounds, as did journalist Diane Divoky. Similarly, antiwar activist Mitchell Goodman's massive tome on the counterculture contains a good chunk of high school material in the writings and cartoons that he amassed in 1970. Finally, some court decisions provide a window into student (and school official) thinking and attitudes.[10]

In another effort to hear from the students themselves, in the fall of 1999 and spring of 2000, I wrote to editors of more than 250 large daily newspapers, some of the largest weekly newspapers, and a number of African-American and Hispanic publications. I described my research and asked readers who were high school teachers or students between 1965 and 1973 to contact me if they had memories to share. I asked no specific questions, preferring to let respondents choose their own stories. Sometimes I suggested subjects I was interested in and often asked follow-up questions. I received more than a hundred replies. The majority of respondents were liberal, left-wing, or not activists while in high school, and only about ten identified themselves as nonwhite. Men and women were fairly evenly represented, and urban respondents outnumbered those from rural areas or small towns. Most people e-mailed their responses to me, and in several cases we engaged in a back-and-forth dialogue for a week or more.

This raises some interesting methodological questions. What kind of research is this? My initial letter was not a survey, questionnaire, or interview, nor did the responses fit into any of these categories. An e-mail message is more immediate and may be less polished than a letter, but it is not as spontaneous as a conversation. Can we consider this "oral history?" If we define oral history broadly as [hi]stories gathered from still-living historical actors, then my research falls within that category. But in an oral interview, the researcher can observe the body language, facial expression, and intonation of the speaker, all of which can be considered part of the communication process. Oral history, which some historians further refine as "aural history," is based on hearing (and seeing, if an interview is conducted in person). An e-mail communication is in some ways closer to a letter than an oral conversation, but the swiftness of the delivery means that, instead of having a week or so to wait for a reply, I sometimes heard back from respondents within twenty-four hours; in some cases, a reply to one of my queries arrived almost instantly. Clearly, the respondent was sitting at his or her computer screen while I was sitting at mine. Moreover, judging by the number of typographical errors in these e-mails as a whole, it is obvious that many respondents dashed off a reply to my query as fast as their fingers could hit the keys and did not recheck or correct what they had written. Rather than resort to the academic condescension of indicating "[*sic*]," I have in most cases simply corrected these typographical errors.

In addition to the peculiarities of communication and interpretation, evidentiary questions emerge. How do I know that writers of these e-mails or letters are who they say they are or had the experiences they claim to have had? My respondents are attempting to recall the events of thirty years ago. Can we rely upon their memories? All historians must face problems of sources and reliability. I found my respondents credible because the stories they shared are corroborated in other sources. This research has uncovered *patterns* of events and attitudes that were common among diverse high schools in diverse settings in the late 1960s and early 1970s. These patterns form the core of my study. Some respondents have been candid about their inability to remember certain details and their uncertainty about the accuracy of their memories. Sharon Bialy-Fox, who attended Glen Cove High School, on Long Island, forwarded to me an e-mail discussion among several members of her high school class, and several of them commented on not remembering certain events until others jogged their memory. One of them thanked the others for validating her memory: "I was beginning to wonder if I was having flashbacks." Most of my readers have graciously allowed themselves to be named and quoted. I have used pseudonyms (and denoted them by using quotation marks) for the few respondents who asked not to be identified.[11]

I have attempted to include as many of the stories my respondents shared as I could reasonably squeeze in. I hope that by telling the story of high school youths in the 1960s those who lived through those days may see their experiences in a broader perspective. Looking at these students gives us a deeper, richer view of the 1960s, and, I hope, may help us to regard young people as active participants in history. In their struggles over rights and identity, they left their mark on public high schools, leaving a different institution to those who came later. Students from the 1960s, like all of us, are shaped by history even as they help to shape it. I hope this book may also shed light on the people who in some ways lived in the shadow of their now-famous college cousins; both groups are now parents, adults, and authorities whose perspectives on the world were often molded in their adolescence in the 1960s.

ONE—THE CHANGING WORLD OF THE

AMERICAN HIGH SCHOOL STUDENT

With ambitions of someday becoming a journalist, Bob Greene kept a diary during the last half of his junior year and first half of his senior year in high school, from January to December 1964. Many of his diary entries center on typically adolescent concerns: struggles with his parents over autonomy, worries about his social life, and dreams of having sex. But, in other ways, his diary places him firmly in historical time and reveals how some current issues touched him but others remained remote. Strictly speaking, the 1960s were nearly half over, yet Greene and his friends can be characterized as one of the last cohorts from the 1950s. He not only paints a vivid portrait of high school life in the waning era of the 1950s, but also provides glimpses of the political and cultural struggles soon to erupt in American high schools.

National politics barely touched Bob Greene. He did not discuss the election of 1964, Lyndon Johnson, or the early stages of the war in Vietnam. He did mention the passage of the Civil Rights Act of 1964 and wrote a column for his school newspaper on the anniversary of John Kennedy's death, but otherwise his concerns were extremely parochial.[1]

Not surprisingly, as a resident of Bexley, a white suburb of Columbus, Ohio, Bob Greene demonstrated shallow interest in or awareness of racial matters. In February 1964, he declared his amazement when Cassius

Clay (later Muhammad Ali) beat Sonny Liston, but he did not elaborate on why he found this so astonishing. Later that year, out of the blue, he reported that his fraternity planned to devote an entire meeting to civil rights. Greene invited a local civil rights leader to speak to the group, but when the man forgot the appointment, Greene dropped the subject. Later that month, when Greene and his friend Jack drove Jack's family's maid Carrie home to a black neighborhood of Columbus, Greene wondered "what they must think—spending their days in nice suburban houses, and going back to their own places at night. In Carrie's case," he mused, "I don't have a hint. She just doesn't seem to be much of a talker." That Carrie's silence might have reflected caution in the presence of two young white men rather than a character trait did not occur to him.[2]

During the summer of 1964, when he worked at a local newspaper, Greene pondered a different type of incident. As his diary describes it, one day when he entered the composing room with Doris, the copygirl, "[a]s soon as we got into the room, all of the printers and linotype operators starting screaming and howling. At first I didn't understand what was going on, but then I figured it out: They were doing it to Doris." When he asked Doris what it meant, she matter-of-factly told him: "It's just how they act around women" and stated that she simply ignored it. Greene made no further comment, but he clearly found the behavior of the other men baffling.[3]

When Greene wrote about life in his high school, his diary makes visible some emerging cultural clashes. He observed that his father seemed to like the Beatles when they appeared on the Ed Sullivan show in February, even though his father had "hated the sight" of Elvis Presley. But when Greene attempted to let his hair grow into a "Beatle haircut," long enough to touch his collar, both his father and his school principal insisted that he cut it. Greene moaned, "That kills me," and swore he would never get his hair cut again, but throughout the year he never openly defied the adult authorities who repeatedly dictated his hair length. The principal even grabbed the shirt of one of his friends and summarily ordered him to get a haircut. In October, Greene tried to convince the principal that black or white Levi's were not the same as "blue jeans," to no avail. In December, he manage to convince the principal to let him wear "Wellington boots," with rounded toes and no heels, on the grounds that they were not "Beatle boots." But the principal had the last word: "Get a haircut." Greene and his peers argued and delayed, but always backed down in the end.[4]

Bob Greene's world was bounded by school, family, social life, and summer jobs. He chafed under some of its constraints and questioned some of its injustices. His diary provides evidence of underlying tensions in race and gender relations and suggests where adult authority pinched teenagers the most. Greene's acceptance of the world as he found it contrasts sharply not only with the critiques voiced by other high school students just a few years later, but also with their optimism about the possibility of change and their passion and energy to carry out these changes. Other students echoed

Greene's complacency. Ellen Skultin Gillenwater graduated from high school in Cambridge, Ohio, in 1967, shortly before high school unrest became a visible national phenomenon. She explains, "To me, getting my homework done, enjoying friends and matching angora yarn (for my boyfriend's class ring to be wrapped in) to the next day's outfit was as heavy as my thoughts ever got." After his ten-year high school reunion in 1970, reporter Steven Roberts affirmed Gillenwater's comments, recalling his high school days in the late 1950s as "marvelously uncomplicated." Minority cultures of dissent existed both in the wider society and in high schools, but students like Greene, Gillenwater, and Roberts predominated. Unrest would soon ripple through American high schools, however, bringing to the surface much of the subterranean rebellion of the 1950s and ending the passivity of many students. In 1964, high schools unknowingly rested on a historical fulcrum, a moment of suspenseful equilibrium before the wider society slowly, but with gathering momentum, tilted. A number of cultural, political, and demographic pressures had been inexorably building. Under their combined weight, American society bulged, distorted, and ultimately cracked open. In many ways, public high schools bore the brunt of these pressures. To understand why this was so, we must look further back in time.[5]

MANDATORY EDUCATION

Perhaps the greatest change in American high schools since the turn of the century was the number and socioeconomic class of students. Whereas in 1900 mostly white youths whose families did not need them to work attended high school, by 1960 it had become well-nigh universal for American adolescents of all races and classes. From the late nineteenth century through World War I, Progressive reformers persuaded a number of states to pass laws mandating compulsory education, usually until age sixteen. Still, in 1930, only about half of working-class youths attended high school.[6]

During the Great Depression, some hoped that compulsory education would keep young people out of the job market so they would not compete with adults for the few available jobs. A million boys and 750,000 girls of high school age wanted or needed jobs and could not find them in the 1930s. New Deal legislation did provide jobs for some, but the belief that young people should be in school shaped the programs designed for them. For example, the National Youth Administration (NYA), established in 1935, ran training camps for poor and unemployed youth but focused primarily on providing part-time work to cover high school expenses, not to support a family. At the height of the Depression, millions of teenagers were neither in school nor working.[7]

During World War II, new opportunities beckoned, keeping substantial numbers of teens out of high school. Social mobilization for the war effort included all age groups, and, although the government promoted scrap drives, bond sales, and Victory Gardens as appropriate for youthful patriots, large numbers of underage boys joined or attempted to join the military while both girls and boys sought jobs in war industries. The number of young people between fourteen and seventeen years of age in the workforce increased 300 percent during World War II. "Victory Girls," teenaged girls who slept with men about to ship off to war, frightened many contemporary observers who wanted to believe that prior to the war teens did not have sex. The end of the war, many people hoped, would resettle youths in the more acceptable environments of family and school.[8]

Indeed, in the 1950s school enrollment did increase. With the majority of American youngsters now attending school, educators and other experts targeted high school students, now dubbed "teenagers," as a particular challenge. Sociologists and psychologists recognized in the early decades of the twentieth century that adolescence was a difficult and troubled life passage. Propelling young people through an extended education and preventing them from assuming adult roles, especially in the workforce, created both a new stage of life and increasing role tension. Young people became sexually mature well before society permitted them to take on adult roles and responsibilities. Moreover, they had to establish an independent identity—the function of adolescence—while still economically dependent and living under their parents' care. To further complicate matters, "identity"—once a relatively stable constellation of occupation, values, sexuality, and gender roles—progressively fragmented into a smorgasbord of choices called "lifestyles." Teens, educators feared, faced a bewildering array of decisions, some with momentous consequences. High schools, then, would play a crucial role in forming students into "well-adjusted" adults. Because parents of all social classes now sent their children to high school, school officials had the further job of steering students into their appropriate educational niches (college preparatory for the middle class and elites; vocational or general education for the others) while managing and defusing class-based antagonisms.[9]

Sorting students into the right curricular box presented few difficulties for educators, because various tests neatly and scientifically classified students, who could then be placed into corresponding "tracks." Lifestyles, however, depended less on educational attainment, social class, or occupational rung than on self-image and self-presentation, based on consumer choices. Here advertisers, not educators, played the crucial role in promoting different lifestyles. In contrast to reformers and educators, whose efforts to keep teens in school and out of the labor force invested the adult world with a certain allure, advertisers ultimately packaged youth itself as a desirable commodity. In the early twentieth century, editors of youth magazines and advertisers emphasized adult values—hard work, thrift, and deferred gratification—in the hopes of making the young into respectable and responsible consumers. But, in the late 1930s and 1940s, youth preferences prompted new approaches in advertising. Their passion for swing music, for example, catalyzed a major change both in how teens viewed themselves and how marketers portrayed and pursued them. Abandoning the sober virtues of a bygone era, advertisers emphasized pleasure and sociability through consumption. Recognizing that the young collectively had an enormous amount of money at their disposal (spending more than $25 billion annually by 1964), advertisers increasingly targeted teens as a special market and set about convincing them that they constituted a separate culture, with its own style and appeal. Already restricted from much of the adult world, forced together with their cohorts in high schools, young people willingly embraced the notion of their distinctiveness.[10]

Elements of the emerging youth culture alarmed adults. Increased teen pregnancies, gang violence, and the rebelliousness of a few middle-class white youths fanned the flames of the great "juvenile delinquency scare," which began in the immediate postwar years but peaked in the early 1950s. In several instances, much discussed in apocalyptic terms in the media, middle-class youths ran amok at parties with no adult supervision, senselessly breaking windows and tearing up furniture. Crime rates began to climb, and in 1953 the U.S. Senate began hearings to investigate juvenile delinquency and, in particular, the influence of the mass media. Both domestic anticommunists and experts testifying on juvenile delinquency used metaphors of contagion and infection, highlighting the vulnerability of the nation. Paradoxically, in an era often regarded as the height of American power, citizens worried about internal rot as much as they did communist aggression. By the late 1950s, black musicians and lower-class white "hoods" exerted a powerful fascination for middle-class white youths as part of a "teen rebel cult." Hollywood movies that romanticized young rebels like James Dean, and the emergence of Elvis Presley, a lower-class white rebel who sang black-inspired music, further encouraged the young to feel that they had values and ideals not shared by adults.[11]

EARLY ACTIVISM IN BLACK SCHOOLS

Whereas some white youths frightened their elders with their affinity for the cultural styles of the wrong sorts of people, a number of black youths took up arms in a far more serious rebellion against social norms: the postwar civil rights movement. Blacks had never passively accepted their second-class status, but the postwar struggle distinguished itself from previous freedom movements by its mass base and adroitness in playing to the national media and sounding traditional American civic and religious themes. Although a proposed 1943 march on Washington, orchestrated by A. Philip Randolph, demonstrated the usefulness of mass pressure to force action by the federal government, the refusal of returning black GIs to accede to Jim Crow rules provided the spark to set a new movement alight. Veterans and independent black farmers and businessmen, who did not have to rely on whites for their livelihood, initiated community organization to fight for their rights.

Black high school students backed veterans and adult activists, supplying the élan and daring that electrified the movement. In Mississippi and Louisiana, young blacks played important roles in groups such as the Student Non-Violent Coordinating Committee (SNCC) and, through its Youth Councils, the National Association for the Advancement of Colored People (NAACP). As early as 1953, southern black high school students actively protested racial discrimination and segregation, sometimes recruiting their parents into the struggles. Even in the North, while Bob Greene drifted along in his suburban cocoon, black students in New York City and Chicago boycotted the schools, demanding integration.[12]

Just as the black freedom struggle inspired and fueled other movements for social justice in the 1960s, so black high school students simultaneously ignited a struggle for student rights. In the late 1950s and early 1960s, black students in the segregated South clashed—not only with whites, but also with their parents and school administrators—over their right to march and demonstrate, wear freedom buttons, sing freedom songs, and engage in door-to-door canvassing for SNCC and the Council of Federated Organizations (COFO). These issues of autonomy and political participation paralleled those raised by high school student activists in the late 1960s, yet the linkages between the earlier and later stages of the student power movement are by no means direct or obvious. In light of the lack of any institutional means of passing their history down to future cohorts of high school students, there is no evidence that activists of the late 1960s knew about their predecessors.

The civil rights movement of the early 1960s laid the groundwork for later developments in American high schools in another way as well. SNCC created its first "freedom school," known as "Non-Violent High," to accommodate students in McComb County, Mississippi, who had been expelled from Burgland High School for taking part in civil rights demonstrations or for boycotting Burgland because of those expulsions. A later freedom school established in Madison County did away with the normal hierarchies of power and authority, encouraging teachers to learn along with their students, who were to have "maximum participation." Eventually students gained the confidence to run their own workshops at a freedom school conference in Meridian, Mississippi. This emphasis on teachers learning and students teaching in an atmosphere of mutual respect characterized the alternative school movement in the late 1960s, and the implied critique of hierarchy, bureaucracy, and traditional curricula formed the core of later high school student attacks on public education.[13]

CHARACTERISTICS OF 1950S HIGH SCHOOLS

In the late 1950s and early 1960s most American high schools in no way resembled the relaxed and informal freedom schools. At best, they were tightly organized institutions with strict rules of dress and behavior. At worst, they were rigid, uptight, buttoned-down, lockstep factories run like fiefdoms by principals who had few checks on their power and could be as tyrannical and arbitrary as they wished. Dress codes, which a number of schools adopted at the behest of parents at the height of the juvenile delinquency scare, exemplified the schools' rigidity. Some schools spelled out in inordinate detail how a student's hair should be cut, what constituted appropriate attire, and how this clothing was to be worn. In addition, most schools attempted the bodily control of students through hall and bathroom passes and rules about absences and skipping classes ("cuts"). Officials would not permit students to form the fraternities and sororities so popular on college campuses, on the grounds that such organizations were elitist and undemocratic. This is undoubtedly true, but the bans (not enforced for older students) effectively eliminated one form of free association for high school students. Other regulations restricted students' physical mobility. For example, students at the elite Bronx High School of Science in New York City could not use its beautiful glass front doors, even though they opened directly onto the auditorium where students had to report at the opening of each school day. Joshua Mamis, a junior high school student who in 1968 successfully sued his school for the right to petition, criticized a rule about "silent passing," which meant students had to move quietly, without talking, from one class to the next. If they failed to perform this maneuver to the satisfaction of the principal, he would turn on the intercom and demand that students "pass" again until they got it right. Rules such as these invited rebellion—indeed triggered it. Whereas students in the 1950s and early 1960s rebelled surreptitiously and individually, rolling their skirts up when no teacher was looking, smoking in the bathrooms, and pushing to see how long they could go without a haircut, by the late 1960s students replaced clandestine rebellion with head-on confrontation.[14]

Public schools' emphasis on rules, hierarchy, and authority in the 1950s—not new in themselves—coincided and conflicted with a more democratic family life. Middle-class white families evinced this trend more than others, and it may be more accurate to state that family life became more expressive rather than necessarily more democratic. Fathers still headed their households, but experts now counseled them to do so through logic, reason, and affection rather than by simply invoking their status as patriarchs. The "permissive parenting" characterized by the advice manuals of Dr. Benjamin Spock and vilified in the late 1960s did not mean unlimited freedom for children. It meant, rather, greater sensitivity to children's needs and clear explanations of boundaries. Childrearing experts increasingly frowned on corporal punishment for misbehavior and emphasized communication between parents and children. Children raised in such families understood the necessity of rules, but they expected the rules to be both rational and somewhat flexible. Unfortunately, many of the rules of the high schools were neither, and this combination of arbitrariness and rigidity ultimately set students and school officials on a collision course.[15]

Other than tradition, a number of factors underlay the strict rules of high schools in the 1950s and early 1960s. Overcrowding plagued many schools. The postwar baby boom pushed larger classes through the school system at a time when there was no federal aid to education. Desperate districts enlarged their schools if they could but otherwise housed students in prefabricated "bungalows," shoehorned them into existing classrooms, or operated in different shifts. Strict rules were simply a form of crowd control. The impersonality of the schools, too, grated on students from child-centered homes. Rapidly changing racial and class demographics—caused by the mobility spawned by World War II and heightened by school desegregation—further increased the necessity of controlling the students. No longer the homogenous group of half a century earlier, students now identified and divided themselves into categories such as "jocks," "dupers," and "greasers" (roughly translated as "athletes," "precollegiate," and "working class"). Later students added more political categories, such as "radicals," "straights," "hippies," "soul brothers and sisters," "Toms" (as in "Uncle Tom"), "Oreos" (black on the outside but white on the inside), and many others. The fact that some of these students attended high school only because of legal compulsion increased intragroup tension and heightened the volatility of the student population as a whole.[16]

In addition to desiring control over a large, heterogeneous student body, the narrow, cramped nature of high schools in the 1950s reflected general political trends. The superheated atmosphere of the cold war lent urgency to education, putting schools on the front lines in the domestic battle against communism. Unfortunately, rather than explore and express American freedoms and democracy, most schools settled for tepid conformity to social norms. Outside pressures confirmed the wisdom of this choice. The House Committee on Un-American Activities, for example, investigated schools, curriculum, and teachers. Parent-Teacher Associations (PTAs) and neighborhood groups carefully scrutinized school library shelves. In the late 1950s, members of the right-wing John Birch Society, established in 1958, examined their community schools to make sure nothing that smacked of communism, including sex education, had insinuated itself into the schools. Written polemics such as "How Red Is the Little Red Schoolhouse?" amplified educators' anxieties, as did loyalty oaths for teachers. Right-wing attacks on schools continued into the late 1960s. In 1969 the Tucson, Arizona, Movement to Restore Decency—also known as "Motorede," an offshoot of the John Birch Society—sponsored public meetings where speakers linked communism, rock music, and sex education. A student writing for a high school underground newspaper in Tucson asked pointedly, "How did the Communists manage the very difficult task of brain-washing all the sex education teachers in Arizona? (Are the Commies really that smart?)" But many adults believed that communism was a serious threat, not only to American security but also to traditions and "decency."[17]

The 1957 launching of the Sputnik satellite by the Soviet Union further threw the American public and educators into a frenzy. Well before Sputnik, critics had attacked progressive education, which, inspired by educator and philosopher John Dewey in the 1920s, emphasized accommodating schools to children's needs and interests, rather than forcing children to adapt to schooling. This meant getting rid of straight rows of bolted-down chairs, the classical curriculum, and traditional lectures. Instead, Dewey asserted, learning should be hands-on and discovery-oriented; it should promote active engagement by the students. Rising hysteria about communism and the suspicion that Soviet schools, for all their repressiveness, turned out students who were better prepared to compete in the cold war arms race, gave the enemies of progressive education the ammunition they needed to insist on a "return to basics." In 1958, *Life* magazine published a five-part series titled "The Crisis in Education," which began with an explicit comparison between Soviet and American high schools. The publication of the Conant report bolstered the view of traditionalists. James Conant, a former president of Harvard University and participant in the Manhattan Project, the wartime project that built the first atomic bomb, visited a number of American high schools in 1958 and expressed dismay at what he found. In his report, published the following year, he argued that high school students needed more emphasis on English, math, and science and should be assigned about fifteen hours of homework per week.[18]

In addition to a renewed emphasis on the "Three R's," educators also attempted to indoctrinate students in patriotism. A number of studies written in the 1950s and early 1960s emphasized that by age eight children adopted core political values, which stayed with them all their lives. Therefore, many Americans believed that, beginning in elementary school, teachers had an obligation to mold students' political values. At first, many schools resisted discussing communism in the classroom, but by the early 1960s some legislators pressured them to pair discussions of democracy with a teaching unit on communism. For example, the Florida legislature declared in 1961 that all public high schools had to include a six-week course on communism. Several other states had similar laws or at least recommended teaching such a course. It is not clear, though, how many students actually gained a working definition of communism. David Super, who graduated from Sturgis High School, in South Dakota, in 1965, recalls critically: "What had we been taught about communism? It was evil. Bad. Nasty." Super learned little about capitalism either. "Susan Snow," a student at Academy High School, in Erie, Pennsylvania, had the same experience.[19]

Even when schools hesitated to teach about communism, they employed courses in "citizenship training" to indoctrinate students in American values. Ironically, just as the strict rules of dress and behavior eventually created a student backlash and rebellion, citizenship training ultimately caused educators grief. Not only did conservative communities censure schools for teaching anything about communism, but also what the schools showcased as "American values" eventually raised serious questions for some students. They readily embraced ideals of openness, tolerance, fairness, and democracy, but the discrepancy between these ideals and reality both within the schools and in society became apparent more slowly. From an early date, black students, who were already living the lie, pointed out the hollowness of rhetoric about equality and democracy. For white children, beginning in the mid-1950s, television competed with teachers as sources of education about their world. The televised events and vivid images of contemporary history itself ruptured the walls between innocent childhood and the wider world, until many white students, like their black counterparts, could no longer blink away the chasm between textbook bromides about democracy and a society at war with itself.[20]

THE INFLUENCE OF NATIONAL EVENTS

Any number of events contributed to the awakening of young people and prepared the way for the later student movements. The watershed Supreme Court decision of *Brown v. Board of Education of Topeka, Kansas,* in 1954, constituted one such event. Although the immediate impact of the decision fell primarily upon African-American and white schoolchildren in the South, where the battle over whether and how to implement it was fought—often literally—by the mid-1960s, many schools across the country had become or were becoming integrated. But white resistance to *Brown* and other efforts to desegregate the South, in contrast to the dignified, determined actions taken by African-Americans to promote desegregation, provided telling lessons to young people. Before their eyes, both "tradition" and duly constituted authority suffered body blows. African-Americans defied state and local governments and southern mores in support of the ideals of equality, freedom, and justice. White Klansmen, Citizens' Council members, and local and state officials defied the federal government and the Supreme Court in *opposition* to those ideals. Although many high schools emphasized obedience to authority as a social value, the struggle over desegregation prompted students to ask, "Which authorities?" and to see some rules and traditions as simply wrong. Authority, with a capital "A," fell off its throne.

By 1960, the civil rights movement intensified, and numbers of young, more militant activists brought their courage and their creativity to the struggle. Images of young African-Americans and their white allies being beaten, set upon by dogs, burned out of buses and churches, even murdered while police and state, local, and federal governments looked on could not help but raise questions about the legitimacy of those authorities. Similar events punctuated the lives of children growing up in this era. A child who was seven when the Greensboro sit-in took place would have been eight when the Freedom Riders tested the desegregation of interstate travel, nine when James Meredith tried to register at Ole Miss, and ten when Martin

Luther King, Jr., staged his March on Washington and President John Kennedy was shot. Two years later, when this hypothetical student would have been an impressionable twelve, Watts burned and the "long hot summers" began. By the time high school activism began to blossom in 1969, this student would have been a sixteen-year-old junior who had witnessed both stirring and troubling episodes in race relations.

Along with the civil rights movement, the Vietnam War eventually raised questions about the values of the nation and the legitimacy of its authorities and institutions for inquisitive high school students. Because policy makers feared the nuclear consequences of an all-out war, they did their best to keep the conflict off the front pages of the newspapers while they attempted to win it on the cheap—cheap, that is, in terms of American lives, if not in dollars. Even when the war's escalation and stalemate forced it into the headlines, the government refrained from the total mobilization and propaganda blitzes it had used to such good effect in World War II. President Lyndon Johnson in fact feared popular mobilization, believing that the American public and Congress would never allow him to wage war while implementing his comprehensive domestic reform program, the Great Society. He preferred reform to the war. Unfortunately for him and the Nixon administration that followed, many Americans nevertheless mobilized themselves to oppose the war. As the numbers of men serving in Vietnam increased, so did the numbers of Americans marching against the war, although the marchers never equaled the numbers of men in uniform. As the war in Vietnam escalated, so did the rhetoric and actions of the antiwar protesters at home. Most high school students paid little heed to the war, but, again, they must have been struck by the spectacle, brought into their homes via television, of thousands of Americans protesting the war.

As blacks rebelled and an unpopular war gradually created public opposition, college students protested against the rules that hemmed them in. In 1964, students at the University of California at Berkeley reacted to a campus ban on political activities by launching the Free Speech Movement. During the rest of the decade, college students demanded to be treated as adults; they challenged university rules about dress, behavior, and political activism, and they generally won. They further won the right to evaluate their teachers and to have more voice in matters of curriculum, discipline, and university governance. Chaperonage and the close confining of female students came to an end.[21]

Rebellion against college rules and governmental authorities took place worldwide. Countries in Latin America, the Far East, and Europe all experienced major upheavals on college campuses that sometimes spilled outside the walls of academe. In France, students and workers joined hands in a general strike in 1968 that briefly paralyzed Paris and threatened to bring down the government. That same year, government troops in Mexico gunned down hundreds of protesting students. Similar social, political, and demographic conditions sparked these international rebellions, and high school students took part in many of them. Whereas other events shaped how high school students regarded their country, the college rebellions may have led them to examine their own schools and to draw parallels with the ways in which administrators treated them.[22]

The growing militancy of public school teachers hit closer to home, and it, too, must have influenced high school students. A teachers' union of sorts, the American Federation of Teachers (AFT) had existed since 1916. Between 1916 and 1960, the AFT limped along, often with fewer than ten thousand members nationally. Few teachers thought of themselves as workers. Rather, they identified themselves—and the public concurred—as professionals. Consequently, many teachers found strikes and other tactics of working-class unions demeaning and inappropriate. "Mrs. Natalie N.," a business education teacher from 1934 until the early 1980s, expresses this viewpoint clearly: "When the chips were down," she asserts, "no one would think of going to ask for a raise. It was, in a way, beneath our dignity. It was genteel poverty that we had taken on."[23]

This self-sacrificing, even masochistic, attitude began to change among teachers in 1961 when the New York City AFT affiliate, the United Federation of Teachers (UFT), staged a strike and won the right to bargain collectively. This victory inspired locals in other large cities, aided by professional organizers from the AFL-CIO's Industrial Union Department, to strike as well. Teachers wanted, among other things, higher pay, smaller class sizes, and greater participation in decision making. Teacher strikes became common in the mid-to late 1960s. The U.S. Department of Labor reported only five in 1965, but in 1969 there were 183 strikes involving more than one hundred thousand teachers. Watching their teachers defy principals and school boards and picket the schools must have shown students the effectiveness of such tactics.[24]

Moreover, attentive students realized that younger and older teachers often clashed over pedagogy, professionalism, and curriculum. Here we need to be careful: the contemporary notion of a "generation gap" exaggerated differences between people of different ages while ignoring the ways in which the adult and youth worlds mirrored each other. Elements of the counterculture crept into adult fashions and mores, for example, and opponents and supporters of the Vietnam War spanned any generational divide. Nevertheless, teachers in the 1960s sometimes fell into "old school" and "new school" categories. Interviews with "old school" teachers revealed that few felt sympathy for teachers' unions and many waxed nostalgic about beating their students in the good old days. One even bragged about using a garden hose. These teachers complained that as their physical power over their students decreased, their moral authority had simultaneously waned.[25]

Changing ideas about appropriate school discipline, however, was only one source of generational conflict within the schools. Young teachers fresh from college campuses clashed with older teachers, administrators, and school boards about unionism, professional attire, and the introduction of controversial topics—like the war in Vietnam—into their classes. Some older teachers recoiled when young women teachers came to class in miniskirts and young men wore facial hair. Guitar-toting teachers who sang folk songs to their classes became a stock joke. Moreover, older and younger teachers often disagreed about how much latitude and freedom students ought to have. High school students and young teachers not uncommonly supported one another in their respective battles against age and authority. Some students eventually favored egalitarian relations between students and teachers, turning this into an element of their critique of education.[26]

In addition to these unsettling developments, the feminist movement challenged gender roles that many Americans regarded as traditional, if not eternal and divinely inspired. During World War II, women's roles underwent dramatic changes, but most Americans understood these to be "for the duration" only. Efforts to return to "normal" were only half-successful, and fissures quickly opened between gender beliefs and practice, highlighted by the profoundly mixed messages the popular media sent women in the 1950s. Movies, magazines, and experts generally emphasized the primacy of the woman's role as wife and mother. Despite this prescription, increasing numbers of married women—even women with children—worked outside the home, and popular media and advice columns often celebrated their accomplishments. The numbers of women working dipped briefly after the end of World War II, reflecting layoffs of women to make room for returning veterans, but the female labor force regained its wartime strength by 1947 and steadily expanded thereafter. Many Americans today believe that the feminist movement of the 1960s and 1970s propelled women into the workforce. In fact, the opposite was true: inequities suffered by women already in the workforce and limited opportunities for women planning to work awakened the feminist movement. It is also true that, despite the laments of those who yearn for the 1950s as a lost Eden, television's placid, domestic June Cleaver did not typify American women in the 1950s.[27]

Public consciousness of the internal contradictions in women's roles did not surface visibly until 1963, with the publication of a report by the Presidential Commission on the Status of Women and Betty Friedan's *The Feminine Mystique*. The commission's report focused on women in the workforce and argued that women who worked faced pervasive discrimination. They earned less than men even when they performed identical work, performed personal services for their bosses that no man would be asked to do, and found themselves systematically barred from promotions and high-paying, prestigious positions. The report recommended laws against sex discrimination in the workforce.

Friedan's book, in contrast, focused on women's lives in the home, where things also looked bleak. Friedan described the home as "a comfortable concentration camp" that turned women into brain-dead cooks and maids. She argued that bright, capable, college-educated women wasted their lives baking brownies, driving the kids to various activities, ironing their husband's shirts, and worrying about the whiteness of their laundry. Ironically, considering the report of the Presidential Commission on the Status of Women, Friedan argued that paid work could open a way out of this domestic dead end. She clearly had touched a raw nerve for many American women, for *The Feminine Mystique* became a bestseller.

By the late 1960s, the effects of the dawning feminist movement palpably touched American schools. Teaching epitomized much of what feminists decried: while women taught in the classroom, men trained and supervised teachers, theorized about education, and dispensed advice. Men were the education professors, the principals, the superintendents, and the majority of the school board members. They earned more money, had more power, and enjoyed higher status than the average female teacher. As female teachers began to critique the male-dominated nature of the profession, they simultaneously cast baleful eyes on their school texts and prescribed curriculum, seeing for the first time how books and courses reinforced sex roles and gender stereotypes for girls and boys. By 1970, women teachers were beginning to demand a broad array of changes that would allow for greater equality of the sexes within the world of education. Although these demands did not exactly parallel changes that high school militants (with the exception of feminist students) sought in curriculum, they constituted yet another salvo against traditional authorities.

Thus, by the mid-1960s, the forces of change were already in motion. As the winds of action and reaction quickened, public high schools found themselves buffeted by rising storms. School officials had not found the 1950s a particularly placid era. Between attacks on progressive education, loyalty oaths and security investigations, worries about school finances and overcrowding, administrators found their jobs extremely challenging. But they seldom viewed their students as part of their problems. In the educational journals of the late 1950s and early 1960s, "students" seem amazingly abstract. The magazine for school administrators, *School Management,* for example, does not give any indication of the initiative and agency of students themselves until 1965. Tellingly, these references to students as independent actors appeared in a new feature of the journal, a column called "Administrators' Clinic"—soon renamed "Administrators' Forum"—in which the editors culled real problems from the newspapers and then asked a panel of educators how they would respond. In the first month of the column, the theme was "Discipline," and two of the examples involved a white student with a Beatle haircut who had gotten a court injunction against the enforcement of his school's dress code, and a black student who attacked a white coach who called him a "lazy nigger." More appropriate examples, foreshadowing much of what lay ahead for the public schools, can hardly be imagined.[28]

By 1965, the schools had unwittingly assembled the components necessary for a student movement to coalesce—a large, heterogeneous student body, weaned on democratic values, and nurtured by images of vigorous, effective social activism by different segments of society. The bureaucratic and hierarchical schools of the late 1950s and early 1960s were ill prepared for the new cohort of students now thronging their halls. Although only a minority of high school students became activists, their numbers sufficed to turn many high schools into battlefields over race, student rights, curriculum, authority, and even the direction of the nation. Because race relations were the most inflammatory issue, when desegregation brought already active black students into previously all-white schools, match met tinder, kindling both high school rights and identity revolutions.

Dozens of reporters, lawyers, and observers thronged the courtroom in the Supreme Court building, murmuring excitedly among themselves on a May afternoon in 1954. From the moment two years earlier when the Supreme Court had agreed to hear five school segregation cases consolidated under the name *Brown v. Board of Education of Topeka, Kansas,* tension over the outcome had steadily mounted among supporters and opponents of desegregation. No one could predict how the Court, led by the recently appointed Chief Justice Earl Warren, might rule. Now reporters and other interested parties assembled anxiously for what was, in the days before Internet postings, the Monday ritual of reading Supreme Court decisions. Refusing to provide reporters with a copy of the decision in advance, as was usually done, heightened the suspense. After listening to Chief Justice Warren read several pages of the decision, the intent listeners still could not discern which way the Court had swung. Warren reviewed the history of the Fourteenth Amendment, mentioned contemporary rulings against segregated higher education, and summarized the role of education before asking the key question: "Does segregation of children in public schools solely on the basis of race . . . deprive the children of the minority group of equal educational opportunities?" Warren answered simply, "We believe that it does," before delivering the unanimous verdict of the Court: "We conclude that, in the field of public education, the doctrine of 'separate but equal' has no place. Separate educational facilities are inherently unequal."[1]

The drama of the case and the self-congratulatory way it is usually depicted have tended to distort the actual history of school desegregation. Popular memory credits—or more quietly blames—the Supreme Court for ending segregation in public education, but the suggestion that the nine white men on the Court accomplished this on their own erases the centuries-long struggle of African-Americans to gain education. This history stretches back to the days of slavery when southern laws forbade educating blacks, and free black communities in the North created their own schools because local white schools barred the attendance of black children. After the Civil War, the newly freed people flocked to schools established by educated blacks and sympathetic whites, despite the efforts of hostile southern whites to destroy the school buildings and terrorize the teachers. In the late-nineteenth century, the celebrated black educator Booker T. Washington carved out a niche for his college, the Tuskegee Institute, by publicly endorsing segregation and preparing his students to accommodate it. Elsewhere, hundreds of black schoolteachers struggled on without Washington's fame or support from whites. They worked in exceedingly trying conditions, with little money and limited resources, but they did their best to impart education and pride in black culture to their pupils. These teachers, students, and their parents in no way saw *Brown v. Board of Education* as a first step. It was simply the *next* step, and not necessarily a welcome one.

Hailing *Brown* as the case that ended segregation also ignores the previous legal victories of the National Association for the Advancement of Colored People (NAACP). Between 1938 and 1950, courts had struck down segregation in higher education in cases that exposed the petty, mean-spirited attitudes that underlay Jim Crow: they ruled that southern states could not take up a collection and send a prospective black college student to a non-segregated state for education; they could not hastily throw together a black law school and call it "equal" to the long-established and prestigious state law school for white students; they could not admit a black student to a state college or university and then make him or her sit behind a screen in classrooms, the cafeteria, or the library. Flushed with these triumphs, the NAACP decided to stop pursuing violations of "separate but equal" education and attack the concept directly, ripping out the legal underpinnings that sanctioned segregated schooling.[2]

Rather than repeat the often-told history of school desegregation that focuses on the role of the courts, school officials, politicians, community leaders, and parents, I tease out the effects of integration on American high schools more broadly, to suggest the ways in which black and white students determined the forms integration actually took. Whatever the Supreme Court's intent in ordering desegregation, white students and officials worked together to maintain structural and social segregation in the schools. Their collusion—often tacit rather than overt—weakened the possibility that public schools might meaningfully desegregate and establish the basis for a new era in race relations. Instead, the white response to desegregation led students of both races to create racialized identities and played a key role in turning increasing numbers of black students toward Black Power and militancy. The Black Power and, later, Brown Power movements fed racial tension and violence as well as the broader, sometimes interracial, push for student power. But both the complex and fragile alliances between white and minority activists that occasionally developed and more straightforward racial enmity required contacts among students of different races.

ASSESSING THE SIGNIFICANCE OF *BROWN*

Three flaws in the widely held belief that *Brown v. Board of Education* ended school segregation become obvious. In the first place, racial segregation in schools did *not* end—not in 1954; not the following year when the Supreme Court, in a ruling known as *Brown II,* declared that schools must desegregate "with all deliberate speed"; not in 1969, when the Supreme Court lost patience and testily ordered schools to desegregate "at once" and to "operate now and hereafter only unitary schools"; and not even in the early twenty-first century when, ironically, American schools are more segregated than they were before *Brown.* School desegregation failed for a number of reasons, but the initial *Brown* decision and the follow-up ruling, *Brown II,* bold as they seemed at the time, lacked the solid, broad-based support necessary to translate the Court's orders into action.[3]

The second questionable implication is that adults—jurists, legislators, public pressure groups, civil rights organizations, even the National Guard—ended school segregation. True, adults ordered desegregation, and drew up plans to enforce it or tried to evade it—yet *students,* ranging in age from five to twenty-something, carried it out or worked with adults to stymie it. Contemporary media coverage and historical accounts have focused on the first efforts to integrate all-white schools, especially when whites resisted violently, as they did in Little Rock, Arkansas, in 1957, Lamar, South Carolina, in 1970, or Boston, in 1975. Emphasizing "extraordinary integration" not only ignores the far more widespread mundane integration, where little drama attracted the media spotlight, but also tends to cast adults as the heroes or villains, disregarding the heroic or villainous roles played by students. Overall, integration proceeded in a painfully meandering path, thanks to courts' toleration for incredible amounts of foot dragging and diversionary tactics by large numbers of school districts, but where it occurred, students helped determine its shape.[4]

Finally, crediting the *Brown* decision with ending segregated education implies an unalloyed victory for blacks; however, even with the limited accomplishments of desegregation, blacks gave up perhaps more than they bargained for. Thousands of black teachers and principals lost their jobs, despite their hope that desegregation would open up white schools to them as well as to their pupils. Black schools lost their status as central community institutions, because most were forced to close. Often outnumbered by whites, black students found themselves in schools that disparaged or ignored their contributions to history and culture. Racial prejudice did not disappear just because schools were desegregated; it lurked or brazenly paraded in classrooms, hallways, and cafeterias. After school, football games, dances, and student clubs became arenas for further racial confrontations. Segregated schools, for all of their shortcomings, had provided a layer of insulation between black students and a hostile society. Stripped of this protection and largely bereft of allies, not all black students regarded *Brown* as a victory worth celebrating.[5]

This is not to suggest that the *Brown* decision did not move the United States closer to "complete freedom and equality between black and white Americans," as black leader W. E. B. DuBois put it. But casting *Brown v. Board of Education* as the triumph of good over evil obscures some painful truths. Even at the time, critics objected to the grounds on which the case was decided. Rather than condemning racial segregation as fundamentally wrong or in violation of American ideals of equality and justice, the Supreme Court agreed with the defendants that segregated schools injured black children for life by making them feel inferior. Thus, the Court transformed a moral issue into a matter of sociology, psychology, and pedagogy. Moreover, the *Brown* decision angered thoughtful blacks because it implied that the weakness of Jim Crow schools stemmed less from their underfunding and pitifully few resources than from their status as *black* institutions. Novelist Zora Neale Hurston argued that, with equal funding, black schools could offer everything that white schools could; she feared that attending white schools under legal compulsion would injure black students far more than attending segregated schools.[6]

HIGH SCHOOL STUDENTS AND DESEGREGATION

Despite *Brown*'s critics, liberal black and white activists assumed that desegregation would advance the black freedom movement. This ideal was tested in practice as students of different races began to attend the same schools. When an interviewer spoke with twenty black high school students from three anonymous rural towns in the heart of the southern black belt in 1967, their stories revealed isolation and tension. Several noted that blacks who did not attend white schools taunted them about beating up or dating whites. This juxtaposition of possibilities—violence versus intimacy—demonstrates fears common to blacks and whites about the consequences of integration. White teachers sometimes punished black students for cultural differences, such as responding to teachers with "yeah" rather than "yes, ma'am," and were not averse to leading or at least colluding with white students in harassing the black students. These black students also received little support from their white classmates. One student, when asked whether he trusted white people more or less since attending the integrated school, responded, "Well, I don't trust white people at all, because they'll pretend that they are your friend and when you turn your back then they'll hit you and call you some silly name. They'll turn their back and pretend they don't know nothing about it."[7]

For other high school students, integration remained abstract. Some white teens living outside the South, for example, felt only mild sympathy for the civil rights movement. Connie Brown grew up in Maumee, Ohio, a suburb of Toledo, and graduated from Maumee High School in 1969. Reflecting the racial isolation of white suburbanites, she comments, "Because few of us had ever even talked to a black person much less knew one (or Hispanic or Asian people) [sic], there was no way we could comprehend the black experience. . . . Although we believed they deserved civil rights, we weren't otherwise involved or concerned about their problems." David Super, from Sturgis, South Dakota, concurs. Only one African-American family lived within a two hundred–mile radius of his home, but, he adds, "That said, the issue of civil rights was visible and something that did get discussed, at least a little bit in school and at home, but only by my mother. I recall feeling sympathetic that African-Americans were badly treated, but that was about it. The problem belonged to people in the south and in major cities; it wasn't important to our community's life."[8]

Where only token integration occurred, white students found the experience positive, at least from their perspective. Val Tabor's Norte Vista High School in Riverside, California, enrolled its first black student in 1967, when Tabor was in the eleventh grade. "Everyone loved her," Tabor declares and suggests that the community apparently accepted integration "because the person was nice and everyone liked her, so it made it easy for all. The family cared about their children and their environment. I am sure there were some that were prejudiced, but it was not shown around my school. I learned some of my best dance steps from her."[9]

Susan Bowman Prendergast, from a rural school in New Jersey, echoes Tabor's story. When she was a freshman, in 1968, her class included only four black students. Thinking back to how whites reacted to their presence, she recalls, "I think the general consensus at the time was 'what's the big deal?'" But she notes that one moved, and one dropped out, so only two of the four black students graduated with the class. One of them was popular because he played football, basketball, and ran track. Prendergast observes, "Whenever he seemed to be injured we all held our breath, nobody wanted anything to happen to him."[10]

We may wonder, however, how these individuals would tell their own stories. As the token black students, they faced enormous pressures. They had to get along with the white students, succeed academically, and serve as representatives of their race, all the while knowing that one misstep would have the white community shaking its collective head, its prejudices confirmed. The popularity of the black students described above stemmed from their conformity to white stereotypes: they could dance and play ball. Moreover, black students shared their talents, instructing whites in the latest dance moves and contributing to athletic victory for their schools. When Frank Petroni and Ernest Hirsch, sociologists from the University of Arizona, interviewed black, white, and Mexican-American students at the fictive "Plains High School" in "Center City" in 1970, the students agreed that the playing field was the most integrated spot on campus, but only during a game. They further noted that, although black students willingly taught whites how to dance, they danced alongside them, rather than with them, and returned to their own side of the dance floor once the lesson was over.[11]

Val Tabor admits that some prejudice existed but dismisses it because "it was not shown around the school." Similarly, Susan Bowman Prendergast criticizes the "very sheltered," "very opinionated" family next door, who did not permit their daughter to go on a hayride for Prendergast's sixteenth birthday party because one of the black students was invited. At least Tabor and Prendergast found ways to include the few black students in off-campus social life; other whites exerted less effort. Judy Brown grew up in Kansas City, Missouri. The few black students at her high school, she remembers, "made an effort to fit in and we made an effort to include them in school-related activities. Although no one gave them a call at home or invited them to the movies like you might other friends. . . . Once they arrived there seemed to be genuine empathy for their plight—who would want to be bused across town to attend school with a bunch of strangers? Simultaneously, there wasn't the effort to get close to them either."[12]

The apparent failure of white students to notice prejudice did not mean that blacks were immune to racial slights. Perhaps manifestations of prejudice escaped them, too, but it seems more likely that they were hyperaware of the emotional currents swirling around them. Without strength in numbers, conforming to white expectations may have seemed their best bet. These students worked harder at fitting in, by attending dances, ball games, and the occasional party, than whites did at welcoming them. Other blacks chose to confront rather than to endure subtle racial snubs. When Betty Walker integrated Handley High School in Roanoke, Alabama, in 1965, she acknowledges that whites acted with restraint. Nevertheless Walker states: "I remember pep rallies every Friday afternoon during football season. The white students had an enormous amount of school spirit and confederate pride. At the end of each pep rally they would stand and sing 'Dixie.' I made a special point of sitting during that song and making other African-American students aware of its meaning during the following years." She further notes that no blacks were elected cheerleader or class officer. Only Handley students could attend dances, restricting the dating pool for the few blacks at the school, because interracial dating was unthinkable. A student at another school noticed that the school newspaper published interviews with all of the white candidates for student council, but not the sole black candidate. Perhaps whites did not intend to exclude black students, but their actions indicate a gross insensitivity, to say the least.[13]

On other occasions, whites deliberately sought to make black students feel unwelcome. In 1969, Charles Caldwell was a fourteen-year-old student in an integrated school in Lebanon, Texas, one of eighty-nine African-Americans among 1,245 whites. Trouble began when a white girl harassed him in the band room, sneering that "the room was too dark" and "there was a dirty nigger present." Charles fought back by refusing to play "Dixie" with the band. School officials threw him out of the band and fired his mother, who was a teacher's aide. Students taunted him by whistling "Dixie" in the halls. When the American Civil Liberties Union sued to contest Charles's expulsion from the band, enraged whites stoned the Caldwell's home and car. Similarly, after the court ordered Dixie Hollins High School, in St. Petersburg, Florida, to desegregate in the fall of 1971, an eighty-car motorcade of whites waving Confederate flags drove up to the school, sparking a race riot. Eleven black students were arrested. The following day, new fighting between black and white students broke out on the school steps. Although the student council attempted to ease the tensions by voting to remove the Confederate flag as the symbol of the school, more than half of the designs suggested by students to replace it bore a close resemblance to the flag, signifying continued white resistance to desegregation. White students in Florida who opposed desegregation were aided by the state legislature, which had banned any school action prohibiting the song "Dixie."[14]

These two symbols—the Confederate flag and "Dixie"—appeared repeatedly in racial confrontations in newly integrated schools. From the 1950s, southern states had used them to express defiance of the federal government, which, segregationists argued, once again wanted to trample states' rights and enforce its own vision of a moral racial order on the South. Outside the schools, segregationists used the flag more often than the song to deride and intimidate civil rights activists. Inside the schools, students and officials colluded in creating a hostile atmosphere for blacks by using both of these symbols. Even beyond the states of the old Confederacy, schools such as Southside High School, in Muncie, Indiana, adopted the name "Rebels" for their athletic teams and designed a school flag to mimic the Confederate flag.[15]

Southside High School students only adopted their Confederate insignia in 1962 when the school was built, although it was integrated from the outset. In other places, blacks found Confederate symbols already in place when they integrated the schools. In light of the historical legacies the symbols evoked—slavery and white supremacy—their use was never an innocent expression of "heritage," as some claimed. Continuing to sing "Dixie," cheer the Rebels, or fly the Confederate flag after schools integrated sent pointed messages of hate. Students such as Betty Walker and Charles Caldwell responded by refusing to honor Confederate symbols.

Other black students countered with symbolic messages of their own. At Tuscaloosa Senior High School, in Tuscaloosa, Alabama, for example, the principal negotiated a compromise between black and white students, in which black students promised to stop raising their fists in the Black Power salute at pep rallies if the white students would stop waving Confederate flags. The principal apologetically told the black students that he would limit the number of times the band played "Dixie," although he could not simply ban the song for fear of further riling whites.[16]

Even where officials or white students exhibited some sensitivity to black students, others angrily clung to the disputed symbols. Brainerd High School, in Chattanooga, Tennessee, named its football team the Rebels, flew the Confederate flag, and played "Dixie" at pep rallies until 1966, when it integrated. Controversy over the continued used of these symbols grew increasingly heated, with school disruptions, demonstrations, and a four-night citywide curfew in October 1969. A school-appointed committee of local citizens met to consider a solution and decided that, although the school would retain the team name "Rebels," it would abandon both the controversial song and the flag. Outraged by this decision, Rod Melton, a white student, came to school with a Confederate flag on the sleeve of his jacket, for which he was suspended. Melton sued, but lost. Incidents like these around the country, where whites used provocative symbols to taunt black students, heightened a sense of strong racial identity for both groups.[17]

Whites who tried to reach out to black students found, to their surprise, that they could become targets of criticism, even in schools with few blacks. Eve Levin attended Vestal High School in a suburb of Binghamton, New York, and graduated in 1971. Less than two dozen black students went to Vestal, but one of Levin's white friends was upset about Levin's friendship with a black girl. In 1970, however, the students elected a black homecoming queen. Marsh' Fenstermaker had a somewhat different experience at her West Virginia high School, where whites accepted black boys as athletes but rejected the notion of black cheerleaders. Moreover, Fenstermaker's white peers, boyfriend, and parents all condemned her for having black friends. She relates this story:

> I can remember some friends (???) told me people were talking about me, because I was seen with some black girls going to school lunch at the local hotdog joint. My boyfriend . . . told me it didn't look right. And believe it or not, later I was in a car with some friends, and a local police officer who knew my mother had the NERVE to go to my mother's place of business to tell her I was in a car with BLACKS. . . . Can you believe it? Like I was with gangsters or I had broken some horrible law!! I was GROUNDED . . . I cried and could not make my mother understand there was nothing wrong and I wasn't going to hell for this. . . . Oh it just makes me so angry to even think about all this over again.[18]

Fenstermaker does not make clear whether she held her ground and kept her black friends or succumbed to the pressure of white friends and family members and renounced them.

Some black students, perhaps not fully understanding the strains on white students, dismissed them as cowards and hypocrites. One black student complained in an interview, "They [white students] all seem to be afraid of what someone else might think. They can't seem to think for themselves. They can't even follow their own moral right." Others agreed with a black girl who explained, "You can't be sure where you stand with them ever. Some of them will smile in your face, and some of them really mean it, I think, but they don't want any other white person seeing them talk to you because they're afraid they'll be called Nigger lover or something."[19]

The rude welcome that many black students faced intensified their racial awareness. Some experienced a more gradual racial awakening. Skywalker Payne was one of two black students attending St. John's Catholic Junior High School, in Panama City, Florida. She describes this minimal integration as "uneventful." The death of a childhood friend confirmed her desire for a religious vocation, however, and, because all of the high schools in Panama City remained segregated, her parents permitted her to enter the all-girls Resurrection High School in Chicago. There, she explains, "I did not feel racially isolated. . . . I was socially isolated because I was part of a select group of girls who were candidates for the order. We lived on a separate wing of the convent and had a Prefect over us. So, my feelings of being different stemmed from my spiritual aspirations, not my race." But she did experience her "personal thrust into racial consciousness" while attending Resurrection High. "I remember my shocked disbelief that girls I sat next to in class were opposed to open housing." Open housing meant selling or renting property to residents regardless of their color or the color of the neighborhood. Payne assumed that Christians would share her support for open, as opposed to segregated, housing. Later, as she stood watching a parade of antiwar protesters, a black man asked her if she was a "soul sister." She had never heard the expression before. "'Well,' he asked, 'Are you Negro or Puerto Rican?'" Then she understood and agreed, "I guess I'm a soul sister."

By her junior year, in 1967, Payne no longer wanted to become a nun and she returned to Panama City to find that the schools had desegregated. She states, "Since I had consistently placed in the top ten academically at Resurrection, I placed myself in honors classes and signed up for Yearbook. I never had more than one or two black students in any of my classes, except for Home-Ec[onomics] and Communism vs. Americanism." These years, she says, "were more bitter than sweet" as "prejudice was outfront and obvious." When her class performed the play *Our Town*, she and "the only other light-skinned black in my classes" played the roles of dead people.[20]

When a handful of blacks integrated a school, racial prejudice might be muted. But "outfront and obvious" prejudice and hostility frequently confronted those who enrolled in large numbers in previously white schools. Roscoe Reeve was a white social studies teacher at Southern High School in Durham County, North Carolina. In his second year of teaching (1966), the school desegregated. He describes what happened:

> The county schools had been the "white schools" and they did not take desegregation well. The first black students caught hell, every day, in class and out. The first day a black student entered my class (midyear) a white student raised his hand (isn't that ironic) and asked why he had to "sit in the same room as a nigger?" I thought I had been punched in the stomach. I'm afraid I launched a diatribe about how he would feel if he were treated like that and had he learned nothing in my US history class . . . blah, blah, blah. Silence.

Sympathetic to the plight of the new students, Reeve recognized that his intervention had no effect. He was also painfully aware that merely refraining from violence or overt discrimination did not guarantee black students a warm environment.

> Most of the schools I had contact with desegregated slowly and the process was universally painful, even in Chapel Hill. Only Charlotte, I think, moved rapidly due to court order. Black students tried hard to be invisible and we on the faculty and those who were administrators did little or nothing to help much. Most of Southern's students came from blue-collar, tobacco farm backgrounds so they were very conservative. Most white students simply ignored the black students, which is its own brand of hell, but they had been told by their parents "to behave."[21]

Mary Alice Cook tells a similar story. Her high school in Lufkin, Texas, managed to hold out against integration until 1969. The following year, however, a federal district judge ordered schools to desegregate at once. At that point, Cook recalls,

> The honchos running the schools in our town finally had to admit that, in 1970, sixteen years after *Brown v. Board,* the jig was up. Plans were hastily made to close Dunbar High School [the black school]—after all, the white kids couldn't be expected to go school there—and ship every last one of its students to formerly white Lufkin High School. The school year 1970–71 would be the first year that blacks would attend Lufkin High en masse. That was my junior year.

Paralleling the passivity of officials at Reeve's school, Lufkin administrators created chaos for students of both races. Cook continues bitterly:

To say that was a rough year would be putting it quite mildly. To say that the whites hated the blacks, and vice versa, is a gross understatement. Rather than accept the inevitable years earlier, plan for it and make a reasonable transition, the school administrators had instead waited to be forced to act, at which time they simply dumped one entire school population into another, stirred them together, and waited for the pot to boil.[22]

The pot indeed boiled over. Unlike the situation at Handley High School, where whites expected blacks to accept the school and its racist customs, Cook claims that Lufkin High threw out some of its "longstanding traditions," angering the whites without placating the blacks. To integrate the sports teams, coaches created an uproar by cutting both blacks and whites who had previously played in the segregated schools. Blacks and whites of opposite sexes could not converse with one another without causing "talk and damaged reputations." White faculty and administration dominated the integrated school and looked down upon the few black teachers hired from Dunbar High School as "ignorant and 'only there to fill a quota.'" In the spring, administrators cancelled a much-loved talent show and "roast" called the "Senior Assembly." Cook cannot remember the precise reason, although she suggests several possibilities—whites did not want the assembly to be held if blacks were allowed to participate; blacks did not want to participate but did not want whites to have any fun, or perhaps, Cook speculates, the administration decided "that it would have been too divisive and disruptive (so many things in those days, previously harmless and fun, were called 'disruptive')."[23]

Mary Alice Cook's narrative points out two important facts about school desegregation. First, integration nearly always entailed transferring blacks to white schools; white officials found it unthinkable to require whites to attend formerly all-black schools, which they assumed were inferior. Indeed, many of them were because whites had withheld money and resources. Consequently, the logic of the day dictated that the inferior schools would close down and their students would integrate the white schools. Officials at Lufkin High threw the black and white students together with callous disregard for any of them. In other places, blacks resisted school closings. In Hyde County, North Carolina, for example, eight hundred black students boycotted classes for more than a year to demand that their schools be integrated by whites, in contrast to the county's plan to integrate only the white schools. The local black community supported the boycott and joined with students at sit-ins and marches to the state capital in Raleigh in an effort to save their schools. In the end they won: formerly black schools were integrated, rather than being closed and essentially thrown away.[24]

Students played a pivotal role in the Hyde County protests. The initial boycott was led by Golden Frinks, an older member of the Student Non-Violent Coordinating Committee (SNCC), but high school students gradually took over the daily details of organizing and sustaining the boycott. Dudley Flood, appointed by the North Carolina Division of Desegregation

Assistance to arbitrate the debate between the black and white communities, found the students to be "incredible visionaries, good planners and thinkers." Without the determination and tenacity of these black students, their schools would have been forced to close. Following their victory, the students formed a planning committee with equal numbers of black and white members, with the hope of easing the integration of white students. How different school desegregation could have been had more people exhibited the sensitivity and sensibility of these Hyde County students. Ironically, despite the mature approach of the black students, one of the black schools was paralyzed by violence in 1972 after whites integrated it, because the honor society refused to admit blacks.[25]

When school officials accepted the *Brown* decision, moved to integrate early according to a plan, and maintained good communications between the black and white communities, fewer problems surfaced. Fayetteville, Arkansas, was the first southern city to obey the *Brown* edict. The principals of the black and white high schools (both of whom were women) worked together on a program of gradual integration and minimal publicity in 1954. It worked. On the first day of integration the white high school drew one lone protester (also a woman), who marched around with a sign whose message has now been forgotten, shouted briefly at the school building, then disappeared. Despite her role in the peaceful integration, the black principal's school closed, and she had to find a job elsewhere. The handful of black students who carried out integration were "prepared" during a six-week summer course offered by the League of Women Voters to "'close the gap,' both academically and culturally." Apparently, no one dreamed that white students might benefit from similar preparation.[26]

Even whites who accepted desegregation assumed that black students would bear the burden of assimilating and accommodating to their new schools. Carole Palmer, who grew up in a small east Texas town and graduated in 1967, remembers being "incensed at our local school authorities," because when the high school integrated in 1965, they "were exceedingly insensitive and did not offer any sort of orientation *for the black kids* prior to the start of that school year" (emphasis added). School integration, then, was generally a one-way street: whites viewed African-American students as guests or interlopers, welcomed them with varying degrees of warmth or coldness, but expected them to adopt the habits and traditions of their reluctant hosts. By the end of the 1960s, when blacks grew tired of their marginal status and demanded to be treated as full-fledged members of the school, conflicts between whites and blacks escalated rapidly.[27]

SEGREGATION IN INTEGRATED SCHOOLS

The second key fact about desegregation that Mary Alice Cook's story highlights is how many schools *resegregated* within their walls, through explicit policies. One student, who later became a teacher, explained that, until she complained to the U.S. Department of Justice and triggered an investigation, her "integrated" southern school established separate study halls for black students and set aside separate bathrooms and tables in the cafeteria. John Canfield, a white teacher in a Chicago ghetto, observed that, once the population at his school became more than half black, the administration cancelled the student court, which had previously been consulted in disciplinary cases. Other students reported separate lunch and gym classes and even different bell ringings, to prevent black and white students from using the halls at the same time. Another student told interviewers that black football players carried the ball "to about the 99 yard line," and then the coach sent in a white player to score the touchdown. Student government and cheerleading squads often remained white or integrated only after another battle.[28]

School policy shaped resegregation in a number of ways. The most important of these was the use of "tracking," assigning students to precollegiate or general diploma pathways based on officials' perceptions of a student's life trajectory or skill level. Many white officials believed that black students lagged far behind white schoolchildren in academic achievement and that black teachers were incompetent. White students sometimes agreed. Jennifer McKee regarded some of the teachers from the formerly segregated black school as "practically illiterate" when they transferred into her newly integrated high school in Greenville, South Carolina. In a 1972 study of the tortuous path to integration in Inglewood, California, one of the white teachers claimed that student achievement scores had dropped since his school desegregated. Black students wanted higher-level math classes to prepare for college, but the teacher did not believe they were ready. He complained that letting black students into his class would lower standards for all students. If he barred them, they would call him a racist. If he offered special summer sessions in math to allow the black students to catch up, the extra work would upset them and some white students might have resented blacks getting special help.[29]

Sometimes integration exposed the inadequacies of segregated education. Donald Reeves was admitted to the prestigious High School of Music and Art, in New York City, in 1968. In his memoir he laments that, after the first week, "I fell flat on my academic face." Although he had graduated from junior high with honors, he concedes, "The truth of the matter was that I had not been prepared for academic work. I was an average student placed in competition with people who had little interest or ability in studying. At Music and Art, faced with real competition, I was unprepared to handle academic life."[30]

To what degree these perceptions of academic weakness in black students and teachers were accurate is impossible to weigh. Supported by tiny tax bases and parsimonious, prejudiced local and state governments, black schools prior to *Brown* in no way equaled white schools. With less money per student and woefully inadequate facilities, they were often forced to use castoff textbooks from the white schools. Focusing solely on the physical and financial shortcomings of the all-black schools, however, ignores the human element, for even under these less-than-ideal circumstances, many children received adequate and even good educations. It is also doubtful that the majority of teachers were as bad as some whites asserted. Teaching had long been the primary occupation for middle-class black women, who were trained by numerous black colleges and normal schools. Like preachers, black teachers enjoyed great respect in their communities. The white assumption that Jim Crow education had produced a sorry breed of teachers denigrated their professionalism.[31]

Relying on standardized tests or course grades as the measure of students' abilities is risky business. Educators understand that many social and economic factors—including teachers' attitudes and expectations—explain the disparities between minority and white students in integrated schools. In light of the chilly reception of black students as they integrated white schools, and the racial tension and even violence that sometimes followed, it seems logical that some students' grades would drop. If white students had been forced to transfer into hostile black schools, how many of them would have maintained good grades?[32]

A widespread presumption of black academic inferiority permitted school administrators to justify the practice of tracking. In addition to routing black students toward a "general diploma," which Donald Reeves called "nothing but a ticket to the army," school counselors steered them toward vocational tracks or "compensatory" classes, the latter designed to "compensate" for the "cultural deprivation" that whites assumed they had suffered. Brent Coatney, a white student in Hopkinsville, Kentucky, found these classes "a terrible joke." Coatney's academic performance and defiant attitude prompted school officials to assign him to what he remembers as "classes with large numbers of blacks and whites alike, who were not at all interested in academics, but reveled in conflict, disruption of class, and all sorts of rebellion." In the college preparatory track, the "upper echelon" of students, he notes, was "mostly white." Both tracking and compensatory education, as Coatney makes clear, tended to resegregate students within school walls. Studies of tracking have revealed that it also influences the scheduling of common courses and electives so that students in different tracks rarely share classes. Special education and bilingual classes, which target students of color far more often than whites, serve to further segregate students.[33]

Bright black students like Skywalker Payne, who managed to "track into" college preparatory classes, suffered isolation of two types. Not only were they outnumbered by white students in these classes, but other blacks who regarded them as "Uncle Toms" for taking "white classes" cold-shouldered them. Some students criticized the entire system of tracking. N. K. Jamal, for example, an activist student who chaired the New York City Black High School Coalition in 1970, attacked college preparatory tracks, because in his opinion they turned blacks into "half-white members of the black middle class, where they [would] serve as examples of 'those who made it.'" Others, like Paul Gayton, a black student at East High School, in Denver, found the general courses into which many blacks were channeled just as offensive. The general track often included classes like woodworking, which, Gayton argued, would not help students get jobs after graduation. These criticisms highlighted a dilemma for school officials. Offering black students the same high-level, precollegiate education available to whites struck black radicals as an effort to "whiten" them. But these same critics scorned compensatory or remedial courses as transparent means of maintaining racial segregation within the schools. While some officials were undoubtedly guilty of tokenism and racism, those who genuinely wanted desegregation to work and who wanted the best for their students felt stymied.[34]

A more insidious form of resegregation masqueraded under the guise of discipline. A 1973 report sponsored by the Southern Regional Council revealed that black students in all parts of the country were two to five times more likely than white students to be suspended from school, were suspended for longer periods, and were more likely to be suspended multiple times. According to one study of these "pushouts," in many places "the suspensions of black students were most pronounced in racially balanced schools that had recently undergone desegregation; previously integrated schools that experienced little change in black enrollment underwent little change in suspensions." The study further noted that black students were more likely than whites to be disciplined for "subjective" offenses, such as disrespect, profanity, or violations of the dress code, and found a strong correlation between numbers of students suspended and numbers of students who dropped out of school altogether.[35]

Resegregation extended beyond the classroom and school as a whole to effect extracurricular activities. Some school events disappeared or moved off-campus. At Janet Gray Carstens's high school in Greenville, North Carolina, class dances moved into private white clubs where blacks could not follow. Tim Galliher, who graduated in 1967 from a high school in Kannapolis, North Carolina, recalls that, although there were only four or five black students in his class, "[b]ecause of their presence the local school board forbade our class from having a prom that year, which really upset parents as well as students. The unofficial reason was that they were scared a black boy would ask a white girl to dance." Marsh Fenstermaker had a number of black friends in high school in West Virginia who told her later that, with regard to dances and extracurricular activities, "they never felt a part of the school and didn't feel welcome at the functions."[36]

Resegregation in school also reflected population shifts in the neighborhoods that served the schools, a phenomenon known as "white flight." Many school districts in the larger cities in the United States began losing white students in the years following World War II, in part because of the national trend toward suburbanization. But was white flight a response to school desegregation? Whites did move for reasons other than fear of desegregation. Yet the evidence leads one to suspect desegregation was a key factor. Contemporaries saw a clear link: some argued that a "tipover" point occurred when a school became 30 percent black; after that, whites would flee and the school would rapidly become all-black.[37]

The period of transition as a school's population changed was frequently marked by stronger racial lines drawn within the school, as those whites still attending voluntarily withdrew from school activities and black students established their own presence. In these cases, students—not school officials—heightened resegregation. During an interview with a representative of the U.S. Commission on Civil Rights in 1971, for example, an anonymous student with the pseudonym "William" commented that, at his mostly black high school, "The white kids don't play basketball or nothing because the colored kids take over, so the white [sic] join ROTC." Terre Hanson Burkhart, from Dayton, Ohio, reports the same phenomenon at her school, when the white student population dropped from 59 percent to 40 percent. This internal white flight helped eliminate some violence, perhaps, but it did not create much in the way of school or interracial solidarity. As Burkhart comments, "There weren't really fights about how many white/black cheerleaders there would be. The white girls just didn't try to make the team in the same numbers the black girls did. Many white girls didn't want to 'risk' being the only white or in the minority. There was a strong apathy. The white boys stopped going out for the major sports as well. Only baseball continued to be mostly white." One white girl told Kenneth Fish, a high school principal who wrote about high school unrest, "If anybody thinks I'm going to the Junior Prom, they've got to be crazy. Do you think I'm going to be one of about four white kids there with ninety black kids?"[38]

In other schools, student resegregation occurred not because white students withdrew, but instead because they staunchly maintained barriers to black participation in school activities. "Rosa," a Mexican-American student, told an interviewer, "The colored girls complained that they couldn't try out for 'Letter Girls' because they would never make it. Every year they try out. The colored girls would get together and pick the best looking ones that had the best figures and were the lightest [in skin color], and still they would never make it." Appealing to the school's counselors had no effect; the counselors either sided with the whites or refused to intervene. In this case, although black girls attempted to accommodate to white standards of beauty, whites simply locked the door. Administrators sometimes quelled black students' protests without addressing their grievances. When black students in a Saginaw, Michigan, high school protested the all-white homecoming court in 1968, school officials suspended eighteen of them.[39]

Other schools established racial quotas to permit black student representation in various extracurricular activities and hopefully to forestall racial violence. Janet Gray Carstens relates that at her high school, the students elected two cheerleading captains—one white, one black—so that the cheerleading team would be integrated under their joint leadership. At John Tyler High School, in east Texas, the principal designed a segregated ballot to allow students to vote for two black cheerleaders from a list of four candidates and four whites from a list of ten. It is not clear whether the lopsided numbers reflected proportional representation of black and whites or the principal intended this tactic to maintain white dominance over cheerleading. In Hyde County, North Carolina, the integrated Student Planning Committee carefully stipulated that all candidates for student government pick a running mate of a different race and agreed to elect two homecoming queens—one black and one white. Although such schemes illustrate a greater will to inclusivity than many integrated schools exhibited, they simultaneously show that the colorblind society of which Martin Luther King dreamed was nowhere in sight.[40]

In 1969, *Life* magazine commissioned pollster Louis Harris to survey Americans on various issues relating to high school life. One question touched on integration, although, tellingly, it asked about "admitting black students into all-white schools." The responses showed clearly that students and teachers embraced this far more enthusiastically than parents did. Fifty-six percent of students and 60 percent of teachers polled stated that they supported integration; a mere 32 percent of parents felt the same way. Only 18 percent of students and 16 percent of teachers responded negatively, compared to 31 percent of parents. Unfortunately, the poll did not break down responses by race, making a more nuanced analysis impossible. When black students arrived on campus, however, particularly as their numbers grew, racial tensions simultaneously increased.[41]

LATINO STUDENTS IN INTEGRATED SCHOOLS

Because blacks were the largest nonwhite racial group in the United States and court-ordered desegregation primarily pinpointed them, most racial tension in 1960s high schools involved blacks and whites. In the same years, Native-Americans generally attended reservation schools, or—as part of the "termination" policy enacted by the Eisenhower administration, which aimed to end their status as wards of the federal government—Indian schools off the reservations. California, Mississippi, and Virginia laws permitted the segregation of Native-Americans, but it is not clear how many in fact attended separate schools, especially in the years after *Brown*. Asian-Americans did not constitute a large group and at this time identified themselves more as members of their specific ethnic group (e.g., Chinese-Americans, Japanese-Americans, or Korean-Americans) than as "Asians." Moreover, there is little evidence of collective action by Asians in the high schools in these years. Latinos' experience, however, often paralleled that of black students.[42]

In 1848, when the United States wrested from Mexico the southwestern states that later became New Mexico, Arizona, California, Utah, and Nevada, the Mexican government attempted to safeguard the rights of its nationals still living on these lands. The Treaty of Guadalupe Hidalgo pledged that Mexicans in the United States would be accorded fair treatment and permitted to keep their religious faith and the Spanish language. But from the beginning, Americans ignored and violated these promises. Schools for Mexican-American children were often segregated. States such as Texas and California did not *require* segregation for Latinos, but they did permit it, and most Mexican-American children attended segregated schools. California segregated Mexican-American children on the grounds that they had Indian blood. Indians and "Mongolians"—meaning the Chinese—could be legally segregated. Sometimes officials justified separate schools on the grounds that the children did not speak English. In *Mendez v. Westminster School District* (1946), a U.S. district court judge struck down segregated education in several Southern California school districts. He accepted school officials' claim that non-English-speaking students should be temporarily separated from other students but held the wide pattern of such "separation" to be discriminatory.[43]

New immigrants from Mexico flooded into the United States in the twentieth century, especially under the World War II–era bracero program. Initiated in 1942 by the federal government, this plan to combat labor shortages in agriculture permitted some two hundred thousand Mexicans to reside and work in the United States temporarily. When the government terminated the program at the end of the war, illegal immigrants continued to enter the country. Meanwhile, American schools continued to discriminate against students of Mexican descent, placing them in the first or second grade regardless of their academic levels, providing fewer hours of instruction, and appointing neophyte teachers to the schools until they had sufficient experience to transfer to more desirable positions.[44]

By the 1960s, Mexican-Americans were the second largest nonwhite group in the United States, and, along with African-Americans, they accelerated their long-standing struggle for rights and equality in education. In 1966, African-American and Mexican parents in Los Angeles joined in a suit to force all city schools to desegregate, but this demand was not met until the case reached the California Supreme Court ten years later. Similarly, a group of minority parents, including Latinos, sued to desegregate the Denver, Colorado, public schools. The federal district court ordered the schools to desegregate in 1969 and again in 1973, but litigation over language programs available to Mexican students dragged on until 1983. Movements for equal access to education and desegregated schools occurred in every city with a substantial Latino population.[45]

Mexican-Americans who attended high school with white students often encountered prejudices. Kenneth García had already dropped out of high school in the late 1960s, but thirty years later he still recalls his outrage upon hearing that a high school teacher had told his students—including some Mexican-Americans—that "if you ate beans you would 'grow up to be stupid like the Mexicans in the class.'" Berdie Sánchez grew up in Crystal City, Texas, forty miles from the Mexican border. Crystal City was predominantly Mexican, but the teachers were all white, and, Sánchez reports, school policy forbade the students to speak "even one word in Spanish."[46]

Officials banned Spanish to force Mexican children into the English-speaking mainstream as quickly as possible, despite the hardships this created. Beginning in the early 1960s, however, some halting efforts at change emerged. Following Fidel Castro's revolution in Cuba, large numbers of Cuban exiles began pouring into the United States. In 1963, one elementary school in Miami, Florida, initiated bilingual education, teaching Cuban children in Spanish while preparing them for English instruction. Within two years, a handful of schools in Texas and New Mexico followed suit. Title VII of the Education Act, signed into law by President Lyndon Johnson in 1968, appropriated $7.5 million for bilingual education. This meager sum encouraged at least some school districts to exhibit greater sensitivity to the needs of Spanish-speaking students. Moreover, when director of the federal Office of Civil Rights argued that school districts that failed to provide adequate services for Hispanic children denied these children equal educational opportunities and thus could have their federal funding reduced, Title VII actually grew some teeth.[47]

Most schools, however, complied slowly, if at all. In any case, although students and parents welcomed bilingual education, it did little to relieve the racial humiliations that students endured. Berdie Sánchez recalls a particularly belittling ritual: "Three or four times a year, all the Hispanic children were called to go see the school nurse, none of the white kids were, and we had our hair literally whitened with louse powder. We were not even examined to see if indeed we had lice, it was just assumed that we did." Her high school banned dating between Mexicans and whites, and the counselors did not encourage Mexican students to think about going to college. "We had no counselors and we certainly were never told that we could earn scholarships."[48] Sánchez continues,

> Although we got along with the White kids, the racism was alive and well. I remember the year we had a talent show. I sang, and we held the show in the auditorium in the evening. I went into the girls' bathroom to get ready, put on my formal and do my hair. I forgot my hairbrush and there were bags of rollers, brushes, and other girl paraphernalia all about and I looked over and just picked up a hairbrush to use. I was only fourteen and quite naïve about a lot of things. As I was brushing my hair, a few of the White girls came and one of them saw me using the brush, which turned out to be hers. She got this shocked look on her face and raced out to get a teacher. When the teacher arrived, she didn't say anything to me for using the brush; she merely instructed the White girl to "throw it in the trash," and walked out. I didn't have to be punished any further. What stayed in my mind was that the White girl had always been friendly with me, but obviously that was just surface stuff.[49]

In the pleasure of primping for her talent show, Sánchez stepped over a line that "the surface stuff," the superficial "getting along" with white students, had blurred for her. The girl with the brush and the teacher emphatically redrew the line. As American schools technically desegregated, white students and adults collaborated in segmenting them racially. Some racial lines demarcated physical territory: separate tables in the cafeteria, space on the dance floor, or seats in a classroom. Other lines maintained racial hierarchy, privileging white claims to brains, beauty, and leadership while excluding students of color. White students whose compassion or bravery compelled them to reach across these lines were abruptly yanked back or chastened by white peers or adults. Race was thus inscribed into the very routines of high school life, and students lived their race in ways they had not done in segregated schools.

When the Supreme Court struck down segregation in schools in 1954, it intended, in part, to repair the injury segregation allegedly caused students of color. This step toward equality and simple justice moved the United States closer to its avowed ideals. It may also have bolstered the country in its fervid competition with the Soviet Union for allies and influence among the decolonizing nations in Africa and Asia, a consideration that prompted a great deal of civil rights legislation. For all the illusion of forward movement or progress, however, a powerful riptide pulled race relations in the opposite direction. Continuity, not change, marked the interactions between students and adults of different races in the public schools. Far from ameliorating the humiliation of racism, school desegregation probably made things worse, particularly for students of color, whose welfare had ostensibly been the chief concern of integrationists.

Several consequences stemmed from the inability or unwillingness of whites to make the public schools open and inclusive, apart from the violence that disrupted education throughout the late 1960s and early 1970s. The transparent efforts of whites to maintain the racial status quo permitted students of color to understand how power undergirded rules, policies, and traditions. Witnessing whites use their power to defend their own interests helped to delegitimize that power. Comprehending how white power operated suggested strategies to oppose it. Finally, emphasizing whiteness made it inevitable that blacks and Latinos would marshal the same tactics in their battles to make the schools institutions that would serve rather than oppress them.

High school students of color quickly found life in white-dominated high schools intolerable. Enduring insults and physical assaults, encountering subtle and overt prejudice, and getting the message in a thousand ways that they did not belong in the schools sparked a rebellious fire in black and Latino students. While in the early stages of desegregation, white administrators, teachers, and students had the upper hand, eventually, buoyed by their rising numbers and the birth of a more aggressive racial spirit in the society as a whole, minority students began to push back. As one black student told an interviewer in 1967, "When we have about an equal number of students we'll see if we can get in a fight over there. We will have the same number in our color as they got in their color so we probably have a better chance fighting[.] [I]f they're looking for a fight this year then I'm going to fight." The failure of desegregation to end racism, in tandem with the new forms of segregation that white adults and students created on every inch of school property fed a rising tide of black and brown militance, leaving whites—for a change—fearful and defensive. Militance sprang to life at different times in different places, but the assassination of Martin Luther King, Jr., on April 4, 1968, is a convenient historical milepost. Changes in race relations that had already begun intensified and coalesced following King's murder. A still more difficult era in race relations followed.[50]

THREE — **IT'S NOT PERSONAL,**

IT'S JUST THAT YOU'RE WHITE

BLACK AND BROWN POWER IN THE HIGH SCHOOLS

Upon learning of Martin Luther King's assassination in April 1968, Jacque Switzer and her friend Marsha Patterson were the only white students who joined their black classmates from Lima Central High School, in Ohio, in a walkout. Switzer and Patterson sympathized with the integrationist aims of the civil rights movement. By participating in their classmates' spontaneous demonstration of mourning for Dr. King, the girls figuratively crossed the color line. Switzer does not relate how her black peers responded to the gesture of solidarity, but in other places, blacks sharply rebuffed white condolences. When officials at the Bronx High School of Science, in New York City, invited representatives of the newly formed student Black Cultural Society (BCS) to address what they intended to be a healing memorial assembly for Dr. King, BCS member Marilyn McIntosh instead emphasized racial differences, addressing her classmates divisively as "brothers and sisters and other students." Indeed, some whites offered no condolences. One white girl told interviewers bluntly, "I didn't like King at all. I never have and I never will, I just thought he was such a hypocrite. I don't see why they were so upset when he was killed."[1]

The disparate reactions of these high school students to King's death reflect the growing divisions in American society and in its high schools. Civil rights activists had, by 1968, accomplished many of their legal goals. New laws forbade segregation, discrimination in housing, public accommodations, and employment, and the federal government promised to safeguard black voting rights in the South. Changing blacks' legal status, however necessary and overdue, was only part of the task of achieving equal opportunity and full citizenship. Civil rights victories barely affected northern ghettos, where legal rights had not been the issue, and there race riots multiplied alarmingly. In the summer before King was murdered, riots broke out in nearly 150 cities as black frustration with poor living conditions, unemployment, and police brutality repeatedly boiled over. King himself had lost stature. His critique of the war in Vietnam for siphoning off much-needed domestic resources and for putting too many blacks on the front lines alienated his white supporters just as younger black activists marched past him, hearing a different, more martial drummer.

Not only had King lost black and white supporters before his murder, but his dream of a color-blind America had also been challenged by the ideologies of black nationalism and Black Power. King hoped to win access to economic, educational, and social opportunities on equal footing with whites, but black nationalists favored pulling away to form exclusively black institutions. In this way, they believed they could control the politics, economics, and culture of the black community and gain a measure of autonomy from whites. Black Power advocates disagreed with King that racial subordination was a moral problem best addressed by nonviolent Christian witness. Blacks' problems, they argued, stemmed from their lack of power; power would have to be seized. How blacks were to seize power, and what they would do with it once they had it, remained obscure. Malcolm X, assassinated in 1965, had been the most famous advocate of both black nationalism and Black Power, and his slogan "By any means necessary" was taken up by those for whom Martin Luther King's dream no longer held appeal.

Black nationalism and Black Power philosophies attracted increasing numbers of minority high school students. Whites had responded to desegregation by racializing the social and physical spaces within the schools, relegating nonwhites to the fringes. Now students of color attempted to claim spaces of their own, remapping the schools as places that both accentuated and valorized racial differences. They also placed race at the center of their identity and made it the core of their interactions with other students and administrators. In the unfamiliar terrain created by minority student activism, some whites trod timorously, some ferociously defended white power and privilege, and others sought common ground. For radical students, King's assassination proved the futility of peaceful change, while shaking the faith of those who still hoped for evolution rather than revolution. It further strengthened the racial consciousness of both black and white students, spurred activism and protests by black students, and sharpened existing antagonisms in the schools.

THE IMPACT OF KING'S DEATH ON HIGH SCHOOLS

President John Kennedy's assassination in 1963 had signaled for many Americans the end of an era of innocence. Stunned by the rapid succession of events—Kennedy's death, Lyndon Johnson's hasty swearing-in, and the televised murder of assassin Lee Harvey Oswald—Americans drew together in sorrow. By contrast, King's murder five years later deepened the cleavages. Riots broke out in more than two hundred cities, as blacks, convulsed with grief and rage, burned, looted, pitched rocks, and shouted their defiance of white America. The sound of shattering glass, the *whoomp* of Molotov cocktails exploding, and the wails of police and fire sirens provided menacing theme music for the intensification of racial hatred.

In the high schools, too, broader societal divisions manifested themselves. Whereas few schools had been integrated when Kennedy was killed, by 1968 desegregation forced together members of two very different communities who often had very different reactions to Martin Luther King's assassination. Each of these communities, in turn, was increasingly riven by ideological differences, as liberal, conservative, and radical Americans of all races disputed the possibility and desirability of the changes King had sought.

Black students, especially those in urban schools, typically reacted with shock and anger. In some instances, adults managed to channel their emotions into productive channels. In Greenwood, Mississippi, for example, when between six hundred to seven hundred students took to the streets the day after the assassination, a local minister led them into his church and convinced them to organize and support an ongoing boycott of racist merchants. A school administrator in Northfield, Illinois, permitted black students to run seminars on white racism and allowed one teacher to incorporate studies on racism and ghetto violence into the coursework. In other places, however, officials either did not try or failed to contain student outrage. According to the Riot Data Clearinghouse at Brandeis University, "civil disorders" broke out in ninety-one schools around the nation. In Washington, D.C., one hundred black high school students sought out college student Joe Miles, vice chair of the D.C. Black Antiwar Antidraft Union, and persuaded him to lead a march to Howard University, where two hundred other high school students joined them. Black students in some schools refused to salute the American flag. Most of the schools in New York City briefly closed, both out of respect for King and fear of more violence.[2]

Some students interpreted the turmoil in high schools following King's death cynically. "Velma," a black student at an urban high school, observes, "Right after King died, a lot of the kids here just made hay with that. But they weren't really followers of King. King didn't mean that much to them." It pleased Velma that these students (both black and white) stayed away from school for a few days after the assassination. "Boy, was it nice when King died," she crows. "All of those radicals and nuts were gone." Another student from the same school echoes her sentiments: "All of the trash stayed home, including white trash, who look for any kind of excuse to cut their classes." What these students meant by "radicals," "nuts," and "trash" is not clear, although they may have referred to the students who, by 1968, considered themselves political radicals, or advocates of racial power. In any case, their name-calling reveals rifts among blacks as well as between blacks and whites.[3]

White students were also internally divided, and their responses to King's death ranged widely. Gary Carnog, a white first-year teacher, found the indifference of his white students "shocking": "They did not like what he stood for; they thought they had no obligations to consider Negroes as their equals; they felt that the burden of proof was on Negro shoulders: when they acted in an acceptable way, then they could receive the respect of whites." A white student at Shaw High School, in Cleveland, Ohio (which was 70 percent black), provoked a fight by wearing a button that taunted, "Happy Easter, Dr. King." (King had died ten days before Easter.) Robert Rossner, who taught English at the Bronx High School of Science, relates that after a number of spontaneous eulogies for Martin Luther King, one white boy complained about the "disruption" of his classes. Other white students felt appalled by King's assassination but struggled to find a way to express their sympathy to black classmates. Because King's murder was both political and racial, in contrast to that of John Kennedy, whites also wrestled with inchoate feelings of guilt. Another student at Science confesses, "I wanted to say something but what could I say? *I'm sorry?* But I hadn't *done* anything, had I—so what was I sorry for?"[4]

The responses of white teachers mirrored those of their students. Some, seemingly unmoved by King's death, took the attitude that nothing that occurred outside school walls should have any bearing on the school's everyday functions. Teachers at the High School of Music and Art, in New York City, expressed annoyance when some students tried to prevent others from entering the day after the assassination on the grounds that it should be a day of mourning. The teachers objected to mourning activities that would disrupt school. John Canfield, a young teacher in a mostly black Chicago school, wrote that after King's death, white teachers who disapproved of his school's newly formed Afro-American Club began harassing the teachers who sponsored the club, by "putting unsigned letters, cartoons and even African coins into their mailboxes."[5]

Many white students reacted more strongly to the subsequent riots than to the assassination itself. Although King's death seemed distant, the riots often touched them personally and left vivid memories. The bus Susan Lindholm took to work passed through a black section of Minneapolis the day after King's assassination. "I was sitting by a window and petrified," she recalls. "We were stopped at a red light, I could see fires and people throwing things. An angry black youth was screaming at the bus, looked like he was going to throw a rock through the window next to me. I just sat there, frozen in disbelief." Jan Weiland's Southside Chicago school, where the student population was changing from Polish and Jewish to black, became the target of violence after King's death. Weiland relates, "[T]he school was up for grabs. Sitting in health class, bricks flew through the window, hitting the girl in front of me. We all fell to the floor and crawled out on our bellies. No SWAT team to save us, that's for sure."[6]

Whites whose encounters with the riots were less direct felt the same vulnerability. Jan Scarbrough had been in Washington, D.C., with her high school band to play in a Cherry Blossom Festival. Terrified of the raging mobs, officials cancelled the festival, and Scarbrough and her peers were "suddenly rushed aboard the buses, and told we had to get out of the area fast. Riots were taking place nearby and our buses had Tennessee license plates on them!" David Wachtel, then in eleventh grade in Ambridge, Pennsylvania, saw a handgun for the first time. His boss, a baker, "was afraid rioting blacks might break in as we worked late at night" and so brought his gun to work.[7]

Witnessing violence, fearing they might become its victims simply because of their race, was a new, terrifying experience for white students. Jan Weiland declares that years later, as a mother, she "made sure [her] daughters grew up in a nice suburban area," so they would never know "the fear of walking down the street facing a group of black girls who thought it would be fun to kick the blond girl just for laughs."[8]

Martin Luther King's assassination rocked the nation, but officials in its high schools generally proved unwilling to grapple with the tragedy. "Pauline" asked her principal for an official show of respect for King's passing, particularly in light of the two-minute silence students had previously observed for a former student killed in Vietnam. But, to her disgust, "Ewing [the principal] said to me, 'Well, you know, Pauline, people die all the time for all kinds of causes, you can't disrupt the schedule.'" Teacher Eleanor Fuke laments the missed opportunity to explore racism directly at her inner-city Chicago school. Black and white students already regarded one another with suspicion and hostility, and in the days after King's death, some unknown student (Fuke assumes) repeatedly set off the fire alarm. After the fire department investigation, Fuke remembers, many students simply went home "in order to avoid possible violence at school." On the day the school held a memorial for Martin Luther King, however, someone again pulled the alarm. The upperclassmen had already had their assembly, but "the freshmen and sophomores, who most needed such a memorial to calm them down, were gaily at home before the first assembly ended." The school ultimately ignored all fire alarms except those sounded from the main office. "This put an end to early dismissals," Fuke recalls, "but it did not give the students a chance to tell the faculty and administration what was on their minds." Race relations continued to be troubled.[9]

At many schools, once the initial shock of King's death passed, racial tensions escalated. Gail Richardson, a young white teacher at Belden High

School, in Chicago, asserts that in the first shock of grief, black and white students seemed united. "[T]aps was played after homeroom," she states, "and a minute of silence was observed, a silence in which you could have heard a pin drop throughout the big old building. A memorial display appeared in the main corridor display case; plans for an assembly were begun." White students and teachers, however, felt tense, nervous, and "inadequate" as African-American students "gathered, threatened to walk out, [and] talked with the administration."[10]

Deteriorating race relations within the schools sometimes exacerbated school-community friction. Teacher John Canfield reports that, when the police came to disperse a group of students outside his school in Chicago, one officer, shoved by the crowd, "lashed out in an uncontrolled fit of anger and began to strike the people nearest to him, seriously injuring one male student and unnecessarily beating several other girls who happened to be near." Police then arrested a number of the students. A parents' meeting in the community revealed fissures between the more affluent parents, who, according to Canfield, "said that they were sure that the students who had been arrested probably deserved it in the first place," and the poorer parents, who expressed outrage both at the violence of the police and the attitude of the other parents.[11]

Canfield's narrative makes clear that the rifts in American high schools mirrored those in the larger society. Racial divisions dominated, yet class and ideological gaps also widened. High schools, however, did not simply passively reflect American society—they actively engaged with it. Using school property as the staging ground for mourning King's assassination and protesting the racism that caused it was one way students interacted with society beyond the school. When these demonstrations drew in outside forces, the collision between students and white adult authorities contributed to the racial polarization of the era, as events in the neighborhood of Detroit's Core High School show. Core High was virtually all black (there was only one white student among more than two thousand African-Americans), and its student leaders threatened to walk out if officials did not close the school the day after King's death. Although the administration convinced most of the students to keep the school open and attend a memorial service, a small group attempted to string up a white effigy with a placard reading "Hang Whitey" slung around its neck. The administration called the police, who arrested one boy with what student onlookers criticized as unnecessary force. The principal hastily dismissed school to avoid further trouble, and the Detroit police and Michigan National Guard (predominantly white) arrived to help restore order. When the Guard left, however, students and administrators discovered that, in addition to looting several hundred dollars worth of athletic and audiovisual equipment, the Guardsmen had chalked on the walls their own vicious messages to the students and community: "Glad you're dead, Martin Luther King," and "Martin Luther King M_____ F_____ [sic]."[12]

BLACK STUDENT ACTIVISM

King's assassination and the violent aftermath also accelerated black high school student activism, which dated back to the 1950s. When principals punished students for volunteer work for the Student Non-Violent Co-ordinating Committee (SNCC) or the Council of Federated Organizations (COFO) after school hours, black students walked out and boycotted their schools. In 1966, two of the first students' rights cases were heard in the U.S. Fifth Circuit Court of Appeals. Both involved the right of black students to wear "freedom buttons" in school. High school activism did not occur solely in the South. In 1962, more than two hundred thousand black students boycotted Chicago schools to show their loathing for the segregationist policies of Superintendent of Schools Benjamin C. Willis. Two years later, a similar boycott occurred in Boston, and nearly half a million black students walked out of their New York City schools.[13]

Early on, high school students either protested discrimination in all aspects of black life, or else they demanded that schools desegregate. By the late 1960s, activism focused on changing the conditions *within* the high schools, which had already integrated. Because students left few records and administrators did not document the precise details of their confrontations and negotiations with activist students, it is difficult to know how they organized to carry out these activities. Both the creation of black student unions and the numerous collective protests students staged suggest a high degree of organization. Black students presented their objectives to principals through petitions, lists of grievances, or—more provocatively—sets of demands. Articulating what they wanted through these means further underscores students' organization, but we cannot know how they chose their leaders, decided which demands to include, or settled upon any particular approach to school authorities.[14]

Paralleling events in many traditionally black universities, as well as newly integrated universities and colleges, black high school students' demands centered on winning institutional recognition. Typically, students wanted more black teachers, principals, and administrators; the teaching of African-American and African history; courses in Swahili or other African languages; "soul food" in the cafeteria; and the freedom to wear dashikis and Afros and display their black pride. They often wanted to establish black student unions. Sometimes they went as far as seeking the dismissal of white teachers or principals accused of racism. In one case in 1969, students disrupted a board of education meeting to demand that their Detroit junior high school and a high school on the same grounds be renamed after Malcolm X. The board voted down this proposal, but it was close—3 to 2. In another instance, students wanted the Black Nationalist flag to replace all American flags. Still another group of activist students pushed for the right to investigate old guidance records, to see whether black students had been discriminated against in the past. Students did not state what they would have done with this information.[15]

White teachers and administrators fielded these demands with varying degrees of finesse or hamfistedness. Some believed that no students, black or white, had the right to issue demands; others hesitated because of the nature of the demands. In part, students' growing emphasis on black identity discomfited white officials. When it came to establishing black student unions, for example, some principals argued that by excluding whites, the unions practiced reverse discrimination. The Cincinnati superintendent of schools flatly condemned black student unions, saying they were "as racist as the Ku Klux Klan." Blacks countered that high school French clubs excluded non–French-speaking students. But many principals regarded racial categorization as a different and unacceptable means of screening club members and insisted that the unions, if permitted at all, be open to interested whites. Some black student unions did open up to white members, but doing so did not necessarily make the organization palatable to school officials. One black student, whose school was half black, told interviewers that when her classmates agreed to open black student union membership to any interested student, the principal next demanded that the student executive council approve the plan. Students secured this approval, but the principal wavered, Hamlet-like: "Well, I don't know, I really don't think so." In the end, students had to stage a rally before he gave in. Possibly the principal had hoped that the students would not meet his conditions, but their persistence forced his hand.[16]

Administrators found it more difficult to brush off demands for courses in black history and yielded reluctantly. Few rushed to establish such classes. The black human relations expert hired by the Inglewood, California, school district claimed that he "had stacks of material [on black history and culture] waiting to be given out as soon as the school expressed an interest." To his disappointment, only three schools asked for the materials. School administrators argued that no qualified teachers existed among the faculty, that an additional class would strain an already overcrowded curriculum, or that black history was a passing fad, not a serious academic subject. Students in Academy High School, in Erie, Pennsylvania, preempted their principal's opposition by creating an after-school course on minorities history and identifying two teachers willing to lead it. But, after a couple of weeks, the teachers' commitment flagged. Conceding that perhaps the teachers lacked the energy to teach additional classes after school, "Susan Snow" still expressed disappointed that the teachers dropped out.[17]

In other instances, high school administrators attempted to put off black students' demands—forever, if possible—by alleging that they were impractical. James Brown, a student at Central High School, in Peoria, Illinois, recalls his disgust when his teachers told him that the school could not offer black history because "a white teacher or a black teacher would have to study for so many years just to get this information across to you and explain it the way it was." Brown found this excuse unconvincing. When he and some friends requested a school meeting for all black students, the superintendent refused, claiming that they "were trying to overcome the school, take over the administration, and threaten all the white kids."[18]

Sometimes those in power resorted to the classic tactic of telling students that they had to "follow procedures." When the school board instructed students of Long Island's Malverne High School to "follow procedures" in response to their request for more black faculty and staff and an investigation into alleged discrimination in the honors society, they concluded that the board had no intention of acting. They then stepped up the pressure by staging a sit-in with three hundred black students in the school's lobby; 137 of them were arrested when the principal called the police, but in the end students won more than half of their demands.[19]

BLACK PRIDE AND THE POLITICS OF RACE

Carving out an institutional niche for themselves in the high schools constituted only a portion of black activists' agenda. By "thinking black" (a term used by Malcolm X) and expressing "black pride," they foregrounded racial consciousness and transformed blackness from an inherited set of physical characteristics to a deliberate political and cultural stance. Politicizing race pushed many white students off-balance. Connie Brown, a white student from Ohio, observes, "Black militants were not afraid to express their presence through afro hairstyles and dress, and the raised fist. I liken it to spreading their wings and flying, just as white students did in their ways. Black militants actually scared a lot of white kids—we weren't sure what to say or do. White kids got to see what it was like to be intimidated for a change."[20]

Brown provides insight into both the symbolic politics of the late 1960s and the shifting power dynamics between black and white students. Opponents of school desegregation had reached back to the Confederacy to find symbols of white supremacy and Southern heritage—by which they meant a racially bifurcated and hierarchical society. Black activists countered by adopting symbols of their African ancestry, such as colorful dashikis and natural (unstraightened, unprocessed) hairstyles. Marcus Garvey's back-to-Africa movement in the 1920s provided another compelling symbol: the Black Nationalist flag. Raising the flag with its three stripes of red, black, and green representing blood, race, and land, black activists repudiated not only the Confederate flag of the segregationists, but also the stars and stripes of the American nation. These symbols and the clenched fist, which activists of all races brandished, rejected both white supremacy and black assimilation. They spoke the language of power and separatism rather than compromise and accommodation.

Black pride and nationalism unsettled whites, but they also divided blacks. Throughout most of the twentieth century, the key strategies for upwardly mobile blacks had been accommodation and assimilation. Middle-class blacks with light skins and "good hair" had been favored both within and outside the black community. By the mid-1960s, these physical attributes drew condemnation, as radicals valorized dark skin and natural hair, attacking as "race traitors" those who had light skin, straightened their hair, worked for whites, or had attitudes that radicals deemed "insufficiently black." To be authentically black became highly subjective and depended very much on the eye of the beholder. Black adults who imagined that their race would better enable them to communicate with and control black students sometimes discovered, to their sorrow, that they were mistaken. James Ross Irwin relates an incident in which black students roughed up a black regional assistant when he attempted to break up a fight. He had believed the students would accept his authority, but, as he ruefully commented to Irwin, "Even my blackness didn't save me!" In another school, students derided their black assistant principal as a "Tom" and an "Oreo." They had protested to force their school to hire this man, but once the school hired him, the students criticized him as not militant enough.[21]

Militancy had in fact become the touchstone of blackness in the high schools. The precise meaning of the term is difficult to nail down because contemporaries used it to mean different things. It could mean racial activism, separatism, overt expressions of racial pride, or simply animosity toward whites. Whites used the term "black militant" to convey strong disapproval of such individuals, while many blacks embraced the label proudly. However one defined black militancy, observers agreed that it had increased among high school students. One study by Charles Billings, a New York University professor, claimed that black students' political attitudes showed "a strong tendency to adhere to the black nationalist 'line.'" It was, Billings asserted, a matter of differing degrees of agreement. Betsy Fancher, a white journalist and civil rights activist, interviewed black students in four southern cities. She concluded that, although black students who embraced militancy were in the minority, "many are clearly being edged toward separatist views by a combination of factors, foremost among which were their humiliating experiences in desegregated classrooms; their sense of their own government's betrayal in enforcement; and finally, though not always in readily determined ways, the influence of 'black consciousness' thought that has been articulated by some black leaders for some time now."[22]

These hardening attitudes among black high school students across the nation included a growing belief in the efficacy of violence. A 1970 study of black high school activists and nonactivists showed that nearly half of the activists agreed with the statement "violence is cleansing," as did more than a third of the nonactivists. More significantly, only 7 percent of all black students surveyed agreed that whites could be "persuaded" to change. Another study showed that black students felt a greater sense of personal and collective power than did white students; this may well have reflected—or caused—their increased militancy in the late 1960s and early 1970s.[23]

Militancy not only drew sharp lines between the races but also served as a means of disciplining black students as a whole and policing the boundaries of blackness. Just as fear of being called "nigger lover" had prevented whites from offering friendship to black classmates, the scathing epithets "Tom" or "Oreo" kept less-militant, less-separatist black students in line. The insults reveal how decisively militant blacks had turned away from the ideals of Martin Luther King. "Tom" referred to "Uncle Tom," the saintly and long-suffering slave in the nineteenth-century novel *Uncle Tom's Cabin*. In the eyes of contemporary blacks, Uncle Tom represented shameful, cowardly servility to whites. Oreos, the popular cookies with two black wafers sandwiching a white filling, were "black on the outside but white on the inside." Racial identity had acquired both absolute and disturbingly malleable characteristics. It was both a biological fact and a matter of political position.

WHITE STUDENTS: JUDGED, CONVICTED, AND CONDEMNED

Fear of being deemed "not black enough" pulled moderate black students into supporting, or at least not openly challenging, the dominant militant ethos. Militant blacks also succeeded in exerting a certain amount of power over their white colleagues. Many whites had previously been impervious to what blacks thought of them—indeed, had expected blacks to measure up to *their* standards—now the epithet "racist" could burn through to a sensitive white soul. In her Chicago high school, Jan Weiland feared that someday a black or Latino male student might "talk dirty to me in the hallway, or physically grab me." She complains, "I couldn't fight back because then I would be 'racist' for turning down their advances." Weiland does not state whether this ever happened to her, but her fear speaks volumes about white attitudes. While voicing traditional stereotypes of racial others as hypersexual and aggressive, she apparently regarded being labeled a racist as fearful a fate as an actual sexual assault.[24]

Blacks exerted power over whites by means other than accusing them of racism. Terre Hanson Burkhart, a white student at Colonel White High School, in Dayton, Ohio, joined the school's cheerleading squad in her freshman year, one of two white girls on a squad of six. Before the year was over, she was the only white cheerleader. She explains the perverse terms of her relationship with her teammates: "As the only white cheerleader I did not have a seat on the bleachers when I was not cheering. I had to sit on the floor. Yet my team did like me. *It was not personal, it's just that I was white*" (emphasis added). Jacque Switzer had a parallel experience. She recalls that, at school dances, she and her friend "would have to 'wade' through what seemed like a sea of young black males [who] would feel us up." Switzer asserts that the black students who "felt her up" singled out white girls to "humiliat[e] and intimidat[e] them" just because of their race. If they had known about her racial liberalism, she imagines they might have treated her more respectfully. In the context of contemporary racial politics, Switzer, like her black classmates, made race the central frame for her experience. She does not mention how she would have interpreted similar abuse from white boys.[25]

Whatever white students may have believed about their own racial attitudes, black students pounced on any vestige of white racism they perceived and dragged it into the daylight. Burkhart relates this story about her sophomore year at Colonel White High School:

> As I told you before the black cheerleaders liked me. Yet my sophomore year I did not try out for cheerleader. Mainly because my father (who I not so affectionately called "Archie Bunker" at the time) would not let me try out for the squad because there were so few whites. Instead I tried out for the drill team, which was almost all white. The black cheerleaders were furious with me. They said I thought I was too good for them, and attacked me in gym class. It was terrible for me, because I truly did want to stay on the cheerleading squad. I couldn't tell them why my father wouldn't allow it. I remember sitting in the principal's office trying to explain to them that my Dad just thought drill team was better for me. So still without saying the real words my father had said, which I think was something like "I don't want you on the squad with a bunch of niggers," they still knew. I never completely mended my friendships with most of the girls, however, they didn't attack me again. Still I always avoided some of them and was afraid [that] given the right opportunity that they would attack again.[26]

Torn between loyalty to her black friends and a sense of family solidarity, albeit shot through with shame, Burkhart could not admit her father's racism to the other cheerleaders. In the charged atmosphere of the times, she might have been able to maintain these friendships if she had denounced her father and distanced herself from him. Because she would not do this, the black girls, knowing full well what motivated her father's refusal to let Burkhart cheer with them, ostracized her. Militant black students turned every contact between blacks and whites into a litmus test of racial attitudes: Burkhart failed. Class president Joe Griffin spoke for many blacks when he said, "When a white teacher says 'I'm with you people all the way,' that's his first mistake. I'd much rather have him get up and say 'I'm a racist' than have him pretend to be the great white father bringing light to all us little darkies." Griffin suggests that on some level all whites were racists and ought to stop kidding themselves; other activist black students agreed with him.[27]

From the perspective of some white students, blacks wanted to dominate them and overemphasized racial issues. "Roxane" claims that discussions with the half dozen black students in her English class "always ended up with something to do with Black Power or the difference between white people and the colored, the Negro. Some things don't even pertain to this, but they find a way of bringing it out." The paucity of evidence about what actually took place in the classrooms makes it difficult to evaluate white opinions. Influenced by what one black administrator called "the glory in our blackness," black students did overemphasize race. White students, however, were not always inclined to listen to anything relating to black life. One white student countered the claim by a black student that studying black history would help whites understand contemporary race relations, arguing, "If you bring too much colored—Negro—history into the school, white kids will stop listening and say, 'Who wants to hear about some nigger?'"[28]

These stories expose how politicized and pervasive race became in integrated high schools. Blacks who made race central to their identity simultaneously took it on themselves to classify other students: Who is truly black? Who is a racist? There is no evidence that they ever considered their own practice of judging others by their race, skin, or hair to be racist. In addition, they set the bar for whites impossibly high. If blacks believed that even explicit statements of support for their freedom struggle masked hypocrisy, whites were destined to lose.

As blacks became the arbiters of race and racism, white students lost the comparative advantage they had enjoyed in the early days of desegregation. Many black students on and off campus reveled in making whites feel uncomfortable, if not downright scared. One report on high school violence put it bluntly: black students wanted revenge. "Numbers of black students told us one way or another," the report stated, "that 'it's whitey's turn to take some heat.'" Black students effectively turned the tables on whites, and they did so from a position of relative weakness. White adults still controlled the school system and had far greater access to the legal instruments of violence and repression: they could suspend or expel students and call in police forces. Nevertheless, black aggression in the high schools threw white adults and students onto the defensive. The white principal of Calumet High School in Chicago bitterly commented to interviewers in 1969: "If you're white, you're wrong." It was almost as if for many black students King's death loosened the restraints of courtesy and forbearance and justified, even demanded, acts of hostility and intimidation toward whites. Adopting a bellicose attitude, black students put the onus on whites to prove—if they could—that they were not racists.[29]

For militant black high school students, the psychological pleasures of getting in "whitey's" face and forcing him or her to metaphorically step off the sidewalk must have been considerable. But doing so further complicated race relations. Well-meaning people who wanted to bridge the racial divide in the high schools sometimes approached interracial encounters with great tentativeness and circumspection. James Ross Irwin, the white principal of Core High School in Detroit, for example, was surprised when his black vice principal told students that they could not wear African garb to class, even though the school had approved it for a special dance on school grounds. Irwin attributed this ban to the vice principal's presumed middle-class values, but it seems equally likely that the vice principal believed he was carrying out Irwin's own policies, or that any signs of black pride made him uneasy. In a delicate maneuver that showed the fragility of relations between the races, Irwin consulted with the superintendent of the Division of School-Community Relations—also black, as Irwin hastily notes—before overruling his vice principal.[30]

The sensitivity Irwin and his vice principal displayed shows how convoluted race relations had grown. Under black students' glowering gaze, moderate and liberal whites wrestled with mixed feelings of guilt, fear, and sympathy. White students, no less than adults, sometimes quailed, or, like Jacque Switzer and Terre Burkhart, found ways to excuse black aggression and hatefulness.

RISING FEAR AND VIOLENCE

In response to the demands and aggressive presence of black students, many whites in the high schools recall being afraid. Elnore Grow, a white chemistry teacher in Seattle, Washington, claims that he felt secure enough inside the school, but he "did not always feel safe in the neighborhood." Students often had different memories: they *did* feel threatened within the school walls. Alice Krause Young went to school in southwestern Ohio. In her junior year, a choir from a predominantly black high school performed during an assembly, perhaps, she recalls, for Black History Week. She remarks, "I cannot recall specifically any of the songs [the visitors sang], but I remember that the songs became more and more frenzied, with a message of 'down with whitey.' I recall feeling very uncomfortable, close to fear if not actually there."[31]

Violence and fear of violence, including sexual harassment or assault, underlay white anxieties about blacks in their schools. Some white students noted the inability or unwillingness of adults to protect them. In relating her story about being groped at school dances, Jacque Switzer complains, "I don't know how the teachers didn't know about it, but they seemed not to be around anytime this happened." Terre Hanson Burkhart claims that, in her freshman year, students from a neighboring black high school "came in and started a riot. Students were punched, shoved to the floor and then jumped on by others who stood [on] tables to get more force. There was no way out as the entrances were blocked—the adults I turned to for help were just as frightened, and were really no help." In the end, a black football player who had a lot of white friends rescued Burkhart and several other white girls.[32]

Switzer and Burkhart suffered real assaults on their persons and their dignity, but both also seem to have comprehended the complex motivations of their attackers. Many whites, however, regarded black pride, Black Power, and black separatism as equally illegitimate. In their eyes, all of these simply manifested black racism, a thirst for revenge, and a conspiracy to "take over," with violence as their common denominator. "Bill," a black student interviewed by sociologists Frank Petroni and Ernest Hirsch, reports that, when he brought up Black Power to a white classmate, "[s]he became really afraid. She said, 'Why do you want to kill me? She doesn't know that Black Power is social and economic power.'" In the face of this ignorance, even the elements of Black Power that constituted little more than posturing alarmed and offended whites. They fed right into the paranoia of those whites who feared that any gains for blacks necessarily came at their own expense. What Donald Reeves sardonically termed the "fascist-honky-motherfucker-revolutionary" talk of some blacks, paralleling the "riot-rape-robbery-revolutionary" code words used by some whites to suggest the nature of the black threat, foreclosed the possibility of a mutual accommodation. It provided white perpetrators of violence against blacks with a measure of legitimacy and intensified the white backlash. Blacks had succeeded in giving white racism a bad name and forcing some of its worst manifestations underground; now some whites argued that blacks themselves had become racists.[33]

Name-calling and intimidation made white students nervous. Increasing instances of racial violence intensified the friction. Because it coincided with other types of high school unrest, violence drew considerable attention from people outside the schools. The *New York Times* began tracking stories of high school violence and racial protest around the nation. Some of these incidents can be labeled true race riots, whereas others were simply fights between individual students that got out of hand. A survey by Urban America, Inc., found that high school racial disorders hit in a wave, beginning in the academic year 1968–1969. The following year, more than six hundred violent episodes took place. A 1970 study by the Policy Institute at Syracuse University found that 85 percent of the nearly seven hundred urban high schools investigated had experienced "disturbances"—which it did not define—during the past three years. Race, the study claimed, figured prominently in many of these disturbances. People outside the high schools initiated or amplified some of the confrontations, but the majority erupted because of events and tensions generated by the students themselves. While black and white students felt the influence of racial polarization in the wider society, they acted as historical agents, in response to circumstances in their own locales.[34]

Students' perception of local events could cause seemingly minor conflicts to spiral out of control. At Vailsburg High School, in Newark, New Jersey, the sight of a black girl dancing with a white boy at a school dance triggered several days of demonstrations, including a "White Power" boycott by about 150 of the school's white students and the firebombing of the guidance center. The principal identified a white boy as the instigator but noted that the blacks, who comprised 20 percent of the school's student body, became "very defensive and retaliatory." It turned out, however, that at least some of these alleged incidents never took place. In one instance, white students in Trenton, New Jersey, angry in response to allegations, demonstrated with "White Power" buttons and signs reading "Kill Black Men." The whites refused to attend classes until the administration could protect them against black violence. A couple of weeks after the demonstration, two white girls finally admitted that they had invented the story of the attacks. Late for class and fearing detention, they had cut themselves with broken glass and blamed their injuries on black students.[35]

Though illustrating the willingness of both black and white students to come to blows, both of these incidents raise more questions than available evidence can answer. In the first incident, why did the black students at Vailsburg High apparently support the girl who danced with a white boy? Did this not mark her as a "race traitor," or did the violent objections of whites obligate black students to retaliate regardless of the precipitating cause? In Trenton, did whites believe the story about blacks cutting the two white girls because similar assaults had already taken place? Were the girls credible witnesses?

Although we cannot answer these questions without knowing considerably more about the specific circumstances and individuals involved, both cases do reveal that some whites, like blacks, had begun to redefine their racial identity. White supremacy slid out of sight, replaced by white disadvantage or defensiveness. The slogan "White Power" suggests, astonishingly, that whites had somehow become the underdogs and lacked power. In the wider society, white resentment of blacks' legal gains and their new social and cultural visibility helped tilt the balance of political power away from the Democratic Party toward the Republicans. Both Independent George Wallace and Republican Richard Nixon tapped this wellspring of white victimhood among adult voters; it had its counterpart in integrated high schools.

Violent racial confrontations became so common at some schools that black students organized themselves to monitor the halls and keep order. High school groups calling themselves the Black Legions, Black Panthers, Black Patrols, and Black Elite Troops attempted to use their own muscles to rein in unruly students. Teachers and administrators, however, recoiled from this student "help." Detroit principal James Irwin comments laconically that any principal whose school was "invaded by uniformed youth patrols" would have to "question his own sanity" if he seriously considered using them to restore order.[36]

White students also yearned for order in the schools, but instead of forming vigilante squads, they sometimes organized counterdemonstrations opposing black demands or called for the punishment of black protesters. In Xenia, Ohio, for example, one hundred black students staged a sit-in in the lobby of their school in 1969, protesting the expulsion of a black girl from the cheerleading team. Her crime was applauding a visiting high school's all-black wrestling team after overhearing white Xenia fans make racist comments about their competitors. The protesters pointed out that the cheerleader had not been wearing her uniform when the incident occurred and the behavior of white Xenia fans had provoked her. Indeed, other than overt racism, it is difficult to explain why officials punished the cheerleader but not the jeering whites. School superintendent Frank Mayer met with the students and agreed to reduce the punishment to suspension for one game and probation. This concession not only failed to mollify the protesters, who felt that the girl should not be punished at all, but also infuriated many whites, including the cheerleading coach, who resigned. Threatening to boycott classes, whites argued that blacks were "getting away with too much" and demanded that all those who participated in the sit-in be punished along with the cheerleader. In the end, the administration called upon the school board to mediate. Once again the scales of justice were adjusted; the board voted to increase the cheerleader's suspension to two games and to implement a new policy of a three-day suspension for any student who disrupted classes.[37]

Events followed a similar pattern in Malverne, New York. When the school board refused to respond to their list of demands, black students began an extended protest. Four hundred students held an eight-hour sit-in, while a squad of protesters attempted to seize control of the school's public address system and other activists—including supportive parents—marched outside. Police ended the sit-in by threatening to arrest the students if they did not leave the school grounds and guarded the school over the weekend. The following week saw a student takeover of the cafeteria, peaceful picketing, and more than one hundred arrests. Rather than endure further disruptions, administrators ultimately granted more than half of the students' demands. They agreed, among other concessions, to create a black history course, hire more black school personnel, use the word "black" rather than "Negro" in the student newspaper, and establish a student advisory committee to the school board. In retaliation, a thousand whites from the school and community signed a petition against dropping the charges for those arrested. School officials granted this demand, too.[38]

In yet another incident, described by Detroit high school principal James Irwin, white students formed a "reactionary organization" and pledged to "protect" the school from any ceremonies honoring the late Malcolm X in February 1969. Black students regarded Malcolm X as a hero of their community whom the schools should celebrate. They also felt threatened by increasing white aggression. Matching militancy for militancy, black students vowed not to retreat from a confrontation with whites. Seeking a way to defuse the growing tension, the student council proposed that the administration hold seminars on Malcolm X to educate whites about his life and beliefs. The administration rejected this proposal as provocative.[39]

As order and discipline disintegrated, black and white students had different views on the officials' responses. Some whites indignantly claimed that black students "got away with murder." Harold Saltzman, a white teacher in primarily black Franklin Lane High School, in Brooklyn, New York, claimed that administrators advised all teachers to look the other way rather than discipline black students. Black students, in contrast, believed that they were singled out for punishment. According to one, "If you start to even question some of the rules, even if you know they are directed against you, you are called a Communist, or you are just a black militant that is going totally insane." Another black student from a school near Chicago states that "[a]nytime more than about five or six Negro guys walked together, the police would spray them with mace. . . . That's what really made the black students mad. After that, every opportunity we had, we tried to just tear this place down." It is not clear whether these police attacks took place on or off campus.[40]

Studies of school discipline support the views of black students that officials punished them more harshly and more often than white students; interpretations of why this was the case have varied. Black students and their parents believed that sheer discrimination explained it. Others argued that white officials failed to understand black cultural norms and inappropriately applied their own rigid views of proper behavior. On the other end of the spectrum, some claimed that black students misbehaved more often, so naturally they were punished more. The evidence suggests that a more complex dynamic underlay the problem. In light of the touchy relations between blacks and whites, the fact that few whites had worked at making black students feel welcome in integrated schools, and the paucity of black school administrators, few black students felt inclined to trust the fairness of white authorities. Moreover, the logic of Black Power convinced black students that they had "taken it" long enough. In turn, the willingness of black students to confront school officials justified, in the eyes of many whites, efforts to crack down on black militancy.[41]

Opposing interpretations of school discipline by blacks and whites sometimes set off cycles of disruption. Mary Ann Kennedy reports that the problems in her Erie, Pennsylvania, high school erupted when, under unclear circumstances, a white teacher knocked down a black student but the school suspended the student. When black students protested with a petition, the administration responded by suspending *them* and thus created what Kennedy calls a "ludicrous chain reaction" of new protests from the black students, answered by a backlash white riot. At Miami Central High School, white students boycotted classes, demanding that twenty-five African-American students, who had been suspended following a cafeteria riot, be expelled. Teachers soon adopted student tactics. In Los Angeles, teachers organized a walkout to protest the earlier walkout and general militancy of their students at the mostly black Jefferson High School.[42]

TENTATIVE BLACK-WHITE ALLIANCES

On some occasions, however, white students supported black demands for changes. Susan Worley attended Chapel Hill High School, in North Carolina. The school, which Worley claims "always had the reputation of being one of the best schools in the state," integrated in 1966. When black students from Lincoln High School transferred to the previously all-white school, "the traditions of old Lincoln High were lost when Lincoln was shut down." Specifically, Worley notes that "[t]he name of the school, the school mascot, and school colors all remained that of the white school." But in the academic year 1969–1969, in what Worley calls a "controversial vote," black and white students agreed to readopt the Lincoln mascot, the tiger. She comments, "I always thought that vote showed that white students had a better understanding of what black students had lost than did white administrators."[43]

White students similarly supported demands for black cheerleaders at Seaford High School, in Delaware. The administration refused to agree until April 1969, when the black students organized a sit-in. Then the principal finally permitted the entire student body to vote on the issue, which "easily resolved" it, when black and white students voted in favor of integrating the cheerleading squad. The Seaford Board of Education dampened the students' sense of victory by voting to punish future protesters with suspensions or expulsions and, when necessary, to summon the police.[44]

The interracial violence that accompanied desegregation in many schools sometimes induced students themselves to resolve tensions. Black and white students in New Brunswick, New Jersey, staged a "walk-out, walk-in" in which they left the school building, linked arms in mixed-race groups, and marched back in. They had insisted that they could resolve the racial violence that had led to the closing of the school for a week, and indeed an interracial committee of forty-two students had conceived this demonstration of unity. This committee also proposed the creation of a democratically elected committee with ten students of each race who would work together to maintain racial harmony in the school. The students permitted three faculty members to serve as "consultants," but not, they carefully stated, as "monitors" or "advisors." At the unity demonstration, students read a statement asserting that the earlier unrest had been "misrepresented by many people in many ways and . . . this demonstration is proof of the willingness of both black and white students to peacefully work out problems."[45]

In a Washington, D.C., high school, students formed a biracial coalition and called for a weeklong school boycott. They demanded a new principal, recognition of their own coalition as a legitimate student organization, and a free breakfast and lunch program at the school. It is not clear whether officials granted their demands, but black and white students proved that they could sometimes work together for a common goal. In another case, a high school principal in Atlantic City organized a "Peace Corps" of black and white students to work on easing racial tensions. The students recommended interracial home visits and programs to prepare junior high school students for integration when they entered high school. Atlantic City was also the site of a federally sponsored effort to soothe troubled waters. In

1968, the government hosted a group of seventy-two New Jersey high school students—chosen from more than four hundred volunteers—for several weeks at a "luxurious" hotel for extensive seminars on race relations run by the head of the Atlantic City NAACP.[46]

Unfortunately, some school officials objected to letting students attempt to bridge the racial divide. Indeed, interracial unity may have seemed a greater threat than simple student militancy. Paula Smith, a white student at a girls' Catholic school in Chicago, claims to have been radicalized politically when she attended the 1968 Chicago Democratic Convention and had her "head beat in" by police. She put most of her energy into the group she had founded, "Concerned Students Against the War," but she and three white friends also supported the demand of the "Black Young Ladies of Longwood" (another school organization) that the library acquire black literature. At that point, the principal expelled Smith, calling her "militant, defiant, [and] revolutionary" and accusing her of stirring up racial hatred. Smith believed that her efforts to unite with black students, not her other political causes, led to her expulsion.[47]

NEW YORK CITY: A SPECIAL CASE

In the fall of 1968, several teacher strikes occurred in New York City, contesting an educational experiment in the Ocean Hill–Brownsville district. Analyzing this event from the perspective of students rather than adults not only brings into focus the roles both played in politicizing race, but also reveals the potential for a new kind of black-white unity. Although racial issues permeated the strikes and their aftermath, other identities—student, teacher, radical—complicated the seemingly straightforward black-white divide. When white students supported the demands of black and Puerto Rican students in New York, some race-based and others not, they simultaneously hinted at the possibility of an alliance based on their shared student status. This alliance never quite solidified, but the vision of a broad-based, interracial high school student coalition entranced some high school activists even as it threatened school administrators. In the alternative schools that sprang up during the strikes, teachers and students also glimpsed the possibilities for a new type of education based on more egalitarian relationships between adults and teens.

The Ocean Hill–Brownsville experiment explored the concept of "community control" of the schools. Community control meant decentralizing authority over schools and giving parents and community leaders a role in running them. Some black activists thought that only community control would allow black students to receive a sound education without becoming "whitened" by racist teachers and a curriculum that neglected their history and culture. High school activists from Chicago to Mobile embraced the idea of black community control over their schools, but New York City officials actually tried it in the Ocean Hill–Brownsville schools.[48]

Conflict in Ocean Hill–Brownsville surfaced in 1968 when the black supervisor of the school district, Rhody McCoy, announced his plan to involuntarily "reassign" nineteen teachers, transferring them out of the Ocean Hill schools. McCoy believed he possessed the power to hire and fire in his district. New York's newly powerful union, the United Federation of Teachers (UFT), however, argued that permitting McCoy to reassign teachers against their will violated union rules about tenure and seniority. On one level, the conflict was a turf battle between McCoy and UFT president Albert Shanker. On another level, most observers believed that racism lay beneath the jousting over rules and power. Because all of the nineteen teachers McCoy wanted transferred were white and Jewish, white New Yorkers interpreted his action as evidence of black racism and anti-Semitism. McCoy claimed that the teachers in question were themselves racist and, further, that disregarding his personnel decisions undercut community control and revealed the racism and duplicity of whites. When McCoy and Shanker failed to agree or work out a compromise, the UFT struck three times between Labor Day and Thanksgiving, keeping one million students out of school. Donald Reeves, a student at the High School of Music and Art, remarks contemptuously, "I saw those same teachers who had so righteously spoken about their duty, their responsibility to teach [after Martin Luther King's assassination] marching on a picket line."[49]

Politically radical white high school students sided with black students and community activists in the debate over Ocean Hill–Brownsville. They agreed with McCoy that true community control entailed letting him run his own school district. In addition, they rejected Shanker's charge of black anti-Semitism, pointing out that of the teachers McCoy hired to replace the original nineteen as well as others on strike, half were Jewish. Radical whites collaborated with black students to keep their schools open during the three strikes. At the prestigious Bronx High School of Science, a handful of students managed to get in through the back door when the janitors, who supported the UFT, refused to admit them at the front, only to have policemen chase them out. Ultimately, two black students from nearby DeWitt Clinton High School came up with an ingenious argument that kept the school open. These students, Guy Oliver and Harold Young, combed the state legislature's report and discovered that it had left the "special" schools, like Science, under state jurisdiction, not under the control of the local school board. The state of New York, they concluded, did not support the strike—since it was illegal by state law—and therefore the school was open. The superintendent of the special schools, Seelig Lester, confirmed the students' interpretation and ordered the police to allow the nonstriking teachers to open the school. Todd Gitlin, a Science alumnus and former college activist, visited the school during the strike and commented sarcastically, "Once the liberators convinced the cops that they, who wanted the school open, were the duly constituted authority, the cops switched sides to enforce the opening. Servants of the law after all."[50]

The coalition of radical white students and black students was joined by a small number of white teachers, who stood with these students as well as their black colleagues by defying the UFT call to strike. Robert Rossner, a white teacher at Science, crossed the picket line to open the high school. Like the students, he endured the racist taunting of the strikers who called him "nigger lover." Rossner claims that the strikers' hostility intensified a few days into the strike, when the nonstriking students and teachers reorganized the school day and designed new classes that reflected student suggestions and interests. Strikers specifically targeted Don Schwartz, a social studies teacher who had made himself conspicuous the previous year by growing a beard, coming to class in a turtleneck shirt, and serving as the faculty sponsor for the Black Cultural Society. Now the strikers screamed at him, "Hey, Schwartz! What are you teaching in there—African history?" Their jibes highlighted the growing divisions between blacks and Jews, reminding Schwartz of where, in the strikers' opinion, his loyalties ought to lie and scornfully dismissing the teaching of African history.[51]

Racial identity loomed so large for blacks and whites by late 1960s that it almost obscured everything else. Yet identity based on something other than race never completely faded from view and sometimes competed with race for primacy. Shared political beliefs could potentially create a solid bond among students of different races as well as between students and teachers. Black and white students had worked together to open some of the schools. Schwartz had evidently gravitated to the black student camp before the strikes. For Rossner, running the gauntlet of his erstwhile colleagues moved him further to the left politically, while his relationships with students inside the school made him increasingly sympathetic to the emergent student power movement.

By late November, 1968, the UFT and city officials reached an agreement that ended the strikes. The nineteen teachers McCoy had tried to remove were restored to their jobs, although all of them quickly transferred—voluntarily, this time—out of his district. The state education department took over the management of the Ocean Hill–Brownsville schools, and the state legislature drastically curtailed the powers granted to local school boards. This outcome was no compromise. It was a thorough defeat for those who had supported community control. Shanker's vindictiveness, as he sought to have those legislators who had backed the black community voted out of office, was imitated by striking teachers, who returned to work eager to punish those who had crossed their picket lines.[52]

The aftermath of the strikes and forced school openings demonstrates the complex interplay between divergent identities. Race continued to dominate as relations between students and teachers—especially between black students and white teachers—chilled considerably. Adults rarely attributed student hostility to recent events. Some teachers, for example, felt threatened by their students' dashikis, Black Power emblems sewn to their clothing, and Afros. Others, perhaps because of the roles students played in the strikes, worried about conspiracy and rebellion. When someone reported to Max Bromer, principal of Wingate High School, that confrontations in the school cafeteria had diminished in recent weeks, he suspected that black students were "massing" for some kind of attack. When no attack occurred, he interpreted this as a form of "psychological warfare." His paranoid response shows the erosion of trust between pupils and adults.[53]

In contrast to the failure of adults to link the frosty atmosphere in the schools to the strike, many black students in New York City drew direct connections. Some believed that the strike had mercilessly exposed their teachers' racism. Billy Pointer asserts that he had heard his teachers screaming "nigger!" during the strikes. Another black student comments disgustedly, "As soon as they get the cops behind them, they show how racist they are." Jackie Glover was a senior at Taft High School, one of the schools kept open during the strike. She, too, claims to have had her eyes opened by the teachers' behavior, particularly their threats against their colleagues at Taft who refused to join the strike. Afterward, Glover admits that her attitude had changed. One of her teachers plaintively noted that Glover never smiled anymore, like the "good, sweet girl" she had once been. Glover explains, "I'm not sweet anymore because I saw for the first time what was really going on in that school."[54]

For activist high school students in New York City, although the Ocean Hill–Brownsville conflict exacerbated racial friction, it simultaneously allowed limited black-white unity, opening the possibility of a broad student alliance in pursuit of common goals. Protests broke out among students when officials lengthened the school day by forty-five minutes so they could make up the classes missed during the strikes and the teachers could earn back their lost pay. The egregious unfairness of the situation aroused bitter sentiments among students, so that when the Black and Puerto Rican Citywide High School Council issued fifteen "nonnegotiable" demands, the white-dominated New York High School Student Union (NYHSSU) lent its support. With individual chapters in more than a hundred New York public and private schools, the NYHSSU was the largest high school student union in the United States. It linked an endorsement of the Citywide Council demands to its campaign for the adoption of a student bill of rights. NYHSSU activists recognized the importance of racial identity, keeping a respectful distance between themselves and the black and Puerto Rican students' movement. According to the Student Union's leaflet explaining its position, "Whites have to realize that Blacks must lead their own people in the struggle for liberation." At the same time, the leaflet pointed out that *as students,* whites could benefit from the changes the black students wanted. Students of color called for several changes that were race-based, such as hiring more nonwhite faculty and celebrating the birthdays of Martin Luther King and Malcolm X, but they also made demands that would empower all students, regardless of their race. The latter included items such as ending "automatic suspensions" for certain offenses, eliminating the police presence on campus, and creating a student-faculty council to advise on curriculum, school rules, and discipline. John Birmingham, a white student in Hackensack, New Jersey, and author of a book on high school underground newspapers, asserted that black and white students in New York City were among the most united in the country. Although the students' demands were not met, Birmingham claims that their actions "did show the city just how much muscle the New York City high school underground had acquired."[55]

THE LIMITS OF BLACK-WHITE UNITY: THE CASE OF CUBBERLY HIGH SCHOOL

If the peculiar circumstances in New York City allowed for a tentative interracial coalition, black high school students in other places rejected the aid of white liberals and radicals, which they perceived as patronizing or presumptuous. White activists who sought common cause with black students were compelled to tread very cautiously, as events at Cubberly High School, in Palo Alto, California, reveal. The student body at Cubberly High was fractionalized in 1968. Whites were at loggerheads over radicals' efforts to enact a student bill of rights through an organization called the United Student Movement (USM). Tensions also bristled between middle-class blacks who lived in Palo Alto proper and the "sneak-outs" who lived in poorer East Palo Alto but attended Cubberly High with a white family "sponsor." The sneak-outs regarded the more affluent blacks as hopeless "boojies" (slang for "bourgeois"), whereas the "boojies" themselves felt torn between a desire for class status and racial authenticity.[56]

In the spring of 1968, the USM attempted to organize a student strike against the Vietnam War and, almost as an afterthought, racism. In a move that probably startled the whites, black students from both sides of the tracks responded angrily, resenting the effrontery of the whites in claiming to speak for them. A series of events heightened both the unity and truculence of black students: a black girl lost a disputed cheerleader election; students and administrators clashed over the organization of a black students' union; officials hired a black militant, who habitually wore a "Free Huey [Newton]" button on his suit coat, to run a new "multicultural program"; and students formed a new organization called Black Men for the Protection of Black Women (BMPBW).[57]

In the spring of 1969, two incidents precipitated a crisis. First, a group— or maybe an individual pretending to be a group—calling itself the Society for the Prevention of Niggers Getting Everything (SPONGE) issued a memo denouncing any concessions to black demands. Second, two white male teachers entered the girls' restroom to break up a fight among some black girls. The administration suspended Norman Morgan when he and several other members of the BMPBW attempted to "protect" the girls in the restroom. The suspensions enraged black students, who claimed, with some justification, that the white community would never have tolerated black men entering the girls' restroom. The students staged a sit-in and, with the support of white radicals—whether they wanted it or not—went on strike.[58]

Cubberly's administrators held a series of meetings with students, teachers, and parents, which revealed the vastness of the racial divide. One black parent related that when her daughter's white teacher asked her to erase the chalkboard, the girl had refused, asserting, "I don't want to do your dirty work." The teacher, in contrast, believed she had honored the girl with this request. Sylvia Williams, a white teacher who wrote a book about the school's ordeal, noted that whites felt they were always six steps behind the blacks, did not know what they wanted, and felt perplexed at their own failures to communicate. Blacks resented whites presuming to understand and to speak for them, but they also grew weary of having to educate whites about their own racism. For their part, whites found it hard to comprehend black rage or accept that it had any legitimate basis because— despite the nasty SPONGE memo—many white students supported the black students and their demands. White students had even formed their own group, Students Concerned with Aiding the Multicultural Program (SCAMP), to demonstrate their support.[59]

After a weeklong strike, most of the suspended students were allowed to return to school, and, for the moment, the troubles at Cubberly High School, died down. Black students won a mixed victory. The administration had granted most of their demands, including the creation of courses in black history and Swahili and the hiring of more black personnel. But it had not rescinded the expulsion of Norman Morgan (during his suspension, Morgan had gotten into a fight and had been expelled) and could not legalize the "sneak-out" program. White radicals, who had tried to hitch their campaign for a bill of rights to the black students' demands, lamented that the student strike had yielded so little for them. The USM's poststrike issue of their unauthorized paper, *Serve the People,* sneered that the strike had ended in "meaningful dialogue. You know about meaningful dialogue. It's when some loudmouth bullshitter opens his mouth and you fall asleep. A favorite game of the administration."

White radicals did not achieve their policy demands, but in the end they managed to cobble together a fragile alliance with the black students. The USM's seizing the issue of racism had annoyed the black students, who quoted Malcolm X to the effect that whites should stop trying to lead the black movement and work on ending racism in their own community. Nevertheless, blacks had accepted the USM's stalwart support of their strike.

In both New York City and Palo Alto, radical whites snatched at the tail of the black student movement as it blazed like a comet across their sky. Around the country, some whites envied the unity and sense of purpose black students seemed to have. "Norman," a white student at a white school, declares that black students "really have something that they want and are fighting for it." He concludes wistfully, "I kind of envy them because

I don't have anything like that." At other schools, rather than envying blacks, whites sometimes felt that they and the school administration had bent over backwards to understand black students and to support their demands. Hostile reactions from black students and their escalating demands led whites to conclude that blacks rebelled merely for the sake of rebellion and that acceding to any of their demands merely emboldened them to issue new ones. Black students, for their part, often distrusted whites who trumpeted their solidarity with black students. They suspected that whites wanted to run everything, including the black revolution. Other blacks thought the time for blacks and whites to work together had run out— whites had delayed too long, while blacks had to work too hard and sacrifice too much just to obtain basic rights and decent treatment. Now it was payback time.[60]

BROWN POWER AND STUDENT "BLOWOUTS"

Black-white friction garnered the most attention, yet militancy and clashes with whites occurred among other students of color in the late 1960s. Testifying before a U.S. Senate Subcommittee on Education in 1971, L. Ling Chi Wang, the director of youth services in San Francisco's Chinatown observed that, despite the widespread perception that Chinese students were more docile than white or black students, in fact disciplinary problems had recently skyrocketed. Chinese students demanded more Chinese teachers and an end to their second-class status. In New York City, Puerto Rican students often made common cause with black students in promoting their own desire for recognition. In many other parts of the country, notably Los Angeles, Denver, and several Mexican-American-dominated towns in Texas, Mexican-Americans—or as many called themselves in that era, Chicanos—began to borrow current tactics to push for demands that paralleled those of black students.[61]

The first stirrings that captured newspapers' attention took place in East Los Angeles in March 1968, when students at Lincoln High School walked out and staged a rally at a nearby park. The students, led by a Mexican-American teacher, Sal Castro, and a handful of Chicano college activists, protested the discriminatory treatment of Mexicans and Mexican-Americans. They demanded classes in Chicano history and literature, as well as more Chicano teachers and administrators. In addition, they demanded freedom of speech and the press for students, Mexican food in the cafeteria, improved school facilities, more counselors and electives, better school-community relations, and an end to corporal punishment. When the movement spread to the predominantly Mexican-American school, Roosevelt High, the administration attempted to intimidate the students by surrounding the school with police cars and allowing police officers to harass those attempting to leave. When students threw bottles at the patrol cars, the police jumped two Chicano male students and beat them down.

The beatings helped to unify the Mexican-American community, even as violence between Chicanos and the Los Angeles Police Department (LAPD) increased. Behind the scene of these heavy-handed tactics, however, educational officials worked to meet some of the students' demands, particularly hiring more Mexican personnel and providing workshops on Spanish and the Mexican-American culture for white public school teachers.[62]

High school "blow-outs," as Chicanos referred to their boycotts, occurred elsewhere in the country as well. In the Lower Rio Grande Valley in Texas, students staged a two-day school boycott and demonstrations after the school administration refused to consider their list of fifteen demands, including the right to speak Spanish at school and the addition of Mexican history and culture in the curriculum. The school expelled some sixty students, but, with the help of the Mexican-American Legal Defense and Educational Fund (MALDEF) and a federal district court, they were reinstated and their records cleared.[63]

MALDEF, established in 1967, was part of a new wave of militant, nationalist organizations that arose to challenge the assimilationist posture of earlier groups, such as the League of United Latin American Citizens (LU-LAC, founded in 1929). César Chávez and Delores Huerta organized a union, the United Farm Workers, and led strikes by Mexican migrant workers and boycotts among the white consumers of the produce they grew. Although not overtly nationalist, their movement drew heavily upon Mexican Catholic imagery and rhetoric. In Arizona, the fiery Reies López Tijerina, nicknamed "King Tiger," led an armed movement that attempted to seize land lost to Mexican nationals when the United States took over what became the southwestern states in 1848.

By 1969, the Brown Power movement spread beyond the Southwest, and two of the key movements worked closely with Chicano high school students. In Denver, Colorado, Rodolfo "Corky" Gonzáles, a former featherweight boxer, who had been a Democratic ward captain before his disenchantment with liberal white politics, organized a group called the "Crusade for Justice." When a teacher at West High School in Denver, which was predominantly Chicano, disparaged the "stupidity" of Mexicans, outraged students contacted the Crusade for Justice, asking Gonzáles to speak to the administration on their behalf. They wanted the teacher fired. The Crusade sent Kenneth García, Corky Gonzáles, and others to investigate. When they arrived, they found police already guarding the front of the building. The older activists called to the students to come out. When some did, the police told all of them to move off the school steps, so they adjourned to a park across the street. Kenneth García recalls,

> I'm not sure of just what started it all. I remember there was a cameraman from a local news channel there with his equipment and at one point a cop tried to shove him off the stairs (it was a black newsman). Anyway when the cops began to push and shove him as he filmed the confrontation they say he

turned and used his camera as a weapon, swinging it at the heads of several cops. By that time all hell had busted loose. Cops were kicking and beating anyone and everyone on the school steps. Then when that was over they arrested dozens of them and charged all with several "crimes."[64]

The demonstrators picketed the school for several days, the crowds growing larger and larger. Eventually violence broke out. García suggests that "the sight of the heavily armed cops was too much for the [students]," who threw the first rocks and renewed the confrontation with the police. Several patrol cars were turned over as the violence escalated. The authorities, though outnumbered, were better armed than the students and their allies. García continues:

> I also remember that towards the end of this demonstration we thought a helicopter was attempting to set down inside [the] park across from the school and so we ordered a portion of the crowd to stand in the middle of the park to prevent the copter from landing. Only problem with that strategy was the copter was not trying to land in the park. It was intending to hover over the park and spray all of us with a substance we knew nothing about, at that time. It was mace and it burned like hell.[65]

Spraying the neighborhood with mace enraged local residents, many of whom opened the doors of their houses so that the demonstrators could escape. In the end, the school board did not fire the offensive teacher but merely transferred him to another school. Still, García insists, "The demonstrations ended but not the fire that was lit that day." Gonzáles called for a nation-wide school walkout to protest the treatment of minority students, which ultimately became an annual "Mexican Independence Day" celebration.[66]

In that same year, 1969, a high school protest in Crystal City, Texas, over the refusal of school authorities to permit Mexican-American girls to be cheerleaders, galvanized the entire Mexican population (which was numerically dominant) and allowed a new political party, La Raza Unida, to take over not only the school board but the city council as well. The high school subsequently reflected Chicano nationalism and pride: classes taught Mexican and Mexican-American history, the band played nationalist songs, and the cafeteria used only produce grown by the United Farm Workers.[67]

The experience of Crystal City inspired similar protests in other predominantly Mexican and Mexican-American towns in Texas, and again high school students took the lead. Students in Uvalde, Texas, staged a boycott in February 1970 and pressed a list of demands for better schooling, better communication between school and parents, better equipment, and improved safety measures for students coming and going to school. According to José Uriegas, a member of the Texas State Advisory Committee on Civil Rights, the students "stated that the principal had done a very poor job, that his methods were outdated, and that he completely disregarded their wishes." Whites in Uvalde responded with a display of powers at their command: they brought in an entire company of Texas Rangers, the Texas Department of Public Safety hovered over the demonstrating students in helicopters, the local draft board reclassified draft-age students, and parents of the boycotters were either fired or threatened with dismissal from their jobs.[68]

In March 1970, students in Los Angeles erupted for a second time. Chicanos from East Los Angeles' Roosevelt High School "blew out" again, in protest of what they saw as racist educational policies and the fact that none of the students' demands from the 1968 protests had been met. Once again the LAPD reacted with violence, beating the students and even pulling girls around by their hair. Tactics like these and the murder of a Mexican man during a police raid that summer inflamed the community. In this tense atmosphere, the National Chicano Moratorium, planned as a protest of the number of Mexican-Americans being killed in the Vietnam War, was held on August 29, 1970. During the protest, a group of Chicano high school students unwittingly sparked a riot when they supposedly stole soft drinks and then threw rocks at the police, who chased them right into the midst of the demonstration. The police thereupon declared the moratorium an illegal assembly and violently tried to disperse it, which may have been their goal all along. In the melee that followed, the police arrested more than one hundred people, injured forty, and killed three, including the popular Chicano journalist Rúben Sálazar.[69]

High school blowouts garnered substantial press coverage, but, even where they did not occur, Latino students resisted racism they encountered in school, particularly from teachers and administrators. These students agreed with black students that "[t]he best teachers are the ones that come from a similar background and know the kids' problems" and not "one that goes in there thinking he is going to tear all those little ignorant people up." They paired demands for more Spanish-speaking teachers and administrators with cries for better education. "Edgar," a Mexican-American student, told interviewers, "We wanted to improve the curriculum to be able to compete with other students. We wanted algebra taught in the ninth grade and chemistry made available. We wanted a program for calculus and maybe computers. . . . We wanted a voice. . . . We were asking for so little."[70]

Chicano student activists received strong support from their parents, many of whom had suffered the same indignities their children now refused to accept. In the case of Crystal City, the high school protests catalyzed the creation of a proud, self-consciously Mexican-American political party, La Raza Unida, and led to community-wide demands for justice. In Denver, high school students had a similarly dynamic relationship with Corky Gonzáles's Crusade for Justice. The crusade predated high school unrest, unlike La Raza Unida, but it did not create nor could it entirely control dissenting students. Gonzáles in fact attempted to draw the most effective high school student activists into his organization, as did La Raza Unida. For Latino and black students, discrimination in choosing cheerleaders or the disparaging remarks of a teacher allowed them to grasp both the theory and the practice of racism as it impinged upon their daily lives. These lessons were not new for black and brown students, of course, yet in the social and political context of the 1960s and early 1970s, they perceived that, through collective action and protest, change was within their reach. Like the activists outside the high schools, these students seized the initiative.[71]

Students of color wrung some concessions from school administrators, primarily in hiring more diverse personnel, teaching history and culture more inclusively, and allowing assertions of racial and ethnic pride and solidarity. Simultaneously, they served notice that white students and administrators could no longer expect black and Latino students to move like silent ghosts through their high schools or bear the sole burden of making integration work. In one interview, a black girl complained, "I'm sick of the white students saying, 'All right, you can sit with me.' I feel, 'Well, why don't you come sit with me instead?'" Why, these students wanted to know, should all aspects of school life be on white terms?[72]

When Sylvia Williams concluded her book on the black and white movements at Cubberly High School, she noted that after the school returned to "normal," several things had changed. There were new classes on black history and culture, more black adults working in the school, and, through the expansion of the sneak-out program (now more demurely called the "black transfer program"), more black students attending. The multicultural program and black student union continued. Moreover, three of four student body offices were filled by blacks. "Normal" had been redefined. The election of black students to student body government may indicate a color-blind ethos among the students, but the other changes signaled that racial consciousness had become heightened, institutionalized, and made permanent.[73]

Whites had organized desegregation by closing black schools and grudgingly admitting blacks into institutions they continued to dominate. When students of color sought power and expressed pride in their own heritage, they not only broke the white monopoly on power and pride, but also fundamentally reordered—but did not eliminate—the racial system. White students and officials had previously regarded whiteness as the norm, a universal standard against which others, who were "colored," were measured. Activism by black and brown students turned *white* into a color, no better and sometimes worse than the others. Race, however, continued to shape the identity of many students.

Radical white students, sometimes clumsily, offered gestures of support. In response to the Los Angeles Chicano students' walkout in 1970, two hundred white students from the wealthy Beverly Hills High School on the other side of town boycotted classes for one hour in sympathy with the Chicano students' demands. This symbolic protest indicated a potential for solidarity based on their common identity as high school students. When the issues black and Hispanic students raised touched on matters of curriculum and students' rights, they affected a much broader constituency among students and could sometimes unify students across races against teachers and administrators. Although race continued to divide high school students, countervailing demands for student rights and power cut across race. Far more high school students took part in the students' rights movement than in the Black and Brown Power movements, and, although it may be that racial disturbances had more serious consequences (being more likely to involve violence or use of police), high school unrest that centered on rules and students' rights proved equally challenging to teachers and administrators. Two broad categories of agitation emerged: the rights of high school students (especially First Amendment rights) and student power and participation within their schools. These categories often overlapped; to draw too sharp a distinction between them is misleading. Nevertheless, some of the things high school students wanted pertained to their status as citizens of the United States while others focused more narrowly on students as members of the high school community and participants in the educational process. In the former case, students often painted a broad critique of American society; in the latter, they took aim at prevailing rules and educational content in the high schools. We will look at each in turn.[74]

FOUR—THE HIGH SCHOOL

STUDENT RIGHTS MOVEMENT

Brooklyn Technical High School, founded in 1922, was one of a handful of "special schools" for gifted students in New York City, training them in math, science, and engineering. In 1969, when the student body was more than 80 percent white, its black students were highly politicized and clashed repeatedly with the white principal, Isador Auerbach. In one instance, Auerbach ripped down a picture of Black Panther Eldridge Cleaver that students had posted in the cafeteria, claiming that Cleaver was a "fugitive from justice," not a positive role model. The following year, Auerbach called the police to remove a Black Nationalist flag from campus. Why the incident required police involvement is not clear, but the principal justified his action by citing the law, asserting that state law forbade schools from flying any banner except the American flag. His claim was pure fabrication, for no such law existed. Ira Glasser of the New York Civil Liberties Union remarked that this incident typified "the lawlessness of principals." Although students may not have had a right to post portraits of their heroes on school grounds or to hoist the banners of their particular causes, in this case and others principals often proceeded as if students had no rights and schools could impose any rules they wished, including rules that had little to do with education and reflected instead the class, race, and ideological biases of the authorities.[1]

Public high schools, in addition to teaching the "three R's" and preparing students for college or work, tried to provide experiences that would let them practice being citizens of a larger polity. To that end, most schools had a school newspaper and some form of student government. Curricula included courses on civics and government to teach students about their rights and responsibilities as American citizens. Educators argued that such classes allowed the student to "appreciate the nature of democratic citizenship and to develop social skills with which he [sic] can improve his civic competence as he moves gradually into the adult world." After all, "[t]he young adolescent is putting away childish things." These classes, as well as courses in American history, lauded U.S. democracy and freedom and contrasted "our way of life" with the unfortunate lives of people enslaved by communism.[2]

Classes on the theoretical rights high school students possessed, however, sometimes raised their expectations higher than school officials were willing to meet. As long as students conformed to broader societal and political norms and exercised their rights within the limits established by school authorities, the mock democracy of the high schools—the school newspapers, the student government—remained intact. But when students began to question social norms and school rules, discuss controversial issues, or explore and express political views at odds with those of the administration or the community, they were shocked to discover that, in the end, they possessed only as many rights as the school officials would grant them—or as many as they could win through pressure, demonstrations, or lawsuits.

Although many high schools claimed to treat students as adults-in-training, they simultaneously imposed rules and restrictions that relegated teenagers to the status of children. Educator Charles Silberman's popular book *Crisis in the Classroom,* published in 1970, noted sarcastically that one California high school's student handbook emphasized students' "responsibility of becoming your own man or woman," but then insisted upon "a dress code with *sixteen* separate regulations" on hair styles and apparel (his emphasis). Although Silberman's critique had many supporters, few adults believed that students possessed the same as rights as adult citizens or could be trusted to make wise decisions. Educators shared this opinion and doled out rights and freedoms piecemeal. To students, studying the freedoms asserted in the Bill of Rights in particular but being permitted to exercise only a portion of those rights while in school smacked of hypocrisy or even tyranny. Rules that seemed arbitrary, like those at Brooklyn Technical High School, motivated students to scrutinize all rules and eventually to demand a voice in creating and enforcing them.[3]

Drawing sustenance from the contemporary rights revolution, students demanded the right to dress as they pleased, publish and distribute their own newspapers, form their own extracurricular clubs, and invite outside speakers to campus. With the aid of the American Civil Liberties Union

(ACLU) students won some battles in court, helping to clarify—to some degree—the legal status of schoolchildren. They won other battles through demonstrations, petitions, and boycotts, by wearing down administrators' will to resist. In still other cases, school officials quelled student insurgents with draconian punishments. Student rights activism divided students less sharply than did racial issues, for most agreed that the First Amendment, in particular, applied to them. Yet, because some moderate and conservative students disapproved of the activists' tactics, school officials could sometimes isolate the activists and undercut support for their demands.

One of the hottest points of contention between students and school officials in the late 1960s concerned students' right to choose their own clothing and hairstyles. According to a report on student unrest released by the U.S. House of Representatives Subcommittee on General Education in 1969, although the most serious disruptions had to do with race, the majority of high school protests involved dress codes and student discipline. By the late 1960s, many American schools had fairly elaborate sex-specific dress codes. The codes laid out how boys could wear their hair, mandated collars and tucked-in shirts, and banned blue jeans. For girls, pants were proscribed entirely, and the codes dictated the lengths of skirts. Neither boys nor girls were permitted to wear boots or sandals. Rules about footwear had some logical justification: boots could mar the finish of a floor (especially a wooden floor) and sandals made toes vulnerable to injury. Many of the other rules could not be justified on such grounds, although official sometimes employed contorted reasoning to prove that the taboo styles posed a risk to the physical environment or to the students' health, or disrupted the classroom. At base, most dress codes represented a muddled and not always articulated set of beliefs about class, gender, and discipline, buttressed by issues of power, control, and authority.[4]

Unlike dress codes, censorship of student publications and limits on their abilities to speak and write freely affected smaller numbers of students— everyone dressed, but fewer wrote or challenged political restrictions on speech—but drew larger numbers of outside supporters. Adults generally regarded skirmishing over clothing and hair as trivial but believed that speech and writing involved substantial First Amendment rights. When some students evaded censorship by publishing unofficial newspapers or magazines, they launched new battles with officials over ownership of school property and the purposes of education. Administrators defended dress codes as essential for creating the proper atmosphere for education, but they could hardly say the same about restricting students' freedom of expression. When they defended censorship by emphasizing the youth of the students, they pressured the courts to establish the precise age at which citizenship rights applied. The courts declined, but they did expand the First Amendment rights available to teenagers.

Student activists drew heavily upon the First Amendment in asserting their rights to dress, write, and speak freely. They were on shakier ground when they criticized student governments for not exercising meaningful power, for nothing in the Bill of Rights or existing laws suggested they had a right to govern themselves. Adults understood that student governments were the creations of school officials, who alone decided how they should be structured, who should participate, and what powers they should have. Nevertheless, when officials violated the very regulations they had set in place, students were outraged and demanded more genuine power.

Contemporary commentators generally regarded the high school student rights movement as an imitation of the college movement. Some went further, insisting that college dissidents themselves stirred up unrest in the high schools. Certainly high school students recognized the changes sweeping over American society in the 1960s and early 1970s and were inspired to activism, but awareness of their lack of rights sprang from their own experiences. Radical high school students who assailed capitalism, the war in Vietnam, or other off-campus issues may have been more influenced by college students, but activists for student rights had their feet firmly planted in local soil. Like students of color, who forced high schools to be more responsive to their needs, the student rights movement succeeded in curtailing the arbitrary power of administrators and claimed a number of rights they had not previously enjoyed.

THE GREAT HAIR DEBATE

The battle over long hair on male students highlights many of these issues and lays bare the contending values that undergirded both sides of the divide. Historically, beards, mustaches, wigs, and queues (single braids or ponytails in the back of the head) had gone in and out of style among American men over the previous two centuries; by later standards, nineteenth-century men were exceedingly hirsute. By the era of the cold war, however, terms such as "clean-cut," "clean-shaven," and "wholesome" indicated new standards of appearance. Many people interpreted short hair on men as a sign of conformity with social norms, whereas facial hair or longer hair became associated with nonconformity, homosexuality, or even communism. Even in the mild 1950s, however, some high school boys scorned the crewcut for the DA (duck's ass), combing their longish hair into a V at the back, a style linked to rebellion against middle-class respectability. Adults regarded rock musician Elvis Presley as the Demon King of cultural rebellion, and indeed Presley's greased-up hair, eye shadow, loud clothing, and shimmying hips assaulted conventionality. A more significant impetus toward the long-haired trend came from the Beatles. When, in the mid-1960s, high school boys wanted to imitate the hairstyle of their British idols, many adults reacted explosively, and battles raged until well into the 1970s. During this time, what was considered "long hair" grew from merely grazing the shirt collar or eyebrows to hanging well over the shoulders.[5]

Adult hostility toward long hair on boys stemmed from several sources. In part, adults interpreted long hair as defiance of cultural norms and their own authority. Some connected long hair to the countercultural attack on tradition, or even to political radicalism and the antiwar movement. In addition, long hair on boys—just like pants on girls—violated deeply felt beliefs about appropriate sex roles. Boys should be boys, and they should look the part. The school board at Oswego Community High School, in Illinois, for example, claimed in 1969 that "since there is so much similarity in the dress of male and female students who wear slacks and sweaters, there should be some way by which teachers could easily distinguish the boys from the girls." The board solved the problem by banning "the wearing of a girl-style hair-do by boys." The argument that only differing hairstyles could enable adults to distinguish adolescent boys from adolescent girls is laughable. We might also ask for what purpose did boys and girls need to be distinguished? Administrators claimed that they needed to know the sex of their students to prevent "malicious boys" from sneaking into the girls' bathrooms, but this is difficult to take seriously. It seems that adults in Oswego merely imposed their own ideas about gender on the students. The belief that long hair was intrinsically girlish and that gender boundaries needed strict policing lay behind many rules establishing permissible male hairstyles.[6]

In addition to ruffling adults' sensibilities about gender, long hair offended because it violated norms of respectability. The fashions of hair and clothing from the 1950s exuded formality and conventionality. Hats, gloves, industrial-strength undergarments, lipstick, and stockings were de rigueur for women. For men, clothing choices also reflected class position. Except on informal occasions, middle-class men of all races wore hats, tight collars, neckties, wingtips, and suit coats. Working-class and poor men wore this type of attire to church but not to work. By the late 1960s, however, informality had gone public, working-class styles crossed over, and young people led the way in adopting relaxed clothing and hairstyles. Blue jeans—not the elaborately detailed designer pants of the 1980s but the sturdy denim apparel of working men—epitomized the shift. Banned by school officials, the pants symbolized all that was cool, countercultural, and comfortable, the direct inverse of 1950s fashions. City officials in Norwalk, Connecticut, reacting to skirmishes in their high schools over long hair, expressed disdain for the new fashions with a billboard: "Students of Norwalk—Beautify America—Get a Haircut." In one instance, a principal suspended a high school student because he did not like the boy's faded jeans or "general appearance." But what adults saw as neat and "beautiful" appeared to many young people as stifling and oppressive.[7]

Long hair also angered school administrators and parents who drew connections between student dress, attitudes, and behavior. If students dressed in a neat, respectable (i.e., middle-class) way, their manners would mirror their attire and they would be better students. Conformity seemed particularly important given the heterogeneous student body of the postwar era.

When Jim Turley sued his Iowa high school in 1971, claiming a right to wear his hair long, school authorities countered by asserting that "there is a definite correlation between a student's hair length and his academic achievement, his discipline, his general opinions, and the way he conducts himself in school." As proof, the assistant principal submitted a study of eighteen students that he had conducted. The judge dismissed the study as "not only unsupported . . . but border[ing] on the ridiculous." Other judges, however, either agreed with officials or were willing to let them set standards for students' hair.[8]

Administrators did not draw up rules about hair in a vacuum. They shared ideas about hair, gender, sexuality, and discipline with other adults around the nation, but they also responded to specific pressures. One official argued that attitudes of the local "political constituency" were such that any "failure of the . . . school district to promulgate and enforce the rule [against long hair] would cause the school to lose support required for its welfare." Whether local taxpayers could impose their values to the degree that some officials claimed is open to question. Teachers also supported dress codes, at least early on. A poll of one thousand teachers in 1965 revealed that nearly 97 percent favored such rules.[9]

High school students did not necessarily share the values of adult educators and resisted the hair codes in a variety of ways. Some boys complied by keeping within a whisker (literally) of the regulations. Geoff Burkman, for example, characterized Mariemont High School, in Cincinnati, which he attended in the late 1960s, as "fairly liberal," although it did have dress and hair codes. He brags, "We pushed things as far to the limits as we could without actually trashing those limits. For instance, if the code said no sideburns below the bottom of the ear, then we all made sure we grew our sideburns (those of us who could) right down to that line."[10]

Other boys rejected the dress codes outright. A number of long-haired high school rock-and-roll musicians engaged in tests of strength with school authorities. They might have fared better had they claimed to be imitating Ludwig von Beethoven, an unkempt classical musician. Violating school rules to mimic rock stars, whom many adults loathed, heaped rebellion upon rebellion. James McNamara attended a wealthy, virtually all-white school outside Columbus, Ohio. Although his school's dress code specified short hair for boys, he grew his long to fit his rock band persona. On at least one occasion, school officials physically held him down and forcibly trimmed his hair. Phillip Ferrell, Stephen Webb, and Paul Jarvis were all students at W. W. Samuell High School, in Dallas. They too grew their hair long to play in a rock band called Sounds Unlimited. Jarvis cut his hair to attend summer school, but the other two boys allowed their hair to grow, and in the fall of 1966 the school denied them entrance. They filed for an injunction against the school, lost, appealed, and lost again.[11]

The boys' case, *Ferrell v. Dallas,* the first appealed to the federal circuit courts of appeals, sheds some light on the divergent attitudes of students and administrators. Judges in the district and appellate courts found themselves juggling claims about contractual agreements, the function of education, and the right to privacy. The students and their agent, Kent Alexander, submitted their contract into evidence, for it stipulated, that as members of the band, they were required to wear their hair long. Alexander claimed that he had invested thousands of dollars in the group, which might be jeopardized if the boys had to clip their hair. The courts rejected this reasoning on the grounds that contracts were unenforceable for minors.[12]

For their part, school authorities argued that male long hair disrupted education. The school's principal, W. S. Lanham, testified that short-haired boys had tried to pick fights with the "long hairs," made disparaging and sometimes obscene comments (which Lanham claimed upset girls), and on one occasion took it upon themselves to act as barbers. Lanham argued that, in light of the turmoil long hair caused, the school's rule against it should be upheld. Both the district and the appellate courts agreed. In district court, Judge William Taylor wrote, "One of the most important aims of the school should be to educate the individual to live successfully with other people in our democracy." Taylor interpreted "living successfully" to mean abiding by group norms. To many students in the 1960s, however, democracy meant nothing if it did not mean individual liberty. Here the values of the 1950s collided with the emergent values of the later era.[13]

While the adults fought over contracts and education, the students regarded their hair length as a private matter over which school authorities should have no control. After they were suspended, but before their case went to court, Farrell, Webb, and Jarvis wrote a rock song called "Keep Your Hands Off It" that got some local radio airtime in Dallas and succinctly expressed their views:

> Went to school, got kicked out
> Said it was too long, now we're going to shout.
>
> [Chorus] Keep your hands off of it,
> Keep your hands off of it,
> Keep your hands off of it,
> It don't belong to you.
>
> Bopped upon the steps, the principal I met,
> You're not getting in, now what do want to bet [sic]
>
> [Chorus]
>
> Went this morning, tried to get in,
> The kids were for us, but we still couldn't win.
>
> [Chorus]
>
> HAIR, THAT IS![14]

In addition to declaring hair to be private property, this song suggests generational solidarity on the question of hairstyles—"the kids were for us." In fact, although dress codes formed a core issue for students' rights activists, short-haired boys frequently harassed those with long hair, of their own accord or egged on by adults. School officials like W. S. Lanham then used the disruptions to justify rules mandating short hair.

Whereas some boys claimed long hair as a professional necessity for their rock-'n'-roll image, others wanted to follow the fashion, and a few explicitly rejected adult authority. Chris Corley challenged the hair regulations of Forest Heights Junior High School, in Little Rock, Arkansas, to show his opposition to the American war in Vietnam. John Pepple simply felt "ugly" in the short haircut his parents imposed upon him. He remarks, "A chance remark from my sister made me aware that she and both my parents thought of me as cute in that awful butch haircut. So, when I began rebelling and demanding to grow my hair, they must have thought that I was rebelling simply to rebel. Maybe if they had understood how ugly I felt in that type of haircut, they might have been a little more understanding."[15]

Other students historicized hairstyles, noting that societal norms of appropriate styles for men varied in different times. Therefore, they argued, administrators who insisted that the cuts popular in the 1950s be worn into the late 1960s simply demonstrated their preference for one style over another. Questioning their school's dress code, two students from William A. Workman High School, in La Puente, California, pointed out in an underground newspaper,

> On page 28 of the Workman Student Handbook . . . it states that a haircut should begin at the bottom of the ears and be tapered up. But on page 14 of this same publication, there is a picture of William A. Workman, whose appearance is not in accordance with this rule. Yet the school is named after this "undesirable." Mr. Workman's hair seems to be hanging over his ears.

Workman had been a leading California citizen in the mid-nineteenth century, and his hair reflected the fashions of that time. Tongue in cheek, the students suggested renaming their school "Yul Brynner High" after the bald actor or altering the dress code. Calling attention to the long hair of the school's namesake undermined administrators' rationale—whatever it was—for the rule.[16]

Facial hair posed a different challenge to school authorities. If long hair was effeminate and blurred gender lines, the same could not be said of beards and mustaches, biological markers of male physical maturity. Nevertheless, administrators often adamantly opposed facial hair on students or teachers. David Super recalls that one of his friends had to shave off his "quite conservative" mustache upon graduation to take a teaching job in a small town in South Dakota in 1970. John Pepple's best friend began growing a beard just before graduation. Infuriated, school authorities announced that they would not permit him to graduate and directed him to bring his parents in for a conference. When the friend's father walked in sporting a beard of his own, Pepple says, "[T]his so staggered the administrators that they . . . said that Chris could graduate, but they insisted that he couldn't be in the ceremony unless he shaved off his beard. The administrators thought of this as a punishment, but at least some of us thought of this as a privilege instead."[17]

Beards divided younger and older teachers, men and women. When his principal told John Canfield, a first-year teacher, that his beard caused some of the older women teachers lose their appetites, he retorted, "Fine. . . . Maybe they'll die of malnutrition and be replaced." A fellow teacher told him his beard was a "bad example" for the students. What this teacher meant is unclear; perhaps only that if the teachers wore beards, students would want them, too. Teachers with long hair or facial hair prevented adults from maintaining a united front and weakened the official rationale for hair regulations.[18]

High school rules about hair clearly had more to do with school officials' beliefs about masculinity, conformity, neatness, and obedience to authority than to genuine pedagogical or health issues. But, unlike students from earlier times, who unhappily accepted school dictates, high school boys—and more rarely teachers—in the mid- to late 1960s and into the 1970s often took their cases to court. Courts generally upheld the rules if the school authorities could convince them that long hair, beards, or mustaches disrupted the educational process or endangered the students' health or safety. When Edward Gfell sued his Ohio high school in 1969, for example, the court dismissed his complaint with the observation that long hair could be a dangerous nuisance for boys in industrial courses or sports. The court also emphasized that students themselves had devised the dress code at Gfell's school. Democracy, not mere adult authority, partially legitimized the short hair rule in this judge's opinion, which indicates the sea change taking place—although erratically—in many high schools and in the courts, where some adults began to embrace the idea of empowering high school students.[19]

In fact, some judges repudiated arguments that students had to learn to obey authority. Colfax Community School, in Iowa, justified its hair stricture by asserting (as Judge William Cook Hanson summarized their view) that the rule "promotes good citizenship by teaching respect for authority and instilling discipline." Judge Hanson denounced this belief in scathing terms: "If such an argument were accepted, then any rule, no matter how arbitrary, capricious or abhorrent to our democratic process, could be justified by school officials." Moreover, courts rejected rules that were not carefully drawn, as was the Connecticut case of *Crossen v. Fatsi*. There, the court assailed the dress code as "too vague and overbroad. It leaves to the arbitrary whim of the school principal, what in fact constitutes extreme fashion or style in the matter of personal grooming and permits his own subjective opinion to be the sole measure of censorship."[20]

Some contemporaries scorned the hair wars as unimportant, but neither students nor administrators acted as though the issue did not matter. Hundreds of students sued their schools, claiming a right to wear their hair long. When they lost, students and administrators alike appealed. More than a hundred of these "hair cases" were heard in the federal circuit courts of appeals, where the ten appellate circuits split in their decisions—half upheld the right of students to choose their hairstyle, and half upheld the school's responsibility to maintain an atmosphere conducive to study. Losers in the appellate courts asked nearly a dozen times for the United States Supreme Court to issue a ruling and decide the matter finally, but the Court declined to hear the cases. The legal status of the high school students weighed heavily with judges who heard hair cases. Those who regarded teenagers unambiguously as children tersely dismissed their arguments and complained about the waste of time. Others wrestled to define the students' status in a more nuanced way. Although the courts carefully maintained that students did not possess rights identical to those of adults, some judges did agree that hair length fell within the range of personal and private decisions that should be left up to students. These judges located that right in the First Amendment, defining hair as a form of expression, or in the Fourteenth Amendment, as a right of privacy protected by the due process clause. Others found it reasonable for school districts to establish rules about grooming to carry out their educational mandate. The latter conceded that hair regulations infringed on personal liberties to some degree but argued that the need for order and discipline outweighed the negligible harm that students might suffer. Ultimately, students' legal rights with regard to their hair and attire remained shaky. If a boy wanted to wear his hair long during the school year, he had to live in one of the circuits that granted him this right, know the law in his state, and sometimes be willing to lock horns with the administrators to do so. In broad terms, however, principals and school boards could no longer count on students or their parents to accept passively any rules the schools decreed, nor the courts to automatically support the adult view.[21]

GIRLS' BATTLES: SKIRTS AND PANTS

High school girls in the late 1960s also wore their hair long and untrammeled. The fact that few school officials regarded this as unsafe or unhygienic underscores that these were not the real reasons that they opposed long hair for boys. On rare occasions, adults reacted to girls' long bangs. Marsh' Fenstermaker remembers an art teacher taking scissors and personally trimming a girl's bangs after repeatedly asking the girl to do this herself. Susan Sims, of Colfax, Iowa, took her case to court in 1968—the only girl's haircut case in this era—and won after the testimony of Sims's teacher that she could not teach typing if she could not see the students' eyes failed to convince the judge. But in general, girls did not participate in the great hair debate. Their dress codes battles with school administrators involved the length of their skirts and whether they could wear pants.[22]

Fashions for women and older girls in the 1950s sent conflicting signals about femininity, sexuality, and self-control. Following World War II, pants remained permissible for women and girls, but only within a narrow range of public places, which did not include school. Journalist Brett Harvey observed that the dresses of the 1950s highlighted women's sexuality and availability by accentuating prominent breasts and tiny waists, while interposing layers of cloth and rubber in what amounted to a tease. Gradually, fashions in the 1960s maintained or even enhanced the aura of women's sexuality while stripping away the physical barriers to access. Skirts began to climb skyward and undergarments such as bras and girdles thinned, lightened, or disappeared altogether.[23]

When miniskirts became the fashion in the mid-1960s, high school administrators tried as long as they could to hold hemlines down. Girls literally had to kneel before school officials to demonstrate that their skirts reached the specified length. But, while high school boys had to abide by rules about hair length or defy them—and take the consequences—girls found it easier to flout the skirt length rule and get away with it. Kathy Grant, of Sturgis, South Dakota, who felt pressured to be "the perfect kid," because of her father's position on the school board, describes how she and her classmates "rolled the waist so that we could shorten them at least a little. Then if challenged on the skirt length all we did was grab each side and pull down. It was a constant maintenance thing, go to the bathroom and roll the waist every hour or so."[24] Skirt rolling involved not only "constant maintenance," but also constant low-intensity conflict with adults. School officials could not have been completely blind to the games girls played but, like the girls, seem to have preferred guerrilla sniping to full-scale battles such as the ones they waged with long-haired boys.

Some teachers, however, found the role of dress code cop distasteful or a waste of time. Sharon Breitweiser, who attended Central High School, in Cheyenne, Wyoming, from 1969 to 1971, recalls one teacher who mocked the rules by feigning zealous enforcement. He "used valuable class time to make girls kneel down so that he could measure the lengths of their skirts and to measure boys' hair in regard to their ears. He would then make a big deal out of any violations." Breitweiser and her friends understood his actions as sarcastic. Just as male teachers wanted to wear facial hair or hairstyles not permitted to the students, some women wanted to wear their skirts above the knee. Administrators tried to play on these teachers' sense of professionalism, but they did not always succeed.[25]

Again it is clear that officials sometimes invoked authority for its own sake in making rules about girls' fashions. In 1965, just as hemlines crept above the knee and some schools began issuing rules about skirt length, two girls in New Jersey were sent home from a school dance for wearing long-sleeved, high-necked, floor-length garments called "granny dresses."

Upon questioning, the assistant principal declared that any clothing not appropriate for school could not be worn to an after-hours dance. His decision is doubly odd, for not only were the girls' dresses excessively modest, covering virtually their entire bodies, but other students attended the dance in "after school clothes" (dungarees and sweatshirts for the boys and slacks for the girls) and were not reprimanded.[26]

Pants were another commonly disputed item of apparel for girls and women teachers alike. Officials had a hard time parrying the arguments of those who claimed that pants disrupted school less than miniskirts and kept the legs warmer than tights or stockings. It is interesting to note that, although boys who violated hair codes seem to have done so as individuals, girls often struggled collectively for the right to wear pants. Gail Marsh, who graduated from Morgantown High School, in West Virginia, in 1971, remembers that her class held a sit-in until the principal agreed to permit girls to wear slacks. Diane Arave, a student at Brooklyn's Sheepshead Bay High School has a similar story: "The girls in all grades [in the high school] organized, risked getting sent home, and called for days where we all wore pants (jeans/bell bottoms) to school. I was surprised when even my mother supported this one!" Sometimes teachers joined the rebellion. Sharon Rab, who graduated from college in 1964, then taught at Fairmont West High School, in Kettering, Ohio, relates that in 1969 or 1970 "[t]he female teachers staged a coup and we all broke the dress code and wore 'pants suits' to school on the same day. The kids were so proud of us."[27]

Pantsuits gradually gained acceptance as public attire for women and girls. Blue jeans, on the other hand, remained for a time beyond the pale. Long associated with the working class and the poor, blue jeans became part of middle-class wardrobes when civil rights activists in the South began to wear bib overalls or blue jeans in their work with rural blacks. It is not clear whether these activists sought to fit in or used jeans as an expression of solidarity with poor blacks, but when the fashion spread and was taken up by teenaged boys and girls, some schools cracked down. The principal of Robbinsdale High School, in Minnesota, defended his decision to suspend one hundred boys and girls for wearing jeans on the grounds that the rivets might damage school furniture, even though it was formica rather than wood.[28]

Although official objection to blue jeans seems to have had a class basis, other elements of dress codes aimed at sexual containment or the maintenance of firm gender boundaries. In addition to rules about clipped hair for boys and no slacks for girls, some schools required that boys wear their shirts tucked in and cinch in their pants with belts, securing their clothes against their bodies. Others decreed that girls could not come barelegged to school. A principal sent one girl home on a hot day for wearing sandals—which the school permitted—without socks. According to her, "Even my conservative mother thought that was going too far."[29] It is striking, however, that evidently no school had written rules specifying that girls must wear brassieres, the quintessential gear for sexual containment. Either school officials could not imagine that girls might not wear bras to school or they found the subject too embarrassing and indelicate to mention. One cartoon from a student underground newspaper suggested that periodic "bra-checks" were carried out by gym teachers, so it may be that schools had tacit rules about bras and enforced them informally. But when going braless became the fashion, at least one school administrator spoke up. Sharon Bialy-Fox, from Long Island, recalls with amusement that her school scheduled a special girls-only assembly. There, the dean of girls told them, "Girls, when I see those of you without bras go running down the hall, it looks like two squirrels fighting under a blanket!" Bialy-Fox didn't mention whether the lecture had the desired effect.[30]

Many dress codes targeted boys and girls separately, yet race-specific rules were less common. Some schools did forbid African-style dress or limit the length of an Afro hairstyle. Because this evidence is extremely sparse, however, the rationale behind the rules remains obscure. Did officials regard dashikis as too "feminine" to pass as male attire? Did they see Afros merely as "long hair" to be regulated like long hair on white boys? Did they fear inciting white student or community rage if so-called black clothing highlighted their blackness? Or did they object to African clothing and Afros as nonconformist in exactly the same way they objected to white students with long hair and blue jeans? One article in the *New York Times* asserted that teachers identified students in African dress as "hard-core militants." In that case, did administrators believe banning the clothing would dampen black militancy? Although administrators left little record of the motivations behind their actions, some students protested rules against sartorial displays of black solidarity. In Philadelphia, more than three thousand Philadelphia high school students boycotted classes to "crash" a board of education meeting. The confrontation turned violent, with twenty-two injuries and fifty-seven arrests. School officials responded by permitting African-style dress, which ended the turmoil, although only a handful of students in fact adopted the controversial garments.[31]

THE DECLINE OF DRESS CODES

By the early 1970s, school officials found it difficult to maintain their dress codes from the 1950s intact. In some cases, administrators modified dress codes themselves. More commonly, they consulted with or allowed students to vote on the question. Woodward High School, in Cincinnati, modified its dress code after the student council recommended it. Though not all students opposed the dress code *per se,* they usually favored liberalizing it. On the rare occasions when students opted for more stringent dress codes, adults considered this newsworthy. When students at Cheboygan High School, in Michigan, asked for a stricter code, the *New York Times* carried the story in its front section. In some schools where students did not relax the dress code, it either slowly faded from existence or collapsed all at once.[32]

Courts played an important role by rejecting arbitrary rules based on conventionality or sheer authority. Educational experts summarized court decisions in professional journals and advised public schools to alter their dress codes, giving sound advice on what kinds of rules would pass judicial scrutiny. Some officials were simply worn down by resistance from students and younger teachers. Repeated student protests distracted administrators from other problems and could require enormous energy to repress. At Venice High School, in Los Angeles, for example, when officials refused to modify the dress code, students Shasta Hatter and Julie Johnston spearheaded a boycott of the school's fund-raising chocolate sale. The wrathful principal suspended Hatter for distributing leaflets off campus in favor of the boycott and Johnston for wearing a button that said "Boycott Chocolates." Undaunted, the girls sued and won in a federal court of appeals. Negotiation came to seem easier to many principals and school boards than these protracted struggles with determined students. Alice Krause Young points out that, despite the disparaging comments from older teachers at her high school in southwestern Ohio, "as more young male student teachers came to the school with longer hair, it was like holding back the tide." After giving up on hair length, when girls persisted in wearing pants, the administration stopped enforcing the pants ban as well. Administrators believed that drugs and pregnancies were more important problems than dress code violations.[33]

Although the specific issues in disputes over dress codes seem trivial, the bottom line, as sociologist and educator Edgar A. Friedenberg observed, was "adolescents' right to a reasonable degree of respect, privacy, and freedom to establish their own tastes and govern their own actions in areas where they interfere with no one." Adults argued bitterly about whether high school students had such rights. In New York City, for example, even after State Commissioner of Education James Allen forbade dress codes, some high schools ignored him, continuing to enforce their own codes. Children's rights activist Helen Baker claimed that a school superintendent told the principals in his Ohio district to "ignore" *Goss v. Lopez,* the U.S. Supreme Court's decision affirming the right of high school students to due process, unless they were specifically challenged on it. A major problem for the students' rights movement was that, even when the courts, supervisors, or educational commissioners upheld certain rights for students, compliance remained in the hands of local school administrators. No mechanism of oversight or enforcement existed to bring them into line. Student James McNamara comments wryly that knowing about successful legal challenges to dress codes did not necessarily benefit students. Administrators at his school adopted a standpat "so, sue us" attitude. Unless a student had the brains, courage, money, and adult support to initiate a lawsuit, school officials could hang tough and ignore courts, educational experts, parents, and students. Moreover, they did so in the knowledge that they enjoyed the support of at least some parents, students, and members of the wider community.[34]

STUDENTS AND SMOKING

In addition to the freedom to dress and style themselves as they wished, some students wanted the right to smoke cigarettes on campus. Even non-smoking students often supported demands for a smoking space on campus because they hated choking on the air in the bathrooms, where most of the illicit smoking took place. The hazards of smoking were becoming clear. The surgeon general issued the first warning about smoking in 1964. The following year, tobacco companies had to include warning labels on cigarette packages. School officials, however, banned smoking because they believed students were too young to smoke, not for any health considerations. Teachers and administrators could smoke in their own lounges, although not in the classrooms. This exception struck students as hypocritical, and sometimes they protested. In one working-class high school in New York, the principal removed cubicle doors so that bathroom monitors could easily spot smokers. Students protested and gave the principal three days to restore the doors. When he failed to act, "thirty very tough white guys lined up in front of the bathrooms," according to one of the teachers, and succeeded in rehanging some of the doors. The administration responded by calling an assembly and comparing the thirty students to college radicals, which the conservative student body found hilarious. At Niles Township High School, in Skokie, Illinois, a student-faculty-administration cooperative committee conducted a study and recommended creating a smoking area for students. The board of education, however, rejected the recommendation, deciding instead to continue the total ban on student smoking and hiring five new security personnel to enforce it. In other high schools, students won their demands for a "smoking court," a specified campus location for smokers that some called "cancer court."[35]

CENSORSHIP AND THE FIRST AMENDMENT

The assertion of a right to dress as they wished or to smoke failed to convince many adults, but students stood on firmer ground when they attacked censorship of student publications. Whereas the former involved custody and control of students' bodies, the latter concerned control over their thoughts and expression, raising substantial First Amendment issues. Federal courts, divided over hair and clothing regulations, found students' claims to free speech and a free press far more compelling. Early in the 1960s, however, high school principals exercised broad censorship powers. Some schools required graduation speeches to be submitted for prior approval. Almost all monitored school plays and student newspapers.

Obscenities often triggered censorship and provided a justification for it. Marilyn Hall attended North High School, in Bakersfield, California, and graduated in 1968. She remembers the drama teacher having to cut the word "bitch" from a school play. Failure to censor a play at Wellesley High

School, in Massachusetts, led to community outrage and a riot. The school sponsored a special program about racism and poverty, which included a portion of the LeRoi Jones play *The Slave*. Later, a huge crowd of parents and community members showed up at a school committee meeting to denounce the performance. One student—a member of the student council and an athlete—defended the play and quoted lines that contained the word "fuck." Some of the adults in the audience subsequently "went ape," in the words of one onlooker, assaulting the student while screaming "kill him!" Incredibly, police arrested the student, not the rampaging adults. One shocked high school student commented, "Here was America right before our eyes. . . . This is what America really is."[36]

Official censorship went beyond cracking down on obscenities. Administrators also restricted students' freedom to discuss controversial issues such as race relations, the war in Vietnam, and sexuality or birth control in school newspapers. On other occasions, students wrote critiques of education. Some of them were broad and philosophical, but others went so far as to accuse specific teachers or administrators of doing a poor job. Administrators justified censoring these kinds of articles on the grounds that they were libelous, biased, or simply inappropriate. Moreover, they argued, censoring bad articles helped high school students learn responsible journalism. Paralleling their arguments about hair and dress, some further contended that ill-considered articles could harm school-community relations. What officials deemed irresponsible, however, often trampled students' First Amendment right to a free press. As restrictions on obscenity in public language gradually loosened in the wider society, some students believed they had the right to publish words that still offended many adults. Students also asserted their right to comment on current events and critique their schools, curricula, faculty, and education in general.[37] When Susan Bowman Prendergast dug up some old high school newspapers from the late 1960s, the contents astonished her:

> Besides jogging my memory it was also a revelation. Our paper was not only extremely well written, but [I] was struck at the pureness of reporting, unbiased. . . . Everything was covered: politics, the war, apathy, sex education in the school (that caused quite an uproar), our rights, should we concern ourselves as a student body with our rights in our school community where we could have an effect instead of school government focusing on what was going on outside where we couldn't bring about a change.[38]

Prendergast and other contemporaries demonstrate that the extraordinary events of the era penetrated the allegedly separate, self-absorbed world of the high school student. Ted Fox, who published an underground newspaper, the *New Times*, with his brother Nicholas, boasts that his publication "had three times the circulation of the regular high school paper." Buyers must have shared his interest in the Vietnam War, the draft, pollution, and police harassment of citizens, or else enjoyed reading anything that adults sought to ban.[39]

Students reacted in different ways to official censorship of their publications. Geoff Burkman edited his Mariemont High School newspaper. He remarks,

> Our ideas were rarely censored, only our modes of expression. Mostly our attitude was that of typical smartass teens: in one issue we printed a fake classified ad with the first letters of each word spelling out "fuck the system." We enjoyed hiding marijuana leaves and peace signs and the like inside drawings. We wrote a parody of Dracula substituting Mayor Daley for Dracula and Chicago policemen for vampires. We criticized Nixon constantly, and his henchmen.

Nevertheless, when the faculty advisor objected to something he wrote, Burkman "penned a satirical attack on her censorship and resigned."[40]

Other students confronted censorship directly and sought to have the rules changed. Believing that censorship violated their constitutional rights, they took their cases to court. District and federal appellate courts heard a number of high school censorship cases and generally confirmed students' rights to a free press. Though conceding that the rights of students could be abridged in ways not permissible for college students or adults, most judges insisted that the freedoms embodied in the First Amendment were so significant that the schools had to bear the burden of explaining why they should be limited. Even the use of obscenities in student publications could pass muster if they did not "tend to excite sexual desire or [constitute] a predominant appeal to prurient interest." One judge advised school officials that they could stamp "not approved by school" on a troubling issue of the student literary magazine, but they could not impound it and prevent its distribution. The threat of a lawsuit sometimes sufficed to convince school officials to end censorship. Editors of the *New Free Press,* in Skokie, Illinois, consulted the ACLU, which forced the administration, the students crowed, "to finally recognize students' constitutional right of freedom of press."[41]

THE HIGH SCHOOL UNDERGROUND PRESS

John Birmingham took an alternate route in response to censorship at New Jersey's Hackensack High School, where he edited the school newspaper. He argued that few students submitted articles that truly tested the boundaries of "responsible journalism" because they assumed the administration would censor them. Despite what Birmingham saw as his paper's blandness, school officials refused to let him publish an advertisement for draft counseling or an article about a proposed cut in the school's budget. Taken aback, Birmingham numbly accepted the censorship. When he attended the Columbia Scholastic Press Association Convention in February 1969, however, he discovered that he was not the only high school editor battling official censorship. This galvanized him into action. On returning home, he wrote a letter to his principal asking him to stop censoring the student paper. When the principal ignored the letter, Birmingham created an underground newspaper called *Smuff*.[42]

Where censorship caused John Birmingham to shift from public to underground publication, others found the underground press appealing for different reasons. Some regarded undergrounds as an alternative to what they saw as the narrow ideological biases of official school newspapers. Toby Mamis, who attended New York City's Stuyvesant High School, argued that the official coverage of the 1968 election campaign exposed the school paper's slant, because only the Republican and Democratic candidates received any press. This, Mamis claimed, convinced some students that "the radicals had been right all along" in their critique of the paper. Mamis also pointed out that, in some schools, only students who took journalism classes or were active in student government were permitted to write for the official newspaper. Such restrictions could also prod students to establish their own papers.[43]

It is not clear how many such underground newspapers flourished in the late 1960s and early 1970s. Writing for the *Saturday Review* in 1969, Diane Divoky claimed that there were "nearly 500." Others dispute this number, with estimates ranging from a thousand to more than three thousand. It seems fair to say that hundreds of these high school undergrounds existed, although some published only one or two issues. Few lasted more than a year. Rapid turnover of high school writers contributed to the short lives of student undergrounds, but putting out an underground newspaper was also hard work and few students could maintain their own commitment, let alone pass their vision along to the next cohort of students.[44]

In addition to underground newspapers in individual schools, citywide high school undergrounds existed in New York City, Berkeley, and the San Francisco Bay area, along with short-lived efforts to establish a nationwide press service for the high school underground. In the spring of 1968, New York City students organized a citywide underground paper called the *New York High School Free Press*. Paul Steiner, who in 1965 had begun one of the earliest high school underground newspapers, *Sansculottes,* now organized the High School Independent Press Service (HIPS) to provide copy to the *New York High School Free Press* and the plethora of independent underground papers, both in New York City and farther afield. Toby Mamis claims that this first HIPS "never really got off the ground." A second incarnation of HIPS, which appeared in the fall of 1969, operated out of the same office as the college students' Liberation News Service and enjoyed greater success than the first. According to Diane Divoky, HIPS was distributed to sixty high school newspapers and four hundred individuals, often free. HIPS charged high school independent papers $2 a month and all others $4 a month, but rarely collected and provided "a weekly packet of news and illustrations of high school uprisings, busts, dress codes, discipline, and politics."[45]

By its own admission, HIPS was "just as bad as the [New York] *Times* in being biased," although where the *Times* was "straight," HIPS was "in the revolutionary bag." In addition to this confessed bias, the very individualism that characterized high school underground newspapers and their readers could militate against their using HIPS as a press service. The editors of the Waukegan, Illinois, *Minstrel,* for example, experimented with different formats to attract readers. The third issue borrowed heavily from materials provided by HIPS. In the opinion of one of the editors, "We were no longer our own publication, but merely a soap box for HIPS. After review of their material and the typical crap that they gave us, we abandoned the idea of using anything else from HIPS, thereby enabling us to have better rapport with the students and the particular situation at our school." It is also not clear how many underground newspaper editors had even heard of HIPS. In Chicago, students created their own news service called FRED in February 1969, but this folded after seven or eight months for lack of financial support. John Schaller founded another high school news service called Chicago-Area High School Independent Press Syndicate (CHIPS), which spread to "nearly twenty states" by late 1969 and changed its name to the Co-Operative High School Independent Press Syndicate, thus maintaining the acronym CHIPS. It is not clear whether FRED and CHIPS were related or whether their founders even knew of the other's existence.[46]

Student underground editors had a hard time gaining access to machinery for duplicating their papers or money to fund them. Sharon Breitweiser and some friends in Cheyenne, Wyoming, put out an underground newspaper called *Candor.* This group had the paper "professionally printed at an out-of-state printer" for the three issues that constituted the paper's run. Breitweiser remembers, "We went all over town getting ads from local businesses. Many of them were shocked when the newspaper came out and they realized what it was, and I am not sure that we had any ads after the first issue!" Other undergrounds, in addition to seeking advertising revenues, solicited donations from their readers. The *New Free Press,* published by the Niles Township (Illinois) Student Coalition, appealed to its readers for donations so it could continue its policy of giving away the paper rather than charging for it. The editors of the Waukegan, Illinois, *Minstrel* found that circulation doubled when they stopped trying to sell the newspaper and gave it away instead. Thanks to reader donations, the editors finally broke even on their fourth issue.[47]

Time, money, and means posed problems for editors of high school undergrounds, but school officials threatened both the existence of the papers and the scholastic records of their editors. Only a few schools permitted open distribution of underground newspapers on their campuses. John Birmingham, who sought out as many editors as he could for his book on the high school underground press, could name only three schools that officially tolerated underground papers. Far more common was the reaction of officials at a Washington, D.C., high school, who sent around a memorandum ordering teachers to confiscate any copies of the *Washington Free Press* and report any student caught selling or distributing it. These students would be immediately suspended. In a Queens, New York, high school, the principal threatened to suspend any student seen reading, carrying, or even *suspected* of possessing the *High School Free Press*. In another case, student editors of the Mahwah, New Jersey, *Oracle* got in trouble for printing a photo of a nude student—a photo that had previously been published in *Newsweek* magazine. Sharon Breitweiser thinks that she blunted official wrath by being first in her class of four hundred and, probably more important, by carrying a tape recorder with her when the principal called her in for a meeting.[48]

High school undergrounds did not anger school officials alone. Stuart Steffan, John B. Koskinen, and Richard Shadden, editors of the *Minstrel,* mention that, in addition to minor flak from the school administration, "we did receive other threats. Threats in the form of threats against our person, crosses burned on lawns and on top of doghouses (really!), and threatening phone calls." It is hard to imagine administrators burning crosses on doghouses when they possessed more potent powers to punish; more likely conservative students or community members were behind these incidents. In another case, a New York City teacher who had been mocked in an underground newspaper seized an opportunity during the emotional Ocean Hill–Brownsville strike to punch the student who had written the article.[49]

Ironically, when students attempted to use the underground newspapers to bridge the communication gap between themselves and authorities, they were often ignored. For example, the *New Free Press* solicited articles from the Skokie, Illinois, school superintendent and a board of education member, clearly offering them a forum in which to express their own views to the students. When neither responded, the editors wrote hopefully, "Maybe next issue?"[50]

As with dress codes, the inquisitorial fervor of some school administrators with regard to student underground papers calls for an explanation. What offended or threatened them so deeply? What Geoff Burkman called the "typical smartass teen" element in the newspapers undoubtedly irked their elders, but this is a timeless feature of adolescents. A more likely explanation is that adults opposed the undergrounds for two reasons: their content and their very existence. Specific attacks on administrators and policies as well as philosophical critiques on the purposes and practices of contemporary education made officials see red. Students were children, and as such they had no right to criticize their elders. When they tackled the sexual revolution, the war in Vietnam, civil rights, Black and Brown Power, feminism, urban riots, government policies, and the counterculture, the liberal-left perspective of the undergrounds often enraged conservative principals and school boards. The tone of the papers—ranging from sharp critique to exuberant optimism about social change—their freewheeling illustrations, and their caustic cartoons gave them a vibrancy that the more sedate aboveground newspapers lacked but rubbed officials the wrong way.[51]

Beyond finding their content offensive, the appearance of underground papers threatened the authority of school officials, who feared that members of their community might interpret a lenient policy on unauthorized publications as evidence that the school principal did not fully control the students. In one instance, a lawyer for the local school board told student underground editors that the community might think the board condoned "dirty" language if it failed to crack down on their paper. School-sponsored papers could be monitored for content, language, and even political perspective. Underground newspapers eluded adult control. They created a free space for students to explore their own ideas and beliefs, take up issues that interested them, and set the agenda for the student rights movement. They were, in short, autonomous zones. Most principals and school boards responded as they did to all other challenges to their control over students: they clamped down.[52]

In clamping down, adults clearly sought to maintain their own power and control. The judges of the Fifth Circuit Court of Appeals took this view when five seniors from San Antonio, Texas, sued their school for suppressing their underground newspaper, *Awakening*. Declaring that this publication was "probably one of the most vanilla-flavored ever to reach a federal court," the judges heaped scorn on the "school board's bootstrap transmogrification into Super-Parent" and ruled for the students. Diane Divoky reported the sense of betrayal students in a Long Beach, New York, high school felt when the administration denied their request to publish an independent newspaper, *Frox*. The students had offered to refrain from using obscenities, publish multiple points of view, and "accept a faculty adviser who is not a censor." Divoky observed that, once the students decided to hire a lawyer to defend their First Amendment rights, the administration suddenly began to view them as "rebels confronting the adults who control their education."[53]

In his book on high school undergrounds, John Birmingham analyzed their popularity with students and the adult response. He noted that, although he would happily make his paper, *Smuff*, into an "aboveground" newspaper if his school officials would relinquish their powers of censorship, he believed that other students, lacking avenues for truly independent expression, reveled in this free space. To some journalists and their readers, the illicit nature of the publication added spice to it. Birmingham argued that the few high schools that did allow uncensored aboveground student newspapers showed "their desire to communicate with the students." Overall, however, he believed that many adults would rather simply squash independent student expression. He also noted that student charges of hypocrisy angered school officials.[54]

Indeed, students were quick to note the difference between the rhetoric they learned in civics class and the way their schools operated with regard to freedom of the press. Drawing upon the language of cold war indoctrination, Toby Mamis commented sarcastically, "Sometimes the 'commies' [students affiliated with an underground paper] are lucky. They get off with confiscation, a black mark on the record, a letter home, and probation. Lucky. In Russia you have that kind of freedom."[55] Mamis went even further in exposing high schools' double standards. He recruited friends to hand out his underground *New York Herald Tribune* one week then asked "straighter-looking friends" to pass out the official United Federation of Teachers (UFT) newspaper the next. Mamis and his friends photographed the differing responses; the principal "stopped, threatened, and yelled at" the first group, while permitting the second group to distribute its paper freely.[56]

Officials evoked their concern about articles that were libelous, inflammatory, or beyond contemporary standards of decency to justify censorship of the school-sponsored press. Wrestling with journalistic ethics and style without adult oversight, students in the underground press frequently developed their own standards. Many student editors understood that, although obscene words titillated the readers, they did not of themselves constitute good journalism. Birmingham confesses that, until he put out *Smuff,* he had never thought much about obscenity one way or another. "It seemed ridiculous," he observes, "but one major interest of many students and teachers was to see how many four-letter words we dared to print. For this reason, we completely avoided offensive language in the first issue." Later, however, when *Smuff* interviewed some students in a high school commune, Birmingham decided not to edit the obscenities they uttered. Editors of *Links,* a high school underground paper from Madison, Wisconsin, criticized the hypocrisy of adults who used obscenities but told young people they were too young to swear or characterized certain words as "unnecessary" or "unladylike." The editors responded by asking "what the hell's so right and necessary and ladylike about the four-letter words 'kill,' 'rape,' and 'hate' and what they mean?"[57]

Editors of the *American Revelation,* of Elgin, Illinois, had a different response. In the seventh issue of the newspaper, they tackled head-on the question of "Why We Don't Use the Word Shit":

> Many of our friends ask, What's all this shit about no "shit?" Well it's like this, fans, if we used a lot of naughty words the Establishment would get all tinkled-off at us. Also there is a tendency for writers to use naughty words for the sake of naughty words which leads to poor writing, and we don't want any of that poop. However we realize some people see the use of profanity as the Ultimate Freedom. So as a public service we have provided a Do-It-Yourself Underground Newspaper Kit. Cut out each word below and paste it over a word in any newspaper or magazine, even Revelation, and presto! You have a dirty underground newspaper! So don't give none of your B.M. about clean language.
>
> SHIT SHIT SHIT SHIT SHIT SHIT SHIT SHIT SHIT SHIT
>
> Besides if this paper were meant for shit we'd perforate it.[58]

Distributing as well as publishing unauthorized material became points of conflict between students and administrators. In March of 1969, officials at Taft High School, in the Bronx, suspended a black student for handing out the *Black Student Union Press* and incited one hundred black students to protest the school's action. When the school called in the police to quell the disturbance, fights broke out and seven students were arrested. Sometimes students fought back through the courts, often with the aid of the local chapter of the ACLU, which, since 1966, had litigated students' rights cases. Many students knew or quickly learned their rights under the First Amendment and stood up for them. One student calmed his mother, who feared he'd be suspended for distributing an underground newspaper off campus: "It's all right, mother. My lawyer says I can do this." Joe Harris, a radical black student put it more bluntly, calling it "a mother-fucking lie" when his principal told him he could not pass out political leaflets on campus. His lawyer too had said it was "perfectly legal." Birmingham was less certain of his rights when principal told him that he could not distribute the underground *Smuff* on school grounds. Birmingham double-checked by contacting the local ACLU. The representative, Birmingham states, "said that if we were suspended, he would have ACLU lawyers working for us as soon as we called." Bolstered by the knowledge that the law was on his side and activist lawyers would defend him, Birmingham held his ground, although he was careful not to sell the paper in classrooms without the teacher's permission.[59]

Other students, faced with more obdurate school officials, sued to affirm their right to distribute nonschool materials on campus or right outside the school gates. Once again, the resulting court decisions tended to broaden students' rights and limit the power of school administrators. After Charles Quarterman, a student at Pine Forest High School, in Southern Pines, North Carolina, was suspended for breaking a school rule banning the distribution of literature without permission, he sued. Overruling the district court, judges in the Fourth Circuit Court of Appeals struck down the rule because it laid out no criteria for determining whether permission to distribute materials would be granted or withheld and lacked "any procedural safeguards in the form of an 'expeditious review procedure' of the decision of school authorities." Although many judges cited the opinion in *Schwartz v. Schuker,* a case involving both the distribution of unauthorized literature and a libelous attack on a school principal, that the "the activities of high school students do not always fall within the same category as the conduct of college students," still less the category of full legal adults, courts generally insisted that they possessed basic constitutional rights that educators had to respect.[60]

FREEDOM OF EXPRESSION IN HIGH SCHOOLS: THE *TINKER* CASE

The most significant court case involving the First Amendment rights of minors was heard by the United States Supreme Court in 1969 and involved symbolic expression, rather than free speech or free press as such.

The Court's opinion firmly established that teenagers have rights yet ironically failed to clarify what those rights are. It limited the power of school officials while not spelling out the precise boundaries of that power.

In December 1965, just as the nascent antiwar movement began to coalesce, Christopher Eckhardt, a sophomore at Theodore Roosevelt High School, John Tinker, from North High School, and Mary Beth Tinker, a thirteen-year-old eighth grader at Warren Harding Junior High School, all in Des Moines, Iowa, came to school wearing black armbands to mourn the dead in Vietnam. Their gesture violated a recently passed rule against symbolic protest, which Des Moines principals had created after hearing what the students planned to do. Supported by their parents and the Iowa Civil Liberties Union, the students sued in federal district court. When they lost, they appealed to the Eighth Circuit Court of Appeals, which sat en banc, meaning that all of the judges in the circuit heard the case, not just a panel of three. When the Eighth Circuit split in its decision, the Tinkers and Eckhardts appealed to the U.S. Supreme Court, which handed down its decision in 1969.[61]

At first reading, the Court's opinion in *Tinker v. Des Moines* appears to be a solid victory for students. Justice Abe Fortas penned a stirring affirmation of their rights. "It can hardly be argued," he wrote, "that either students or teachers shed their constitutional rights to freedom of speech or expression at the schoolhouse gate." He also rebuked school officials, sternly remarking, "state-operated schools may not be enclaves of totalitarianism." Fortas then reduced the boldness of these statements by hedging them with qualifications. Citing a 1966 decision by the Fifth Circuit that permitted school rules against black students wearing freedom buttons, Fortas upheld the right of administrators to quell student expression that disrupted school. The Court had ruled against Des Moines principals because they had attempted to quash expression that had caused *no* disruption. The schools' need for order could trump the students' right to free expression.[62]

Fortas also punctiliously distinguished Tinker's and Eckhart's political expression—their black armbands meant something—from "regulation of the length of skirts or the type of clothing, to hair style, or deportment." Armbands, Fortas opined, "involve[d] direct, primary First Amendment rights akin to 'pure speech.'" According to the Court's formulation, administrators could prevent boys from wearing long hair because it was fashionable, but not if they did so to express a political belief. Blacks' right to wear dashikis as a protest against racism might be protected but not whites' right to wear blue jeans or untucked shirts.[63]

The consequences of the Court's ruling may be seen in the confusion among the lower courts on the issue of hair. In the cases heard after 1969, most courts cited *Tinker* as a precedent, with the circuits ruling for the students arguing that either long hair was expressive or that schools could not be "enclaves of totalitarianism" and the circuits ruling against the students seizing on Fortas's distinction between real political expression and mere apparel. The latter also drew upon Justice Potter Stewart's commentary in the *Tinker* case. Stewart agreed with the majority but specified that he could not "share the Court's uncritical assumption that, school discipline aside, the First Amendment rights of children are co-extensive with those of adults." Other judges who supported administrators' power referred to Justice Hugo Black's scathing dissent in *Tinker:* "If the time has come when pupils of state-supported schools, kindergartens, grammar schools, or high schools, can defy and flout orders of school officials to keep their minds on their own schoolwork, it is the beginning of a new revolutionary era of permissiveness in this country fostered by the judiciary."[64]

Not knowing where teenagers' rights as citizens began or ended meant that both students and administrators groped in the dark when it came to school regulations. Previously principals and school boards could create regulations and expect that most students would abide by them, most parents would back up the schools, and, if push came to shove, courts would uphold their authority. By the late 1960s, none of these assumptions survived. For the students, challenging school rules could be equally chancy. Maybe authorities' will to enforce the rules would falter if students protested, demonstrated, or sued. On the other hand, if their battles found their way into the courtroom, the outcome was unpredictable. Courts ruled in favor of the students often enough to give administrators pause, but not consistently enough to establish solid parameters for students' rights.

DEMOCRACY AND STUDENT GOVERNMENT

Just as restrictions on publications revealed a deprivation of substantive students' rights, their efforts to exercise meaningful power through student government demonstrated the reality of adult control. *T.R.I.P.,* an underground newspaper in Long Beach, California, described what happened when some students sought to include initiatives on marijuana and the Vietnam War on their school ballot "so that kids at their high school could vote on issues which were important to them and to the world around them, just like grown-up people do in real life." Their school bylaws established that a petition with signatures from 10 percent of the student body sufficed to get any issue onto the ballot. The students dutifully collected more than enough signatures only to discover that the more conservative student council, hearing about the petition, had preempted them by voting that these specific initiatives could not be put on the ballot. The principal refused to back up the student initiatives. The *T.R.I.P.* editors mocked the "play democracy" of the school, recognizing that neither the student government nor the administration welcomed a truly democratic exchange of ideas and that both were willing to violate established procedures to prevent it.[65]

Similarly, Donald Reeves characterizes student organizations put together by school administrators as "buffer zone[s] to cut off student unrest altogether." Initially critical of Black Power advocates at the High School of Music and Art, Reeves began to feel that as the moderate student body president, he was being manipulated by the principal. He comments, "When he [the principal] wanted something said that was unpopular, I'd say it and take the criticism." Reeves hoped that militant and moderate students at Music and Art could be brought together under his leadership, but he gradually perceived the principal's role in "giv[ing] the militant students a legitimate issue to protest about." Reeves's disillusionment was complete when the principal suspended him for advocating a student march to protest cuts in the state educational budget, a demonstration the principal had privately supported, agreeing with Reeves that it might unite students for a common goal. By then, although Reeves still eyed student radicals suspiciously, he scorned student government organizations, which he regarded as powerless mouthpieces for the administration.[66]

The student rights movement, like the Black and Brown Power movements, succeeded in altering the high school environment. Racial activism had decentered the whiteness of the schools and opened the door to cultural pluralism and multiculturalism. The student rights movement now wrote teenagers into the Constitution. It trimmed the arbitrary power of officials and made the schools more democratic. Viewpoints previously unheard or quelled began to be expressed, enhancing the intellectual atmosphere and breaking open the narrow conformity of the 1950s and early 1960s. Publishing underground newspapers and circulating them on campus contributed to this intellectual blossoming, and created spaces in which students could test their ideas and practice citizenship. Defending their hairstyles or publications in court encouraged students to think broadly about the meaning of freedom and the operation of power. Chesley Karr, who ultimately lost his lawsuit and dropped out of school rather than cut his hair, recognizes that his two trials—at the district and appellate courts—provided him with a tremendous education.[67]

For their part, principals, superintendents, and schools boards now had to reckon with students as actors, not ciphers. Few of them applauded the education that student activists made for themselves, because the majority regarded the agitation for rights as disruptive. But although some clung more fiercely to the disciplinary powers they had wielded so effectively in earlier years and a few tentatively sought new ways of interacting with students, all administrators conceded that their environment had drastically changed. Lawsuits put their authority literally on trial, and, like students, administrators were forced to articulate their position within the framework of the Constitution. They too had to consider issues of freedom and power and how these concepts fit into the educational system. The very ambiguity of students' legal and social status—were they citizens? Children? Could they be both?—meant that any official decision or ruling had to be weighed in a manner astonishing to those who had managed the schools in previous years.

Because students' status was so unclear, and because few administrators evinced any willingness to work this through in partnership with students themselves, activists were not satisfied with the limited victories they had won. Like black and Chicano activists, those concerned with student rights concluded that merely possessing rights was not sufficient. Students needed power. Without power, students were helpless to resist principals who ignored democratic procedures, the courts, or the law. Without power, they could not forge new relationships with adults or change their status as children. Thus the student rights movement moved easily into a student power movement. Now students would focus less on their rights and status as citizens and more on their relationship with school officials and role in the educational process.

FIVE—STUDENT RIGHTS, STUDENT POWER, AND THE CRITIQUE OF CONTEMPORARY EDUCATION

The camera pans slowly around the classroom as the teacher reads the 1888 poem "Casey at the Bat." Not a spark of interest shows on the students' faces. Some look blank, others lean on their hands, eyes half-closed. A close-up shot of a student's wristwatch lingers for interminable seconds. In the hallway, an administrator lectures a girl for attending a dance in a short skirt when all of the other girls wore long gowns. He calls her action "individualistic." She is upset by the accusation, nearly in tears. "Oh, I didn't mean to be individualistic," she insists. Elsewhere, the principal scolds a tough-looking boy. "We are out to establish that you are a man," he admonishes, "and that you can take orders." The camera cuts to another classroom. A young teacher is playing a song by popular folksingers Simon and Garfunkel. On the board the teacher has written sentences with blanks for the students to fill in, as they listen for the metaphors and similes that the teacher expects them to find in the lyrics.[1]

These scenes appeared in filmmaker Frederick Wiseman's 1968 documentary *High School*. The film captured one day in the operation of North East High School, in Philadelphia, a large, mostly white, suburban school. Shot in black and white, with no music or voice-over commentary, the seventy-five-minute movie emphasized authoritarian adults and bored students. *High School* was repeatedly screened on public television and was available for rental, so it sparked widespread and heated discussion. Magazines such as *Newsweek* and the *New Republic* published reviews of the film. Journalist Richard S. Fuller saw it in the company of three high school students, who agreed with Wiseman's critique. From a different perspective, a group of school administrators who watched the film before discussing it with Wiseman attacked it as "a brutal distortion and a completely invalid basis for making generalizations about high schools per se." Wiseman clearly intended to depict tedium, joylessness, and regimentation as defining characteristics of American high schools. When asked why he failed to show any lively, creative teaching, Wiseman replied that he simply had not seen any. "I was appalled," he continued, "at the low quality of the teaching." Although some adults angrily rejected his portrait of high schools, others argued that the film was dead accurate and that high schools were in deep trouble. The film paralleled the critique of high schools that activist students were already voicing. Student Donald Reeves comments, "Wiseman has got the overkill, the socialization, the authoritarianism all on film. He missed the political scene, but even without it, he's got it."[2]

However much Wiseman's depiction may have offended educators, the idea that high schools were boring and joyless would neither have shocked nor horrified most adults. Students went to school to be educated, not entertained. A certain amount of boredom was inevitable and would prepare students for real life. Activist students, on the other hand, regarded Wiseman's film as diagnostic of the problems with schooling. Why did teachers force-feed them doggerel from the late nineteenth century? What possible relevance could "Casey at the Bat" have for their lives? Playing a Simon and Garfunkel song seemed aimed at student interests, but the teacher had already decided exactly what the students were supposed to learn from it. Why did school officials value conformity and taking orders? Would this kind of education truly prepare students to live in the complex and difficult world they saw around them?

Students' opinions on contemporary education emerged most fully in underground newspapers. Officials could have easily laid their hands on underground publications and read the student perspective for themselves, but it is not clear how many ever did. Even without delving into high school undergrounds, both professional educational journals and mainstream news magazines repeatedly probed and published the student point of view. In 1969, pollster Louis Harris surveyed twenty-five hundred students, parents, teachers, and principals from across the country for *Life* magazine. He found that, although only 35 percent of teachers and 20 percent of parents thought students should have more say in running the schools, fully 58 percent of students wanted this power. More than 60 percent of students wanted to help make rules and select curriculum, nearly half wanted a voice in discipline and classroom activities, and 40 percent thought they should have a hand in grading. Despite their hunger for a greater role, these students nevertheless overwhelmingly rated both their teachers and schools "good to excellent." Thus, their critique of education was not a nihilistic attack on the entire system. Rather, it was, by and large, a thoughtful assessment of its strengths and weaknesses. Moreover, it echoed the broader push for increased participation by other marginalized groups within the United States.[3]

Adults who pressed to be allowed fuller participation in American society, politics, and economic life couched their demands in terms of simple justice. They argued that as citizens they had a right to be included. For high school activists, claiming citizenship led them onto boggy ground, for no firm definition of the rights of minor citizens existed. Of necessity, demanding to participate—even when participation was confined to the school environment—entailed renegotiating childhood.

Thoroughly redefining childhood would have been a momentous undertaking, with implications reaching well beyond schooling. Student activists seem to have been only dimly aware of how their demands challenged contemporary ideas about childhood. A careful analysis of childhood as a historically invented category, or even an awareness of how much young people in previous centuries had contributed to society, could have bolstered the activists' demand for a greater voice. But they made no such analysis, preferring instead to portray themselves as citizens, despite the shakiness of the claim, or as consumer-clients in the realm of education. As citizens, they insisted on defining and protecting their rights; as consumers of education or clients of the schools, they argued that their role in the schools enabled them to see more clearly the flaws in the educational system and offer suggestions on how to improve it. In both cases, activist students sought to participate as functional adults, without directly confronting the reality of their status as minors.

Students' unwillingness to grapple with their legal and social status is all the more surprising in light of how thoroughly they explored their powerlessness. They attacked student government as meaningless playacting, criticized their subordinate roles, and specified the precise school policies that denied them rights and dignity. Having enumerated the ways in which, in their view, officials oppressed them, many sought the adoption of student bills of rights. Others organized classes or schools of their own, both to educate themselves and to model good education to adults. The student movement gained some victories, but in the absence of a sustained dialogue with adults about their status as children more substantial victories eluded them.

THE NEED FOR NEW FORMS OF STUDENT ORGANIZATION

When officials failed to respond to their demands, activists launched a vociferous, vibrant rights movement of their own. Underground high school newspapers not only expressed students' opinions, but also often spearheaded organizational drives to mobilize them for student rights. Ann

Arbor Youth Liberation hoped its underground *Youth Rising* would improve communication and coordination with student unions throughout the town. The Niles Township (Illinois) Student Coalition declared that, in addition to publishing the underground *New Free Press,* it sought to advance student rights, gain a "definite, decisive voice in school policy," and "unite the student body in support of our objectives." John Birmingham's underground *Smuff* created the Smuff Student Coalition expressly to "represent the students where our student council had failed."[4]

Birmingham and others justified their own activities by highlighting the weaknesses of existing mechanisms for participation in school governance. Because most student governments had a very limited jurisdiction, activists mocked them as useless. "Oh, we're trained for participating in the 'democratic process,'" gibes *New York High School Free Press* founder Howie Swerdloff. "[W]e have our student governments—they can legislate about basketball games and other such meaningful topics." Even within these narrow limits, student government legislation could be dismissed at the whim of school officials. *Common Sense,* an underground paper from Alton, Illinois, reported that, although the student council had voted three times to exclude cheerleaders as homecoming queen candidates, something that surely ought to come under their purview, the administration vetoed the measure every time. In contrast, student governments that adhered too closely to the positions of the administration ran the risk of being labeled "puppet governments."[5]

As they ridiculed weak, toadying student governments, some underground newspapers veered close to a critique of contemporary childhood. Rich Shadden of the *Minstrel,* Waukegan, Illinois, published a mock interview with a fictitious student council president, "Sy Cofant." When asked whether the student council was "a powerless figurehead set up by the administration," "Sy" retorts,

> It's a lie. None of the 15 percent I represent believe this. And the idea that the Student Council is powerless is ridiculous. Look at the power I have, I preside over all the Student Council's democratic meetings and recognize any speaker I want to. I get to ask everyone to stand and say the pledge of allegiance at assemblies and sometimes I even make a speech before the entire student body.

When Shadden asks "Sy" whether there should be a dress code, "Sy" responds, "Positively! I don't know what I would do if the administration didn't show me how to dress, I'm *only* 17. . . . Anyway, why all the trouble? In a year or two they can dress the way they want to in the army."[6]

Shadden hints that restrictions on teenagers are too tightly drawn when seventeen-year-olds, just shy of eligibility for military service, are not permitted to dress as they please. But he does not follow through with a more detailed discussion of how or why adult treatment of teenagers is absurd, and his point gets lost in the midst of his attacks on student governments as unrepresentative, undemocratic, and lacking in real power.

Complaints about student councils suggest that many activists craved genuine democracy and would have worked through the system to redress their grievances had this been possible. Students in Erie, Pennsylvania, for example, first attempted a dialogue with the faculty and administration. When the adults refused to meet with them, they took their complaints to the school superintendent, who, according to "Susan Snow," listened briefly and then got up and left. Only then did a large group of students "quietly and non-violently" leave the school, an act for which they were punished. As Snow points out, the students were punished for mimicking adult behavior. Here again, Snow alludes to an unvoiced critique of childhood. She clearly believes that students were entitled to behave as the adults did, but she does not flesh out her argument.[7]

Although activists often accused them of complicity with school administrators, student governments appear to have become more restive in this period. Educators praised this trend, especially on the national level, which drew greater attention to student organizations. Not only did the National Association of Student Councils (NASC) become more politically active by the early 1970s, but also a National Association of Student Activity Advisers was created to work with NASC, and, in 1972, President Nixon declared the first National Student Government Day celebration. Despite praise and attention from adults, existing high school student governments frequently could not handle or were not permitted to address the serious issues that activists raised. The latter had become dissatisfied with ersatz school democracy and toothless student organizations and would not be satisfied with incremental changes.[8]

Students sometimes expressed their desire for greater participation using the idiom of the day, as a demand for power. The term was an unfortunate choice. Whereas Americans enshrine the concept of "rights," they regard "power" more ambivalently and interpret their own history as the triumph of virtue rather than as the will of the mighty. Even today, many people applaud black demands for civil rights in the 1950s and 1960s while dismissing Black Power as illegitimate. In the same way, high school students' claim to rights garnered them some adult supporters; when they demanded power, school officials branded them radicals, effectively undercutting their position.

Students' hunger for increased power grew out of their awareness of just how powerless they were. Specific events such as conflicts with administrators over hairstyles, clothing, smoking, and censorship revealed the dimensions of their lack of power. Underground newspapers publicized these clashes, influenced the opinions of the students who read them, and helped them to name their condition, which, in keeping with radical theory of the day, students believed was a prerequisite to changing it.

ANALOGIES OF POWERLESSNESS

Naming their condition meant finding an appropriate analogy for high school students' relationship to school and society. Although college students rarely exerted direct influence on high school activists, Birmingham observes that the article most reprinted in high school undergrounds was Jerry Farber's "The Student as Nigger." Farber, a literature professor active in the antiwar and civil rights movements, wrote the article in 1969 for and about college students. Many high school students found that the article described their situation equally well. Farber argued that students were "niggers" because they were "politically disenfranchised," given a "toy government" to play with, and expected to "know [their] place."[9] Some white students were perturbed by Farber's appropriation of the term "nigger" and wondered, "If the student is a nigger, what is the black student?" But other white students saw parallels between the repression of blacks and their own experiences. Michael Marqusee, a sixteen-year-old junior at Scarsdale High School, in New York, argued that students are "niggers" because "we are subservient to all authority and our lives are controlled by that authority from the selection of our careers to the development of our values."[10] The Stuyvesant Radical Coalition, authors of Stuyvesant High School's underground newspaper, the *Weakly Reader* (a play on the title of an educational magazine, the *Weekly Reader*), linked the analogy of racial subordination to America's revolutionary heritage and a worldwide revolutionary surge. In a wide-ranging article that critiqued capitalism, education in general, and specifically the New York United Federation of Teachers, the coalition declared, "We're obedient little niggers that Massa whips with grades, darkies who jump when the Man says Jump! We're sick of it—students, workers, blacks and oppressed people everywhere: We're going to claim our birthright—dig that Manifest Destiny—we're going to be Americans and what's more American than REVOLUTION?"[11]

Other students characterized themselves as infants rather than niggers, particularly when it came to school regulations. Scott Badesch's letter to the Skokie underground *New Free Press* complained that he felt infantilized "whenever I have to ask permission to go to the washroom or whenever I'm punished for whispering to a friend in study hall." He criticized the "dehumanizing process" of school routines, concluding, "I respect the Coalition [publisher of the *New Free Press*] for striving toward some measure of student dignity."[12]

Another common analogy high school students adopted was "prison" and "prisoners," a comparison college radicals echoed. When the Liberation News Service reported rising militance in high schools, it used this analogy, as did raiding parties from Students for a Democratic Society (SDS), who stormed high schools in several northeastern cities in the late 1960s, screaming "Jail break!" Students also called high schools factories, or, in the words of the *Weakly Reader,* "assembly line[s] that [move] the product from junior high school to college with a minimum of contamination by education."[13]

Looking to the barnyard for his analogy, Mike Fox, an activist at a Flushing, New York, high school likened students to cattle, arguing that as farmers cared about their cows only in terms of their milk production, so

"Farmer X" (it is not clear if he means teachers, administrators, parents, or society in general) cared about students only in terms of their grades. Just as a cow would be slaughtered if she could not produce enough, students either "remain[ed] with the herd" in college or were sent "into the army to be slaughtered."[14]

All of these analogies describe asymmetrical power relations. Only Fox's reference to cattle suggested that students had anything to contribute to society, and, even then, they did so under the control of "Farmer X." Students indisputably lacked power, but their analogies are grotesquely exaggerated, even allowing for youthful hyperbole. It is striking that activists never employed positive analogies to express how they wished they could interact with adults and adult society. Was the proper analogy that of apprentice to master? Copilot to pilot? Or did students regard themselves as equal to adults?

The analogies they used in their undergrounds express how indignities in school made students feel. When they explored the concrete dimensions of their powerlessness, they not only made a stronger attack on existing educational policies and practices but also made clearer what they hoped their own activism would accomplish.

ENDING EVERYDAY OPPRESSION

Toby Mamis, founder of the high school underground *New York Herald-Tribune,* bluntly sums up the sentiment underlying the analogies: "High school students are oppressed." Most commonly, students complained of lack of freedom in dress and hair styles, censorship of student newspapers, and student governments that were either powerless or—since they often included only white or highly achieving students—unrepresentative of the student body as a whole. Students also objected to the lack of due process in disciplinary procedures and the ways in which principals flouted directives from higher authorities that would have provided students with some freedom and rights. Some officials exercised vast and ill-defined powers to punish any kind of student behavior or attitudes that they did not like. As "Susan Snow" recognizes, "*[I]nsubordination* can be literally anything, anything that the teacher wants to consider it." Toby Mamis adds that, because school administrators wrote college recommendations for students, they had "considerable control over our lives" even after graduation.[15]

Paradoxically, although students claimed to be powerless, they clearly felt empowered to demand changes in their treatment and status, and they took action. They often attacked school regulations piecemeal, singling out specific offensive rules. They engaged in civil disobedience or mass demonstrations, relying on the strength of their own wills or the size of the crowds they gathered to wear down the resistance of the school administrators. Official responses, however, sometimes led students to see themselves as not so much troubled by one or two bad rules but as hemmed in by an entire system. Consequently, some students began to think more broadly about their status, draw upon their lessons in American civics, and work through the existing system—not only the high school system, but also the legal and political system, which they had been taught to believe represented them.

To widen their reform efforts, some students formed unions with others in the same city or region. In 1969, Marc Libarle and Tom Seligson, two sympathetic twenty-four-year-old teachers from New York, traveled around the country studying the student movement. They made contact with a number of high school unions: the New Jersey High School Liberation Movement, the Minnesota Student Union, the Montgomery County (Maryland) Student Alliance, the Students' Rights Organization (Columbus, Ohio), the District of Columbia Student Coalition for Education, the Democratic Students' Coalition (Hewlitt, New York), the Newcastle County (Delaware) Student Union, the Bay Area Student Union and the Berkeley Student Union (both in California), and the New York High School Student Union (New York City). In their book on student revolutionaries (their term), Libarle and Seligson reported that "virtually all schools where there are blacks" had black student unions; in New York City, the Black High School Coalition attempted to coordinate all black student unions in the city. Other student unions probably existed as well but have left no trace in the historical record.[16]

Sadly, in most cases we know only the names and locations of these student unions. Some were linked to specific underground newspapers at specific high schools. But who joined them? Did they hold regular meetings with elected officers? Did they make decisions based on democratic rule or by consensus? How many survived the graduation of their leaders? Disparate sources suggest that, apart from the black student unions, membership in student unions was primarily white. Black or white, these students were nearly always politically left of center. Some groups met more or less regularly, others only when the leaders called a meeting for a specific purpose. When grievances arose, larger numbers of students could be drawn into the unions, which would ultimately shrink back to the original core of activists. At the peak of high school activism, student groups sometimes outlived their leaders. Donald Reeves remarks that, when Darryl Chisholm, leader of the Black Security Council (in effect, a black student union) at the School of Music and Art, graduated in 1969, although the Black Security Council continued, its members regarded Chisholm as an "outsider." His influence in the high school movement vanished.[17]

With or without a union, students employed two key strategies in their efforts for reform. One assumed that students were citizens with rights and attempted to work through the existing student government, petitions, or negotiations with the school administration or school board. Although these students, who referred to themselves as moderates or liberals, could resort to disruptive tactics—sit-ins, demonstrations, walkouts, or boycotts—if their initial approaches failed, they tried to exhaust moderate and legalistic measures first.

Other students, the radicals, assumed that the administration would never concede anything without a confrontation. John Birmingham (a moderate) disapproved of this stand. In his opinion, "the students who most often use the word 'demand' are also the ones who use words like 'struggle' when they refer to the underground [newspaper] movement. They see the administration as the enemy, an enemy that they don't mind backing into a corner." These were also the students whose strident rhetoric most adults found difficult to take seriously. They seemed intoxicated by their revolutionary spirit, and their demands ranged from the impossible to the outlandish, such as calling for the "integration" of the faculty bathrooms by permitting students to use them. Other far-fetched demands, voiced by activists at Academy High School in Pennsylvania, included an end to compulsory school attendance and lower snack bar prices. Student demands for access to personnel files or a voice in the hiring and firing of teachers, for example, were taken by some as evidence of the irresponsibility of the entire high school student movement. Others accused these young people of mimicking the bombast of self-proclaimed college revolutionaries, whose style and tone was indeed similar.[18]

Despite their overblown rhetoric, romanticization of confrontation and struggle, and simplistic approach to complex problems, radical students were more shrewd than students who hoped to work through the system. The latter often seem curiously naïve in assuming that, if school officials only knew what high school students wanted, they would acquiesce. Radicals also were far more visionary—even utopian—in their outlook than moderate students. Moderates were usually more concerned about local school affairs, whereas radicals drew connections between their school experiences and broader social issues, such as racism, sexism, militarism, corporate capitalism, and the repression of all powerless groups. Moderate students could move into the radical camp, but the opposite movement rarely—if ever—occurred. Activist students at D.C. Everest High School in Weston, Wisconsin, demonstrated this moderate-to-radical trajectory. The precipitating incident was a struggle over a new dress code, but after the administration ignored the students' suggestions for reforming the code, other issues quickly surfaced: students' desire for a school SDS chapter, a "civil rights bulletin board," and the right to circulate literature about their various causes and to sell underground newspapers and "Black Power" buttons. The administration fought back with suspensions, locker searches, and mandatory appointments with the school psychiatrist. Shocked activists likened these "headhunts" to McCarthyism and concluded, "So we're not *asking* anymore, we're *demanding!*"[19]

TOWARD A STUDENT BILL OF RIGHTS

Once students grasped their relative powerlessness and lack of basic rights, moderates and radicals alike agreed that the creation of a student bill of rights seemed a logical next step. These documents often paralleled the U.S. Bill of Rights, although some added rights specific to students in a high school setting. Sometimes students at a single high school presented their bill of rights solely to their principal or student government. On several occasions, notably in Homestead, Pennsylvania, Detroit, and New York City, citywide high school movements pushed for a bill of rights. In 1969, the Student Mobilization Committee, a college organization, met with activist high school students at a conference in Cleveland and hammered out a National High School Students Bill of Rights. Nothing further came of this proposal, but it demonstrated the ambitions some students harbored.[20]

Native-American students, differently situated than others, also sought a student bill of rights. But because they attended schools run by the Bureau of Indian Affairs (BIA) rather than by local school boards, they appealed to the U.S. Senate Committee on Appropriations for redress of their grievances. Students Margaret DeJolie and Lee Luke Begay both testified before the committee, complaining about the lack of due process and attacks on Native-American culture in the BIA high schools. They entered into the record a thirty-page Indian Student Bill of Rights, which the committee recommended the BIA adopt. Whether it did is unclear.[21]

Student bills of rights aimed both to protect the rights students assumed they had and to limit the power of school officials. What the bills did not say is perhaps as remarkable as what they included. High school students apparently found it self-evident that they had rights and did not consider how the mission of the schools—to educate them—might conflict with or support some of the rights they claimed. Although judges who heard lawsuits brought by students generally attempted to weigh the rights of students against the needs of school officials, activists generally avoided this gray area. Even when students could have defended specific rights as contributing to their education, they did not always make the connection.

First Amendment rights, for example, are central to the American conception of liberty, but could also undergird a sound education. High school bills of rights emphasized the First Amendment because school officials so frequently violated it. The La Puente (California) underground newspaper, *Freethinker,* described how a student had been suspended merely for asking another student whether he planned to take part in a walkout. In another instance, two students were allegedly "told by an administrator not to look at each other while making a decision about their walking out." Administrators also violated students' First Amendment rights by banning controversial speakers from campus, punishing students for off-campus political activism, and restricting student publications or distribution of literature on or off campus. In challenging administrators' power to enact these policies, students missed an opportunity to question their educational goals as well as their definition of childhood. Many adults believed that high school students were simply too young to be exposed to political controversies or to engage in any sort of political activism. Educating youth meant deferring these issues until later. Rights activists disagreed, but neither elaborated their reasons why they were old enough for politics nor pushed adults to defend their views.[22]

In the context of widespread denial of students' rights, activists spelled out what the First Amendment meant in the high school environment. To the editors of *Sansculottes,* a Bronx high school underground, it included the right to hand out literature on school grounds and less censorship of student writings. Steve Wasserman, the president of Berkeley High School, in California, and the founder of the Berkeley Student Union, specified that free speech meant "the right to have independent newspapers, the right to assemble and organize ourselves for our own needs, the right to take political action in our own interests without penalty, the right to do all of these things without administrative restrictions, interference, or approval." In its bill of rights for Detroit students, the Student Mobilization Committee (SMC) asserted that they had the right to refuse to salute the flag or attend any assembly, could express their political beliefs and opinions through buttons, armbands, and style of dress, and had the right to strike.[23]

Ironically, while demanding the right to invite controversial speakers— primarily antiwar or left-wing speakers—to campus, some student activists sought to keep prowar or progovernment representatives off campus. The Detroit SMC's bill of rights, for example, insisted that "the student body has the right to be free from the presence of any influence of federal agencies not directly involved in the educational process." This meant that denying military recruiters access to the students, ending ROTC classes, and barring police forces from the schools. The New York High School Student Union similarly condemned military recruiting on campus. But black and white students sometimes differed here. Neither the Black and Puerto Rican Citywide High School Council nor the New York City black student unions, for example, mentioned forbidding military presence. In fact, these students demanded the establishment of student rifle and self-defense clubs, and some black students regarded the military as a legitimate avenue of upward mobility for people of color.[24]

Students' rights activists also focused on discipline and due process. They criticized the fact that students facing disciplinary proceedings—even expulsion—generally had no right to a hearing, representation by counsel, notice of the evidence against them, or even self-defense. Students rarely could appeal actions taken against them by school authorities. Worse, students had little recourse when principals violated directives from higher authorities. The *New York High School Free Press* cited repeated violations of board of education rules that only a principal could suspend a student, parents had to be notified in advance, the suspension had to be written up and filed rather than being issued verbally, and no student could be suspended for more than five days. Donald Reeves claims that, although the New York Board of Education had forbidden principals to punish students for participating in the Moratorium against the War in 1969, many were suspended nonetheless. It is not surprising, then, that one black student union in New York City based its demand for a fair trial by a jury of their peers on the Fourteenth Amendment, following this demand with a long paraphrase from the Declaration of Independence, substituting the word "students" for "people." In Detroit, the SMC's bill of rights included not only a right to a hearing but demanded that students should in effect have a full trial, with the right to question witnesses and to receive a transcript of the proceedings from the school administration.[25]

In some cases, students proposed institutional changes to safeguard their right to due process. Students at Waukegan, Illinois, wanted a student-faculty court, consisting of four faculty members and three students. One of the faculty members would be the student council sponsor; the students would be elected by the student body. An article in the high school underground explained, "It would be an appellate court. It would give the students a recourse to unreasonable administrative action. . . . Appeal can be denied by the court, if the court feels the case does not warrant a hearing. Suspensions and expulsions are given automatic appeals and hearings because of their severity." This is a sophisticated proposal; these students had paid attention in their civics classes. It is unclear, however, whether they won this right.[26]

The U.S. Supreme Court ultimately weighed in on the students' side with regard to due process. It did so, however, in a tentative manner that stopped short of what the most radical students demanded. The case of *Goss v. Lopez,* decided in 1975, was brought by nine students who had been suspended for ten days in 1971 for their behavior during a period of extended upheaval in the Cleveland, Ohio, public schools. None had received a hearing or notice of why they had been suspended. School officials argued that, because the Constitution guaranteed no right to a free public education, students had no legal protection against expulsion and a ten-day suspension was too minor to justify a hearing. Justice Byran White, author of the majority opinion, countered that, because the state of Ohio had created free public schools and required children to attend them, education was in fact a "property interest" protected under the due process clause of the Fourteenth Amendment. The case established the minimum rights applicable to a student facing suspension of ten days or more: notice of the behavior that warranted suspension, and "an opportunity to present his [sic] side of the story." The Supreme Court deliberately refrained from granting students a right to a full-blown hearing, with rights to counsel, cross-examine, and present their own witnesses on the grounds that "even truncated trial-type procedures might well overwhelm administrative facilities."[27]

Paralleling the *Tinker v. Des Moines* decision concerning black armbands, the Court's opinion in the *Goss* case did not analyze how far citizenship rights extended to minor children. By defining education as a "property interest," the justices glossed over the fact that this was a property forced upon its putative owners. The Court simultaneously refused to decide whether, in the words of Justice Stewart in *Tinker,* the property rights of children were "co-extensive" with those of adults. Once again, although the legal system expanded the rights and protections available to students, like the activists themselves it sidestepped the question of their precise status before the law and their role in society.

THE BATTLE FOR STUDENT RIGHTS IN NEW YORK CITY

Well before the Supreme Court ruled in *Goss v. Lopez,* a protracted struggled over student rights took place in New York City between high school activists, school administrators, and city officials. Following the polarizing Ocean Hill–Brownsville strikes in the fall of 1968, black and white student groups separately issued sets of demands. The following spring, a number of high school student organizations, including the New York High School Student Union, the Black High School Student Coalition, the Afro-American Students' Association (AASA), and several black student unions united in calling for a week of disruptions to push for their demands.[28] As Bruce Trigg of the New York High School Union explained to a reporter, students' demands had already escalated. Initially students wanted only to eliminate dress codes and permit student leafleting. In Trigg's words, now, however, "We're . . . demanding an end to all disciplinary suspensions and expulsions. In New York, 95% of these are black and Puerto Rican. All pigs [police] and narcs [narcotics agents] out of the schools. Abolish identification cards. End the tracking system, open admissions to colleges, free housing and meaningful jobs for all high school graduates and power to run the schools." As the stakes rose, the New York City Board of Education publicized a resolution on student rights in October 1969. It drew upon recommendations of the New York Civil Liberties Union but did not include all of the rights the NYCLU had proposed. Even this watered-down resolution upset the Council of Supervisory Associations (a principals' organization), which, according to Donald Reeves, opposed any broadening of students' rights. So the board further weakened the resolution. Activist students were outraged to learn that no student group had been consulted in formulating the resolution and, worse, it granted principals the power to set limits on free speech.[29]

Reacting to the spread of violence in the high schools, as well as the widening gulf between adults and young people, the school board established a citywide advisory council of high school students. To the board's surprise, radical high school students agreed with Reeves that the council was a transparent attempt to coopt students and stifle criticism. Reeves, appointed to the council, criticized the board's motives: "The Board would say: See, look here, we have students on our committees." Reeves also argued that the board of education's "phony" bill of rights helped unify some of the diverse high school student groups in the city. In the spring of 1970, thirteen of these activists, including Reeves, devised their own bill of rights to replace the one proposed by the board. The students borrowed from the United States Constitution, the ACLU pamphlet "Academic Freedom in the Secondary Schools," a proposal by the New York City Government Organization Council (a citywide student council), the New York City Board of Education Resolution on Rights of Senior High School Students, Recommendations to the California State Board of Education, the California Association of Student Councils, the AASA's seventeen demands, and the New York City High School Women's Coalition's article on women's rights.[30]

The bill of rights these students proposed to the board included seven sections: student government, freedom of expression, freedom from discrimination, due process, personal counseling, curriculum, and the amendment process. From the administration's perspective, the bill had several objectionable features. The student government was to be "independent of the administration and faculty advisor," have control over all student organizations and money raised by those organizations, and be allowed to call eight assemblies a year. Students also demanded the establishment of a school liaison board whose decrees would be "final, absolute, and binding on the faculty, administration and student body of each school." This board—to consist of ten students, four teachers, the principal, and five parents at each school—would control student suspensions, use of police forces within the school, the presence of federal, state or city agencies, curriculum, programs, and textbooks. Students facing suspension or expulsion would have full trials, presided over by the school liaison board. Dress codes and censorship—except in the case of defamation or obscenity—would end, and students could receive counseling on birth control, abortion, drug abuse, and the military draft.

Reeves admitted in his book that some parts of the student plan were "unworkable," but insisted that something had to "replac[e] the principal's autocratic rule." He also noted that students had deliberately asked for too much to gain some negotiating room. A public hearing on the matter in February of 1970 drew seven hundred people but ended in chaos when the board of education refused to let any other students speak following Reeves's call for democracy in the schools and the trimming of principals' power. Representatives of the AASA seized the microphone, concluding ominously, "You people gotta learn to respect us—'else you gonna die." This was clearly an empty threat, but it allowed the media and school officials to paint the activists as dangerous radicals. Nevertheless, the liberal student government organization rejected the board of education's bill, and after some debate, the student city council adopted the student-written bill of rights. At its next meeting, however, the city council condemned Reeves's group, the High School Student Rights Coalition, as the puppet of outside agitators—in this case, the Student Mobilization Committee and the Third World Committee, both college associations. Reeves countered that principals had packed the city council meeting with compliant students and pointed out that representatives of only thirty-three of the city's ninety-one schools had voted to condemn his coalition, but twice as many had previously voted to approve the bill of rights.[31]

Even as activists threatened a student strike to force the issue, whatever unity they had thus far had begun to dissipate. The rise of the Black Panther party and escalating violence between blacks and whites distracted the black student organizations. At a meeting to plan the strike, an adult Black Panther scolded black students, saying, "You high school kids got to become part of national struggles and forget all this high school shit." At the same time, radical whites were wrapped up in plans for a demonstration against the Vietnam War. The most they could agree upon was a half-day strike on behalf of the bill of rights in the morning, devoting the afternoon to the antiwar protest. Although a number of high school students attended the antiwar demonstration, few others evinced interest in their parochial struggles.[32]

In May 1970, Reeves confronted Walter Degnan, president of the Council of Supervisory Associations, for a debate on local radio, which highlighted the chasm between activist students and school officials. The broadcast, moderated by WCBS/TV news education editor Robert Potts, was part of a series titled "Public Hearing" and aired midday on a Sunday. Reeves criticized the board of education's bill, pointing out, "Their bill was not formulated by students, it was not voted on by the students. And, in all honesty, it was not a bill designed to give students the opportunity to change things peacefully within the system." The students' own bill of rights, by contrast, included "the problems of drugs, of racial polarization, and a number of other problems that the Board of Ed's [sic] document left out."[33]

Degnan denied Reeves's charge that principals did not want students to have any rights. As a substitute for the bill of rights proposed by the students, he suggested a student advisory board. Reeves wearily noted that he had sat on a similar advisory board, which was completely ineffective. "These things are all advisory, and they still do not provide students with any legitimate grievance machinery," he said. Degnan countered that Reeves did not represent all high school students. The debate degenerated rapidly from that point. Degnan emphasized the immaturity of high school students, citing their threats of violence if their demands were not met. Reeves was exasperated by the reference to violence. In his book about this struggle for student rights, he observes that the media loved to play up student violence. When Reeves appeared with a panel of students, teachers, and administrators on the *David Susskind Show,* a television talk show whose host enjoyed baiting his often controversial guests, he noted how Susskind "took advantage of the overemotional student panelists," and then "the cameras rolled in so that America could see just how crazy high school students are."[34]

The issue of violence haunted activists in New York City. Reeves is correct that adults exaggerated the threat, using it to divide liberal and moderate students as well as to depict activists as "crazy." But violence really did break out repeatedly in America's high schools in this era, and students were not above using adults' fear of violence to pressure concessions to their demands. Even the generally levelheaded Reeves at one point attempted to incite students to "take over" the headquarters of the board of education. Whatever Reeves may have meant by the phrase, adults may be excused for interpreting it as a call to violence.[35]

In the summer of 1970, the board of education quietly abolished the student city council. Outraged, one student asked, "How can you ignore our attempt to work within the system, to use legal channels, and to express a wish to negotiate our Constitutional rights?" According to Reeves, a representative from the Council of Supervisory Associations replied, "Students have no legal rights." None, anyway, that officials were prepared to protect and enforce. Ultimately, the board of education simply issued its student bill of rights in July 1970 as if the events of the preceding year and a half had never occurred. It labeled the policy "limited and moderate" but insisted that it was also "one of the most advanced ever proposed by any public school body in the United States." The *New York Times* editorialized that it established a "new trust" between students and administrators, but the NYCLU was more accurate: "Once again the Board has confirmed the students' belief that their so-called rights are granted and withdrawn at the sole discretion of the Board of Education and that any appearance of student participation in such decisions is a cruel hoax." Neither the board of education nor the *New York Times* editors could envision students as meaningful partners.[36]

This extensive confrontation is better documented than most, in part because a key participant, Donald Reeves, wrote a book about the experience, in part because of the relative unity of New York City high school activists, and also in part because the *New York Times* paid attention to elements of the struggle, even while distorting them. Conflicts of similar intensity and magnitude may well have occurred in other places, for, although the New York City students were arguably better united than students elsewhere, their actions and attitudes reflect a student zeitgeist that was far more widespread.[37]

STUDENT RIGHTS AS ADULTS SAW THEM

In contrast to bills of rights written by students, adult-generated bills of rights for high school students often linked rights to responsibilities. The bill of rights issued over the protests of New York City students by the board of education, for example, bore the title "Rights and Responsibilities for Senior High School Students." Yet, in these documents, student responsibilities appear more as limitations upon their rights than as positive obligations. In terms of free speech, the board declared, "Students may exercise their constitutionally protected rights of free speech and assembly so long as they do not interfere with the operation of the regular school program."

With regard to student clubs, "Students may form political and social orga-nizations, including those that champion unpopular causes, providing they are open to all students and governed by the regulations pertaining to stu-dent government regarding extracurricular activities." The final provision struck at black student unions, which excluded nonblacks. Moreover, regu-lations often stipulated that student organizations embody multiple per-spectives, undermining student antiwar organizations. With regard to stu-dent dress, the board said that students could wear anything as long as it was not "clearly dangerous" or "so distractive as to clearly interfere with the learning and teaching process." It added that "This right may not be re-stricted, even by a dress code arrived at by a majority vote of students."[38]

These policies are not unreasonable. In fact, they concede a good deal of what students demanded—or perhaps more saliently, what federal courts had already granted them. The recognition that students indeed had rights represented a step forward. Nevertheless, the bills left unstated both how the lines of what was permissible would be drawn and who would do the drawing. Who decided, for example, whether student speech or assembly interfered with the operation of the school? Who judged whether a stu-dent's dress was "distractive to the teaching and learning process?" The board of education mandated the creation of a parent-student-faculty council and gave student government representatives opportunities to meet with administrators, but the powers granted to these groups were not spelled out. The balance of power remained with the administration.[39]

This itself would not be so troubling—after all, administrators were adults and students were legally children—if it had not been for the fact that there was still no effective check on administrative power. If teachers and administrators generally exercised power lightly and judiciously there would be no problem. Ample evidence shows that, on the contrary, adults in schools all too commonly used their power capriciously. Consequently, even after this bill was adopted, students still had to go outside the school system, either to the streets or to the courts, for redress. If the largest, most united high school student movement could achieve no more than this, what was the fate of other student movements around the country?

In other places, movements for student rights also yielded mixed results. The bill of rights in New York City angered principals; in Philadelphia, it was the Philadelphia Federation of Teachers (PFT) that opposed the bill written by the city's board of education. The PFT and students had previ-ously clashed when students demanded that a certain white social studies teacher be transferred to another school on the grounds that he "was not able to relate to the black student body." The PFT regarded this demand as a violation of teachers' rights and due process in transfers. More important, it flatly rejected giving students a voice in personnel matters. The school board, attempting to placate both groups, dismissed the students' demand but then issued a student bill of rights and responsibilities to give students both a mechanism for venting (if not redressing) their grievances and a more concrete understanding of what rights they had as students. The PFT, however, opposed to the very idea of a student grievance procedure, questioned specific elements of the proposal, demanding to know whether attendance at hearings called by students would be mandatory for teachers and whether attending would cut into teachers' preparation or after school time. In addition, PFT members wondered whether the First Amendment even applied to schools. Accusing the community leaders who had supported the students' initial demands of manipulating students for their own ends, the PFT dismissed the idea of a bill of rights for creating an "atmosphere of disorder and excitement, [and] the encouragement of disruptive activity."[40]

The PFT lost its battle, but it is not clear how much students won. The board of education succeeded in reducing disruptions in the schools, but few students actually used the new grievance procedures. The record does not reveal what students thought of this bill, nor how much voice—if any—they had in producing it.[41]

BEYOND A BILL OF RIGHTS

Calling their proposals a "bill of rights" helped the student movement appear more legitimate. In the context of the rights revolution taking place in the United States in the late 1960s and early 1970s, "student rights" had a logical, inevitable ring. Certainly pressing for rights was more acceptable to adults than issuing demands. The line between rights, understood as inborn entitlements, and simple demands for power—often based on some stated or implicit threat—was not always clear. But some students bluntly labeled their goals "demands," and the things they pushed for went well beyond the rights enumerated or implied in the Bill of Rights of the U.S. Constitution. Student demands, also exposed some of the differences between black, white, and Latino activists. Students of color explicitly connected student rights and community power as white students seldom did. Black students in Detroit, for example, not only demanded that students be involved in discussions of merit pay and review, hiring, and firing of teachers and administrators, but also wanted "complete community control over all schools," in terms of hiring and firing, the physical school facility, and the curriculum. Chicano and Puerto Rican students also linked their struggles to the wider goals of their community, whose support bolstered them in their battles with administrators.[42]

On the West Coast, Chicano students who had taken part in the East Los Angeles "blowouts" (walkouts) in 1968 issued demands that bore little resemblance to bills of rights. They did want free speech and an end to the dress code, but they also demanded free admission to school sporting events, no more student janitorial work, clemency for those who had participated in the blowouts, an end to forced transfers of dissident teachers, smaller class sizes, along with bilingual and bicultural education. These demands juxtapose local issues, such as students' rights, with demands for broader educational change. Activist high school students of all races not only had a strong sense of themselves as Americans and citizens but also shared a vision of American society and the values it ought to embrace and reflect. This vision was largely liberal and inclusive, tolerant, and pluralistic. Demands for separate organizations for students of color and for an expanded role for students at the heart of the educational enterprise, however, pushed the high school student movement toward a more radical position.[43]

White students, too, sought a voice in the hiring and firing of personnel, particularly when they attempted to protect popular teachers from administrators. These teachers were often young, unconventional, and in hot water with their bosses. Students at Niles Township (Illinois) High School staged demonstrations and walkouts, picketed the school, and petitioned the school board in an effort to retain teachers Nancy Tripp, John Palm, and Judy Pildes, all fired for their "radical concepts of teaching," according to the underground *New Free Press*. They failed when the administration came down hard, threatening to suspend participants in demonstrations or expel students identified as leaders. Students in Pima, Arizona, walked out to protest of the firing of a popular teacher, and Susan Russo's art students petitioned to save her after she was fired for refusing to say the Pledge of Allegiance in Henrietta, New York. The fact that these protests rarely worked reinforced students' sense of powerlessness within the schools.[44]

Some students believed that the best way to empower themselves was to reform the student council and give it genuine power. These students may have perceived themselves as moderates working within the system, but the changes they sought were breathtaking in scope. The same Waukegan (Illinois) high school students who proposed creating a student-faculty court recommended that the student council be permitted to override the administration by a two-thirds vote, that the faculty sponsor be reduced to a silent observer, that the grade criteria for running for office be eliminated, and that anyone who could collect one hundred signatures on a petition be permitted to run for office. They suggested that the full election results be published, rather than simply announcing the winners, and recommended the creation of special (student) election judges and poll watchers. There is no evidence of whether these suggestions were enacted. It is difficult, however, to imagine administrators permitting students veto power.[45]

Harkening back to their analogy of schools as prisons, some student activists wanted to reduce or eliminate rules restricting students' physical mobility, or the use of police officers in the schools. Students in New York City, for example, demanded that all police should be taken out of the schools and that rules about hall checks and bathroom and lunch passes be abolished.[46]

Movements for student rights and student power often merged seamlessly into one another, because activists simultaneously wanted to define and protect their rights while increasing their power within the schools. No evidence shows students delineating where, as minors, their rights should

be limited nor at what point, as students, they should defer to adult teachers and administrators. In their bills of rights and sets of demands, students
presented themselves as equal to adults. Those who demanded veto power
over adult policies suggested that they were in fact superior to adults. Here
we see the dynamic interplay between the rights and identity revolutions.
In pursuing their rights as they understood them, student activists rejected
their identity as children and embraced citizenship as the best measure of
their status. When they looked at schooling itself, students again refused to
view themselves as children who were more or less at the mercy of adult
teachers and administrators. Instead, they regarded themselves as equal col-
laborators who had the right to a voice in how they would be educated. In
the realm of education, student power meant partnership.

THE STUDENT CRITIQUE OF EDUCATION

Student complaints about school did not originate in the 1960s, of
course, but activists in this era transformed mere griping into a broad-based
and thorough critique, buttressed by high levels of organization and—
through their publications—communication. They questioned the curriculum, teaching methods, and the means of measuring learning and often
made radical suggestions to improve each of these areas. Adults felt as-
tounded by the depth, breadth, and thoughtfulness of the student critique.
Linda Corman taught at an alternative school, intended to give a second
chance to students who had been either expelled from a regular school or
simply could not perform in that setting. She noted with surprise, "The last
thing I expected from public school rejects . . . was serious, perceptive criticism of exactly what they were expected to learn." She wrote that in the
end she felt compelled to accept these students as more or less her equals,
which was in large part what the student rights movement intended.[47]

In critiquing curriculum, students endlessly reiterated the word "relevance." High school students were highly conscious of living in a time
when the very fabric of society was ripping and being rewoven, and they
argued that education ought to help them to make sense of these changes.
The 1969 *Life* poll revealed that more than a third of the students interviewed wanted "folk rock music," hair and clothing styles, and underground papers and films discussed in class. More than half thought sex and
black rights should be included in the curriculum, and 70 percent wanted
drug usage discussed. Tellingly, the pollsters did not ask about the Vietnam
War or women's liberation, but half of the students believed the right to
dissent should be presented in their classes, and in venues outside the *Life*
poll they attacked the way their teachers either presented or ignored the
Vietnam War. Students on opposite ends of the political spectrum complained that their teachers used their power to punish students whose
views diverged from their own or refused to permit any discussion of controversial matters.[48]

As we have seen, black students often demanded courses in black studies, black history, or African languages, dismissing the white-centered curriculum as irrelevant to their lives. School administrations commonly accepted these demands. Black students at White Plains High School in New York agreed to "do all in their power to establish communication with the administration and to establish order" once the administration granted their request for classes about their own culture. In fact, the principal, Manson Donaghey, stated that he "felt great" upon reaching the agreement and insisted that the students' "demands were educationally sound." Scanty evidence suggests that many white students rejected these new courses—which some blacks wanted to be mandatory for all students—viewing administrators' concessions as craven. On at least one occasion, white parents sought an injunction against classes in black history.[49]

Elements of high school culture encouraged by administrators as fun or appealing to teenagers struck radicals as inane. The sophomore assembly, where students chanted "We're number one!" to the beat of a drum, appalled one student from Long Beach, California. She wrote sardonically, "For a moment I could have sworn it was 1984, and the middle of the Two Minute Hate. That's the kind of school spirit cultivated at Millikan—blind, automatic, and meaningless." For these students, the innocuous pastimes promoted by the schools—pep rallies, football games, proms—were ludicrous at a time when cities burned, an unpopular war ground on, and race relations bristled with tension.[50]

Besides wanting schooling relevant to their lives and times, activist students disapproved of tracking systems, which identified some students as college material and funneled others into less-desirable vocational education or what were called "general tracks"—all-purpose general education. Because school counselors typically placed large numbers of black, Puerto Rican, and Chicano students in the vocational or general tracks, activists of all colors attacked tracking as racist. Students often linked their critique of tracking to demands for open college admissions. As Donald Reeves put it, "Any nation that can maintain armies and navies around the world, pour billions into space exploration and foreign aid, and then throw away 'surplus' food has enough money to build facilities to give every one of us a college education." It is clear that these high school students imbibed the sense of endless possibilities and heightened expectations that characterized this era.[51]

In turn, students linked opposition to tracking and desire for open college admissions to the war in Vietnam. Draft boards exempted college students from eligibility for the draft, but high school graduates from the general tracks lacked the prerequisites for college and thus were prime material for draft boards. Here the class and racial uses of tracking had stunning consequences. Joe Harris, a radical student from Theodore Roosevelt High School, in New York City, declared, "The school will not be used as a cannon fodder supplier."[52]

Administrative procedures that processed students rather than treating them as individuals also angered students. Editors of *Common Sense,* the underground newspaper of Alton (Illinois) High School, resented the fact that computers arranged their schedules. They argued that students should be allowed to make changes to their schedules, and complained, "As the situation stands now, the school is run for the convenience of the IBM computer, not the student." Other students criticized the schools for being wedded to the clock to the point of obsession. Students commonly left the room when the bell rang, regardless of what was happening in class. One student told Mark Libarle and Tom Seligson about a teacher who would stop speaking in mid-sentence when the bell rang, and take up (again in mid-sentence) the following day![53]

Students condemned the way contemporary education was carried out. At the same time, many of them criticized the ostensible purposes of that education. Laurie Sandow of the New York High School Student Union asserts, "Schools are major instruments for the perpetuation of the racism and inequalities of our society." In the opinion of Paul Steiner, another New York City high school student, "The point of high school is that you learn to accept doing things which are meaningless to you so that you can achieve some other goal like college or a job. And you don't really want college or the job either, but you need them, so you can achieve another goal—money. And you don't *need* very much money to live, you just need it for things which you've been taught to want." Steiner identifies the "life adjustment" emphasis in the high schools as wrong-headed. He argues that, instead, the purpose of education ought to be for each individual to "find out for yourself what your real needs and desires are." He simultaneously rejects corporate capitalism and consumerism while defending individual self-fulfillment as a life goal, mirroring the ethos of the counterculture within the high school environment. Radical students, in contrast to Steiner, believed that education should prepare students to change the world, not adjust to it or seek self-fulfillment.[54]

STUDENT ALTERNATIVES TO PUBLIC EDUCATION

Although some students turned to activism to pursue reform, in other instances students organized alternatives to traditional education, bypassing the school system. These alternatives ranged from individual seminars to full-scale schools. The underground *New Free Press,* in Illinois, advertised a "Liberation School" that met on Sunday afternoons. Hackensack, New Jersey, student John Birmingham created an "Independent Study Program," where study groups voluntarily researched whatever interested them and then wrote up their findings for other students. In Royal Oak, Michigan, underground editors publicized their "freedom school," which offered courses in "Foreign Policy, White Racism and Black Power, Myths in American History, Civil Liberties, The New Morality, the Draft, American Indians,

China, and Student Power and the American School System." The school was run by Youth for Peace, Freedom, and Justice, a high school group.[55]

On other occasions, the students organized brand-new schools. Toby Mamis, editor of the underground *New York Herald Tribune,* left high school with twenty others in his senior year to establish his own unaccredited school. A group of students in Minneapolis, Minnesota, also dropped out to found an alternative school. The founders and enrollees were among the brightest students in Minneapolis public schools and were highly critical of public education. Belinda Behne, one of the founders, asserted that students were "pumped through the system like products, never learning to think at all." The student-run school allowed students to sign up for classes that interested them, to be taught by volunteers from the community.[56]

Adults who supported these student initiatives quickly learned that, if they wanted to participate, it had to be on a basis of equality. Activist students had not disengaged from the public schools only to play a subordinate role in alternative schools of their own design. The Minneapolis dropouts persuaded a professor of education to quit his job at the University of Wisconsin at Milwaukee to coordinate their school; he was to be paid by community donations. Administrators in the public schools, unhappy with the new school, noted that under state law students attending the alternative school would be considered truant. One assistant superintendent of schools expressed concern about losing good students, stating, "It makes you wonder what we're not offering to meet their needs." Here again we see a willful refusal to accept what the students themselves were saying. Looking closely at the schools the students set up provided broad clues about what they wanted, but somehow these administrators were not getting the message.[57]

One student-run school in New York City exemplified activists' vision of good education. When a handful of students and their parents met in 1971 to discuss how to establish an alternative school, adults initially dominated. But at the second meeting, the students let the adults know that, because the school was for them, parents should take a back seat. Students liked the school they ultimately created, the Elizabeth Cleaners Street School (named after the storefront into which the school moved), because of the role they had in designing and choosing classes, the egalitarian relations between students and teachers—some of whom were paid, and others were volunteers— and the relaxed environment with regard to assignments and class meetings. By the end of the year, many of the students discovered their own need for structure, lamenting that they had not done as much work as they could have. Adults could have explained that public schools were heavily structured for that very reason, but the students preferred learning for themselves by making mistakes rather than simply being told.[58]

Black students, as well as whites, set up alternative schools. The New York City Black High School Coalition established a number of "liberation classes," which were taught both by students and by black educators. The classes met in the summer and covered such practical topics as first aid and photography, because students "realiz[ed] the need of good photographers in a demonstration." Academic subjects included Maoism, the works of Franz Fanon, Malcolm X, and "the Religions of Man and Women in the Liberation Struggle." Mao, Fanon, and Malcolm X were all radical figures. Radical students embraced Chinese Communist leader Mao Zedong's writings on power, violence, and revolution. Algerian writer and philosopher Fanon's critique of white colonialism around the world and Malcolm X's black nationalist attack on the oppression of blacks in the United States also held powerful appeal. Activist students clearly hungered for education of a type not available in most schools. When they had the freedom to design or choose their own courses, they opted for courses that centered on the most burning issues of their day.[59]

Deliberately planned educational alternatives competed with schools that emerged temporarily out of educational chaos and usually disappeared with the reestablishment of order. During the Ocean Hill–Brownsville teachers' strikes in New York City, for example, a number of "liberation schools" sprang up to provide students with schooling while the strikes were in full swing. Stuyvesant High School began with standard classes in English, history, math, physics, chemistry, and gym, but by the third day of the strike began offering electives in art, music, Swahili, political science, black history, and poetry, a selection that clearly reflected student interest. The liberation school he attended in a church in the Bronx entranced Donald Reeves: no hall passes, no bureaucracy, students choosing their own courses and programs of education, and no grades or tests. Reeves felt that in this school both teachers and parents listened to the students. He comments, "For the first time students felt the beauty of learning what school could be like. The school was ours. We were learning from each other." He believed that the liberation schools radicalized many students, who now saw "the difference between education and indoctrination" and "began to recognize that we had voluntarily relinquished our freedom to the bureaucracy of rules and regulations."[60]

Some teachers shared in the students' excitement. Robert Rossner, who taught English at the Bronx High School of Science, was one of the strikebreakers during the New York City teachers' strikes. After the students opened Science, they began planning their own courses of study. Rossner recalls, "It was tremendously exciting." He felt very proud of the students. After arranging which classes would be taught and when, students posted a schedule on a blackboard in the auditorium and let attending students pick the classes they wanted to take. Eventually, conflict arose between the student "founders" of the liberated school and those students who had initially stayed out of school, but returned before the strike was over. The latecomers worried about college entrance exams and failed to share the enthusiasm of the founders for their newly discovered freedom. The founders and the nonstriking teachers decided to hold daily orientations for newcomers, according to Rossner, to try to "infuse them with the spirit of the *New* Bronx High School of Science, as we see it." The students and some teachers hoped that after the strike was over one wing of Science could be given over to the liberated school. Their hopes were dashed.[61]

TEACHERS RESPOND TO THE STUDENT CRITIQUE

Although some teachers such as Robert Rossner valued the student-teacher collaboration in learning, others felt profoundly threatened rather than exhilarated by their students' critique of education. One particularly touchy point was the issue of teacher competence. Teachers believed that student had neither the expertise nor the right to evaluate teaching. Students, on the other hand, argued that they knew bad teaching when they experienced it. When *New York Times* reporter Nicholas Pileggi interviewed a number of high school radicals in New York City, Margie Glenn, who attended Performing Arts High School, told him bluntly, "Teaching is the only profession where incompetence is not grounds for firing." Teachers at Academy High School in Erie, Pennsylvania, refused to discuss teacher competence and racism in a "Dialog" sought by students. "No teacher was willing to stand before individual students and be questioned," "Susan Snow" remembers. Teachers and administrators alike regarded student demands to have a role in hiring and firing, to examine teachers' personnel files, to evaluate their teachers, or even to raise the issue of competence as attacks on their integrity, professionalism, and power.[62]

Teachers were also leery of student demands to abolish grades. But, according to radical students, teachers used grades as a weapon to force students to conform, in either their thinking or behavior. Deborah Astley claims that her education at Western Heights High School, in Oklahoma City, taught her to "[view] the rule makers as hypocrites. I learned that if I wanted to make a good grade in a particular class, I had to agree with the teachers. Different opinions—thinking—was not encouraged." Student underground writers for the Milwaukee *Open Door* argued that grades were "the equivalent of the caveman's club." Students doubted that grades could really measure learning, and they disapproved of the competitive attitudes that grades fostered. Because poor grades kept students out of college at a time when the draft swept up youths who did not attend college, students' attacks on grades had political, racial, and class ramifications.[63]

RESULTS OF STUDENT CALLS FOR REFORM

Battles for reform in the schools resulted in some victories, and some losses, for students. Administrators frequently granted demands for more black counselors and black history. Many schools worked out ways to channel student discontent or to allow student representation in decision making. The sober demeanor of Detroit students, who marched to a board of education meeting in the rain, convinced the members to allocate more than a million dollars to improve the schools, another peaceful victory. David Wachtel conducted a ten-page survey of student opinions at his Ambridge, Pennsylvania, high school. After presenting the results to the administration, "males were allowed to wear facial hair if trimmed, all students were allowed to wear jeans, girls were allowed to wear pants, and a Russian language class was added as an elective to the curriculum." A survey of more than fifteen thousand high school principals showed that in fully 40 percent of cases where students protested nonviolently, schools made some changes in response. In contrast, where protests were violent, only 8 percent of principals indicated that any "substantive change" had taken place.[64]

There were plenty of failures as well. In some places, administrative repression quashed a student reform movement. The Montgomery County (Maryland) Student Alliance had an ambitious "program for change," which included student participation in teacher evaluation and curriculum matters, the abolition of censorship, the right to distribute literature on campus, and "relevance" in course work. Within a week, a handful of members of this alliance were suspended, and their program came to naught. The student battle for a bill of rights in Homestead, Pennsylvania, was similarly crushed. Administrators threatened Elliott Jones, the leader of this movement, with expulsion and issued a policy of suspending or expelling any student who disrupted school "through actions, behavior, dress, or presence." The deliberate vagueness of the policy shows the broad powers these administrators still claimed.[65]

Sometimes students' struggles for greater rights had surprising outcomes. The alternative school where Linda Corman taught witnessed a student power movement. After a handful of demonstrations, Corman reports that the administration suggested "that the newly formed student council, which had evolved more or less into a Black Power group, have jurisdiction over certain difficult discipline cases, including the mugging of a white student by a black student, and several cases of extortion." The students rejected this idea, complaining that it was "unfair" for the administration to saddle them with this burden. In this case, ironically, students emphasized their youth to evade an unpleasant task.[66]

Pollster Louis Harris may have expressed the student point of view the best after his survey for *Life*. Summing up the survey results, he argued that

> students are willing to be taught, but not to be told. They are willing to abide by rules, but they will not abide by rules which put them down. They are aware of the need for authority, but not impressed by it for its own sake. They are excited by the prospect of living in a fast-changing modern society and they want their high school education to help prepare them for it—not for some society of the past.

Harris emphasizes the essential moderation of the students' position. They sought, at base, respect for their dignity and fundamental rights along with fuller participation in decisions directly affecting their education. They generally accepted formal schooling as the best way to prepare themselves for adult life. Even at the peak of their frustration, activists walked out of public schools only to form their own alternatives rather than dropping out altogether. Student rights and power advocates did not question their status as students, on the whole.

Activists did, however, seek to radically alter the relationship between students, teachers, and administrators. Here Harris missed the student movement's most critical edge. Paralleling the insistence of students of color that high schools cease to be bastions of white privilege, student rights and power advocates challenged adult privilege. It is true that they never launched a frontal assault on childhood as a social category, yet, by redefining what it meant to be a student, they shook up contemporary ideas about the status of both students and children. Activists attempted to strip the role of student of its previous passive, subordinate elements. In their view, students played a dual role: as citizens of the larger polity, with all of the rights appropriate to that status, and as coequals with educators within the schools. These definitions raised compelling questions. If students were citizens and partners, in what ways could they still be considered children? How did their legal minority affect their rights as citizens or their powers as partners?

There is no evidence that student activists even conceded that any specific issue was beyond their realm as students. They never articulated where the line between adult and student might be drawn. They may not have believed there was such a line. Although few adults were willing to recognize students as full equals, court decisions and concessions granted by school officials moved students closer to the seat of power and broadened the rights available to them. Before the combined pressure of racial, rights, and power advocates, American high schools were transformed. Rigid, hierarchical bureaucracies gave way to institutions that were far more responsive to the needs of the diverse students attending them.

For a vocal minority of students, censure of schooling and the school system opened out into a broader critique of American society. For these students, the high school was a mere microcosm of the wider society. As Steven Porter, a senior at Newton South High School, in Newton, Massachusetts, put it, after watching *High School*, "If you think that the movie is sick and the high schools are sick, this is just part of the society." Activist students yearned to reform both.[67]

SIX—HIGH SCHOOL STUDENTS, THE VIETNAM WAR, AND RADICAL POLITICS

When the *New York Times* summarized the graduation speeches of high school valedictorians and salutatorians at five New York high schools in June 1968, the report noted, "a marked disenchantment with the direction that American society is taking." Students expressed dismay over violence in the United States, particularly the wave of political assassinations (Robert Kennedy's assassination had occurred earlier that month), and roundly criticized the war in Vietnam. Some worried about the poor in America; others condemned materialism. Deborah Smullyan, of Mamaroneck High School, accused corporate America of demanding "crewcuts, punctuality, and respectful conformity," while the government sought "patriotic cannon fodder." Smullyan concluded bitterly, "A world like this deserves contempt."[1]

We have no way of knowing how typical the five speeches that the *Times* reported were. There is, however, good evidence that a small but articulate group of high school students across the country assailed their schools, the educational system, and society from a left-wing perspective. These students constituted a distinct minority, and they knew it. Vicki Aldrich, a high school student in Colorado, recalls being one of four or five activists in a student body of some three hundred. Yet Aldrich and others like her took leading roles in the student movement; they drew up the petitions, organized the demonstrations, and created the underground newspapers that larger numbers of students merely signed, attended, or read. Some activists focused on a single issue, such as student rights or the war in Vietnam. Others, like Calvan Vail, were involved on multiple fronts. Vail, a student at Portsmouth High School, in New Hampshire, tried to bring socialist and antiwar speakers to his school and wrote for an underground newspaper, the *Strawberry Grenade*.[2]

Activists often perceived connections between high school and local, national, and even international issues, an angle of vision that encouraged them to analyze different but related systems of authority. Their convictions, no less than their determination to right the world's wrongs, set them apart from their peers and made them the focus of considerable attention from adults. The left-wing opinions of student activists alarmed and puzzled principals and school boards. Students had been conformist and passive in the 1950s and early 1960s. Why, adults wondered, were today's students so different? What motivated them to become politically active?

Believing that high school students were children, adults doubted that activists arrived at their views independently. Indeed, organizations such as Students for a Democratic Society (SDS), the Student Mobilization Committee to End the War (SMC), the Black Panthers, and the American Civil Liberties Union (ACLU) both sought and exerted influence over the high school movement. Students proved difficult to control, however, and none of these groups convinced them to subordinate their own independence to someone else's agenda. Rather than being manipulated by strangers, as adults frequently feared was the case, parents, teachers, and peers had far greater influence.

Specific events such as the course of the Vietnam War, violence on the home front, and the rise of the feminist movement also influenced high school activists. In keeping with their conception of themselves as citizens, these students believed that they had a right and an obligation to express their views and, if necessary, protest the direction their society was taking.

DISPUTING THE ROLE OF SDS

Despite the fact that they constituted a minority, left-wing high school students troubled their elders for several reasons. First, these students often clashed with conservative teachers and administrators, many of whom seemed unwilling to allow students to express dissident views. Second, some administrators feared that in conservative communities these students would harm school-community relations, possibly even jeopardizing school funding. Third, because leftist students embraced activism more than conservatives did, they irked teachers and administrators who preferred order, even passivity, among students. Unable to see students as independent thinkers, educators and the wider public looked outside the schools for its source. Some administrators agreed with the superintendent of the Cincinnati schools, Paul Miller, who asserted, "Few of these demonstrations are spontaneous. They are planned by outside agents. These demonstrations may be part of a national conspiracy, and may be nationally directed." "Outside agents" and "national conspiracy" were heavily freighted words in cold war America and conveyed the siege mentality of some conservatives.[3]

Adults singled out SDS, a college student group, as the instigator of high school activism, branding it a dangerous, radical organization. The American Association of School Administrators even claimed to trace all high school unrest to a Los Angeles student position paper that, it alleged, SDS had printed and distributed nationally to other high schools. The paper, written by SDS member Mark Kleinman when he was a high school student in Southern California, succinctly laid out what ultimately became the standard critique. Kleinman argued that high schools constrained but did not educate students, and he urged students in Los Angeles to organize both within their schools and on a citywide basis. Hardly a revolutionary, Kleinman suggested that, to attain the broadest base possible, student organizers should avoid taking stands on the civil rights movement or the Vietnam War and concentrate instead on reforming their schools. Kleinman's proposals included reducing class size, giving students a greater voice in rules and curriculum, and using an honor system to replace the "oppressive policing" of students. That some adults interpreted this mild manifesto as a blueprint for revolution reveals their suspicion that any concessions undermined their own power.[4]

Kleinman's paper aside, SDS did take an interest in high schools. Born with a liberal spirit of optimism and reform in 1963, by the late 1960s SDS had become disillusioned with American society; radical members touted revolutionary violence as the only way to force changes. Some SDS theorists posited that, as the most oppressed group within society, high school students, especially from the white working class, would form the vanguard of the coming revolution. SDS leader Bernadine Dohrn declared in 1968, "High schools will be the new thrust. They are racist. They are used as babysitting jails. They are used to trap people into the Army, into stupid colleges to train them for jobs they don't want. They are oppressive."[5]

SDS followed Dohrn's declaration with concerted recruiting efforts. In the fall of 1968, its national office printed and distributed instructions on high school organizing. Beyond creating new chapters, the college group also staged a handful of ill-conceived raids, beginning in the summer of 1969. In public high schools in Akron, Chicago, Columbus, Detroit, New York, Pittsburgh and other urban areas, SDS members burst into classrooms, assaulted the teachers, and harangued the students about the need for revolution. In one memorable incident in September 1969, scores of SDS women raided South Hills High School, in Pittsburgh, baring their breasts and waving a Viet Cong flag. Police arrested twenty-six of the women. Despite the dramatic recruitment effort, it is not clear how many students rushed to join SDS.[6]

Though hardly posing a threat to the schools, these disruptions provided wonderful copy for the media, which intensified public anxiety about SDS by playing up stories about its presence in high schools. SDS member Todd Gitlin, who later became a professor of journalism, has described how the media seizes issues and frames them to maximize their shock value. A producer for the Walter Cronkite show, Gitlin explains, "would not propose the mundane, wearisome subject of SDS as a radical group, say, but 'SDS in the high schools,' expecting to draw the reaction, 'What? Those fuckers are in the high schools?'" If SDS reveled in fantasies about imminent revolution, mainstream society both titillated and frightened itself by pretending to believe such fantasies. The Congressional Committee on Internal Security fanned these fears by investigating SDS in the high schools. Even though the testimony of students strongly suggested that few read SDS literature or were impressed when SDS activists invaded their schools, the committee ominously concluded that SDS constituted a major menace: "Because of the dedicated commitment of SDS activists to the use of direct action and violence in attaining their objectives, it can be expected that efforts will be intensified to win recruits of high school age, and increasingly hostile efforts will be exerted to 'shut down' the high schools of our Nation."[7]

Noting and recoiling from the "new thrust" by SDS, many school officials failed to investigate further. If they had, they would have found that SDS had minimal influence on high school activists despite some modest successes. High school SDS chapters did appear as early as 1963, and an internal poll in 1966 showed that high school students made up 10 percent of the SDS membership. Because SDS chapters were known—even notorious—for their independence from the national office, exact numbers of high school chapters or members do not exist. According to the Liberation News Service, high school students in Richmond Hills and Queens, New York, greeted SDS representatives enthusiastically. In Cleveland, SDS succeeded in establishing a number of high school chapters, and New Orleans had a citywide high school SDS chapter. At D. C. Everest High School, in Weston, Wisconsin, the underground newspaper reported a new SDS group. A nationwide survey by the Associated Press in March 1969 identified SDS high school chapters in Boston, Columbus, Denver, and Los Angeles. A 1969 article in *Saturday Review* mentioned high school chapters in Akron, St. Louis, and Seattle.[8]

These lists suggest the wide dispersal of SDS influence in high schools, but not the often tenuous connections between college SDS and high school students. Lynn Szwaja and Susan Pennybacker, leaders of Cleveland's Movement for a Democratic Society (an offshoot of SDS), stated that, in their chapter, high school students met separately from college students. Moreover, although the concerns of high school and college students overlapped—both opposed the war in Vietnam, corporate influence, and poverty—high school students also spent time on problems rooted in their own schools. Kenneth Fish, a high school principal from Montclair, New Jersey, reported that an SDS chapter at Columbia University helped local high school students organize demonstrations and publish an underground newspaper. He noted, however, that, although the college students were "willing and eager to help their high school counterparts . . . for the most part [they] are not initiating the action." He argued that adults exaggerated the degree of SDS influence in the schools. Of the two dozen troubled schools he visited, none of the principals believed SDS had caused the unrest.[9]

In fact, the college group's overtures often left high school students cold. Although SDS theoretically assigned them a key historical role, the organization apparently could not envisage them actually leading a revolution. For that, they needed the enlightened leadership of SDS. In addition, SDS never spelled out just what role students would actually play in the revolution or in the period leading up to it. The group's condescending attitudes, transparent manipulation of students for its own ends, and ignorance of the issues most germane to high school activists lost SDS more students than it ever gained. One high school student in Madison, Wisconsin, laid out the terms for cooperation with SDS in brutally frank terms:

> Whenever SDS has come into high schools we've either said, okay, you can help us in this way: give us your printing press and give us some paper and that is it; or you can help us by giving us this information and getting us these pamphlets that we want. But we've stopped them coming into the high school and organizing for their own, and we've stopped them coming and speaking for the most part.

The student went on to explain why students limited their contacts with the group:

> We've kept them out of high schools because we don't want them there. The SDS of late hasn't been able to relate to high schools and many times they don't relate to their own ideas. They have certain ways of going about things, and it relates to college life and the college system, but it doesn't apply for high school.[10]

Other than recruiting soldiers for a nebulous revolution that existed only in their minds, it is not clear what SDS hoped to accomplish by organizing high school students, many of whom agreed with the Madison activist that SDS was out of touch with their needs. Robbie Newton of the *New York High School Free Press* condemned SDS efforts to ingratiate itself with New York City radicals. When SDS members from Columbia University wrote up a high school version of their program, Newton opposed it. "It was really rhetorical. It talked about antimilitarism as a major issue in the high schools, which it is not. For high school kids who get into the army, the army is getting away from home and away from lousy jobs and it's maybe learning a skill. When the army is the best alternative for some kids, you shouldn't say 'But the army is imperialist and capitalist.'" SDS drew its membership primarily from the college-going middle class; its claims about the political views of working-class high school students held about as much validity as its assessment of the prospects for revolution in America. Jaime Friar, another New York City high school student, put it crudely: "The SDS has really fucked up politics."[11]

High school students also condemned SDS's obvious efforts to manipulate them. Consider the experience of students at Sharpton High School, in Houston, Texas, who had been embroiled in conflicts with teachers and administrators over several issues. Teachers had quelled a protest over the lack of written school rules and refused to let students collect money for Biafra (then in the throes of famine and civil war as it attempted to secede from Nigeria), while demanding that students cough up money to buy plants for the school lobby. When one student refused, a teacher told him his "mind was being taken over by Communists." Two Sharpton students, Dan Sullivan and Mike Fischer, founded an underground newspaper to publicize these issues and to rally student response. They asked the SDS chapter at the University of Houston for assistance, although neither of them "agreed with the principles of the organization." In the first issue, SDS printed its name at the bottom of the front page, without consulting Sullivan and Fischer, who promptly cut the name off before distributing it. In the next issue, SDS planted its name in the middle of the front page where it could not be easily removed. Officials expelled Sullivan and Fischer; their connection with SDS probably hurt them as much as their publication of the newspaper itself. It is unlikely that the Houston SDS won many high school adherents after this incident.[12]

Chicago student Jan Weiland, who was no radical, also criticizes older students' efforts to recruit in the high schools. "Black Panthers and SDS . . . thought it would be fun to raise a ruckus with the teens," she complains. "Get them while they're young! There were chalk drawings and words from the SDS written on the sidewalk all around my high school." However, she adds, "SDS was just out there trying to gain support from us kids, but no one I knew took them up on it." She found the SDS presence, faint though it was, unnerving, and believed that it increased tensions. When, in their misguided attempts to impress working-class students with their toughness, groups of college-age SDS members raided urban high schools, most students reacted with stunned silence or hostility. In Boston, five hundred high school students staged a counterdemonstration against the would-be revolutionaries.[13]

THE ROLE OF THE SMC

The college SMC, formed in December 1966, also deliberately courted high school students, sometimes successfully. Representatives from two dozen high schools attended the SMC's first national antiwar conference at the University of Chicago in May 1967; a second conference the following year drew representatives from forty high schools. By 1970, the SMC had a national high school coordinator and hoped to use the high schools as "major organizing centers" for yet another antiwar demonstration that spring. Eve Levin's high school in Vestal, New York, had a thirty-five-member SMC organization, which was even included in the student yearbook. Although sympathetic to the group's aims, Levin admits that she rarely attended meetings, "finding them to be dull."[14]

In its endorsement and promulgation of a national high school students' bill of rights, the SMC showed a better grasp than SDS of high school activists' interests. But the SMC's primary goal was to end the Vietnam War and to mass bodies in demonstrations for this purpose. Thus, it too sometimes rubbed high school activists the wrong way. In New York City, the SMC supported the students' bill of rights, rather than the one drawn up by the board of education. Student leader Donald Reeves attempted to use the SMC just as it attempted to use him. On one occasion, he permitted an SMC representative to chair a student meeting because his own "knowledge of parliamentary procedure was for shit," as he put it. Later, however, Reeves complained that the SMC had too much control over where and when the student coalition met. In the anticlimactic climax of the students' demand for their own bill of rights, their rally was clumsily tacked onto an SMC demonstration against the war. The SMC—unlike Reeves's group—could afford to rent sound equipment, but it was not willing to stray far from its agenda to ensure the students an audience. In Detroit, a high school Revolutionary Student Coalition issued a leaflet in 1969 to support a walkout called by the SMC to oppose the war and memorialize the late Martin Luther King, Jr. The leaflet added, however, "High school students don't need the issue of the war in Vietnam to walk out of school. School itself is a good enough reason to walk out." The students laid out their complaints about education, which ranged from Eurocentric history classes to lousy cafeteria food, signaling that their interests diverged substantially from those of the SMC.[15]

BLACK PANTHERS AND HIGH SCHOOL STUDENTS

In urban high schools with large black populations, the Black Panthers attempted to establish a beachhead. Long Island City High School, for example, had a Black Panther chapter. Paul Gayton, a radical student at East Denver High School, was a member of the Black Panthers. Nevertheless, the extent of adult Panther influence on students is unclear. When, at a rally in New York City, the Panthers called on high school students to support Lonnie Epps, one of the "Panther 21"(charged with conspiracy to blow up buildings) who had helped organize a high school chapter, a sympathetic observer from the *New York High School Free Press* reported that only about half of the students listened to the speakers and the crowd snickered when someone tried to get a chant going—"No more pigs [police] in our community, Off [kill] the pig."[16]

Black students, like whites, sometimes sought out older allies for their own purposes. The black student association at Central High School, in Peoria, Illinois, sought the support of Bradley College's black student association, believing that no one would listen to the demands of high school students. The college black student association met with high school activists and wrote a letter backing them, but as student James Brown observes, the principal ignored them and "nothing changed." Brown concluded that high school students had to fight their own battles.[17]

COLLEGE ACTIVISTS AND THE HIGH SCHOOL MOVEMENT

Apart from these organized groups, who pursued high school recruits for their own programs, other older activists regarded the younger ones with a mixture of interest, encouragement, and condescension. Susan Jacobson, who had graduated from Niles Township High School and gone on to the University of Illinois, sent the high school underground a letter of praise and a donation ("half of my worldly cash"), commenting that she was glad that "there is finally something happening." Adult underground newspapers, which flourished in the 1960s, sometimes covered the struggles of high school students on their pages. The *Midpeninsula Observer,* for example, wrote sympathetically about the United Student Movement in Palo Alto, California. A New York City underground, the *Guardian,* reported extensively on student strikes in New York, New Haven, and Chicago, expressing satisfaction that high school students were "breaking out." Jack Benning, the publisher of two underground newspapers, gave more concrete support when he taught the editors of the *New York High School Free Press* how to use his typesetter and let them use his office. He told an interviewer from the *New York Times:* "Sometimes I regret that decision. . . . They're kids. They're noisy. They love big meetings and endless discussions, but they are relevant and they are sharp." Benning stated that he opened his office to the high school students because "[t]he high schools were about to blow up. The Establishment was trying to stop them from even distributing their leaflets near schools. I thought it would be better to let them blow off a little steam."[18]

Benning hoped to provide students with an outlet for their frustrations; other older activists tried to agitate them. In addition to the concerted—although rarely fruitful—efforts of groups like SDS, the SMC, and the Black Panthers to mobilize high school students, principals complained about other nonstudents loitering around campus or even entering the schools. Radicals in Seattle bragged about disrupting a "Military Day" assembly at Shorecrest High School and setting up an antiwar table next to the Marine Corps recruiter at Roosevelt High School. School officials fought back in court, where judges generally supported them. The court upheld the arrest of Joe Eugene Start and a group of his friends, for example, when they tried to pass out antidraft pamphlets at Sehome High School, in Bellingham,

Washington. John Young, a lay minister and director of the House of Soul (a settlement house) in Trenton, New Jersey, was convicted of "interfer[ing] with the peace and good order" of Trenton High School. Young claimed that he only wanted to support students who were protesting the suspension of another student for refusing to salute the flag, but the judge believed that Young had caused the student sit-in. In contrast, Robert Mandel won when he appealed his conviction for vagrancy after passing out antidraft literature in two Oakland, California, high schools. Because no disruption occurred, the judge ruled that the First Amendment protected leafleting, even in front of a high school.[19]

In these cases, the initiative of high school students themselves is blurred; we cannot know how students reacted to Start and Mandel's antidraft literature or the dynamics of John Young's relationship with students at Trenton High School. It is clear that both the outsiders and the school officials believed that students could be influenced and led. The presumption that high school students could be influenced made them an attractive target for outsiders with agendas. For the same reason school officials—and often courts—viewed them as innocents to be protected, but the precise lines of influence and initiative can be tricky to trace. Following the high school "blowouts" in East Los Angeles in 1968, Sal Castro, a teacher at Lincoln High School, and a number of college student representatives of the Union of Mexican-American Students (UMAS) were charged with conspiracy to disrupt the schools (disrupting school was a misdemeanor; conspiracy to do so was a felony). Although the legal contest centered on the First Amendment rights of the defendants, the subtext of the trial was that the older youths and Castro, the teacher, had planned the high school walkouts and, like the famed Pied Piper, led the mesmerized students out. Pressed to clarify the role of high school students, Carlos Muñoz, an UMAS defendant and later a historian, insists, "High school activists did not get the ball rolling. It was strictly a college student and young adult community activist movement. Teachers like Sal Castro got the students interested and identified leaders at the various high schools. But college and community activists were their mentors." He adds, "From my perspective, it is difficult for me to think the [high school] students first came up with the idea." Others have argued that, on the contrary, students approached Castro with their grievances. In their view, adults helped shape student activism, but the students were already primed for action.[20]

High school students seem to have played larger roles in other places. Kenneth García claims that in Denver the Crusade for Justice supported activist Chicano students, but the students reached out to them first with complaints about a racist teacher. The Crusade's main role, according to García, "was in disseminating certain information." Moreover, García emphasizes, "the nucleus of both the walk out and the West [H]igh [School] demonstration were the kids. And by 'kids' I mean just that. With the walk out, at least in Denver—in Colorado—it was kids from the age of 10, 12, and the older ones 15 and 16, that made the body move." Organizations such as the Crusade for Justice, in Colorado, and the Mexican-American Youth Organization (MAYO), in Texas, successfully turned student activism into community organization drives, but high school youths provided the catalyzing issues and the righteous anger that drew in the adults.[21]

THE ACLU AND STUDENTS' RIGHTS

The revolutionary aspirations of SDS and its blatant, colorful attempts to woo students made it the favorite whipping boy for those who assumed that older outsiders manipulated high school activists, yet the ACLU and its state chapters also met criticism for unduly influencing the young. Once again the accusations were off the mark. The ACLU, unlike SDS, did not attempt to recruit high school students or to establish high school chapters. Beginning in 1967, however, with the appointment of Ira Glasser as associate director of the New York Civil Liberties Union, the ACLU identified students' rights as a key area of concern. Students knew that, if their battles in school touched upon constitutional issues, the ACLU would fight in their corner. The ACLU backed a number of court cases, including the landmark *Tinker* and *Goss* cases (on black armbands and due process in suspensions), to the Supreme Court, dispatched its lawyers to fight for students, filed for numerous injunctions against school principals who violated students' rights, and reassured activists when administrators threatened them with reprisals. After the principal suspended Richie Cohen for holding silent vigils protesting the Marine Reserve Officer Training Corps program in his Greensboro, North Carolina, high school (despite his having first obtained a police permit), the ACLU represented him. Cohen points out: "The ACLU is pretty powerful in Greensboro, and from then on the principal was afraid to do anything as unconstitutional as suspending me for organizing the vigils."[22]

In 1968, the ACLU also published a pamphlet titled "Academic Freedom in the Secondary Schools" that explained students' legal rights, but how many students knew that this document existed, let alone actually read it, cannot be determined. When schools violated a student's rights, the student or a parent generally contacted the ACLU, not the other way around. Richie Cohen claims that the ACLU "heard about" his suspension and volunteered to represent him, but it is not clear how often this occurred. The ACLU certainly encouraged students who contacted the organization with their concerns, but this hardly constitutes the manipulation of impressionable youths. On the contrary, it reflects sophisticated students reaching outside their schools to find allies with real clout.[23]

THE INDEPENDENCE OF HIGH SCHOOL ACTIVISTS

The notion that outsiders controlled the high school movement did not go unchallenged in its time. Tom Hayden, a founding member of SDS, testified to the House Committee on Un-American Activities that high school students outdistanced college students in radicalism. Nicholas Pileggi, a *New York Times* reporter, dismissed the idea that high school students were under the sway of college radicals. "Generally high school students are far too mercurial for political manipulation," he declared, pointing out the infighting among organized student radicals. Students themselves scorned the idea that older radicals dominated them. David Romano, an activist from Westport, Connecticut, argues, "I disagree with any such analysis that denies the High School Movement the individuality and meaning it deserves. Admittedly there is a lot of similarity between college radicalism and high school radicalism, but it's because we as radicals recognize that we have many goals in common. That is not to say, however, that high school radicalism is just a lower off-shoot of the college movement." Tom Lindsay, of the New York High School Student Union and the *High School Free Press,* gave up high school organizing once he graduated, believing that it was best for students to organize themselves.[24]

Available evidence strongly affirms the independence of high school activists. They both responded to outside influences and acted of their own accord, but were no more malleable than adults. Whether giggling at Black Panthers or arguing against antiwar teachers, they were perfectly capable of resisting any group or individual who attempted to mold their thinking. Although nonstudents sought to and did influence the views of high school students, the sources of this influence were often much closer to home than critics imagined. Many students, perhaps the majority, shared the political views of their parents. Communities of color often stood behind their activist children, and the white students who took their battles to court generally enjoyed their parents' support. Again, however, the dynamics of influence are difficult to read. In Cincinnati, black students in eight high schools staged massive sit-ins protesting racist teachers, the lack of black history in the curriculum, and the transfer of four student leaders to other schools. When the school superintendent cracked down and suspended more than thirteen hundred demonstrating students, the following week the school boycott ballooned to nearly four thousand students, supported by 250 parents, who picketed the board of education. Did the students influence their parents, or vice versa?[25]

Teachers and school officials influenced students as well, some deliberately attempting to mold student opinions, because they believed that shaping minds and attitudes formed an important part of their job. Cincinnati superintendent Paul Miller, while attacking "outsiders" for "tampering" with students, insisted, "This does not mean, however, that the adult world has no responsible role to play in shaping the conscience of youth." Problems emerged only when adults tried to persuade students to embrace the *wrong* sorts of opinions, as defined by the generally conservative educational establishment. This becomes abundantly clear when we examine the most burning foreign policy issue of the late 1960s—the Vietnam War.[26]

THE AMERICAN WAR IN VIETNAM

Before 1965, Americans knew little about the U.S. role in Vietnam, even though it dated back to 1950 when Americans bankrolled the French effort to preserve Vietnam as a colony. Following the French defeat in 1954, a peace conference in Geneva attempted to halt the fighting and allow the people of Vietnam to choose their own form of government through national elections. The conference failed in both aims: Vietnam suffered a de facto division into two opposing states, and a civil war commenced in the south between the adherents of unification and supporters of the new government in South Vietnam. The latter refused to hold the election scheduled at Geneva. Because nationwide elections would almost certainly bring the communist leader Ho Chi Minh to power, the United States, which had declined to sign the Geneva Accords but had promised not to interfere, threw its support to South Vietnam's leader, Ngo Dinh Diem, and began providing him with aid and military advisers, in direct violation of its "hands-off" pledge. Under President John Kennedy, the number of American advisers, whose role extended well beyond giving advice, reached nearly seventeen thousand. American involvement deepened in 1963 after a coup toppled the unpopular Diem and installed a revolving door of would-be leaders in the south. In 1965, Lyndon Johnson reluctantly, and with a deep sense of foreboding, launched the United States into full war with the provision of two Marine battalions, followed rapidly by other ground troops, and initiated sustained bombing of both North and South Vietnam.

At that point, small traditional peace groups joined with increasing numbers of antiwar activists, the most visible of whom were college students. SDS had originally focused on poverty and racism, but in April 1965 it sponsored a surprisingly well-attended rally against the war. Earlier that same year, the University of Michigan held the first teach-in about the war, bringing students and faculty together—in the evening, because the administration would not permit classes to be cancelled—to debate the merits of the war.[27]

The majority of Americans supported the government's policies in Vietnam, but the drumbeat of dissent grew steadily louder. Then, suddenly, the Tet Offensive of 1968, an enemy offensive that caught the American troops and their South Vietnamese allies off guard, turned many Americans against the war. On April 26, 1968, a national student strike against the war brought an estimated one million college and high school students out of their classrooms. Not all who opposed the war supported the antiwar movement, but the collapse of consensus on containing communism in the Far East warned American officials that time was running out. Beginning in 1968 and continuing through 1973, when the United States finally signed a peace treaty with North Vietnam, U.S. policy shifted from an attempt to win the war to a contradictory—indeed doomed—attempt to withdraw its troops without allowing the government of South Vietnam to fall. Both the American war and the protests against it gradually wound down, although President Nixon's brief efforts to reinvigorate the war effort breathed new life into the antiwar movement, especially after his invasion of Cambodia in May 1970.[28]

EDUCATORS AND THE WAR

Adults debated whether to discuss the war with high school students. Some assumed that the war did not or should not concern them. The 1969 *Life* poll on the attitudes of students, parents, and teachers about their schools did not even raise the question. One study of 154 high school sophomores and seniors revealed that, although students yearned to discuss the war, their teachers would not permit it. Getting a C on an English paper she had written about the war shocked Loretta Nunn. Her teacher justified the grade, telling Nunn, "we are not going to talk about this because it is too involved for discussion in English class." Other teachers—usually those who opposed the war—took it upon themselves to bring the war into the classroom, regardless of whether their students wanted to hear about it. At least one group of teachers created a "Vietnam curriculum," a packet of teaching materials about the war. In 1968, one of the originators of the course traveled from school to school distributing the curriculum and, in her own words, "trying to convince them that it was not too controversial to teach about the war." "Martha Zimmerman" taught in a working-class high school in upstate New York. Her principal ordered her to teach her students to conform, because they were all headed for Vietnam or factory work. Zimmerman ignored him and discussed the war and politics in her classes until she was fired, without converting students to her antiwar views. Student Mark Richards recalls that the war was "certainly a topic in sociology and history classes." It is not clear that his teachers orchestrated the discussion in these classes, but at least they tolerated it.[29]

Antiwar teachers' efforts to influence students could edge into bullying. Gary Carnog, thinking back ruefully on his first year of teaching, comments, "In my belligerence for the pacifist cause I had put aside my toleration of their [students'] opinions in order to savor my contempt for their unenlightened right-wing outlook on the world." With some insight, he continues, "My zeal made me wonder whether the real reason I had decided to teach was to have a forum for the propagation of unpopular sentiments regarding morality, patriotism, and authority." From the students' point of view, "Sally" criticized teachers who abused their power over students to influence their views: "Yeah, like there's this German teacher. . . . I'm a hawk and she's a dove. She always marks me down when I oppose her." Some teachers went further, encouraging acts of dissent. Don Schwartz, a young teacher at the Bronx High School of Science, approved of a student-planned antiwar demonstration on April 26, 1968, urging faculty to boycott classes along with their students. Following the U.S. invasion of Cambodia in 1970, the *High School Journal,* a national publication for educators, polled a small group of intern teachers and found that, of the fifty-six who returned the questionnaire, thirty-six had conducted or participated in teach-ins, thirty-six had taken part in "strikes and protests," and fifteen had held class discussions on the war. Twenty reported political activism outside the school, and small numbers listed a smattering of other forms of activism.[30]

Conservatives, who attacked liberal or radical teachers for pushing their ideas onto students, could be just as guilty. Academy High School student Mary Ann Kennedy told interviewers, "Many teachers are like government agents, insuring that we have the United States' opinions instead of our own." Eve Levin recalls arguing with teachers and making fun of "the anti-Communist indoctrination that was part of the curriculum." Other educators enlisted outsiders to make the prowar case to the students. Jacqueline Rummel Groll, who attended high school in central California, observes, "I remember as a sophomore, going to a 'mandatory' rally where an Army recruiter came along and gave a talk about the importance of the United States entry into this war and how we, as Americans, must stop the . . . encroaching communist threat."

Groll remembers her high school years as filled with anxiety, rather than as a carefree time of life. The way adults in school explained the war increased her fears. "Years later, I understood this to be propaganda but at the time as a 15 year old, all I could see were the bad Vietnamese, coming ashore to take our lives on American soil."[31] Jacqueline Groll accepted the anticommunist perspective her school promoted. Only as an adult did she perceive the views she had been taught differently.

Students who instead questioned the conservative view met with chilly responses. Catharine Strahm, an antiwar teacher at Topeka High School, in Kansas, observed what happened when one student silently but publicly challenged conservative wisdom on the war. As an adult, Strahm willingly endured criticism for her antiwar stance but notes, "It was difficult for me to witness harassment of fine young citizens." In 1967, Strahm attended a school assembly whose purpose was to "explain the reason for U.S. involvement in the Vietnam War." As she explains,

> Two journalists shared the stage. Mike Shearer, student editor of the T.H.S. newspaper, *The World,* received an award for outstanding high-school journalist. The other journalist was editor of the *Manhattan* (Kansas) *Mercury,* Bill Colvin, who was the main speaker. Mr. Colvin played a tape made by grade-school children who thanked the combat troops for fighting "to keep them free." Colvin ended his speech by remarking that if one is bothered by rats, one must kill them.

Colvin's words provoked a sharp response from the audience. Some rose and cheered. Others remained seated in stony silence. On stage, the platform guests—including educators and community members—gave Colvin a standing ovation. Only the student, Mike Shearer, kept his seat in an obvious and pointed rebuke. Strahm describes what happened next:

> As Mike Shearer went to his classes following the assembly, teachers and students greeted him with scathing criticism and derogatory remarks. Two teachers, the late Louise Graumann and I, approached Shearer and expressed our admiration for his bravery in upholding his beliefs. He thanked us for our support and said that we were the only two who approved his right not to show acceptance of Colvin's remarks.[32]

Strahm reveals how the debate over the war in Vietnam was fought out in the high schools. Her story shows the polarization of the student body, official efforts to indoctrinate students into a prowar stance, the use of adult power and peer pressure to discipline a nonconforming student, and the mutual support that united left-wing students and teachers, which could turn coercive when left-wing teachers had conservative students.

Peer pressure could silence opponents of the war, but sometimes it worked the other way around. Louise Lancaster-Keim attended William R. Boone High School, in Orlando, Florida. After her boyfriend joined the Marines in 1967, he showed up for the junior-senior prom with his hair shorn. According to Lancaster-Keim, "He might as well have worn a scarlet 'U' for undesirable on his chest because at that point in time, with the war in such disfavor (and long hair so popular), anything that hinted of the military was scorned. I had a miserable time at the prom because, although my family supported the war, like most kids my age, I looked down on people in the military." Susan Lindholm also had a boyfriend who volunteered for the military. She recalls, "He left before I graduated, so I was quite aware of the war and very torn about the way soldiers were viewed, given the fact that the ones I knew didn't want to be there." Thus, a variety of pressures pushed high school students to pick sides, with consequences no matter which choice they made.[33]

THE RANGE OF STUDENT OPINION ON THE WAR AND THE DRAFT

Despite adult ambivalence about the propriety of discussing the war in school, the national debate echoed in American high schools, sometimes outside the classroom. Scanty evidence suggests that student opinions on the war, like those of adults, reflected the divisions in American society. When activists at West Milford Township High School polled their peers on the Vietnam War, 45 percent favored the Vietnam Moratorium of 1969, but 43 percent opposed it. Sixty-one percent approved of Nixon's policy of "Vietnamization"—removing American troops and encouraging troops from South Vietnam to take up the battle themselves. Forty-five percent believed that the United States had a right to be in Vietnam, whereas 37 percent disagreed. Perhaps most tellingly, only 33 percent of the students said that they would consider taking part in an antiwar demonstration, but fully 51 percent said they would not. A larger poll of twenty-five thousand students undertaken by *Scholastic* magazine the same year yielded similar results: only 38 percent disapproved of Nixon's handling of the war.[34]

When educators refused to discuss the war or to encourage students to support it, some students simply ignored it. At a Kentucky school torn by racial violence, Brent Coatney noted, "Kids at school didn't talk much about the war in Viet Nam, since we had our own [war] going on right there at school." Ignorance about the war was widespread. "Susan Snow" claims that high school boys knew they would have to serve in the war but did not understand what it was about. David Super, of South Dakota, agrees. "During the spring of our senior year," he explains, "I very distinctly recall discussing our general LACK of knowledge regarding the war in Vietnam with fellow male classmates. We nervously joked that we should pay more attention. It soon could become our war."[35]

Super's awareness that he might have to fight a war whose purposes he did not understand highlights a stark difference between high school boys and girls. The looming reality of registering for the draft during their senior year in high school made the war more immediately relevant to male students. Some began to ask questions about the war. Pete Biscus, of Gahanna Lincoln High School, in Ohio, recalls, "I was not particularly interested in politics in high school, though about the time I became a Junior ('69–'70) I began paying closer attention to the War in Viet Nam, and remember questions many had of the actions of President Nixon." When the time came, however, Biscus, like the majority of high school boys, registered for the draft.[36]

The draft meant that seniors had to be at least dimly conscious of the war. They did not necessarily discuss either the draft or the war openly. Jean Hartley Davis Sidden observes that, as a girl, she did not know what her male classmates thought of the draft. "If the boys were registered for the draft, I was completely unaware. They didn't project worry about going to Viet Nam and they prepared for college." The fact that a handful of high school and college activists established draft-counseling centers—actually antidraft counseling centers—indicates that students knew the Selective Service stood waiting to escort male graduates into the army and possibly into Vietnam. Taken together, comments from contemporary students suggest that boys occasionally discussed the draft among themselves, but not with girls. What Super describes as "nervous joking" might substitute for candidness about the fears these boys felt. Constrained by a masculine culture of stoical silence and confused by conflicting public debates about communism, patriotism, obedience, and dissent—to say nothing of the social consequences of questioning the war—high school boys wrestled with draft registration privately and alone.[37]

For others, even those who expected to be drafted if they did not go to college, the war was barely an issue. John Pepple, a student in Minneapolis, could not remember any protests against the war in his high school. "It was all pretty remote for us. When I turned 18 in my senior year, I dutifully went to register for the draft, as the law required. It was impossible not to know about the war in Vietnam, but it was still quite remote from our lives." Student awareness of the war, then, depended on whether it was discussed at home or in school, whether antiwar demonstrations occurred in their school or town, and—most important—whether the students themselves took an active interest in national affairs.[38]

STUDENT UNEASE ABOUT THE WAR

For all but the most radical students, questions about the war arose gradually. The steadily rising American casualty rate disturbed students no less than adults. Brent Coatney, who attended school in Hopkinsville, Kentucky, admits, "I was deeply troubled when body bags of guys from our county came back to town. However, I really believed in the war, and saw it as a second Korea, where we were building another line of demarcation against the communist aggressors." To Joyce Mitchel, who graduated in 1970, the war "had become pretty much of a meat grinder" by the time she was in high school, yet "[n]o one openly protested the war at that time as it was not acceptable. It would be like treason. . . . And kids' brothers were being killed and you'd look really bad acting like they weren't great heroes. And nobody wanted to believed they died for nothing." Coatney kept his qualms to himself because he believed in the war's purpose, and Mitchel remained silent for fear of offending classmates or community norms, yet the course of the war itself prompted both students to think about it more critically.[39]

Exempt from the draft, girls frequently found the war too abstract to concern them, unless they knew someone who became a casualty. Carole Palmer asserts, "Vietnam was just a word in the newspaper or on TV. We weren't touched by it—until one of our own became a casualty of the war. Then it was a reality. Pat Lindley wasn't coming home again." Joyce Mitchel recalls a similar tragedy: "A popular older kid from our school had come home in a wheelchair. He had a brother still in school with us. It brought the reality home to all of us. A kid everyone loved, Joe America, whatever, brought down in his prime for what?"[40]

High school students with parents in the military may have had a somewhat different perspective on the war, but they too were exposed to prowar propaganda, antiwar activism, and the human costs of the war. They could not simply avoid uncomfortable questions about the war. Mike Ward, whose father was in the Air Force and who spent most of his youth on military bases in Europe, grew up believing "you were either part of the team, or you were the enemy . . . and that America was always right." He first encountered an American girl with antiwar views during middle school in

Germany but dismissed her because she "said very negative things about Vietnam; and she was shunned. She was clearly misinformed, even though she had talked to Vietnam Vets, we considered her a fool, and she wasn't part of the Team." In 1970, Ward's family transferred to Indiana. He still believed wholeheartedly in the American war effort, but two incidents troubled him: "First, Dad wouldn't talk about his service in Indo China. If John Wayne said we were Right, what bothered Dad so much he didn't want to discuss it?" Second, Ward's history teacher invited a Vietnam veteran to speak to his class. Ward recalls, "He told us, quietly, that Vietnam was a land of horrors, and we were a part of that horror. He would not be specific, but the real gut wrenching instant was when a lovely Indiana farmgirl, whose brother had just been killed in Vietnam, ran crying from the room. She, and all of us, knew in that instant that her brother had died for nothing." By inviting an antiwar veteran to speak to his class, Ward's history teacher helped legitimize opposition to the war in a way that his classmate in the German school—a mere girl, and not "part of the Team"—could not. Just as important, Ward himself had begun to question the war. Although his teacher and guest speaker undoubtedly influenced him, Ward's conclusions were his own.[41]

FROM DISSENT TO PROTEST

Because the majority of Americans supported the Vietnam War in the mid-1960s and most schools—barring the occasional antiwar teacher—either promoted the war or maintained a discreet silence, how did antiwar students arrive at their opinions? What pushed them over the line from feeling troubled by the war to directly protesting it? After all, the questions the war raised for them did not provoke students like Pete Biscus, Mike Ward, or Brent Coatney to take up antiwar activism. Joyce Mitchel did eventually protest the war, labeling her activism "the most noble, unselfish, patriotic thing I had ever done in my life," but not until she was in college. So why did others demonstrate against the war while still in high school?[42]

Conservatives feared that outside agitators brainwashed gullible students. From the perspective of the students themselves, it is clear that inside agitators—parents and friends—wielded far greater influence. Eve Levin credits both family and friends with shaping her beliefs and encouraging her to act on them. As she remembers,

> My entire circle was very concerned about the Vietnam War. Most of us were staunchly opposed to U.S. involvement, and many of us were following our parents in this stance. My parents were active in the antiwar movement from early on, and they volunteered to process mass mailings because they had so many children to do the fold-stuff-and-stamp work. With parental approval, my friends and I went on protest marches and collected signatures on petitions to stop the bombing of North Vietnam. With our parents' support, we convinced school authorities to hold a "teach-in" one day, with guest speakers mostly from SUNY-B[inghamton].[43]

Her parents' initial involvement in antiwar work drew Levin in; later her parents encouraged and supported her as she moved into activism on her own.

Vicki Aldrich was part of a Quaker community in Jefferson County, Colorado. She participated in Saturday vigils against the war at a local shopping center with her parents and adults from her Quaker Meeting. She attended other protests with her friends and took a turn in front of the county courthouse in a twenty-hour-long reading of the names of Americans who had died in Vietnam as of June 1969. Aldrich states, "This reading of the names . . . was for me a type of graduation or right [*sic*] of passage into the adult world." Antiwar adults accepted Aldrich into the antiwar movement. They did not perceive her as too young to hold an opinion on the war nor too young to act on her beliefs.[44]

Whereas the religious convictions of her parents influenced Vicki Aldrich, Elizabeth Harzoff, who attended Charles F. Brush High School, in Lyndhurst, Ohio, found her parents' political beliefs compelling. They had been active in the Progressive Party in the 1940s—a group of left-liberals who disagreed with the anti-Soviet foreign policy of Harry Truman. Harzoff notes that her parents "had Socialist leanings, although to the best of my knowledge they were not party members." Many of her friends had parents of similar backgrounds, and they formed an activist social circle in Harzoff's high school.[45]

David Wachtel credited a wider circle of adults with influencing him: his parents, Mohandas Gandhi, Martin Luther King, Jr., and John and Robert Kennedy. No coercion or manipulation by adults controlled Wachtel's choice of mentors and heroes. His upbringing probably inclined him toward a liberal perspective, but by the time he was in high school he exercised his own judgment.[46]

Peers exerted stronger influence than parents or other adults in some cases. Richie Cohen, for example, initially supported the Vietnam War, but his friends in Greensboro, North Carolina, challenged him to think about it more deeply. They recommended books and articles that reflected their own views. Cohen told interviewers, "The more I read the more I began to agree with what they were saying." In time, Cohen became an outspoken antiwar activist.[47]

THE IMPACT OF NATIONAL EVENTS

Aside from the influences of parents and friends, the tumultuous nature of the times pushed students leftward politically. The police riot in Chicago during the National Democratic Convention in 1968 helped catapult some students into activism. By the time of the convention, the United States had been rocked by a series of body blows. In late January, Vietnamese communists launched the Tet Offensive—a massive enemy offensive on more than a hundred cities and towns in South Vietnam. American troops beat back the attackers, but the offensive exploded the Johnson administration's rhetoric about the progress of the war. In April, Martin Luther King, Jr., was assassinated; two months later, so was Robert Kennedy. Coming on the heels on these traumatic events, college radicals, including SDS and the Yippies, vowed to disrupt the Democratic Convention in August. With every avenue of peaceful protest blocked, they marched anyway and sat down in the street, snarling traffic. Then the Chicago police, many of whom had removed their badges and any identifying insignia, attacked. Nightsticks swinging indiscriminately, they chased, clubbed, and bloodied protesters, journalists, and horrified bystanders. Some of the protesters attempted to fight back, but it was a one-sided battle. More than six hundred people were arrested, and even more were injured.

Witnessing the riot on television shocked high school viewers. But not all students were safely at home. Paula Smith, a Catholic school student in Chicago, went to photograph the convention and demonstration for her school paper. Already a radical, Smith does not explain what else she might have been doing at the site of the riot, but she comments, "Like a lot of other kids, I was arrested. I had my head beat in. I saw a friend of mine shot by the police and killed for nothing." David Romano had a similar experience. Although he wasn't beaten, when he witnessed the brutal excesses of the police, he felt that he had "personally encountered the power structure incarnate." His politics swung sharply to the left after that.[48]

In contrast, a peaceful antiwar demonstration radicalized Jim Gardiner, a thirteen-year-old sophomore at the Bronx High School of Science. Gardiner had been involved in political activism since he was eight years old. His long history of involvement may account for the fact that, despite his youth, in April 1969 he served as a marshal for the Fifth Avenue Vietnam Peace Parade Committee's demonstration. His job was to maintain order among the marchers. In his own words,

> Here were thousands of people with a massive potential for revolutionary action passively marching in docile submission to the limitations set by the power structure. Rather than offer violence to the fascist, imperialist pigs whose malevolent acts perpetrated poverty, fear, and death on masses of oppressed people, they marched pointlessly past scores of policemen bordering their path. Yet I was one of them; I presumed to lead them. The total futility of mere nonviolent demonstrations became clear. The rain came down, baptizing me. I was a radical.[49]

Just as liberal student rights activists sometimes became more radical when their efforts to work through existing channels failed, Gardiner rejected nonviolent protest against a power structure that he characterized as fascist and imperialist. The charged terms students like Gardiner use reflect the extremism of the era. As we have seen, conservatives had their own intemperate language.

The events of the "Cambodian May" likewise roused or increased activists' outrage toward the war and the adults who waged it. In May 1970, President Nixon announced a "limited incursion" in the ostensibly neutral country of Cambodia. The hapless government of Cambodia had desperately tried to stay out of the war by not antagonizing the main combatants but found itself drawn into the conflict nonetheless. Communist Vietnamese soldiers used Cambodia as a sanctuary and transported war materiel through it; the United States had been bombing the country and crossing its borders for years prior to Nixon's announcement. For those who agreed that communism must be stopped at any cost, the U.S. invasion of Cambodia made sense. By 1970, however, strident anticommunism appealed to far fewer Americans. Moreover, Nixon had been elected in 1968 in part because he had promised to end the war, not widen it. When students at Kent State University demonstrated against the invasion, local officials panicked and called in the National Guard. During a tense confrontation with rock-throwing, taunting students, the Guardsmen turned to march away, then suddenly and inexplicably wheeled and opened fire, killing four students and injuring thirteen.

For some high school students, the Kent State killings turned their world upside down. They were incredulous that the armed might of the state could be turned against them. Alice Krause Young had just turned fifteen in a high school in southwestern Ohio. "I was young enough to be shocked and confused when the Kent State incident took place," she recollects. "Part of my shock was the fact that one of the young women who was killed had a name very similar to my own—her name was Alison Kraus, mine is Alice Krause." In fact, some of Krause's friends thought that she had been killed. At an unknown number of high schools, protests succeeded the initial shock. Athens High School, in Ohio, and others around the country closed for several days after the shootings, for fear of student protests. Gretchen Keller Gallucci, a student at Athens High, recalls, "This event made the Vietnam War more real for the high school students and teachers."[50]

Heightened awareness of the war and its effects on the home front cast a harsh light on the pettiness of issues that seemed so important to authorities in the high schools. In the wake of the killings, Alice Krause Young found herself changing. She observes, "I think Kent State started my rebellion, started my thinking for myself. Things we had been taught in school about the right to assemble, freedom of speech—were they all just talk and no show? My god, there were bigger issues in the world than girls wearing dresses to school and boys wearing their hair short." Like more radical high school students, Young began to link seemingly unconnected things—classroom lessons on democracy, dress codes, and antiwar protests that turned deadly—and to ask critical questions about the priorities and values of her elders as she sorted through her own beliefs. Jonathan Wallace did the same. Fifteen at the time of the killings and a student at Brooklyn's Midwood High School, Wallace asserts, "Kent State was my political education. What I discovered that week . . . was that America in those times was perfectly willing to harass, beat and kill its own children if they disagreed with government policy."[51]

The Kent State deaths overshadowed the killing of two black students at Jackson State University on May 14, 1970, then and in popular memory. Tensions over the war, racism, and the Kent State killings gripped the students at the historically black university, and a riot broke out after rumors spread that a black politician had been killed. Local and state police, as well as the Mississippi National Guard, converged on the university. In another murky set of events whose precise chronology and detail have never been established, state troopers peppered a women's dormitory and the street around them with bullets, killing one Jackson State student and injuring twelve. The other student killed was seventeen-year-old James Earl Green, a senior at Jim Hill High School. There is no evidence that Green was an activist of any kind. That evening he had been on his way home from work when he stopped to watch the drama unfolding at the university.

In both of these instances, observers have documented the provocative behavior of the student demonstrators. Yet the brutal response of authorities lacked any sense of proportion. In response to both shootings, antiwar activist Fred Halstead claims that more than four million college students struck, along with "uncounted high school, junior high school, and even elementary school students." High school students in New York City persuaded officials to close the high schools for one day to honor the dead. Jonathan Wallace gave a speech opposing Nixon and the crackdown on dissidents to strikers in front of Midwood High School.[52]

RADICAL STUDENTS' ANALYSIS OF THE WAR AND AMERICA

A sizable number of antiwar students found it difficult to isolate the Vietnam War from other social problems. "Eric Oakstein," a private high school student in New York, recalls that he "felt that something was evil about the war" and found it disturbing that the United States spent billions allegedly to bring democracy to South Vietnam but was unconcerned about conditions in its own ghettoes and rural areas. "It became logical at that point," he observes, "not only to oppose the war but to oppose American racism and poverty at the same time." The indifference of the government to problems at home in tandem with its bellicosity in Vietnam influenced Oakstein to become an activist.[53]

In a like manner, Laurie Sandow, a member of the New York High School Student Union, linked her critique of the American educational system to her opposition to the war. In an interview with a reporter from the national periodical *Nation's Schools,* she argued that schools taught students "perverted forms" of American ideals and that these "racist and imperialistic" values "rationalize wars like Vietnam." She added, "And it is systems like this that speak of our right to dissent but beats us on the streets of Chicago, and the streets of the ghetto, when we exercise it." Sandow's emphasis on an oppressive "system" with tentacles reaching from corporate boardrooms to the government and down into high schools and private life reflects the contemporary leftist critique of the United States.[54]

Radicals in the 1960s commonly analyzed the United States in terms of overlapping and intersecting systems of authority that oppressed various groups on the bottom of society. As his own perspective broadened beyond the plight of southern blacks, Martin Luther King, Jr.—far more radical in life than he is remembered since his death—linked war, racism, and poverty. Members of the Student Non-Violent Coordinating Committee (SNCC), SDS, and the Black Panthers referred to "the system" or "the establishment," but, like King, they perceived a web of oppressive forces strangling liberty and equality.

Thus, this analysis reverberated in the larger society. High school students who were paying attention—and the activists were—could hardly miss it. They appropriated these arguments because they made sense in the light of their high school experiences. Even as high school activists yearned for power within their schools, some of them simultaneously participated in the broader debate over American culture and values. These activists wanted to reform their schools but also dreamed of changing the world. Seeing connections between multiple systems of authority, great and small, sometimes led to odd and humorous juxtapositions. The underground newspaper from Niles Township High School, in Skokie, Illinois, for example, rang in the new decade in 1970 by lamenting how little had changed since 1960 and citing a grab bag of evidence: "A seemingly endless war in Viet Nam drags on, our johns still substitute for smoking lounges, citizens continue to choke on the air they breath [sic], study halls persist as detention camps, political repression continues unchecked at the Conspiracy trial [of the Chicago Seven], suspension is still punishment for truancy, and President Nixon listens only to the voices of silent Americans." This laundry list of woes mingles school and social problems and suggests that student suspensions were on a par with the Vietnam War and the government's crackdown on dissidents. As amusing as their grievances may seem, this is the authentic voice of the high school student movement. No one put these words into their mouths.[55]

HIGH SCHOOL ANTIWAR ACTIVISM

Beyond the urgency of democratizing and reforming their schools, activist students regarded the Vietnam War as the most pressing issue of their time. It inspired in them a number of responses. Many took part in national protests, such as the massive student strike on April 26, 1968, and the Vietnam Moratorium, a series of antiwar demonstrations coordinated around the country on October 15, 1969. Several students from West Milford (New Jersey) Township attended the moratorium in New York City and reported on it for their underground newspaper. Liberals rather than radicals, these students expressed the breadth of student antiwar sentiment, arguing, "We think this proves to the President that long-haired 'weirdos' aren't the only ones against the war. Many people who put him in office are still waiting for him to fulfill his promised of ending that unjust war." Niles Township Coalition members chartered a bus to take them from Illinois to Washington, D.C., for the second moratorium, held a month after the first. Although President Nixon ostentatiously ignored the marchers, claiming that he spent the weekend watching football on television, to the Niles Township Student Coalition members the event was "impressive," a "new and unique life experience," and "beautiful."[56]

All student antiwar protest did not take place off campus. As a response to the Kent State killings, Sharon Bialy-Fox, who attended Glen Cove High School, in New York, recalls, "A large number of students cut school . . . and organized a protest on the front lawn of the high school." Students at New Rochelle High School, in New York, formed the Ad Hoc Student Committee against the War in Vietnam and ran an advertisement against the war in their school newspaper. The advertisement landed them and the editor of the newspaper in trouble with administrators, who found it inappropriate. When the students sued, citing their First Amendment rights, they won. Here again, students connected—or circumstances forced them to connect—their status as minor students with their broader political beliefs.[57]

At least two high school students committed suicide in anguish over the American role in the war. Craig Badiali and Joan Fox were popular students in their New Jersey high school, where he was the president of the drama club and she was a cheerleader. But following the 1969 moratorium, the two students gassed themselves to death in Badiali's parents' car.[58]

High school draft counseling represented an effort to bridge the gap between school and the wider world by providing students with information about the draft and, more significantly, how to evade it. For students with little knowledge of how the Selective Service System worked, draft counselors explained the draft and students' options, both legal and illegal. According to the *New Free Press*, the Niles Township High School underground newspaper, a $100 grant from the Niles Township Student Coalition was "primarily" responsible for the opening of a draft counseling center in a nearby Jewish temple, although the original impetus to do so came from a Harvard University graduate. The paper noted, "The Niles township group felt the necessity for a draft information center in the area after noticing how high school students in the community ineptly faced the draft question." In New York City, Toby Mamis helped start draft counseling at Stuyvesant High School. This group, too, had to meet off campus because, as Mamis told a reporter from the *New York Times*, "our application for a school chapter was denied, even though we had the signatures of more than 1,000 students and 20 teachers."[59]

Walking out of school constituted another act of protest against the war. When authorities at Niles Township refused to excuse students to attend the Vietnam Moratorium or to permit students to hold a teach-in at the school on October 15, the infuriated students called for a "teach-out," rather than a strike, to be held at Northwestern University. Susan Worley was one of the "ringleaders" (her word) who organized a student strike that shut down Chapel Hill High School following the Kent State incident. College students at the nearby University of North Carolina, including some SDS members, aided the younger students, but the high school strike ended when the administration threatened to lower their grades for every day they stayed out of school. Worley did not return for two weeks, with no effect on her grades after all; other students were more easily intimidated.[60]

Worley's story illustrates the determination of conservative administrators to quell antiwar activism within their schools. Although officials occasionally allowed parental approval to excuse student absences for political reasons, others threatened to use their power over grades and records to prevent students from taking part in demonstrations, whether these were held on or off campus. Students regarded these actions as attacks on their right to assemble peacefully and express their views. Students were even more indignant when officials discriminated against some forms of activism but not others. Cynthia Barnes, who attended Wilmington High School in southwestern Ohio from 1968 to 1971, remembered, "Two . . . days stand out in my mind in 1970s. First was the day of protest against the Viet Nam war, when the school issued a preemptive statement that no absences that day would be excused. Later in the spring, when Earth Day occurred, the administration issued a decision that absences for Earth Day would be excused because the local veteran's groups were having a parade and event. I remember those of us who had skipped school the first time were contemptuous of this decision and did not participate in Earth Day."[61]

RACE IN THE STUDENT ANTIWAR MOVEMENT

The racial makeup of the high school antiwar movement is difficult to analyze. In society at large, historians have noted that, although a higher percentage of blacks than whites opposed the war throughout its duration, whites dominated the antiwar movement. Black activists did link the war to racism at home, but the latter seemed more immediate. This was true on the high school level as well. Black students who opposed the war often emphasized the primacy of the civil rights struggle. "Bill" told interviewers in 1970, "I think it's kind of stupid in Viet Nam right now. Here we are trying to uphold the Civil Rights of Vietnamese, when the Negroes don't have their own rights here." Seeking black participation in antiwar protests, sometimes white students used racial reasoning to attack the war and convince students of color to join them. The editors of the *New York High School Free Press* criticized military recruiting: "The only part of the world you'll see in the army is basic training camps and Vietnam. The only skill you can learn is how to survive in a jungle war, against our brother and sisters of Vietnam. The war we have to fight is here."[62]

In contrast to black students, white antiwar activists emphasized the war over domestic racism. Thus, their proclaimed opposition to racism seemed pro forma to observers. Don Schwartz, faculty sponsor for the Black Cultural Society, was angered when white students at the Bronx High School of Science announced a rally against war and racism but ignored racism on the placards they carried. On the West Coast, black students at Cubberly High School, in Palo Alto, California, were annoyed when whites organized a protest against the war and, incidentally, also against racism. For all that radical whites claimed to see connections between war and racism, they regarded the struggles of people of color as secondary, and brought up race primarily to recruit nonwhites to *their* cause.[63]

Nevertheless, high school students of color did take part in the antiwar movement; those who did also linked the war to racism and discrimination at home. One Latina student, Tanya Luna Mount, blamed the war in Vietnam for the meager funding of Mexican-American school districts. "We can't read," she commented sardonically, "but we can die!" Skywalker Payne dated her racial and political awakening to a conversation with a black Vietnam War veteran who told her, "The fight I want to fight is over here, right here." Although Payne did not protest the war while in high school, when she later did she observes, "I saw more hatred directed toward us for protesting the Vietnam War than I ever experienced directed toward me because of my skin color."[64]

CONSERVATIVE STUDENTS AND PROWAR ACTIVISM

Nationally, although a substantial minority of Americans supported the Vietnam War to its bitter end, prowar demonstrations never matched antiwar protests in either size or frequency. The same was true on high school campuses. Limited evidence suggests that the majority of students were in fact politically conservative in this era, but they left a far less visible record than did activists on the left. A poll of one thousand high school students showed that they preferred Richard Nixon to George McGovern by a two-to-one margin, and other sources reveal that both the Young Americans for Freedom and Young Republicans had high school chapters, although, paralleling the problems of documenting high SDS chapters, further details are lacking. Available evidence of conservative high school activism is thin and scattered.[65]

At Niles Township High School, Jeff Schramek and his friends organized a conservative group called "The Etruscans," whose avowed purpose was to "defend our great American civilization from meeting the same fate the Etruscans met." (The Etruscans ruled much of Italy before the Romans conquered them.) There is no way of knowing how many students joined the group, how long it lasted, how it related to other students and the school administration, or how it attempted to achieve its goals. The only surviving evidence that the group existed is a letter from Schramek to the editors of a left-wing underground newspaper, the *New Free Press*. The high school Etruscans identified "Communist Conspiracy" as the primary enemy of "American Civilization," which was no more original than the leftist student critique but reflected the worldview of conservative students.[66]

Opposition to liberal or radical students provides evidence of conservative activism, but it is not clear how well organized conservatives were. At the Bronx High School of Science, they established the Student Committee for Victory in Vietnam, which suggests both organization and an ongoing purpose. In a Dallas school, when antiwar students wore black armbands to show their support for the October 15, 1969, Vietnam Moratorium, others countered by wearing white armbands. Here, both sides formed identifiable groups. On other occasions, however, conservatives simply beat up dissident classmates. More than once, athletic coaches instigated violence against left-wing students; sometimes athletes themselves decided to attack and punish students. Christopher Eckhardt, who joined the Tinkers in their lawsuit concerning black armbands, was threatened by jocks, who told him that if he wore an armband, "you'll find our fists in your face and our foot up your ass." The gym teacher egged them on by making all students chant "Beat the Vietcong" as they exercised. Mike Ward, an Air Force brat, asserts that he "was willing to fight (after school) the weenies that wanted to wear the black armband against the Cambodian invasion." But this form of ad hoc activism left few traces. No underground right-wing high school newspapers apparently existed—perhaps right-wing student papers did not need to go underground—and there were few formal conservative high school organizations. One radical underground newspaper from Brooklyn Technical High School even slyly included a column called "We're Right," which was "set aside so that any right-winger can put his foot into his mouth in print." At least two conservative students took advantage of the offer.[67]

One reason why high school students who supported the Vietnam War left so little record of their beliefs and actions may be because there was little outlet for an outpouring of prowar sentiment. Although schools taught anticommunism and encouraged students to support the war, they did not attempt to mobilize support in a great moral crusade, as they had done during World War II. Apart from letter writing or attacking those who opposed the war, either verbally or physically, prowar high school students remained on the sidelines.

Although high school students differed on national politics and ideological persuasion, on some occasions—like the temporary alliances between black and white activists—students made common cause on local issues. Poll after poll revealed agreement on student rights, dress codes, and the need for student power. When the sixteen-year-old president of the Maine Association of Student Councils was removed from office after calling for "Student Power," Jeffery Hollingsworth, the treasurer of the Teen-Age Republicans of Maine, began a petition drive to have him reinstated. Insofar as students identified themselves as students, they were capable of broad—and to some school administrators, threatening—unity. When students looked beyond the high school, this consensus broke down.[68]

Overall, despite the heated rhetoric of both opponents and supporters the Vietnam War had a muted impact on American high school students. Civil rights, integration, and Black Power evoked the most violent responses on high school campuses. Empowering students within their high schools, defining and protecting their rights, engaged the largest numbers. Although race relations or student power did not concern all students, these were the two most significant issues on high school campuses in the late 1960s and early 1970s. In contrast, although the draft brought the war at least within the peripheral vision of high school males, it seemed disconnected from daily student life. Student reaction to the war ranged from apathy and indifference on one end of the spectrum, to passionate commitment and activism—most often in opposition to the war—on the other. In the middle was the muddled majority, some with reservations about the war, some with faith that the government was doing the right thing, but neither possessing sufficient conviction to take a public stand for or against the war. Here, too, high school students reflected their society.

WOMEN'S LIBERATION AND HIGH SCHOOL GIRLS

Isolating gender differences in the high school movement is far more difficult than identifying fractures based on race or ideology. Boys and girls alike opposed dress codes, with boys most often utilizing the courts to establish a right to wear hair long and girls employing collective civil disobedience so they could wear pants. Definitions of beauty and access to status based on beauty—the ability to run for homecoming queen or join the cheerleaders—animated numerous protests by students of color, both male and female. Race pride more than gender beliefs undergirded the latter movements. High school girls also took action in the antiwar movement. Although they were not drafted and thus not directly affected by the war, peace had traditionally been considered a legitimate female concern.

Thinking about war and peace, however, promoted a reevaluation of gender beliefs and practices among a handful of high school girls. As Alice Krause Young, the Ohio student, pondered the state of American society after the Kent State shootings, she recalls,

> Kent State made me angry. I began questioning things, like my father's blatant prejudice, my mother's submission to him in almost all things. Why were women treated the way they were? Why did my brothers have so much freedom, and my sisters and I were kept at home? Why did my brother's athletic ability mean more than my excellent grades?
>
> I'm still a bit of a "bra burner" today. I think it was started with Kent State.[69]

Once again, when high school students looked critically at their world, some reexamined all of their previously held beliefs.

At the peak of the feminist movement, consciousness of gender moved to the center of many women's thinking, yet this did not happen all at once. Eve Levin admitted that for her and her friends, women's issues were not "nearly as prominent a part of our consciousness" as the Vietnam War. This was the experience of older feminists in the antiwar and civil rights movements as well, as men belittled their initial protests against sexism. The fact that the war and racism literally killed—whereas gender discrimination appeared less urgent—contributed to women's hesitation to raise their own grievances and men's disinclination to heed them. By the mid- or late 1970s, beyond the scope of this study, it seems reasonable to surmise that high school feminism—like feminism in society as a whole—expanded dramatically.[70]

During the late 1960s and early 1970s, students of both sexes learned that their prescribed gender roles were "natural." Some girls, ahead of the curve, questioned these roles. Alice de Rivera challenged the admissions restrictions for girls seeking to enroll in New York City's specialized schools of math and science and won the right to attend Stuyvesant High School. As a guest editor for a student-run daily newspaper, Sharon Bialy-Fox wrote on women's rights. When she joined the paper's staff, she shocked her peers by volunteering to be the sports editor. She ended up sharing the job with a boy, although she did most of the work. Eve Levin recalls "being more conscious than most" about discrimination against women and girls. She and her friends agreed that "women should get equal pay for equal work, but . . . didn't challenge the gender system overtly." Still, when a teacher told her class that boys could be newspaper carriers and girls could babysit to earn money, Levin asked why girls too could not carry papers. The teacher responded that girls were not strong enough to manage the heavy newspapers, and her peers teased Levin for asking the question. Levin's youngest sister, however, sometimes filled in for her brother on his paper route, using a wagon to haul the papers—substituting brains for brawn.[71]

De Rivera and Levin confronted the existing gender system head-on. Other contemporary female students only perceived the discrimination practiced by their parents and in their schools years later, after the feminist movement forced widespread changes in both school and society. Looking back on their high school days, they regret the loss of educational and career opportunities because of gendered beliefs about girls' abilities and proper place in those times. After visiting her alma mater, Western Heights High School, in Oklahoma City, Deborah Astley laments, "I see all these athletic opportunities available to the females who now go to school there. I have to admit I resent that I missed out on this funding, but I am happy for the girls who came after." JoAnne Dickens graduated from high school in 1965. Because her parents assumed that she would simply marry and become a dependent wife, she "begged" them "for a chance to go to nursing school to no avail." They sent her brother to college instead. Betty Ann Hans's parents had similar beliefs. They told her "money spent on college [for her] would have been wasted," because she would "more than likely get married."[72]

Marriage thus remained a key goal for many high school girls throughout this period. "June Stewart" comments, "Any girl who wasn't going to college and wasn't engaged by Christmas of her senior year was in sad shape." She further explains that because of pressure to marry, "many of us clung to boyfriends, accepted the engagement rings and got married for all of the wrong reasons . . . none of us wanted to be left out."[73]

School administrators and guidance counselors bore some responsibility for channeling girls into appropriately feminine walks of life. A Union City, Indiana, student remembers that her school offered only three courses for female students: college preparatory classes, office studies, and home economics. The last option was for the girls not planning to go to college, "since preparing ourselves to be good wives and mothers was considered important." Kathy Goecke, from Aurora Central High School, in Denver, reports that her parents found the idea of college for girls "ridiculous," but the high school counselors "never encouraged me (and other girls) to pursue college" either. Parents and administrators reinforced social beliefs about women's talents and abilities, even after feminist rumblings had begun.[74]

Social class further influenced a girl's fate. In retrospect, "June Stewart" realizes that "there was a definite difference between us that had to do with economics. The girls whose parents were affluent were the ones who were in the college-bound set. Career choices for those going to college were basically going to either become a teacher or become a nurse." Kathy Goecke echoes Stewart's words. An anonymous e-mail respondent comments bitterly, "I think you would do all of society a service by exposing the way girls (especially girls of blue collar parents) were treated in the '60s. We were 8th-class citizens all the way. Told we couldn't go to college, not allowed to use our intellect. Athletics, music, academics—all beyond our reach." These students angrily mourned the fact that the sea changes brought about by the feminist movement came too late for them.[75]

STUDENT ACTIVISTS AND THEIR TIMES

Whatever the issues high school activists embraced, they sharply critiqued those who refused to speak up and lend a hand in shaping their society. In an article for the *New Free Press*, Allen Mott took issue with President Nixon's claim to represent a "silent majority" that backed his policies in Vietnam. "What is puzzling," he wrote, "is how does the President know they support him if they are all 'silent.' Perhaps even more important, why are they silent?" He concluded that if it existed, this group of people was more properly called an "apathetic majority" and argued, "Contrary to the criticism made by many members of the [Nixon] administration, I believe the citizens of this country who do take the initiative to actively demonstrate their feelings against a national policy are more patriotic than those who show no interest."[76]

Mott's point is well made. If one purpose of high school was, as educators claimed, to prepare good citizens, surely those who burned with outrage over injustices, debated how best to resolve to a bogged-down war effort, and tried as hard as they could to improve the world they were about to inherit were better citizens than the apathetic majority. What is striking about high school students in the late 1960s and early 1970s is the number of them who ardently cared about their education, their nation, and their planet.

Students similar to these activists in the 1960s—curious, questioning, restless under adult authority—no doubt have existed as long as there have been high schools. Whatever influences these earlier students may have wielded on the local level, in the aggregate American high school students had never previously constituted a national, identifiable movement. A glance at student movements around the globe and over time suggests that a combination of five preconditions heightens the likelihood of such movements occurring: critical mass, critical issues, social values that privilege either the educated or youthfulness, a shared perception among many educated youths that their elders are not in control of society or actively impede its progress, and at least a rudimentary ability to communicate with youths in different places. All five of these preconditions existed in the high schools of the United States in the late 1960s and early 1970s and helped create a student movement of unprecedented size, consensus, and effectiveness.

Because the majority of adult authorities who, activists argued, had bungled race relations, the Vietnam War, gender relations, and the entire educational system were conservative—and radicals attacked liberals as well for their part in these failures—it is not surprising that most high school activists were left wing. The relative passivity of conservative students is less easy to understand. Perhaps knowing their strength in numbers in the school and American society at large made conservatives underestimate the power and passion of the less-numerous left-wing activists.

American high schools were not well equipped to respond swiftly or flexibly to the challenges posed by the activists. These students felt stymied by the adults who controlled the schools. One student complained, "I'm really so frustrated. It is so hard to force teachers to talk or let you talk about things that are important to you and to the world outside." Rapid changes in the world beyond the schoolroom windows touched the hearts, fears, or imaginations of activist students. They never constituted the majority of students, yet they were visible enough to ultimately compel the attention of adults. The magazine *Nation's Schools* called them a "potent force." However potent they might have been, adults did not fully engage with their calls for thoroughgoing reform or restructuring of American society. Nevertheless, educators, journalists, and government officials did hear and respond to the broad-based criticism of schooling and education these students raised.[77]

SEVEN—COPS IN THE HALLS, STUDENTS ON THE SCHOOL BOARD

EDUCATORS RESPOND TO HIGH SCHOOL TURMOIL

n March 31, 1969, some teachers informed Peter Lawrence, principal of Wilbur H. Lynch High School in Amsterdam, New York, that a group of students was about to stage a walkout. Hastening to the scene, Lawrence found several dozen students putting on their coats. Somewhat to his surprise, the students doffed their coats and returned to class upon his request. Later that evening, however, his wife phoned him at a meeting to tell him that students were planning to demonstrate again the following day. Because his school district had no policies for handling student unrest, Lawrence decided to "play it by ear." First alerting his vice principals, he contacted the student strike leaders and arranged to meet with them at 11 p.m. Then he hurried to a board of education meeting that was coincidentally occurring at that moment and told the board members what was in the wind. Shocked and infuriated, some members reacted harshly, saying, "Let's lock them up!" and "Who put them up to it?" Lawrence was able to mollify them, however, and they agreed to let him handle the students in his own way.

Late that night, Lawrence met with student leaders and elicited their promise not to strike. The next day, he called an assembly to discuss the students' concerns, which centered on a $1.3 million budget cut and rumors that thirty teachers favored by students would be let go. Lawrence permitted the seniors to hold a separate meeting at school and helped them to set up a meeting with the board of education. Following the board meeting, Edwin Hardies, an electrician and board member confessed, "We were astounded at the knowledge, the astuteness, and the awareness of our students. . . . We were proud of the kids. They asked questions more detailed than many of the adults in this town have asked." Lawrence agreed, concluding that the incident had been constructive and educational—and not just for students. He believed that the board's receptiveness improved its reputation and created stronger rapport among students, teachers, and administrators. Buttressing Lawrence's opinion, vice principal Claude Palczak praised his handling of the crisis: "I'm firmly convinced that a straight authoritarian approach would have been disastrous."[1]

Not all high school demonstrations ended so neatly. When student activists wanted substantive changes rather than information or when violence resulted, reservoirs of resentment and bitterness sometimes remained after the confrontations, no matter who won. Journals for professional educators, however, tended to highlight events like those at Lynch High School that exemplified the openness and flexibility in the face of student unrest that these journals touted. But even in this story, published in the *Bulletin of the National Association of Secondary School Principals* (NASSP), opposing viewpoints leak through. Many board members initially took a hard line, and Palczak's defense of Lawrence's actions illustrates his awareness that not all adults would have applauded his stance.

College activism overshadows high school activism in popular memory, yet contemporaries expressed grave misgivings over the state of secondary education and worried that the emergence of protest and dissent among these young Americans signaled the unraveling of society. Parents, teachers, school board members, and school administrators differed in their views of the causes and legitimacy of dissent and advocated various responses, as did those outside the schools, including college and university academics, politicians, legislators, and social commentators. School administrators and members of the educational establishment left fuller records than did parents and teachers, so their views will be overrepresented. Elements of the adult response to high school unrest can be glimpsed in previous chapters; here their own voices grant us entrée into conversations they held with each other, more or less out of earshot of the students.

In general, adults can be grouped into two categories regarding high school unrest: hawks or doves. Contemporaries used the terms to identify supporters (hawks) and opponents (doves) of the Vietnam War. The characterizations work as well in assessing the adult response to high school unrest. Hawks took a hard-line approach to defending the status quo, saw student grievances as part of a broad, illegitimate attack on authority, and recommended using institutional power and force to maintain order.

Hawks were often the people most involved in the daily operation of the schools: principals, school superintendents, and members of school boards. In one study of twenty-three high school principals in New York City, for example, researchers found them "on the defensive, confronting an educational world they neither made nor anticipated; it is not surprising that their model for the future as well as their defense against the present is their vision of the past." Hawkish educators allied with political conservatives, who blamed societal breakdown on the erosion of parental authority as well as the intrusion of government into both family circles and schools. Parents and teachers often joined the hawks in demanding stronger discipline in the schools. Some government officials, viewing school dissent as the product of manipulation by older, outside groups, emphasized restoring order to the classroom rather than restructuring education or allowing students greater participation.[2]

Doves, on the other hand, accepted some elements of the student critique of education and society and recommended allowing students a greater role, within limits that they did not always take care to specify. Doves typically included academics, writers and editors of educational journals, and journalists in the mainstream popular press—that is, people not directly involved in running schools. Parents of activist students often supported their children. Teachers could be found anywhere along this spectrum; they tended to divide along generational lines, with older teachers more likely to identify with the hard-line approach and younger teachers more likely to sympathize with student demands. One book of oral interviews with activist women teachers revealed that most of them were young teachers in the 1960s. In contrast, interviews in 1983 with thirty-eight older teachers showed that most of them could be grouped with the hawks. Nevertheless, the American Federation of Teachers (AFT) supported student rights at its 1970 convention.[3]

Hawks and doves constitute convenient shorthand, yet it is important to keep in mind that these were fluid and dynamic groupings. Adults who were dovish on, say, dress codes, might agree with hawks about black student unions or permitting students to evaluate teachers. Adults also changed their minds. Doves might be pushed by repeated student demonstrations into the hawks' corner, or hawks might find themselves reluctantly persuaded to support dovish policies. Some adults preferred a cautious middle road, arguing that a judicious blend of concessions and firmness would yield the best results. One handbook for administrators recommended "a frank and genuine promise to investigate a complaint" or concessions to student demands "if no legitimate reason can be found to oppose" them, as well as "absolute" action against "ringleaders." The authors warned, "Vacillation will breed further discontent and further disruption."[4]

When the federal government entered the debate about how to handle high school rebels, again hawk and dove factions emerged. The Internal Security Committee and J. Edgar Hoover, director of the Federal Bureau of

Investigation (FBI), blamed outsiders and favored a law-and-order approach. Senator Robert Byrd (D-West Virginia) tried to interest Congress in a bill making the disruption of a school a federal crime, to quell what he called "a wave of anarchy and revolution engulfing high schools and colleges throughout the land." In contrast, the Department of Health, Education, and Welfare's Office of Education, headed in 1969 by Commissioner James E. Allen, established an Office of Students and Youth, run by twenty-five-year-old Toby Moffett. The U.S. Commission on Civil Rights conducted interviews with 277 high school students around the country in 1968–1969. Its dovish report praised students' "sensitivity, perceptiveness, and constructive thought" and sympathetically published their views. President Richard Nixon straddled the divide. Even as he marshaled myriad government agencies—mostly illegally—to investigate, disrupt, and quash domestic dissent, he paid lip service to the "legitimate demands" of American youth and urged school and university officials to give students a greater voice. By the late 1960s and early 1970s, high school unrest unleashed a wave of educational innovation, which at least temporarily amplified the voices of high school students as a group and conditionally admitted them to decision- and policy-making circles. This may suggest that the students won their battle for greater participation; however, as the era drew to an end, the final disposition of forces was by no means clear.[5]

FACING THE STORM AND TRACKING ITS CAUSES

In the early 1960s, the eruption of college student activism caught educators and the public off guard, particularly after the quiescent climate on campuses in the 1950s. High school unrest followed in short order, developing first out of the nascent civil rights movement and then from desegregation. This unrest, however, seemed to reflect community or national problems rather than a student movement as such. The first confrontations involving the rights of students to wear political buttons at school occurred in 1964 and 1965, student defiance of a ban on black armbands that led to the landmark *Tinker* case took place in 1965, and the first lawsuit over hair regulations went to court in 1966. It is surprising that educators did not recognize these disparate events as part of a wider social phenomenon until the late 1960s. As late as 1968, in fact after widespread unrest had already erupted, many educational journals still viewed it as a distant storm on the horizon.[6]

Educators told themselves that, having seen the storm coming, they had time to ready themselves, even though their professional training left them ill equipped to deal with it. Lloyd Peterman, principal of Oak Park High School, in Michigan, commented ruefully that textbooks in "school administration courses in grad school . . . did not even hint that we might face underground newspapers, student boycotts, or even student strikes—complete with picket lines and signs." Some credited college unrest with providing officials with a "primer" or "cram course" on student unrest.

Lawrence Brammer, chair of the educational psychology department at the University of Washington in Seattle, predicted (erroneously, as it turned out) that high school student activists were "destined to become the majority." Journal articles repeatedly admonished school officials to prepare for unrest. Even if administrators did not adopt the plans proposed by these journals, authors exhorted them to work out their own response well in advance. Walkouts or demonstrations, they warned ominously, could suddenly immobilize any school. Administrators should not think that because their school was rural, all white, or in a conservative community that they were immune to unrest. Statistics on high school unrest lent credence to their fears. A number of polls of secondary schools emphasized the depth and breadth of the problem.[7]

Not surprisingly, adults spent a good deal of time investigating student activists, attempting to gauge their attitudes and differentiate among them. School administrators and teachers took sabbaticals and traveled around the country, assessing the climate in the high schools and writing about their experiences. Teacher and administrator Philip Cusick actually attended high school for six months, hung out with the students, ate with them, and tried to understand the world from their perspective. Adults who studied the high schools anticipated that sharing the results of their research with teachers and school administrators would help them make more rational decisions about dissent. The unspoken assumption that administrators did not in fact know their students says volumes about the bureaucratization of the schools and the centralization of authority, which radical students often targeted in their critiques.[8]

Administrators who were completely out of touch with student attitudes could benefit from studying the results of any number of student polls. James Jacob, who worked for the education center of the Cincinnati public schools, polled more than ten thousand students in grades 10 through 12 in his district. The results showed that—surprise!—fully three-fourths of the students wanted a greater voice in school affairs, more than 60 percent believed black students should be encouraged to participate more, and 69 percent wanted race discussed in class. Perhaps more astonishing to beleaguered administrators was Jacob's discovery that 70 percent of the students polled felt pride for their schools. Jacob broke his information down by age, sex, and race, revealing that older students were more likely to support a school dress code than younger ones, and black and white students disagreed profoundly over whether schools should allow black student unions, create black history courses, or celebrate black heroes and holidays.[9]

Other polls, however, muddied the waters. The national *Life* poll in 1969 showed that 37 percent of students approved of cracking down on dissenters although 56 percent recommended "try[ing] to understand them." Yet another poll, published by the NASSP in 1974, revealed profound differences in ways in which teachers, administrators, and students perceived or reported conditions in their schools. More than 90 percent of administrators bragged that their school supported student activities, let students help resolve school problems, and opened student club membership on a democratic basis. Only about half of the students agreed with these statements, with teachers leaning more toward the administrators' view but still with substantially less agreement. Whereas only 16 percent of administrators conceded that they did not permit long-haired boys to compete in athletics, 37 percent of teachers and 71 percent of students claimed that their schools barred long-haired boys from these events.[10]

Observers also attempted to track student unrest in terms of where it occurred, what types of school—in terms of size, location, and the racial make-up of the student body—experienced the greatest degrees of unrest, and what precipitated it. Without a central clearinghouse for this information, however, gathering information proved difficult to do. One NASSP survey, undertaken in 1969, included only one thousand schools and relied on self-reporting. Dr. Alan Westin, of the Center for Research and Education in American Liberties at Columbia University, culled newspaper clippings for his study, which also came out in 1969. Toby Moffett, director of the U.S. Department of Health, Education, and Welfare's newly established Office of Students and Youth, hired a clipping service to scour newspapers for reports of high school unrest. The House Subcommittee on General Education undertook the most massive study, based on questionnaires sent to all twenty-nine thousand public and private high schools, for the academic year 1968–1969. Researchers from the Policy Institute of Syracuse University based their study on visits to twenty-seven public high schools in nineteen states in early 1970.[11]

This cumulative research yielded interesting results. Protests against school policies on dress, discipline, and curriculum made up the bulk of the disturbances across the board, but racial issues shook large, urban schools. In many cases, officials classified these protests as actual riots. According to the survey by the House Subcommittee on General Education, racial unrest occurred four times as often in urban schools as in rural or suburban ones, and half of the reporting urban schools with more than one thousand students experienced racial unrest. Geographically, southern and southwestern school districts endured less disruption than schools in other parts of the country. Dr. Stephen Bailey, chairman of the Syracuse study, summed up other key findings: the size of the student body mattered more than the school's location; well-integrated schools suffered more unrest than schools that were primarily black or white; majority-black schools with substantial black personnel experienced less unrest; and schools with lower daily attendance records had greater problems with disruption.[12]

Academic efforts to measure and categorize student unrest fell short of what principals needed, according to U.S. Commissioner of Education James E. Allen. In a speech to the NASSP in 1969, Allen urged school officials to seek out the causes underlying student militancy. Legitimating much of the student critique, he noted, "Our students are telling us that change is needed in our schools." He argued that student energies could be turned to good purpose if adults responded "patiently and thoughtfully." Outlining the liberal position on student dissent, Allen promoted relevance in course materials, efficiency in running the schools, greater participation by students and parents, respect for racial and ethnic differences, and the creation of channels through which students could express their grievances.[13]

Educators and other adults did ponder the question of why high school students dissented. What, they asked themselves, was causing these youngsters to rise up in rebellion? And why were they doing it *now?* For hawks, the answer was simple: high school students rebelled because college students rebelled, in simple imitation or because college students incited them. A 1969 *U.S. News & World Report* article quoted several officials (none of whom were educators) who categorically stated that outside forces sparked high school violence, as part of what Los Angeles Police Chief Thomas Reddin called "a criminal conspiracy . . . to bring 'the establishment' and the Government to its knees." Other hawks denied that student rebellion had any real substance. As one disgruntled school administrator in Texas told pollsters, "Though many complaints by demonstrators have a legitimate base, the major purpose of the use of these complaints is to challenge the validity of any sort of authority." Another grumbled, "Trouble in the high schools will continue to increase until some of the disciplinary powers are restored to the administration." For these officials and many hawks, the key question was not how schools should be run, but who was in charge.[14]

Doves, on the other hand, advanced a range of explanations for the high school student movement. One of the most common reflected their perception that social change had accelerated and that young people—but not their elders—were changing with it. In an article in the *Saturday Review,* anthropologist Margaret Mead argued that only the young dwelt comfortably in the world, that adult claims to authority had shattered under the impact of rapid social and technological change, and thus it only made sense to allow the young to participate more fully in society. Echoing Mead's analysis, Gordon Cowelti, an official in a professional educators' organization, argued, "The current generation of adolescents is more mature and sophisticated than earlier generations." Don Parker, an educator who interviewed a thousand people in thirty states and the District of Columbia, offered a list of "never befores" that he believed explained the unique perspective of the young, highlighting the unprecedented numbers, education, and wealth of the young as well as their exposure to sex, drugs, technology, information, and multiple political and religious beliefs. Other commentators added that students knew more about the world because of television, which made them more mature. Harold Taylor, one-time president of Sarah Lawrence College and author of a book on student unrest, told an interviewer that students now inhabited a separate sphere of youth and that their values differed from those of their elders. Furthermore, modern young people had "no sense of piety" toward traditional authorities. He declared this new state of affairs "healthy for society." Skeptical, the interviewer probed, "Even in high schools?" Yes, Taylor responded, "in that we have never been able in the high schools to generate a serious set of interests in what is happening in the society as a whole . . . for the first time we've got fifteen or sixteen year olds intelligently interested in foreign policy questions, looking at their lives, looking at their families' lives, looking at their society, both critically and creatively."[15]

High school youths, doves asserted, swam freely and confidently in the new environment while their elders floundered in the mud, trying to seal themselves off from the changes that were rapidly reshaping the world. Montclair, New Jersey, principal Kenneth Fish assailed schools as part of the problem because they "cling to traditions of the past, little heeding the rising aspirations of black people, the growing quest for participatory democracy, and the dynamically different world of the 1970s." Other critics noted the "unnecessarily rigid, authoritarian, old-fashioned, and otherwise unreasonable" rules that constrained students.[16]

Whereas hawks tended to identify with conservatives, doves ranged themselves on the left end of the political spectrum. At times liberals read their own agenda into the high school student movement and supported it for that reason. James Irwin, who identified himself as a "ghetto principal," wrote, "The wonder is, then, not that we have dissidents, radicals, revolutionaries, martyrs and missionaries, but that in a world that can spend billions on spacecraft to a dead Moon, but cannot budget enough money to abolish pollution, war, ignorance, and disease there are so few youths who have actually challenged the establishment." Only a tiny group of high school activists rallied around the causes Irwin enumerated; these were his issues, not necessarily those of high school students. Radical adults echoed the critiques of the most radical students. Sociologist Edgar Friedenberg, for example, called students the most discriminated-against minority in American society, a view few liberals would have accepted. Nevertheless, both adult radicals and liberals tended to approve of the student movement.[17]

WHO IS TO BLAME?

If some adults wanted to understand youthful rebellion, others wanted a scapegoat. In addition to blaming radical college groups, some cast their nets more widely to condemn those who, in their view, failed to understand the schools' mission yet still dictated how they should operate. Ira Marienhoff, a teacher at Hunter College High School in New York City, issued a sweeping condemnation of interfering courts, cowardly administrators, and apathetic parents and community members. Marienhoff attacked the idea that students were citizens before the law as a "grotesque misreading" of "judicial restraints devised for limiting the role of government in depriving [adult] citizens of their liberties without due process of law." He further criticized civil liberties lawyers for encouraging student lawsuits against their schools. Scott Thompson, superintendent of Evanston (Illinois) Township High School, agreed: "Those zealots who want students to play at school all the games of the adult world under the aegis of civil rights, and I particularly point to the American Civil Liberties Union, simply do not understand the Pandora's Box they're attempting so righteously to unlock." Others saw the crisis in the schools as emanating from within the schools, largely because of lack of discipline, but also because of "maverick teachers' feeding militant students with sympathetic support." Some hardliners argued that permissive educators had brought their troubles on themselves. One school superintendent from Michigan opined, "Prompt disciplinary action by all secondary and college administrators would have prevented much of the disruption over the past three or four years."[18]

Doves agreed that schools had created the crisis, but for opposite reasons. Rather than critiquing school officials as too soft, they regarded these officials as harsh and inhumane. Lawrence Brammer wrote that it was surprising not to see more rebellion, "in light of [school officials'] activities which tend to humiliate students and lead them to doubt their personal worth." Kenneth Fish, combining self-criticism with admonition, asserted, "Most of us who are principals act like autocrats. There used to be a time when we could get away with this. But the schools of the 1970s should be run by a coalition."[19]

Other doves assailed the structure of the schools. Newton Fink and Benjamin Cullers, a school superintendent and high school principal, respectively, echoed the radical student analogy of schools as prisons. In an article that compared schools, prisons, the military, and mental asylums, Fink and Cullers argued that all of these were "total institutions" that obstructed—indeed rejected—any possible participation from those living under their sway. In bureaucratic institutions, participation was "fragmented," but at least mechanisms existed to allow employees a voice. In contrast, in schools students were "amassed in a situation in which supervision in the form of surveillance and control is made possible." In a like vein, Frederick Wiseman's 1968 film *High School* portrayed high schools as dehumanizing factories, as did Charles Silberman's widely read polemic *Crisis in the Classroom,* published in 1970.[20]

Yet another liberal explanation for student unrest emphasized the lessons in civics that schools imparted. One high school principal noted self-mockingly, "The students, to our utter despair, are exhibiting—at long last—the very kinds of behavior we say to want to encourage, nourish and develop as responsible educators." Stephen Hess, national chairman of the White House Conference on Youth held in 1971, agreed: "These young people have been taught to take seriously and literally the words of our nation's founding documents, the Declaration of Independence and the Constitution, particularly its Bill of Rights." Joyce Mitchel, who graduated from high school in 1970, asserts that her teachers supported the minor rebellion her classmates mounted over a cancelled pep rally because it showed that "they had done their part as good teachers and taught us to stand up for our rights." These educators, and doves as a group, regarded much of the student movement as constructive and believed it might potentially reform the schools.[21]

ASSESSING STUDENT DEMANDS

Adults judged school policies or student demands by their "reasonableness," a word that reverberates through debates over the best response to student movements. Educators and administrators urged each other to accede to "reasonable" student demands. Courts often based their rulings on how "reasonable" school rules were. The NASSP published a book titled *The Reasonable Exercise of Authority.* Despite widespread use of the word, neither hawks nor doves could agree on what it meant; nor could they agree on whether it was "reasonable" to allow students to help define it.[22]

Hair and dress codes, for example, provided adults opportunities to consider whether their own rules were reasonable and whether student criticisms had merit. Rules about apparel generally caught flak from the educational establishment. Paralleling student arguments, these educators pointed out that hairstyles changed with the times and that earlier generations of American men had worn their hair longer than schools considered acceptable in the twentieth century. Friedenberg labeled dress codes "the basis for indoctrination with the values of a petty, clerical social subclass." One editor of the *American School Board Journal* commented, "Just wondering out loud. Might school boards now want to consider getting out of the beauty business and on with the business of education?" Other educators bypassed the issue of whether dress codes were right or wrong, focusing instead on the practicality of attempting to maintain codes when courts often ruled against them. The rules, they warned, had to be reasonable, and even then administrators could only hope "they stand the test."[23]

Granting student more leeway in how they dressed and wore their hair troubled administrators less than did demands for greater student power within the schools. The courts sided with the students often enough to give administrators pause, and educational journals uniformly recommended that administrators relax these rules. Moreover, as much as hawks hated to admit it, rules about dress were ultimately trivial and barely related to the schools' educational goals. Battles over dress and hair rules were nevertheless often closely fought. When the school board in Evanston, Illinois, debated whether to adopt a more lenient dress code, the board's president had to break the tie with his vote. He voted to liberalize the dress code.[24]

In addition to measuring how reasonable student demands were, adults also often invoked the word "legitimate," thus indicating their openness to some student demands, methods, and forms of organization. The term also signaled the reasonableness of their own stance and suggested that adults rejected students' proposals only when they were illegitimate. Even so hawkish an individual as FBI director J. Edgar Hoover conceded, "Legitimate dissent is part of our tradition." Hoover and others championed "peaceful change through democratic processes" and condemned other approaches, ignoring the fact that few meaningful democratic procedures existed for most high school students.[25]

The First Amendment guaranteed a right to dissent and thus constituted a far more substantive issue than dress codes. Did the First Amendment apply to students? When educators wrestled with student press freedom, for instance, those outside of the high schools embraced libertarian views, while those inside the schools had mixed opinions. Robert Sullivan, professor of journalism at Lehigh University, encouraged administrators to allow the "maximum degree of press freedom that can be accorded to students," even as he acknowledged that students needed to be taught good taste and libel laws. He argued that "knockout solutions" reflected "the authoritarian instinct of administrators who momentarily forget their roles as educators." Because the American Civil Liberties Union's defining purpose was the defense of civil liberties, especially First Amendment rights, the ACLU and its state chapters regularly championed freedom for the high school press, both above and underground. Dave Goldberg of the Chicago Civil Liberties Union estimated that his office fielded one phone call every three weeks concerning high school press freedom.[26]

Hawkish school officials, however, doubted that the right to a free press fully applied to high school students. One man asked Sullivan in disbelief, "Are you seriously advocating freedom of speech for minors?" As the editors of *Nation's Schools* pointed out, "many see an underground newspaper as a direct challenge to their authority and a threat to their standing in the community and school district." Indeed, as the point men for the smooth operation of the schools, officials came under pressure from teachers and communities to maintain their control. Samuel Graves, principal of Wellesley Senior High School, in Massachusetts, noted that his lenient policy on underground newspapers made him the target of angry teachers and the local American Legion. Although Graves stuck to his guns, others yielded to pressure to crack down. Students, quite frankly, were administrators' least powerful constituency.[27]

Because many adults in the wider society valorized press freedom and courts usually protected it, some schools lifted restraints on student publications, even to the point of tolerating underground newspapers. Dovish administrators like Graves tacitly or overtly accepted the presence of underground newspapers. Administrators at Valley Falls (Kansas) High School, for example, permitted students to write and distribute an unofficial paper called the *Draconian,* although they did monitor what students wrote. John Farinacci, principal of Cleveland Heights (Ohio) High School, remarked of his own school's underground newspaper, *Alice's Restaurant,* "The paper has made a lot of progress since the first issue. These kids are the movers, the reformers—and I back them one hundred percent." Few principals apparently went this far, but many did attempt to head off underground newspapers by tolerating, without censorship, a broader spectrum of reporting and commentary in aboveground papers.[28]

Teachers, too, sometimes supported students' right to a free press. Dorothy Settle, the advisor for the official student newspaper at Montgomery Blair High School, in Silver Spring, Maryland, dismissed criticism of the principal's permissive policy because, in her view, the student press could not be "legitimately criticized for expressing student opinion." Another commentator noted that, because the principal respected the student newspaper even after it ran three articles criticizing the school's counseling center, "[t]he editorial page, often overlooked in other school newspapers, became a real forum of ideas for the staff and student body" at Blair High School. Jacquelyn Piraino, a teacher at Niles North High School, in Skokie, Illinois, wrote to the editors of the school's underground paper, gently admonishing them to make their stories accurate and avoid snide commentary, but also praising their "grasp of what the issues are" and analysis, which she found "often good and remarkably in depth." She sent a cash donation with her letter.[29]

Doves praised lenient policies because they turned "a nightmare for many schoolmen into an acceptable outlet for student dissent." Others encouraged administrators to lift press censorship not only to give students a peaceful outlet for their grievances, but also to demonstrate democracy in action. Nevertheless, although educational journals praised liberal administrators, they also reported crackdowns on the student press. Student lawsuits also indicate that hardline policies on student press freedom prevailed at many schools.[30]

The First Amendment not only guarantees freedom of the press, but also allows for free assembly and the right to seek redress of grievances. Student demonstrations vexed administrators, but the courts and educational journals sent decidedly mixed messages. No one defended violent demonstrations, but peaceful ones created a dilemma. On the one hand, the courts struck down any prior restraints on students' right to assemble and voice grievances. As one school principal wrote ruefully, "Unfortunately, it is difficult to make rules about demonstrations on public property that are constitutional." On the other hand, the courts and educators recognized the need to maintain order in the schools, especially in secondary schools, and so upheld quelling demonstrations that did or might cause disturbances. Peaceful or not, administrators hated the publicity surrounding demonstrations, because they broadcast to the outside world how little control over students the officials had. For doves, easing the conditions that might lead to a demonstration was the best tactic; hawks preferred draconian policies spelled out in advance, swift recourse to police powers during demonstrations, and harsh punishments in their wake.[31]

Due process and democratic procedures raised anew questions about students' status and the educational mission of the schools. Hawks found democracy an inappropriate model for high school governance for several reasons. First, students were children, not citizens, and school officials bore responsibility for their education and behavior. Second, implementing due process and fleshing out disciplinary procedures to allow students representation and a chance to defend themselves struck many hawks as time-consuming and unwieldy. Third, they regarded students who complained about injustice as spoiled children and resented accusations that administrators and teachers abused their power.[32]

Doves, on the other hand, believed that, if schools preached democracy, they should practice it as well. Wallace Good, professor of education at Kansas State Teachers' College, mocked the hawks' views: "Of course, school authorities can always maintain that the students are too immature and that adult standards [of rights and due process] do not apply. Undoubtedly, students can learn from these experiences, but one wonders what they will learn." Ira Glasser, associate director of the New York Civil Liberties Union, argued, "In the classroom, we teach freedom, but the organization is totalitarian. The kids learn that when the values of freedom and order conflict, freedom recedes." Glasser further peppered an article on student rights for the educational journal *Phi Delta Kappan* with examples of officials' egregious disregard for students' rights, arguing that "these kinds of violations are *routine*" in public high schools.[33]

Although the U.S. Supreme Court outlined the minimum requirements for student due process in the 1975 case of *Goss v. Lopez* and the ACLU and educational journals repeatedly advised officials to steer to the right side of the law, principals continued to improvise when it came to suspensions and expulsions. Moreover, two years after *Goss,* the Supreme Court moved away from insisting on even minimal due process for students who were paddled at school. The Court asserted that fear of civil lawsuits would deter officials from abusing their authority to paddle and that requiring prior notice and a hearing "would significantly burden the use of corporal punishment as a disciplinary measure and would entail a significant intrusion into an area of primary educational responsibility." Once again, the Supreme Court gave with one hand and took away with the other.[34]

Although adults disagreed about the causes of student unrest and the legitimacy of their demands, they generally condemned the methods that students used to prod resistant administrators to listen to or grant their demands. Some feared that concessions to the demands of militant students signaled weakness, even if the demands themselves were reasonable. More than a hundred teachers in East Los Angeles signed a petition to this effect following the 1968 school blowouts. The fact that students couched their proposals for school reform as "demands" offended many adults, and they typically judged student boycotts, walkouts, and demonstrations—essentially anything that disrupted school—as counterproductive. A poll published by *Nation's Schools* in 1969 showed that 75 percent of administrators agreed with some elements of the students' critique of education but not, they emphasized, with "violent demonstrations." It is not clear whether the term referred to actual physical assaults on persons or property or included threats of violence or merely angry rhetoric. A few doves, however, contended that, lacking legitimate means of voicing their grievances, students had little choice but to disrupt school routines. David Kukla, of the Washington Institute for Quality Education, added that "the faults of student radicals do not excuse the principal from listening to their demands."[35]

RESPONDING TO DEMANDS FOR RACIAL RECOGNITION

When student demanded Black or Brown Power within the schools, adults often divided along both racial and generational lines. When black students at Chicago's Harrison High School walked out, protesting the principal's refusal to meet with them, twenty black teachers went with them and issued a manifesto supporting the students. Chicano teachers backed the blowouts by Mexican-American students in Los Angeles schools in 1970. Politically radical white teachers often championed liberal or radical student demands, no matter what color the student. As Kenneth Fish pointed out, and the increase in teacher militancy reinforces, because many teachers felt that they lacked power within the schools, students' call for participatory democracy hit home with them. Recognizing that teachers too could be "fed up with having to deal with rules made by a few other people," Youth Liberation of Ann Arbor encouraged student activists to seek out sympathetic teachers to support the students' cause.[36]

Teacher militancy, however, cut both ways. Paralleling actions taken by conservative students, conservative teachers sometimes staged counter-demonstrations against students or administrative concessions to their demands. Eleanor Fuke, who taught at a majority-black high school in Chicago, described white student and teacher backlash against the newly formed Afro-American Club, sponsored by three black and three white teachers, the latter freshly graduated from the University of Chicago. When the club sponsored two black nationalist speakers at a Black History Week assembly, a group of white teachers walked out in protest and rejected Fuke's suggestion of student-faculty workshops to air the grievances on both sides. Noting that faculty seated themselves at meetings according to their political beliefs, Fuke identified three groups: older, conservative white teachers; younger black and white radical teachers (Fuke put herself in this group); and moderate black teachers who supported the goals but not the methods of radical students and teachers. Here, race, age, and politics divided teachers and determined their responses to radical black and conservative white student activism.[37]

Because of white opposition and because the most violent or potentially violent high school confrontations stemmed from this deep fissure in American society, racial unrest proved a tougher nut to crack than dress codes or First Amendment rights. With the exception of the military, where, ironically, the viciousness of the war in Vietnam may have actually aided desegregation, no other American institution integrated so thoroughly and rapidly as urban public schools. But as schools desegregated and students of color flexed their muscles, administrators had to respond. Many chose to grant some students' demands by hastily creating classes on black or Chicano history. Permitting soul food or Mexican food in school cafeterias seemed relatively unproblematic, although some educators noted wryly that complaints about the food were endemic to schools of all levels. Others hired more nonwhite personnel, set up biracial committees to wrestle with racial antagonism, or held sensitivity training workshops. Demands for black student unions, however, put administrators in a quandary. Kenneth Fish, a dove, admitted feeling wary about black student unions. Nonetheless, he argued that this "is a road that needs to be traversed and smoothed." Because the road to black student unions was also the path of least resistance, administrators frequently allowed them, unless white students or parents expressed objections.[38]

HANDLING PROTESTS BY EMPOWERING STUDENTS

Debating the origins and legitimacy of student dissent was all very well and good, but beleaguered administrators needed practical means of responding to their restive students. Not surprisingly, the advice that poured from the educational and popular press ran the gamut. Doves urged schoolmen to listen to students and reform their schools accordingly. Lawrence Brammer argued that school programs had to "have a serious and significant social purpose, and must offer them [high school students] full partnership in the adult world." Brammer did not spell out just what a "full partnership" between high school students and adults might entail, nor did he consider legal or practical limitations on this suggestion. Nevertheless, by echoing the students' cry for relevance in their education and their demand to be taken seriously, Brammer upheld the two main pillars of activist student demands.[39]

As a first step toward bringing students into fuller partnership with officials, doves recommended transforming "'Mickey Mouse' student councils" or "sandbox [student] governments" by expanding them to include more than the precollegiate, high-grades crowd and allowing them some real power. But again, doves rarely addressed the question of how much power students or student councils should have and who would decide where the limits to their power lay. Doves hoped that creating—with or without student participation—student bills of rights and responsibilities could resolve these problems. It was a neat solution. On the surface such bills appeared democratic even while adults essentially asked students to collude in limiting their rights by tacking on an enumeration of student responsibilities, which frequently required students to categorize demonstrations, the distribution of unauthorized literature, and even the circulation of petitions as "disruptive," abandoning the very tactics—all of which fall under the First Amendment—that had gotten them the ear of the adults in the first place![40]

Student-written bills did not reject the linkage between rights and responsibilities or the idea that all rights had limits. But, as we have seen, they paid far more attention to spelling out how those rights would be protected and their limits negotiated than did adults. Moreover, doves sometimes missed or willfully refused to see the students' point. In his study of student unrest, principal James Ross Irwin, for example, advised administrators, "Get the local Board of Education to adopt a clear and unequivocal policy regarding student rights and responsibilities, including the right to dissent." He also advised hiring full-time directors of student activities, to "plan, guide, supervise and direct all student activities and student involvement in schools affairs." He urged creating a student advisory council, a student-faculty advisory committee, and a "truly representative student council." But Irwin did not consider consulting students in establishing their rights and responsibilities, nor did he inquire whether students wanted this kind of representation. Students in Baltimore rebuked their school for the bill of rights it created without their approval. Because the judge who heard their lawsuit agreed that parts of it were unconstitutional, school officials were forced to rescind it. In both Irwin's trumpeting of support for a handful of student causes and the unilateral action by Baltimore officials, we glimpse the highhandedness of doves who, while imagining themselves as allies of activist students, nonetheless betrayed them in presuming to speak and act for them. This was not the sort of partnership students had envisioned.[41]

However administrators chose to handle specific student problems such as dress codes, press freedom, racial conflict, or demonstrations, doves encouraged them to make at least token gestures toward including students in decision making. Permitting student participation not only answered their most common demand, but doves also believed it channeled student energies toward constructive goals. The phrase "channeling energies" suggested that students' activism ran like a natural force along the path of least resistance and that adults could contain and direct it for better purposes. Linking students' demand for a greater voice with their pleas for relevance, Fish proposed "setting up massive volunteer coordination programs" to let students tackle broader social problems outside the classroom. Consumer advocate Ralph Nader and other public interest groups agreed and published a manual highlighting the types of community projects high school students might profitably undertake. *Nation's Schools* issued a special report in 1969 detailing the ways in which schools had directed student activism into concrete accomplishments, including using students as curriculum consultants, using older students to teach younger ones, establishing days for students to take over administrative roles, and forming student advisory groups for principals, school boards, or both. In addition, as Fish and Nader had recommended, a number of schools encouraged students in community activism, thus displacing and defusing dissidence in school while satisfying students' desire for meaningful action.[42]

Beyond redirecting student activism into productive paths, doves believed that school administrators ought to listen to students, solicit their opinions, and even negotiate with demonstrators. As Kenneth Fish noted, "'Me negotiate?' [was] all too common a reaction" among administrators. But the advice givers reiterated endlessly the need to keep the lines of communication open. Some recommended enlisting the aid of third-party mediators or meeting on neutral ground.[43]

DOVES IN THE FEDERAL OFFICE OF EDUCATION

Responding to student unrest and the quarrels among educators over how to handle it, the federal Office of Education and its agencies weighed in on the doves' side. In 1969, the White House Fellows Association presented a report to the press titled "Confrontation or Participation: The Federal Government and the Student Community," which stated that the government should encourage student participation in school and politics. The White House Conference on Children and Youth, established in 1909 to permit adult experts to discuss problems relating to the young, became the White House Conference on Youth in 1971. That year, for the first time, the conference invited high school students—who made up nearly 40 percent of those attending—to speak their minds. Student delegates set up task forces on issues ranging from drug use to "Values, Ethics, and Culture." They created an education task force as well, but the sweeping nature of the topics the delegates took up reflected young people's desire to be heard on a broad range of issues. The delegates' recommendations paralleled what activists around the country were saying: a greater voice in school affairs, representation on school boards, updated curriculum, and greater institutional flexibility. They also demanded civil liberties, procedural safeguards of those liberties, and a clearer explication of their rights and responsibilities. The majority opposed the American war in Vietnam, supported the Equal Rights Amendment, and called for improved race relations. A government report on the conference emphasized that delegates sought greater involvement in society and the world, rejected unreasonable restraints on their liberty (especially regarding lifestyles), and embraced a broad humanitarianism. President Richard Nixon apparently read the report and, according to Stephen Hess, the conference chair, "directed all departmental secretaries and agency heads to appoint liaison officers who would coordinate a government-wide response to the Conference [sic] proposals."[44]

The following year, the government issued a follow-up report based on a survey of the thirty thousand business, educational, religious, and political leaders who received the conference report. The results showed the same mixed reactions as other measures of adults' opinion. On the whole, educators occupied the middle ground; businessmen consistently took the most hawkish and religious leaders the most dovish positions, illustrating how divergent community attitudes might skewer educators. Although half of the educators who responded found the report "important," only a third thought the report's recommendations were "realistic and relevant." One-half believed that *some* of the recommendations were useful. In terms of implementation, nearly 40 percent said they had already put these recommendations into effect, whereas a further 40 percent claimed to be still studying the report. Eighty-three percent of educators agreed that youth opinions should be solicited, but not quite 40 percent thought young people should play a role in making decisions. Doves in the Office of Education, then, lacked great influence with schoolmen.[45]

The White House Conference on Youth amplified the voices of the young, yet critics pointed out that even those who sympathized with the young often spoke *for* them rather than listening *to* them. Helen Baker, a youth advocate for the Ohio Civil Liberties Union, noted that the *Harvard Educational Review* published two issues dedicated to the rights of children but failed to consult any student activists: "Youth Liberation of Ann Arbor wasn't there; the Children's Rights Organization of California wasn't there; the editors of the high school underground newspapers were not there. Just a whole lot of professionals picking over the same old bones." This sense that adults advanced their own careers and profited by writing about disaffected students provoked the young founders of the Elizabeth Cleaners Street School in New York to write a book—both to tell their own story and raise money for their struggling free school.[46]

RESTORING ORDER TO THE SCHOOLS

Repudiating the doves' self-proclaimed willingness to listen and bend, hawks invoked an academic domino theory. Students, they insisted, would interpret any concessions as a sign of weakness and press further demands. Thomas Shannon, school attorney for the San Diego schools, warned that student confrontations with adults had but one purpose: to force the "total, blind, and unconditional acceptance of [their] demands." Hawks emphasized projecting authority and communicating firmness to student opponents almost as much as they recommended specific tough and firm *acts*. Martin Kalish, president of the Organization of Detroit School Administrators, argued, "The first priority is to establish order in the schools."[47]

For those who agreed with Kalish, large numbers apparently believed that calling in police forces would be the best way to demonstrate their own authority and bring the activists to heel. A 1968 poll of sixteen thousand school administrators around the country revealed that, despite the warnings they had received, fewer than half of the respondents had made plans to handle student unrest. Of those who reported themselves ready to deal with aroused students, an astonishing 69 percent said that they would immediately summon the police. A poll of school administrators in Bergen

County, New Jersey, where the state board of education *required* plans for handling unrest, likewise showed that 65 percent would use police as the first—not the last—resort. These administrators regarded student unrest as disruption pure and simple; they dismissed even the possibility of dialogue, preferring to brandish the forces at their disposal. Whether shows of force from outsiders convinced students that administrators were in control is an open question.[48]

Doves emphasized communication rather than control, yet they agreed with hawks that administrators could not rule out calling the police to quell unrest and restore order. Because administrators bore responsibility for the safety of students, staff, and school property and because violence against both persons and property had marked some high school demonstrations, adults agreed that—as a last or first resort—police forces could be useful. Whereas hawks looked to the police as their primary line of defense, doves recommended that administrators' plans for handling unrest clearly delineate the point at which the police would be called in, but strongly recommended against letting matters reach this extreme. One teacher argued that violence at his school was averted only because, "in full view of the demonstrating students," the assistant principal asked the police to leave.[49]

Educational journals reflected this ambivalence toward the use of state force. Although agreeing that friendly cops could save troubled youths from lives of crime and that frequent contact with police officers could improve relationships between students and law enforcement workers, they also noted instances when the police presence ruffled community members and parents. In Tucson, Arizona, for example, some criticized a program to place plainclothes policemen in the local schools as "the first step toward a fascist state" or "one more threat to the disadvantaged child in an already hostile world." The Arizona Civil Liberties Union opposed the proposal as well and filed suit to stop it. Other commentators noted the high costs of hired security or the legal and procedural obstacles to police officers questioning students on school grounds. Moreover, although Fish conceded that law-and-order responses were sometimes necessary, he reminded administrators that, once they called in the police, they temporarily relinquished their own authority over the school. George Shepard and Jesse James, writing for the Office of Education of the U.S. Department of Health, Education, and Welfare, argued that, rather than simply assigning police to patrol the schools, it would be better to create "wide-angled community involvement programs" to draw police, students, parents and local residents into an alliance to improve schools and community.[50]

Despite educators' misgivings, numerous school districts throughout the country hired security guards. Newark, New Jersey, had at least one guard in every school, with four or five in every high school. Philadelphia put two police officers in every high school, and Chicago had 270 plainclothes officers in fifty-one schools. These programs cost already struggling school districts millions of dollars, so some turned to community or parent volunteers. Whether they used police officers, hired security forces, or local volunteers to maintain order, administrators attempted to convince students that these outsiders constituted an organic part of the school community, rather than an occupying force. Educational experts advised not only that security forces be dressed in plain clothes, but also that they be young, "hip" in appearance—wear their hair longer than regular police officers, eschew suits and ties in favor of more casual attire—and should befriend as well as discipline students. How effective these individuals were is unclear. Alexander Hamilton High School, in West Los Angeles, employed two security officers, one black and one white. Students referred to them by their last names (Tack and Nevilles) and viewed them with a kind of tolerant contempt, calling them "narcs" (narcotics agents). On the other hand, the racial disturbances that had previously shaken the school receded when this author attended Hamilton, between 1973 and 1976.[51]

Hawkish administrators found some allies in the federal bureaucracy and government. At the same time that the Office of Education embraced the liberal view of high school dissent, other federal agencies reacted with suspicion. In a hearing on Washington, D.C., schools before a subcommittee of the House Committee on the District of Columbia, members grilled the superintendent and assistant superintendent of schools, as well as the president and several members of the D.C. Board of Education about the inclusion of seventeen-year-old Ronald Hughes on a panel to choose the next superintendent of schools and pushed them to define the specific age at which public school students could play such roles. In the fourteen days of the hearings, congressmen fired off hostile questions about security in the D.C. schools, a student bill of rights that the board of education supported, and a freedom school operated by black students. Assistant Superintendent George Rhodes, Jr., bravely argued that students all over the country, backed by the courts, demanded their rights, but by the third and fourth day of the inquisition, he had wilted considerably.[52]

Parents often supported the hawks in school administration, unless their own children were activists. The 1969 *Life* poll found that only a quarter of responding parents thought students should have more say in policy making or valued student participation. Sixty-two percent agreed that "maintaining discipline is more important than student self-inquiry," and 63 percent thought that administrations should "crack down" on "unruly students." One-third of teachers, in contrast, favored greater student participation, and only 27 percent valued discipline over self-inquiry. Half of the teachers polled nevertheless preferred quelling disruptors. Cracking down, however, did not always obtain the desired results. One rural school in Boxholm, Iowa, which had not thus far experienced student unrest, took the preemptive step of hiring a new principal who had headed a boys' camp in California, under the mistaken impression that they had gotten themselves a real disciplinarian. When it turned out that the new principal, Harold Jokela, preferred to chat with misbehaving students over a Coke, the irate school board fired him, sparking the very student demonstrations the board had hoped to head off.[53]

Other school officials attempted to walk a middle line. Administrators in Oakland, California, informed the editors of *Nation's Schools* that having granted the "reasonable demands" of students, they would regard any further student demonstrations as disruption and would hand out Fs and suspensions or prosecute students through the courts, as seemed appropriate. They further announced that police would patrol the school area. The New Jersey State Board of Education condemned violent or disruptive demonstrations while ordering schools to take measures to address students' legitimate grievances.[54]

Hawks found the "knockout" approach, as journalism professor Robert Sullivan called it, more appealing than compromise. Whether they used hired guns in the halls or strict rules and suspensions, their tough stance communicated these administrators' defense of the status quo and traditional hierarchies of rank and power. Some hawks, however firm their commitment to resisting change, nevertheless recognized that the strongman model of leadership might not always work. One very odd internal memorandum to New York City high school principals, which high school radicals allegedly obtained and then published in an underground newspaper, reveals cracks in the hawks' position. In words strikingly redolent of the McCarthy era, the undated memo argued that the student movement intended to destroy American society. "Theirs [student radicals'] is a struggle without quarter, fought with total commitment. It will demand and challenge our best efforts, as total a commitment, all our resources. It is a struggle without second chances." Although this assessment implied that only an equal commitment on the part of authorities could stem the tide, in fact the memo's recommendations to the principals contradicted themselves. In one place, the memo stated flatly, "Discussion perhaps. Negotiation, no," and reiterated, "there is no compromise with and no appeasing those who play confrontation politics." At the same time, it advised administrators to be flexible, reasonable, and accessible and to "keep the lines of communication open." And although students were "totally" committed to destroying society, the memo warned, "[i]t is perhaps as dangerous to overreact as to ignore danger signs." To the principal reading this memorandum, now scratching his head and wondering what he should do, the memo advised delay, because "transient issues may die stillborn." But ultimately, once "[a]ll attempts to resolve the problem have failed," the memo fell back on the liberal solution: "student clamor for an immediate hearing must be granted."[55]

Was this the best (or the worst) the hawks could do? Threaten, delay, and then listen to students in the end? Perhaps it was. It was one thing to handle one or two incorrigible students, but something else to face an enraged and aroused student body. The memo attacked principals who had allowed "the number of disorderly students . . . to go unchecked," but the reality remained that, however reluctantly, principals often had to meet students on their own ground. They were facing a movement, not scattered disciplinary problems.[56]

HOLDING THE LINE VERSUS REFORM OF THE SCHOOLS

As student unrest ran its course, administrators divided sharply over how to respond. A 1969 poll revealed 51 percent of those polled agreed that students should have a greater voice in running their schools, but fully 49 percent disagreed. Looking more closely at the questions pollsters asked reveals how little some administrators were willing to concede to students. Although nearly three-quarters of respondents approved of student advisors to the administration, only about one-third thought students should have a role in formulating rules or enforcing discipline, less than one-quarter wanted students as voting committee members, only 18 percent would grant them a voice in curricular matters, and only about 5 percent wanted students to evaluate teachers or the grading system.[57]

Liberal educational journals drew attention to schools where administrators "opened up" to students, to use contemporary terminology. But because officials, teachers, and parents often preferred "clamping down," these reports may be skewed. One survey by a House of Representatives education subcommittee showed that only 8 percent of principals who reported student unrest claimed to have made "substantive change" in response to it. Without knowing how these principals defined "substantive change," we cannot necessarily conclude that the other 92 percent of principals simply cracked down until they broke the spine of the student movement. If students only demanded minor adjustments, principals might not report substantive change. Moreover, since some administrators regarded any concessions to students as the deathblow to their own authority, they may have simply denied that any changes they agreed to were "substantive."[58]

A good number of schools nevertheless did adopt a more flexible, open stance, even in the face of parental or community opposition. Liberal responses took a variety of forms. Some changed school rules in accordance with student demands or institutionalized greater communication with students. Principals established open-door policies, allowing students access to their offices to express grievances or make suggestions. Some began to meet regularly with students, either with members of the student council or a broader cross-section of the student body. After a cascade of serious demonstrations in Cincinnati schools, the superintendent appointed several student committees to investigate student opinion, define school problems, and propose solutions.[59]

In addition, students began to appear on school boards, boards of education, city councils, and special municipal committees, although just how often this occurred is impossible to tell. These students were usually nonvoting members, although the two Berkeley High School seniors who sat on city committees apparently could vote. In 1969, Barbara Marshmont, a sixteen-year-old high school junior, became the first student to sit on a state board of education, as a nonvoting member, in California. Marshmont was chosen from members of the State Student Council Association, so she was mostly likely a moderate rather than a radical. At one of her first meetings with the board, however, Marshmont disagreed with State Superintendent of Education Max Rafferty that Eldridge Cleaver's bestselling book *Soul on Ice* was "obscene." Newark, New Jersey, brought in a more radical student when the mayor appointed seventeen-year-old Lawrence Hamm, leader of the Newark Student Federation, to the school board. Not all high school students celebrated the inclusion of their peers in adult-dominated bodies. Youth Liberation of Ann Arbor argued that this simply made it appear that students had gained representation without granting them any real power. Donald Reeves, of New York City, regarded the inclusion of students as mere window dressing and as an attempt to undercut the student movement.[60]

A number of secondary schools responded to students' desire for greater participation, more relevant curriculum, innovative teaching methods, and greater respect for students as individuals. These measures—often minimal—may have been exaggerated by liberal educators. Nevertheless, they tacitly acknowledged that some arrows from the students' critique of education had found their targets. Moreover, some administrators agreed to tinker with both the structure and content of modern education with an extraordinary range of experiments. Sweeping aside the stale curriculum and hierarchical authority that had encased the schools like suits of armor, students and adult allies freed educational systems to stretch and reach in new directions.

Many of the new educational experiments paralleled those begun by students themselves, but, whereas student-directed educational innovations, often without significant adult advice, took place outside the formal educational apparatus, here students, teachers, and administrators collaborated to create both new and hybrid forms of education. Students and adults from Hyde Park High School, in Chicago, for example, abolished the despised tracking system, created nearly two dozen new courses, and interspersed large-class lectures with small group work. Students at Concord High School, in West Hartford, Connecticut, designed their own summer school course on the inner city, chose their own textbooks, selected the teachers, and raised money so that both Concord High School and inner-city students could attend. Inner-city students in Los Angeles, frustrated by the lack of relevant written course materials, wrote and published their own anthology, which the school board considered for citywide adoption. At John Browne High School, in Flushing, New York, the senior English course followed the regular curriculum but also allowed students to use class time to carry out studies on subjects of their own choosing.[61]

New institutional forms appeared, either alternative schools that operated on campus alongside the traditional school, or completely new schools. Drawing inspiration both from freedom schools organized by civil rights workers in the South in the early 1960s and freedom schools that sprang up in the wake of teachers' strikes and student boycotts, students from Eastern High School in Washington, D.C.—with the support of school administrators and the school board—set up a part-time freedom school across the street in a Lutheran Church. Students took their required courses at Eastern half the day, and then went across the street for electives that students had designed, taught by teachers the students had hired, and funded with grants from foundations that students had solicited. In Philadelphia, the Parkway School won fame as a "school without walls," because it had no buildings or campus. Students could sign up for a variety of classes taught anywhere in the city. A number of local businesses and museums, including the zoo, a science museum, an art museum, an insurance company, a drug manufacturer, and a television station, cooperated in offering classes. From these examples, it is clear that when administrators opened their doors, students surged in, bringing passion, enthusiasm, and new ideas with them. High school students willingly took on new responsibilities if given some real power to put their ideas into motion.[62]

The significance of the changes that blew across the waters, however, should not be exaggerated. Although these examples spotlight those school administrators who boldly waded into new streams, many did no more than gingerly dip a toe, by introducing a class on black history or putting a student on a faculty committee and letting it go at that. Others, whose stories attracted less attention because they ignored the advice of educational experts, simply cracked down more intensely until they drove the last vestiges of student activism out of sight. One student told interviewers that officials at his school in New York City "pull[ed] out all the stops" to prevent the formation of a student union by threatening to keep students from graduating, withholding or writing poor letters of recommendation for college, and reminding both students and parents that if their sons could not get into college, the draft boards might snap them up. In Maryland, the Montgomery Student Alliance reported several such incidents. We cannot know how often administrators used measures like these, yet they underscore the very real power officials possessed. In addition, although student activism may have been the most legitimate (from the doves' perspective) issue roiling the high school environment, it was not the only one. Schools in the 1960s simultaneously wrestled with the drug culture, student pregnancy, and rising violence and vandalism. Linking all of these developments, as hawks often did, permitted administrators to justify instituting more repressive control of students than ever before.[63]

Doves often linked the concessions they recommended that administrators make to emphatic statements about students' responsibilities. They hoped doing so might assuage conservative fears of liberty run amok. While conceding certain rights to high school students, liberal adults insisted that students recognize and shoulder their responsibilities as students and citizens. The printed word lacks nuances; if we could hear the authors speak these words aloud we might better be able to gauge what they meant. In some cases, the argument that responsibilities must accompany rights sounds almost like a quid pro quo: only bearing responsibilities entitles one to rights. But, when James Allen called on schools to grant students "broader rights and responsibilities," he implied that students *wanted* greater responsibilities. In contrast, some adult commentary carries a subtext that immature students demanded rights without accepting their concomitant responsibilities.

In short, in much of this discourse adults defined rights less as inborn and inalienable entitlements than as the just reward for taking up societal responsibilities. This view sits uncomfortably with the Bill of Rights, which is not, after all, paired with a Bill of Responsibilities. Throughout American history, the powerful have denied full rights to those who did not, or could not, fulfill all of the responsibilities of citizens. In these debates over students' rights and responsibilities, it is clear that most adults believed that minors could claim junior citizenship at best, with a miniature set of rights to go along with their smaller burden of responsibilities. They implied that students had too much of a sense of what was owed to them and not enough of what they owed to society. Diane Divoky, who sympathized with the students, wondered, "To what extent can sophisticated adolescents be considered adults when they are still legally children?"[64]

Conservatives had the easier task when it came to assigning roles and status to students. They believed students should obey parents, teachers, and other adult authorities and prepare themselves to enter adult life. In terms of their status, youths were children. Liberals ran aground on the same shoals that confounded student activists. Both agreed that students were citizens, yet neither took a careful look at how their youth necessarily modified their status as citizens.

As they puzzled over students' status as citizens, adults found even the categories of rights and responsibilities obscure at times. Student demands to evaluate their teachers, to have a say in hiring and firing, to help shape school curricula, and to sit on school committees or boards of education could be construed either as rights or responsibilities. In asserting their right to do these things, students simultaneously announced their readiness to take on greater responsibilities and become partners in the process. Hawks rejected their demands on the grounds that students did not have such rights. Liberals, more lamely, argued that they were not ready for such responsibilities. Logically enough, activist students pointed out that the best way to prepare themselves for responsibilities was to begin taking them on. Hawks appeared oppressive to these students, whereas liberals often seemed hypocritical.

Extremely limited evidence nonetheless suggests that school administrators as a whole edged ever so slightly toward the dovish position over time. A poll of administrators in 1969 revealed that, although 44 percent felt less sympathetic toward student protests than they had the previous year and 39 percent felt their attitudes had not changed, 47 percent reported greater sympathy for student activism. Another poll of school superintendents showed a decline in schoolmen's willingness to use police to break up student

demonstrations. In 1968, 69 percent had indicated that the police constituted their first line of defense, but by 1971 this number had shrunk to 47
percent. Whether this trend continued beyond 1971 is unknown. The fact
that repeated polls showed administrators split nearly evenly between
hawks and doves must caution us against the biases in contemporary literature on education. It is entirely plausible that some school officials attributed diminishing student unrest to their own stern responses rather than to
their openness to student grievances.[65]

Indeed, some administrators accepted activist students' rhetoric of grievances and disempowerment only to reverse the parties they identified as ag-
grieved and powerless. When Toby Moffett, director of the short-lived Office of Students and Youth, agreed to speak on "Student Militancy" to the
National Association of School Boards' 1970 convention in San Francisco,
he blamed student militancy on officials, stating bluntly that "[t]he denial
of basic rights in most of the nation's schools is probably the greatest con-
tributor" to student unrest. He urged administrators to listen to and work
with students. But the speaker who followed Moffett opened his address by
asking plaintively, "But when do we start talking about superintendents'
rights and school board members' rights?" Thunderous applause greeted his
remarks, in contrast to the tepid response to Moffett's speech.[66]

Hawks regarded rights and power as zero-sum operations: students could
only gain them at the expense of adults. Doves, in contrast, shared with activists a sense of expanding possibilities that could provide advantages for
all parties. But because doves agreed with hawks that students were not
quite full citizens, they could not articulate a defense of students' rights capable of silencing—let alone convincing—the conservatives. This boded ill
for the long-term future of students' rights.

In the short term, we may view the debates between hawks and doves
over their respective visions of education as a swing of the pendulum between the poles of tradition, hierarchy, and control, on the one hand, and
innovation, egalitarianism, and freedom, on the other. Such oscillations in
educational trends have marked the history of schooling in America, and
thus it is hardly surprising that the 1950s, an era marked by an emphasis
on convention and conformity in education, would be superseded by opposite trends in the 1960s. From this perspective, we could predict the
swing back toward the basics in the 1970s and 1980s, as indeed occurred.

Casting the history of schools in the late 1960s and early 1970s in terms
of running battles between progressives and traditionalists omits the element of this history that stunned educators on both sides of the divide—
the role of students in moving the pendulum in one direction and their in-
sistent presence in this debate. Adults held many of their conversations
about students and education behind closed doors, in legislative offices,
and on the pages on journals that they alone read, yet the real action was
in the schools themselves or, less frequently, in the courts. Both educational traditionalists and progressives were accustomed to sparring with

one another, yet they had never previously had to justify their views to students or to engage them directly as interested constituents. Had the desks suddenly expressed a preference for how they were placed in the classroom, educators could not have been more taken by surprise.

By refusing to alter their relationships with students and by emphasizing order over reform, hawks took the simpler path. Tradition, precedent, and many teachers and parents were on their side. Defining activists as rebellious children meant that hawks did not need to wrestle with the dilemmas that doves faced. The sheer size and breadth of the student movement and the power of the allies who supported it, however, forcibly complicated the black-and-white world many hawks preferred. What were administrators to do when cracking down, rather than intimidating disruptors into compliance, mobilized ever-larger numbers of students? How should they respond when judges, whom hawks counted on to bolster their authority, accused them of running "enclaves of totalitarianism"? Might not order be established sooner by negotiating with students, as educational journals advised, instead of simply suspending them? Their reliance on tried and true arguments and tactics did not guarantee the hawks an easy passage through this era.[67]

Doves found this passage still more difficult. At least hawks could plainly identify student activists as their opponents. Doves, in contrast, required delicate footwork to maintain their putative alliance with activists without actually embracing them as equals. Few were up to the task. Student activists, as we have seen, foundered when it came to articulating a critique of childhood. Doves proved equally poor at defending it. The lowering of the voting age to eighteen in 1971 provided an opportunity for doves to explain why that age should serve as the cut-off between adulthood and childhood and to explicate what they understood childhood to mean. Eighteen-year-olds won the vote in part because at that age the men could be drafted. Doves nevertheless could have pulled out their arguments linking rights to responsibilities to justify setting childhood below the age of eighteen. There is no evidence that they did so, either in their dialogues and confrontations with students, or in their conversations with other adults. Without countervailing arguments about the necessity of limiting the rights and powers available to those who were legally children, doves left themselves open to attacks from both hawks and student activists.

Because hawks acquiesced in granting student demands only when forced to by court orders or by the sheer determination of student activists and their allies and doves (and their activist allies) could not build a sturdy legal or philosophical edifice to bolster these demands, the victories won by students—which appear to have been simultaneously widespread and thin—stood on wobbly foundations. Pressure by activists of many different types—students of color seeking to create institutions to recognize and nurture their distinctive histories and culture, student rights activists looking to establish the young as citizens, student power advocates yearning to reform education and alter relationships between youths and adults, and left-wing radicals dreaming of global revolution and reform—forced a variety of responses from educators. Yet, if this pressure eased, would the schools revert to their old forms? Had students successfully dealt themselves and their successors into the game as participants? Would there in fact be successors, or would student activism fade over time?

As the late 1960s melded into the early 1970s, few could have discerned the future shape of education. Adults recognized the transformations public high schools had undergone in the span of a decade in terms of the makeup of the student body, composition of course work, electives, and extracurricular activities, and, most of all, attitudes of students and the relationships between adults and students. Yet the continuing standoff between educators of differing philosophies called into question the permanence of these changes. Doves gained the upper hand, ever so slightly, because the turmoil in American society suggested that traditional approaches were obsolete and because student initiatives—polite and lawful or angry and violent—added force to dovish recommendations. Hawks remained in the wings, however, unbeaten and with powerful allies of their own. All it would take was a slight rearrangement of the social forces then arrayed to tip the balance back in their favor.

EPILOGUE

Susan Bowman Prendergast attended Hunterdon Central High School, in Flemington, New Jersey, from 1968 to 1972. The *Lamp,* her high school newspaper from these years, provides a composite snapshot of a single rural high school that encapsulates and reflects many of the social forces that tore through American high schools—urban, suburban, and rural—in the late 1960s and early 1970s. In 1968, the school paper revealed Hunterdon students to be a fairly docile and conservative group. A mock election in 1968 resulted in a victory for Republican presidential candidate Richard Nixon, with independent conservative George Wallace coming in second, and liberal Democrat Hubert Humphrey trailing behind. With the approval of adults, Hunterdon students protested the proposed building of a jetport in neighboring Solberg but otherwise exhibited little activism in the pages of this official paper. Five Hunterdon graduates had already died in Vietnam, but student memorials on their deaths emphasized honor, God, and country. Only about fifty students attended a program on the war that was held in December 1968. The paper did not cover local issues such as desegregation, student rights, or dress codes.[1]

By 1970, however, changes had begun percolating. The *Lamp* took an editorial stance against the draft, arguing, "No one should be forced to fight against their will." A student union formed, and the student council, which had previously supported administration views, wrote a student constitution and

pushed for and won a student-faculty review board to hear student grievances about discipline. Some students attempted—without success—to forestall the firing of two popular teachers. Girls began to take boys' shop
classes. The paper now paid more heed to national issues, including the
trial of the Chicago Seven and the painful last years of the Vietnam War.
One Hunterdon teacher returned from the war, and though he wrote in the
Lamp that military service was his duty and upheld the bombing of Vietnam, he also asserted, illogically, that the United States should not be in
Vietnam. Astoundingly, he added, "I am not a draft dodger, but I feel if a
man wants to go to Canada or any other country of that kind and stay, it is
alright." The tenor of this school-sponsored paper shifted perceptibly leftward in these years.[2]

Despite this shift, Hunterdon Central students never became as radicalized as students at some other high schools. They decided against sitting in
to protest the firing of the two teachers and opted for petitions to the
school board instead. The *Lamp* editorialized against student protests. In
May 1970, the student council voted down a proposed student strike to
show "concern over President Nixon's policy in Vietnam and Cambodia,
and as a protest to the shooting deaths of four Kent State college students
by National Guardsmen [*sic*]." Moreover, racial unrest did not trouble Hunterdon Central High School, largely because the student body was overwhelmingly white. Blacks appeared in the *Lamp* only on the sports pages,
and even there, as of 1970, the school had only one black football player.[3]

On the other end of the spectrum, in 1968 when SDS leader Todd Gitlin
visited his alma mater, the Bronx High School of Science, he found the
students in the midst of a heady, though brief, experiment to create the
school of their dreams in partnership with sympathetic teachers during
the Ocean Hill–Brownsville teachers' strike. Gitlin characterized these students as "restless and inventive and taken with the radical possibilities of
their generation."

The distance between the experiences of Hunterdon and Science students cannot disguise the fact that a certain restlessness and inventiveness
characterized many high school students in this era. Cheri Yannuzzi observes that her rural Pennsylvania high school lacked the "huge unrests" of
the times, but when one hundred students protested the dress code it
"made quite a stir." When 250 rural students at a youth leadership work-
shop in Stevens Point, Wisconsin, met President Nixon's Secretary of Defense, Melvin Laird, the reporter who covered the event pointed out that
they framed their questions "earnestly" and "politely" but nonetheless let
Laird know that they opposed dress codes, censorship, "outmoded sex
laws," and the war in Vietnam. But Marilyn Hall, who graduated from
North High School, in Bakersfield, California, found her high school
"incredibly straight" and the high school experience "very insular." Sandra Kral graduated in 1969 from a Chicago high school and recalls, "Unrest is too strong a word. A small group of students chafing under the

rules, cutting classes, trying to be more free" better described the atmosphere at her school. Some schools felt merely a ripple, and others were
nearly swamped by tidal waves of activism and dissent, but few public high
schools were completely untouched by the tumult of the times.[4]

HIGH SCHOOLS AND THE 1960S

Indeed, broader social trends nurtured the development of high school
unrest. As Samuel Huntington, an advisor to the U.S. State Department, observed in 1975, "People no longer felt the same compulsion to obey those
whom they had previously considered superior to themselves in age, rank,
status, expertise, character, or talents. Each group claimed the right to participate equally—and perhaps more than equally—in the decisions which
affected itself." Huntington's remarks could well have applied to high
school students, for, like other contemporary groups, they too pushed for
participation and questioned their elders' insistence upon deference and
obedience. One veteran high school teacher stated, "The boy who's sure he
knows better than me and the President of the United States how to end
the war [in Vietnam] is not going to take without protest my order to trim
his hair. . . . He is no longer in awe of me or the President."[5]

High school dissidents attacked the status quo largely because of its distance from what they believed were core American values. The black revolution initiated the process of ripping away the lies and myths that en-
shrouded race relations in the United States. A convergence of events and
intellectual trends—including World War II, the black migration, the militancy of black veterans, the cold war, new ideas about race, and the rise of
new media, especially television—created the conditions under which black
voices could finally be heard by the white mainstream. Black youths took
active roles in the subsequent rights revolution, which inspired numerous
imitators among other social groups who made similar critiques of American society. Mexican-American, Native-American, and to a lesser degree
Asian-American high school students played similar roles in their own
racialized movements, which owed much to the black example. In all of
these cases, what originated as calls for inclusion and access to power and
opportunity evolved into demands that their racial and ethnic differences
be highlighted and respected in the high school environment.

The war in Vietnam provided another impetus for high school unrest.
Even though very few high school students actively opposed the war, its
unpopularity made it not only possible, but for some young people impera-
tive, to question society's authorities. The fact that many school officials
would not permit the subject to be discussed in the classroom raised troubling questions about the war and the relevance of the curriculum. When
officials permitted only the expression of prowar views, some students perceived not indifference to pressing contemporary issues, but rather an un-
derhanded, and thus illegitimate, desire to manipulate student opinion. As

the public debate on the war grew more heated, young Americans could see that adults did not always agree and, further, that ideas could have life-and-death consequences. Moreover, if adults could be wrong about Vietnam, they could be wrong about other things as well. For a handful of high school activists, the war revealed American imperialism under the mask of benevolence and supplemented the critique raised by people of color.

College dissenters also attracted the notice of high school students. Although high school activism did not simply mimic college activism, nor did college students lead it, the older students' revolt against constraints imposed upon them by university administrators inspired high school students, who saw that their own school rules hemmed them in still more tightly. Witnessing the stormy passage of slightly older students through the educational system helped high school students define their own issues and provided models for collective action, as did the other social movements of the time.

Finally, the counterculture provided many high school students with an issue that seemed particularly germane. As long hair, blue jeans, and casual attire became increasingly fashionable, the power of administrators to dictate how students would dress and wear their hair brought home to them the dimensions of their own powerlessness. Here the personal and the political merged. In demanding control over their own persons, students challenged the broad powers school officials possessed. Conversely, having awakened to an understanding of their powerlessness, some students began to look beyond dress codes to see how the educational system as a whole shut them out of decision making and representation.

In these ways, high school students absorbed the lessons and messages drawn from outside societal conflicts at the same time that local conditions galvanized them to respond to specific issues. Desegregation forced students to confront racism and race relations in their own schools; students collectively attacked school regulations once grudgingly obeyed or surreptitiously violated; and rhetoric about democracy, power, and rights encouraged students to envision new types of education and new relations between students and educators. A few students looked beyond the high schools to address issues such as the war in Vietnam, feminism, or the environment. In sum, a substantial number of students served notice to adults that neither they nor their schools were hermetically sealed off from the wider world. However we choose to define "the sixties"—as a quest for true democracy, a hunger for authenticity, a revolt against authority—high school students played an active role, contributing to both the dynamism and turmoil of the age.

THE SIGNIFICANCE OF YOUTH DISSENT IN THE 1960S

But what exactly did students contribute? How does examining their experiences add to our understanding of the 1960s? In part, it depends upon how we choose to look at this era or which perspective we adopt. If we gaze broadly over the events and trends sweeping the nation in the 1960s, high school activism exhibits something of a tag-along quality. College students rebelled against old-fashioned rules and curriculum; so did high school students. Nonwhite adults demanded rights, access, and inclusion while emphasizing their racial and ethnic differences; so too did young students of color. Adults protested the war and contested the rigid gender system; high school activists did the same. From this perspective, hawks who derided the student movements as little more than "monkey see, monkey do" have a point.

The degree to which high school dissent reflected other forms of unrest was less a result of simple mimicry than a demonstration of how thoroughly dissident ideals and practices permeated American society. Moreover, despite the historical amnesia that has blurred these events, high school unrest rattled adults as deeply as other contemporary movements for change—and sometimes more deeply. When Toby Moffett began his new job as director of the federal Office of Students and Youth, he assumed he would concentrate on minority youths or work with street gangs. He was astonished, and not greatly pleased, when he was ordered to drop these issues and focus on turmoil in the high schools.[6]

Moffett believed that the impetus to study and understand youth unrest came from elite policy makers whose children challenged their rules and worldviews. This explanation hardly seems sufficient, because very few dissidents had parents who were important figures in the government and many activists shared the views of their parents. There were, however, celebrated cases where high-ranking officials found themselves at odds with their children. Vice President Spiro Agnew played the heavy-handed father when his teenaged daughter Kim wanted to wear a black armband to observe the 1969 moratorium. Although he would not permit her to do so, his reasoned arguments in favor of the war failed to convince her. "All right," Kim said, "but why not just get out of there?" Robert McNamara, Secretary of Defense from 1961 to 1968, had a son in a private high school through the late 1960s. Although Craig McNamara did not then openly protest the war, he began questioning it as early as 1966 and at age seventeen developed an ulcer, in part because of his conflict with his father. Similar clashes between youths and adult authorities—parents, teachers, administrators, and government officials—reverberated throughout the United States in this era, at the dinner table as well as in classrooms and courtrooms.[7]

If we substitute a close look at youth and childhood for the bird's eye view of the 1960s, a different vista unfolds. The history of young Americans has yet to be written, but a swift glance at the twentieth century reveals the whipsawing movement of teenagers in and out of adult (or quasi-adult) status: as workers (or managers in training) before the Great Depression; competitors to be removed from the job market and defined as dependents during the New Deal; patriots mobilized to do their part in World War II; and children to be forced back into institutional care in the postwar era. We do not know much about their own roles in contesting, negotiating, or embracing these adult initiatives, but their activism in the 1960s suggests that we should look more carefully and search for the precursors of youthful dissent.

A fruitful place to begin such a search is in the youth cultures of the twentieth century. A youth culture appeared among working-class Americans in the early 1900s and spread to the middle class by the 1920s. This youth culture distinguished itself from the adult world by its emphasis on fashion, entertainment, and sociability. Youth culture was in fact the vehicle for the consumerist challenge to the older ideals of thrift and economy. Derailed by the Great Depression and World War II, youth culture was reborn in the postwar era of affluence. In both the 1920s and 1950s, some of its elements were subversive of the established order. The dawning consumer age of course eventually became the established order, but youth culture in both eras tacitly questioned society's views about female agency and initiative, race relations, conventional morality, and adult authority.

In the 1960s, youth culture broke out of the narrow confines of consumerism and became politicized. High school students became self-aware in ways absent from the earlier eras. They identified themselves as a cohesive group not simply in their choices of fashion, music, and dance, but in terms of their subordinate status in school and in society. Moreover, whereas youth culture in the 1950s mocked adult values and conventions, activists in the 1960s sought to change them. Dissidents in the 1950s shrieked and fainted when Elvis Presley appeared, combed their hair into beehives and duck's asses, and read *Mad* magazine. As forms of rebellion, these constituted little more than disgruntled mutterings under the breath. Rebels in the 1960s not only met authority head on, but also did so armed with cogent arguments in defense of their rebellions.

By their very emphases, youth cultures place a premium on youthfulness, understood more as a set of attitudes, sense of style, and relationship to the consumer market than as a matter of chronological age. When adults dip into youth culture, they send a message that the world of youth, with its focus on pleasure, is more attractive than the adult world. Adults who affirm the positive elements of youth culture may consequently persuade the young to avoid premature admission into adulthood and responsibilities. Activists in the late 1960s and early 1970s, however, understood that real power accompanied adult responsibilities. Whether they sought to change the world or merely change their schools, activists recognized their need for power. Adults who toyed with youth culture—growing their hair half an inch longer, learning to dance the watusi, or hemming their skirts above the knees—did no more than take a vacation from adulthood, maintaining intact the two distinct spheres, whereas high school dissidents longed to merge or at least smudge the boundaries between their world and that of adults. They certainly did not reject youth culture, but they simultaneously reached out for adult powers. This mass mobilization of youth *as* youth demanding to be consulted about the laws and social customs that defined their status has no precedent.

THE LEGACIES OF HIGH SCHOOL ACTIVISM IN THE 1960S

Beyond examining the place of high school unrest in the larger narrative of 1960s history or focusing on the history of youth, we may also consider the significance of these student movements in terms of the legacies they left behind. If we stop the story in the mid-1970s, high school students clearly won some important victories and broadened their powers and rights. Demands of black and brown students to establish social groups based on racial classification were ambiguously granted—depending very much on the attitudes of local officials. Classes on black and Latino history, however, became commonplace. Today many mainstream textbooks include these histories and some high schools offer specialized courses on them. The *Tinker* decision affirmed the citizenship of students, and numerous other cases on dress, hair, student newspapers, and political activism expanded students' First Amendment rights. The *Goss* case increased students' rights to due process and to hearings and appeals in matters of school discipline. Courts increasingly placed the burden on educators to justify their regulations, and professional journals warned school administrators to move cautiously, because courts, parents, and communities could no longer be counted on to uphold administrators' authority. Critics of the content and methods of public high school education added to students' pressure to reform curriculum and teaching practices.

The state of secondary education in the early twenty-first century reveals both continuities and changes since the mid-1970s. The erosion of students' status seems easiest to document. If some adults accepted the possibility of more egalitarian relations with students a generation ago, the majority have moved decisively in the opposite direction since then. According to one study of American teenagers, 146 of the 200 largest cities had teen curfews by 1997. Malls and other quasi-public places have enacted restrictions on their presence, making clear that control, not partnership, is the dominant paradigm for adult-youth relations once more.[8]

Adult control extends beyond physical mobility. Restrictions on dress and appearance flourish. In a report published by the Education Commission of the States in 2001, every state except Massachusetts permits some form of dress code, including the imposition of school uniforms. Students are sent home for hairstyles that officials deem outlandish. Other schools have wrestled anew with how to handle provocative dress, such as Hooters T-shirts, Confederate flag paraphernalia, and gang colors, often resorting to simple bans of the offending articles. It is not clear whether students have any voice in creating these rules, a key demand of students in the 1960s. Student rights to free speech and free press have shrunk. Although court decisions continue to play lip service to the *Tinker* formula for determining when students' First Amendment rights can be curtailed, they have considerably broadened the scope for official censorship. Searches of students' persons and possessions are routine at some schools; others use metal detectors or urine testing.[9]

The diminution of students' legal rights as citizens, moreover, occurs in a vastly different high school milieu. While secondary schools in the late 1960s and early 1970s were under pressure to desegregate, that pressure has recently eased as courts have lifted mandatory integration orders for schools in the South, giving them so-called unitary status. In the North and Midwest, thanks in part to a Supreme Court decision that decoupled suburban schools from metropolitan schools and exempted the former from the requirement that they pursue racial balance, high schools are far more segregated by race than they were thirty years ago. By 2000–2001 a study conducted by the Harvard Civil Rights Project reported that 80 percent of the average white student's classmates are white. At the same time, minority enrollment in public schools has expanded dramatically. In this context of largely resegregated schools, interracial violence in the schools, not surprisingly, has diminished as a social concern, and few people mourn the de facto defeat of an earlier vision of interracial schools. Because racial nationalists in the 1960s and 1970s promoted separatism, perhaps this could even be read as a victory; however, because nonwhite schools generally serve the poor and are drastically underfunded, it is a difficult victory to celebrate.[10]

Today's school segregation results not only from court decisions and white flight from the central cities, but also from the retreat of middle-class and rich children into private schools or their own homes. One study estimates that nearly 900,000 children were homeschooled in 1999, and the numbers of students attending private, charter, or homeschools continues to grow. The majority of children not attending public schools are white and, in light of the commitments of income and parental involvement that the alternative schools (especially homeschools) require, at least middle class. Charter schools, publicly funded but privately run, and special academies for minorities provide new educational institutions for poor and minority students. Although some have claimed that competition from these alternative schools will prod the public schools to clean up their act, it is more likely that the broader societal retreat from public spaces and institutions will continue, leaving public schools starved for funds and students alike. Whatever the consequences for students' educational attainments, it is certain that the lack of a common school experience will fundamentally alter the fabric of American society. This is not to romanticize the common schools. The public schools of the 1960s, with their sort, grade, and pack approach to education, created the conditions that, in conjunction with other trends, sparked the student movements of the 1960s and early 1970s. But Americans in that era still mostly shared the belief that public schools served—or should serve—the common good, an increasingly alien concept in our time, with its impulse to privatize everything.[11]

In conjunction with changes in society as a whole, students themselves may have changed. A survey of high school teachers in 1978 asking about disciplinary problems with students revealed five key trouble areas: fighting, drugs, insubordination, profanity, and vandalism. Strikingly, categories of disruption such as boycotts, walkouts, petitions, and underground publications—which would have ranked high on teachers' lists before 1975—disappeared. In short, all of the problems cited in this 1978 poll are individual; the collective actions taken by students of the earlier era vanished. Or did they? Another study of 159 widely scattered high schools in 1977 revealed that only 47 percent of high school principals believed student dissention and activism were decreasing, while 50 percent thought it was increasing. Forty percent of reporting schools had experienced some kind of student demonstration or confrontation since 1972, whereas nearly 60 percent had not; depending on what poll one consults, these figures are not that different from those of the late 1960s and early 1970s. Catalyzing issues for students after 1972 continued to be racial discrimination, dress codes, and student publications. This evidence, maddeningly, leads in two directions: either student dissent degenerated into individual rowdiness or it continued to be collective and aimed at specific school problems.[12]

Questions about the outcome of high school unrest parallel the debate about the fate of the 1960s. Did the era come to a definitive end, as marked by the "Days of Rage" staged by the Weather Underground in 1969 (itself a spin-off of the defunct SDS), the Kent State shootings in 1970, or the end of the American war in Vietnam three years later? Or instead did the 1960s become transformed into multiple movements that carried the spirit of the 1960s into the subsequent decade and even into the present? If we define the 1960s as a constellation of specific power and rights movements and—most crucially—the antiwar movement, then clearly the 1960s came to an end. Alternatively, if we define the era by its spirit of restlessness, yearning for reform, and utopian hopes for a world reborn, then we must recognize that such sentiments are never completely absent but rather surge and recede in different historical moments.[13]

We may read the results of high school dissent in much the same way. More research needs to be done on teenagers in the late 1970s and 1980s before we will have a good sense of how the 1960s played out in public schools, but the extraordinary awareness of a collective identity among high school students—however fractured by race, class, or ideology—and their collective faith in the possibility of change clearly diminished at some point after 1973. It may well be that the divisions eventually overwhelmed their fragile but palpable unity as students; the identity politics that have fragmented the larger polity may have divided high school students as well. As optimism about social change dimmed in the 1970s and grand projects of revolution gave way to more modest, locally based reform movements, high school student activists too may have lowered their sights. Shocks such as the Watergate scandal and OPEC oil embargo, both climaxing in 1973, may have disillusioned students and robbed them of the energy needed for continued agitation and protest. It is also possible that high school administrators adopted draconian tactics to drive wedges between students and prevent cohesion and organization. In the study of 159 schools discussed above, 71 percent of school principals favored the use of suspensions in handling student disruption. As long as they adhered to the legal niceties, a legacy of the 1960s, principals could probably get away with this.[14]

Despite the erosion of some of the gains made by students in the 1960s and their diminished group cohesion, those who imagine that public high schools have once again become holding tanks for passive teens (as they were reputed to be in the 1950s) or that school officials have regained all of their former power are deluding themselves. High school student activism and dissidence do continue, sometimes following older issues, sometimes breaking new ground. Some students today, like those of the past, possess an actual or intuitive sense of their rights. Before the Iraq war began in 2003, Bretton Barber, a junior at Dearborn (Michigan) High School, was sent home for wearing a T-shirt that lampooned President George W. Bush as an "International Terrorist." The principal cited the *Tinker* dissent rather than the majority opinion in an attempt to convince Barber that he had no right to wear the shirt to school, but Barber had already read the case on the Internet. "I knew that wasn't how the case came out," he told a reporter, "but I didn't argue with her." Knowing the law and his allies, Barber contacted the Michigan Civil Liberties Union. The following November, a federal judge ruled in Barber's favor.[15]

While students continue to fight for free speech and the right to dress as they wish, they have also branched out into new realms. Some students have fought against prayers in public school ceremonies, and others have demanded the right to religious expression in schools; both have won some victories. Gay rights have surfaced as an issue for high school students, as they have demanded the right to organize into clubs and attend school functions in same-sex pairs. Other students have challenged drug testing and punishment for what they publish on the Internet on their own time and computers.[16]

Today's activists have outside allies, as did their counterparts in the 1960s. The American Civil Liberties Union and its branches remain the most important ally in legal battles. The ACLU maintains a students' rights page on its website and posts news about impending cases and their outcomes. It identifies specific trouble areas for students, such as discrimination, dress codes and uniforms, drug testing, due process, freedom of expression, off-campus conduct, privacy, religion, and sexuality, revealing the ways in which new and old issues continue to shape the high school environment. The National Scholastic Press Association focuses on student press rights, and it too helps students understand and obtain their rights when school officials violate them. Its website points to specialized information about a variety of student publications. The Internet itself allows curious students access to information about their status and rights, which would have required sustained research thirty years ago. The Internet also permits students across the nation and around the world to contact one another far more easily than was the case in the 1960s.[17]

Just as high school students today have identified new issues to tackle, so too have they developed new strategies for making themselves heard. One of the most intriguing of these is radical cheerleading. Two sisters in Florida are credited with inventing this new form of activism, which includes girls and boys (both often dressed in conventional girls' cheerleading outfits) and which has spread across the United States and even internationally. As the Radical Cheerleaders website explains, "It's activism with pom poms and middle fingers extended. It's screaming FUCK CAPITALISM while doing a split." The site includes the words to their cheers, in categories that include "Girl Positive Cheers," "Queer/Sex-Positive Cheers," "Environmental Cheers," and "Anti-Authority Cheers," showing both legacies from the 1960s and the emergence of new concerns.[18]

In addition to campus issues, events in the United States and the world continue to engage a minority of high school students. We know that political activism on college campuses continued, albeit with a lower profile, into the 1980s and 1990s. Some of the key issues included apartheid in South Africa, women's rights, workers' rights, the role of the Central Intelligence Agency, Ronald Reagan's foreign policy, especially in Latin America, and the first Gulf War. It would be astonishing if no high school students participated in these movements, but, with little media coverage of college activism, high school activism again flies well below the media radar, unless it involves students with guns. The invasion of Iraq in March 2003 sparked a number of high school student protests. Just how many is difficult to tell, because the news media exhibited a marked reluctance to cover stories about opposition to George W. Bush's foreign policies. Nevertheless, students from Los Angeles, California, to Normal, Illinois, debated the war, walked out of school in protest, carried signs opposing the war, and, in one case, discussed it with English-speaking Iraqi students in Baghdad through a satellite link-up. In some cases, students acted after being prompted by adults; in others, they defied adult bans on voicing their opinions. It seems likely too that prowar students conducted counterprotests or rallies in favor of the U.S. preemptive war, although the media did not cover these, either. Activism may not be the dominant mode among today's students, but the potential clearly exists. A catalyst, such as the reinstitution of the military draft, may well be all that is lacking.[19]

The most active students on high school campuses still appear to be liberal or left leaning, but conservative groups are more prominent today than they were in the late 1960s and early 1970s. Again, the Internet provides instant access to national groups such as the Young Conservatives or National Teenage Republicans. These groups' websites, however, do not indicate that students are active in their schools or that they focus on school issues. Their emphasis instead appears to be on national politics and international current events. Nevertheless, insofar as school officials violate the First Amendment rights of conservatives, the ACLU fights for them as well. In May 2004, for example, the Michigan Civil Liberties

Union pressured a high school in Detroit to stop censoring student year-book entries that included passages from the Bible.[20]

LOOKING BACK ON THE 1960S

Reflecting on their experiences in high school in the 1960s, former students attempt to fit those experiences into the broader perspective of their own lives and the historical trends in the country at large. Some look back fondly. Jean Hartley Davis Siddon found much that was good in the 1960s. She points out that the environmental and natural foods movements emerged from concerns of that era, human and civil rights moved onto the national agenda, and the nation as a whole became more "casualized." Elizabeth Harzoff agrees, noting that her high school days "set the tone for the rest of [her] life." Sharon Breitweiser comments that she has remained politically active as an adult. Susan Worley recalls feeling "that I was living in a time of such great upheaval and change that anything was possible. I would not have been at all surprised if the government had been overthrown, much less our educational system." She believes, "it was a great time to be a teenager." For Gail Marsh, high school students in the sixties "had a PASSION for what was going on around us, and I think there's a lot of that missing now." Marsh and Worley seem to believe that the distinctive era they lived through has ended, though Siddon, Harzoff, and Breitweiser perceive continuities, both in their own lives and in other social trends.[21]

Contrasting with their positive recollections, Deborah Astley observes, "While I am sometimes surprised by the actions of teenagers today . . . I still think this is a better time. Even with the school violence. The 'good old days' were not especially good. They were restrictive and the sixties came as a result of all the restrictions. I think what scares us now, as then, is all the freedom of choices we have. Freedom is terrifyingly wonderful." Astley approves the sixties' legacy of greater freedom, yet other students characterize the era as one of excess and self-indulgence. Susan Bowman Prendergast admits, "Unfortunately for many of us at that age we didn't realize the responsibility that came with many of the issues we were demanding." Paul "Gene" Kohli, a teacher rather than a student in the 1960s, links Elvis Presley and the Beatles with a downward slide in students' work ethic and achievement. These differing views reflect the divisions among Americans at the time, who similarly regarded the era in terms of opposites: freedom versus order, pleasure versus responsibility.[22]

Recent violence in the high schools leads some respondents to consider their own experiences. Kathy Goecke, denying that our society has made great progress on problems that existed in the 1960s, adds, "BUT I ALWAYS FELT SAFE AT SCHOOL!!" School violence, she implies, is a contemporary concern. As a student at a mostly white, suburban school, Goecke's experience did not match those of students like Jacqueline Rummel Groll, who vividly recalls instances of violence and fear. Jan Weiland concurs.

"High school was terrifying," she states. "When my daughters . . . ask me if the '60s were cool and fun, I say no. Those years were the most frightening of my life and I wouldn't wish them on anyone." "Claire Johnson" believes that handling student unrest and violence absorbed all of the time of her school counselors, so that she got no help in her quest to attend college out of state. Saralee Etter remembers both violence and drug use as influential forces in her Riviera Beach, Florida, high school.[23]

The bittersweet recollections of former students highlight the traumas of their coming-of-age. Those who study adolescents emphasize their physical and hormonal changes along with the psychological difficulties of establishing separate identities. Rarely do they consider the impact of specific historical moments in terms of how they aided or complicated the passage of youths through adolescence. Although teenagers during the Depression or World War II endured experiences that rivaled those of the 1960s in intensity, at least a sense of national unity and purpose gave meaning to the hardships. In contrast, students of the 1960s confronted disunity and profound confusion about the national purpose. Youths in the earlier eras fought against poverty and fascism, but activists in the 1960s battled other Americans over issues of race, rights, and reform. If the survival of the nation was at stake in the 1930s and 1940s, by the 1960s its very soul seemed in jeopardy. High school students asked adults some penetrating questions. What does it mean to be an American? Who can claim this status? Can people who are different—in race, ideology, or gender—still be Americans? How can abstractions such as freedom, equality, and democracy be lived in everyday life? Do they even apply to young people or the high school setting?

High school students prior to the 1960s had not audibly asked these questions, for several reasons. To begin with, until the end of World War II their numbers would not have sufficed to make their voices heard. High school attendance was still largely a middle-class practice. Black and Latino students, who may well have found questions about citizenship, equality, and democracy compelling, were far fewer than whites and attended segregated schools, muting their critique still further. Students most likely to ask such questions in fact may not have been in high school. They might have been working to help their families survive, or might have joined the military by concealing their real age. Moreover, although the era of the 1930s temporarily permitted some forms of anticapitalist dissent, wartime security concerns and propaganda stifled much critical inquiry, as did the anticommunist furor of the immediate postwar years.

The events of the 1930s through the 1950s, however, helped to set the stage for the later explosion of high school unrest. Official rhetoric suggested that on some levels both poverty and racism were un-American. Although the 1950s emphasized conformity, the social and geographic mobility spawned by the war, the stricter enforcement of school attendance laws, and the gradual enactment of school desegregation began to put together high school student bodies that were anything but uniform. As these diverse groups of students sat through classroom instruction about American values, they simultaneously faced sharp limitations on their own freedoms and watched the nation's fragile unity disintegrate. What happened in high schools in the late 1960s and early 1970s was in some senses the educational equivalent of a perfect storm, the congruence of precisely the right—or wrong, depending on one's perspective—mixture of internal pressures and external stimuli.

In the early twenty-first century, having achieved some distance from the 1960s, we are better able to view the era as part of a broader historical narrative. No longer regarding the sixties as a kind of historical mutation, a deviation from the standard story of triumphal progress, we may increasingly point both forward and back to examine this time. The 1960s did not burst unheralded onto the scene, but, rather, represented the surfacing of deep trends in race and gender relations, state-citizen relations, capitalist development, and consumer ideologies. High school youths were both caught up in these events and helped give them shape. Their actions, moreover, forced the consequences of these long-term trends to be examined within a core American institution: the public school.

Students, teachers, administrators, and educational reformers were not the only Americans in the 1960s who took an interest in the schools and their operation. The concept of the common school and the fact that formal education was a nearly universal experience for postwar Americans meant that few segments of society exhibited indifference toward the public schools. One administrator grumbled, "Whenever there is a conflict in a high school . . . the armies gather. Poverty groups show up. . . . The press shows up, young radicals, community people, everyone."[24] Officials' complaint about outside influence and pressures contained a significant truth: those who wanted to reform or revolutionize American society saw public schools as a key locus for their energies. In contrast, those who wanted to conserve the status quo regarded the schools as a place to stand pat. No one argued—in fact, no one believed—that the dozen years that children spent in the public schools were inconsequential. Rather, their debate focused on what the results of school attendance were, whether and how those outcomes should be changed for the benefit of society, and who had the right and power to decide such things.

Anxiety over the public schools and the students they produced was not new in the late 1960s and early 1970s. The voices of high school students clamoring to be heard in the circles of power *were* new, and, backed by educational reformers, high school students won significant victories in some, perhaps many, schools. These victories, ironically, occurred at the high tide of public schools' centrality as social institutions and hence today ring somewhat hollow. In the 1960s, Americans believed that public education could raise individuals from poverty, erase centuries of racism and discrimination, and strengthen the United States in its war against communism. Today, few tout education as the cure to the nation's ills and multiple institutions compete with public schools. The disruptions of the 1960s may in fact have hastened the flight of parents and students into alternative institutions. Societal attitudes have changed, with weariness and cynicism replacing the optimism of the 1960s. Whereas both the Johnson and Nixon administrations showered public schools with federal money, improving education today means demanding that students perform well on standardized tests without providing additional resources. Repeated exposes of unequal school funding and shocking conditions in inner-city and rural schools leave the public yawning.

With the public seemingly indifferent to the fate of education, common schools no longer function as the primary socializer of the young. Time will tell whether this is a positive or negative development. For high school students today, lack of a common educational experience may make it impossible—despite all advances in communications—to create a unified movement capable of challenging adults and the educational system as a whole in the way their predecessors in the 1960s managed. In many ways, this book tells the story of conversations started but not completed, of projects imagined but not undertaken. High school students of the 1960s, by dint of their noise, persistence, and careful arguments, captured adult attention. They elbowed their way to the table where decisions affecting them were made and demanded to be included in these debates as well as broader ones about policy, identity, and purpose. Since that time, somebody has stolen their chair.

NOTES

INTRODUCTION

1. Subtitle comes from Beatrice M. Gudridge, *High School Student Unrest* (Washington, D.C.: National School Public Relations Association, 1969), 1.

2. *National Association of Secondary School Principals [NASSP] Bulletin,* cited in Ronald L. Abrell and Charles C. Hanna, "High School Unrest Reconsidered," *High School Journal* 54, no. 6 (March 1971): 396–404; Dale Gaddy, *Rights and Freedoms of Public School Students: Directions from the 1960s* (Topeka, Kans.: National Organization on Legal Problems of Education, 1971), 2–6; Irving G. Hendrick and Reginald L. Jones, eds., *Student Dissent in the Schools* (Boston: Houghton Mifflin, 1972), 4; F. K. Heussenstamm, "Public High School Dress Regulations: Some Sociological and Legal Implications," reprinted in Hendrick and Jones, *Student Dissent,* 194; Tom Wells, *The War Within: America's Battle over Vietnam* (Berkeley: University of California Press, 1994), 297; *New York Times,* May 1, 1969, 1:2; Toby Moffett, *The Participation Put-On: Reflections of a Disenchanted Washington Youth Expert* (New York: Delacorte Press, 1971).

3. Leonard L. Baird, "Who Protests: A Study of Student Activists," in Julian Foster and Durward Long, eds., *Protest! Student Activism in America* (New York: William Morrow, 1970), 123–33; Charles Anrig, "Trouble in the High Schools," *American Education* (October 1969): 1–4; Christian Bay, "Political and Apolitical Students: Facts in Search of Theory," in Edward Sampson and Harold Korn, eds., *Student Activism and Protest: Alternatives for Social Change* (San Francisco: Jossey-Bass, 1970), 60–88.

4. Alan E. Bayer, Alexander W. Astin, and Robert F. Boruch, *Social Issues and Protest Activity: Recent Student Trends* (ACE Research Reports, 8, no. 2, February 1970), 24, table 3.

5. Kathleen Casey, *I Answer with My Life: Life Histories of Women Teachers Working for Social Change* (New York: Routledge, 1993), 80.

6. *El Paso Times,* August 9, 1970, A-8.

7. Craig McNamara interview in Joan Morrison and Robert K. Morrison, eds., *From Camelot to Kent State: The Sixties Experience in the Words of Those Who Lived It* (Oxford: Oxford University Press, 1987), 161–70; Melvin Small, *Antiwarriors: The Vietnam War and the Battle for America's Hearts and Minds* (Wilmington, Del.: Scholarly Resources, 2000), 88–89; Wells, *The War Within,* 107–110, 374.

8. *New York Times,* January 9, 1969, 71:1.

9. Sylvia Williams, *Hassling* (Boston: Little, Brown, 1970), 188.

10. Marc Libarle and Tom Seligson, eds., *The High School Revolutionaries* (New York: Random House, 1970); John Birmingham, *Our Time Is Now: Notes from the High School Underground* (New York: Praeger, 1970); Mitchell Goodman, comp., *The Movement Toward a New America: The Beginnings of a Long Revolution (A Collage)—A What?* (Philadelphia: Pilgrim Press, 1970).

11. Sharon Bialy-Fox, e-mail to author, June 20, 2000.

1—THE CHANGING WORLD OF THE AMERICAN HIGH SCHOOL STUDENT

1. Bob Greene, *Be True to Your School: A Diary of 1964* (New York: Atheneum, 1987), 160, 262.

2. Greene, *Be True,* viii, ix, 53, 271, 282–83.

3. Greene, *Be True,* 172.

4. Greene, *Be True,* 30, 32, 42, 50, 74, 240, 300, 308.

5. Ellen Gillenwater, letter to author, June 22, 1999; *New York Times,* December 6, 1970, 6:46; Margot A. Henriksen, *Dr. Strangelove's America: Society and Culture in the Atomic Age* (Berkeley: University of California Press, 1997), 148–82; William Graebner, *Coming of Age in Buffalo: Youth and Authority in the Post-War Era* (Philadelphia: Temple University Press, 1990), 13–84; Maurice Isserman, *If I Had a Hammer: The Death of the Old Left and the Birth of the New Left* (Urbana: University of Illinois Press, 1993), 146.

6. James Gilbert, *A Cycle of Outrage: America's Reaction to the Juvenile Delinquent in the 1950s* (New York: Oxford University Press, 1986), 18.

7. Grace Palladino, *Teenagers: An American History* (New York: Basic Books, 1996), 53; T. H. Watkins, *The Hungry Years: A Narrative History of the Great Depression in America* (New York: Henry Holt, 1999), 267–72; Kathleen Thompson and Hilary MacAustin, eds., *Children of the Depression* (Bloomington: Indiana University Press, 2001), n.p.

8. Palladino, *Teenagers,* xii, 73–76; Arlene Skolnick, *Embattled Paradise: The American Family in an Age of Uncertainty* (New York: Basic Books, 1991), 65, 71, 207; Gilbert, *A Cycle of Outrage,* 17–19.

9. Palladino, *Teenagers,* 52; Skolnick, *Embattled Paradise,* 78.

10. Palladino, *Teenagers,* 195, 39–45.

11. Gilbert, *Cycle of Outrage,* 75–76; Palladino, *Teenagers,* 53, 117–35; Skolnick, *Embattled Paradise,* 80.

12. John Dittmer, *Local People: The Struggle for Civil Rights in Mississippi* (Urbana: University of Illinois Press, 1994), 126; Adam Fairclough, *Race and Democracy: The Civil Rights Struggle in Louisiana, 1915–1972* (Athens: University of Georgia Press, 1995), 156, 214; Charles M. Payne, *I've Got the Light of Freedom: The Organizing Tradition and the Mississippi Freedom Struggle* (Berkeley: University of California, 1995), 225, 271; John Egerton, *Speak Now against the Day: The Generation before the Civil Rights Movement in the South* (Chapel Hill: University of North Carolina Press, 1995), 594–600; Diane Ravitch, *The Great School Wars: A History of the New York City Public Schools* (New York: Basic Books, 1988), 276.

13. Dittmer, *Local People,* 126, 258–60, 332.

14. Kenneth L. Fish, *Conflict and Dissent in the High Schools* (New York: Bruce Publishing, 1970), 8, 86; Richard Fuller, "A Discussion of the Film 'High School,'" *Colloquy,* March 1970, reprinted in Mitchell Goodman, comp., *The Movement Toward a New America: The Beginnings of a Long Revolution (A Collage)—A What?* (Philadelphia: Pilgrim Press, 1970), 278–79; Gilbert, *Cycle of Outrage,* 16; Thomas Hine, *The Rise and Fall of the American Teenager* (New York: Avon, 1999), 166; Robert Rossner, *The Year Without an Autumn: Portrait of a School in Crisis* (New York: Richard W. Baron, 1969), 194; Joshua Mamis, "The Right to Petition at Eleven," in Marc Libarle and Tom Seligson, eds., *The High School Revolutionaries* (New York: Random House, 1970), 153.

15. Dominick Cavallo, *A Fiction of the Past: The Sixties in American History* (New York: Palgrave, 1999), 43–78.

16. Almost any volume of the journal *School Management* includes advertisements for mobile or temporary classrooms; the July 1965 issue (9, no. 7) focused on the issue of school building, and included an article titled "Take Advantage of Overcrowding."

17. Diane Ravitch, *The Troubled Crusade: American Education, 1945–1980* (New York: Basic Books, 1983), 81–113; J. Ronald Oakley, *God's Country: America in the Fifties* (New York: Bembner Books, 1986), 72–73; *Mine,* no. 7, Tucson, Ariz. (a student underground newspaper), quoted in John Birmingham, *Our Time Is Now: Notes from the High School Underground* (New York: Praeger, 1970), 248.

18. Ravitch, *Troubled Crusade,* 72, 79; Palladino, *Teenagers,* 170–71; "The Crisis in Education, Part I," *Life,* March 24, 1958, 25–37.

19. Richard P. Kleeman, "How One School District is Teaching About Communism," *School Management,* September 1962, 54–59, 127–28; Doug Owram, *Born at the Right Time: A History of the Baby-Boom Generation* (Toronto: University of Toronto Press,

1996), 128, 134–35; David Super, e-mail to author, May 17, 2000; "Susan Snow," "My Teacher is a Racist," interview in Libarle and Seligson, *High School Revolutionaries*, 90.

20. Jack Allen, "The Role of Ninth Grade Civic in Citizenship Education," *High School Journal* 44, no. 3 (December 1960): 110–11.

21. Edward K. Spann, *Democracy's Children: The Young Rebels of the 1960s and the Power of Ideals* (Wilmington, Del.: Scholarly Resources, 2003), 74.

22. Seymour Martin Lipset and Philip G. Altbach, eds., *Students in Revolt* (Boston: Beacon Press, 1970); Victor Kobayashi, "Confusion and Hope: Student Unrest in Japan," in William W. Brickman and Stanley Lehrer, eds., *Conflict and Change on the Campus: The Response to Student Hyperactivism* (New York: School and Society Books, 1970), 359–66.

23. Alice Duffy Rinehart, *Mortals in the Immortal Profession: An Oral History of Teaching* (New York: Irvington Publishers, 1983), 260.

24. Myron Lieberman, "Teacher Militancy," in Dwight W. Allen and Jeffrey C. Hecht, eds., *Controversies in Education* (Philadelphia: W. B. Saunders, 1974), 404–11; Elsie Y. Cross and Irving Rosenstein, "Do Teachers Want What Students Need?" in Allen and Hecht, *Controversies in Education*, 385–403; Mary A. Golloaday and Jay Noell, eds., *The Condition of Education, Statistical Report* (National Center for Education Statistics, U.S. Department of Health, Education and Welfare, 1978), 182–83.

25. Rinehart, *Immortals*, 321.

26. David Schimmel and Louis Fischer, "Second Class Citizens: The Civil Rights of Teachers," in Allen and Hecht, *Controversies in Education*, 423–33.

27. Maxine L. Margolis, *True to Her Nature: Changing Advice to American Women* (Prospect Heights, Ill.: Waveland Press, 2000), 3–4; Joanne Meyerowitz, ed., *Not June Cleaver: Women and Gender in Postwar America, 1945–1960* (Philadelphia: Temple University Press, 1994).

28. *School Management* 9, no. 3 (March 1965): 80–84.

2—MAINTAINING THE COLOR LINE IN DESEGREGATED HIGH SCHOOLS

1. John Egerton, *Speak Now against the Day: The Generation before the Civil Rights Movement in the South* (Chapel Hill: University of North Carolina Press, 1994), 586–611; *Brown v. Board of Education of Topeka*, 347 U.S. 483 (1954).

2. *Missouri ex rel Gaines v. Canada*, 305 US 337 (1938), *Sipuel v. Oklahoma State Board of Regents*, 332 US 631 (1948), *Sweatt v. Painter*, 339 US 629 (1950), *McLaurin v. Oklahoma State Board of Regents*, 339 US 637 (1950), *Henderson v. United States*, 339 US 816 (1950).

3. Pansye Atkinson, Brown vs. Topeka: *An African American's View: Desegregation and Miseducation* (Chicago: African American Images, 1993), 1–2; J. Harvie Wilkinson, III, *From Brown to Bakke: The Supreme Court and School Integration: 1954–1978* (Oxford: Oxford University Press, 1979), 81.

4. *New York Times*, October 23, 1971, 43:1, 2.

5. Van Dempsey and George Noblit, "Cultural Ignorance and School Desegregation: A Community Narrative," in Mwalimu J. Shujaa, ed., *Beyond Desegregation: The Politics of Quality in African American Schooling* (Thousand Oaks, Calif.: Corwin Press, 1996), 116; Adam Fairclough, *Race and Democracy: The Civil Rights Struggle in Louisiana, 1915–1972* (Athens: University of Georgia Press, 1995), 446–47; Vanessa Siddle Walker, *Their Highest Potential: An African American School Community in the Segregated South* (Chapel Hill: University of North Carolina Press, 1996); Alvis V. Adair, *Desegregation: The Illusion of Black Progress* (Lanham, Md.: University Press of America, 1984); Atkinson, Brown vs Topeka; David S. Cecelski, *Along Freedom Road: Hyde County, North Carolina, and the Fate of Black Schools in the South* (Chapel Hill: University of North Carolina Press, 1994).

6. W. E. B. DuBois is quoted in Egerton, *Speak Now against the Day*, 610. For Hurston's views, see James T. Patterson, *Grand Expectations: The United States, 1945–1974* (New York: Oxford University Press, 1996), 390–91.

7. Mark Chesler, *In Their Own Words: A Student Appraisal of What Happened after School Desegregation* (Atlanta: Southern Regional Council, 1967), 2–3, 12, 13, 52.

8. Connie Brown, letter to author, June 14, 1999; David Super, e-mail to author, May 17, 2000.

9. Val Tabor, e-mails to author, May 11, 2000, and May 17, 2000.

10. Susan Bowman Prendergast, e-mail to author, May 22, 2000.

11. Frank A. Petroni and Ernest A. Hirsch, with C. Lillian Petroni, *Two Four, Six, Eight, When You Gonna Integrate?* (Morningside Heights, N.Y.: Behavioral Problems, 1970), 10, 142.

12. Val Tabor, e-mail to author, May 17, 2000; Susan Bowman Prendergast, e-mail to author, May 22, 2000; Judy Brown, e-mail to author, May 17, 2000.

13. Betty Walker, e-mail to author, June 3, 2000; Kenneth L. Fish, *Conflict and Dissent in the High Schools* (New York: Bruce Publishing, 1970), 110.

14. *New York Times,* February 14, 1969, 33:3; February 26, 28:1; and March 9, 1969, 41:1; *Caldwell v. Craighead,* 432 F. 2d 213 (1970); *New York Times,* October 14, 1971, 27:1.

15. *Banks v. Muncie Community Schools,* 433 F. 2d 292 (1970).

16. Roger Rapoport and Laurence J. Kirshbaum, *Is the Library Burning?* (New York: Random House, 1969), 132.

17. *Melton v. Young,* 465 F. 2d 1332 (1972); Fish, *Conflict and Dissent,* 10–11.

18. Eve Levin, e-mail to author, June 18, 1999; Marsh' Fenstermaker, e-mails to author, June 16, 1999, and June 18, 1999.

19. Chesler, *In Their Own Words,* 12, 52.

20. Skywalker Payne, letter to author, September 24, 1999.

21. Roscoe Reeve, e-mail to author, May 10, 2000.

22. Mary Alice Cook, e-mail to author, May 15, 2000.

23. Ibid.

24. Cecelski, *Along Freedom Road,* 58–82, 86–102, 133–34, 150–61.

25. Cecelski, *Along Freedom Road,* 100, 149, 160–61, 172.

26. Juliane Lewis Adams and Thomas A. DeBlack, *Civil Obedience: An Oral History of School Desegregation in Fayetteville, Arkansas, 1954–1965* (Fayetteville: University of Arkansas Press, 1994), 1–22.

27. Letter from Carole Palmer to author, May 2, 2000; Fairclough, *Race and Democracy,* 444; Jennings L. Wagner, Jr., "School Relationships and Activities in Desegregated Schools," *High School Journal* 54, no. 3 (December 1970): 200.

28. Kathleen Casey, *I Answer with My Life: Life Histories of Women Teachers Working for Social Change* (New York: Routledge, 1993), 126; John Canfield, "White Teacher, Black School," in Kevin Ryan, ed., *Don't Smile Until Christmas: Accounts of the First Year Teaching* (Chicago: University of Chicago Press, 1970), 40; Betsy Fancher, *Voices From the South: Black Students Talk about Their Experiences in Desegregated Schools* (Atlanta: Southern Regional Council, 1970), 5; *Dunn v. Tyler Independent School District,* 327 F. Supp. 528 (1971).

29. Janet Eyler, Valerie J. Cook, and Leslie E. Ward, "Resegregation: Segregation Within Desegregated Schools," in Christine H. Rossell and Willis D. Hawley, eds., *The Consequences of School Desegregation* (Philadelphia: Temple University Press, 1983), 126–62; Jennifer McKee, interview with author, June 7, 2000; Edna Bonacich and Robert F. Goodman, *Deadlock in School Desegregation: A Case Study of Inglewood, California* (New York: Praeger, 1972), 43.

30. Donald Reeves, *Notes of a Processed Brother* (New York: Pantheon Books, 1971), 58–59.

31. Emilie V. Siddle Walker, "Can Institutions Care? Evidence from the Segregated Schools of African-American Children," in Shujaa, *Beyond Desegregation,* 211.

32. David B. Tyack, *The One Best System: A History of American Urban Education* (Cambridge, Mass.: Harvard University Press, 1974), 281–82.

33. Reeves, *Notes of a Processed Brother,* 159; Brent Coatney, letter to author, September 7, 1999; Eyler, Cook, and Ward, "Resegregation," 130, 141–43.

34. N. K. Jamal, "Right On," in Marc Libarle and Tom Seligson, eds., *The High School Revolutionaries* (New York: Random House, 1970), 32; Paul Gayton, "Keep On Pushing," in Libarle and Seligson, *High School Revolutionaries,* 73–74.

35. Eyler, Cook, and Ward, "Resegregation," 141–43.

36. Janet Gray Carstens, interview with author, June 2, 2000; Tim Galliher, e-mail to author, May 5, 2000; Fairclough, *Race and Democracy,* 438; Marsh' Fenstermaker, e-mail to author, June 16, 1999.

37. Christine Rossell, "Desegregation Plans, Racial Isolation, White Flight, and Community Response," in Rossell and Hawley, *Consequences of School Desegregation,* 13–57.

38. U.S. Commission on Civil Rights, *What Students Want: A National Survey Prepared by the U.S. Commission on Civil Rights* (New York: Emerson Hall, 1971), 99; Fairclough, *Race and Democracy,* 453; Alexander M. Bickel, "Desegregation: Where Do We Go From Here?" *New Republic,* February 7, 1970, reprinted in Sol Cohen, ed., *Education in the United States: A Documentary History* (New York: Random House, 1974), 5:3223–27; Terre Hanson Burkhart, e-mail to author, June 15, 1999; Fish, *Conflict and Dissent,* 110.

39. U.S. Commission on Civil Rights, *What Students Want,* 33; *New York Times,* October 17, 22:6.

40. Janet Gray Carstens, interview with author, June 2, 2000; *Dunn. v. Tyler Independent School District,* 460 F. 2d 137 (1972); Cecelski, *Along Freedom Road,* 161.

41. "What People Think about Their High Schools," *Life* 66, no. 19 (May 16, 1969): 23–33.

42. Bernard D. Reams, Jr., and Paul E. Wilson, eds., *Segregation and the Fourteenth Amendment in the States: A Survey of State Segregation Laws, 1865–1953; Prepared for the United States Supreme Court in re,* Brown v. Board of Education of Topeka (Buffalo: W. S. Hein, 1975), 43, 342, 695.

43. Abbas Tashakkori and Salvador Hector Ochoa, eds., *Education of Hispanics in the United States.* Vol. 16 of *Readings on Equal Education,* ed. Charles Teddlie (New York, AMS Press, 1999), 3–8; *Mendez v. Westminster School District,* 64 F. Supp. 544 (1946).

44. Tashakkori and Ochoa, *Education of Hispanics,* 10–12.

45. *A Generation Deprived: Los Angeles School Desegregation: A Report of the U.S. Commission on Civil Rights* (Washington, D.C.: U.S. Commission on Civil Rights, 1977), 4–12; Tashakkori and Ochoa, *Education of Hispanics,* 163.

46. Kenneth García, letter to author, September 7, 1999; Berdie Sánchez, e-mail to author, May 10, 2000.

47. Thomas Weyr, *Hispanic U.S.A.: Breaking the Melting Pot* (New York: Harper & Row, 1988), 53–57.

48. Berdie Sánchez, e-mails to author, May 10, 2000, 2:19 p.m., and May 10, 2000, 4:54 p.m.

49. Berdie Sánchez, e-mail to author, May 10, 2000, 4:54 p.m.

50. Chesler, *In Their Own Words,* 71.

3—IT'S NOT PERSONAL, IT'S JUST THAT YOU'RE WHITE

1. Jacque Switzer, e-mail to author, June 22, 1999; Robert Rossner, *The Year Without an Autumn: Portrait of a School in Crisis* (New York: Richard W. Baron, 1969), 12; Frank A. Petroni and Ernest A. Hirsch, with C. Lillian Petroni, *Two, Four, Six, Eight, When You Gonna Integrate?* (Morningside Heights, N.Y.: Behavioral Problems, 1970), 99.

2. Charles M. Payne, *I've Got the Light of Freedom: The Organizing Tradition and the Mississippi Freedom Struggle* (Berkeley: University of California Press: 1995), 326; "Special Report on Student Unrest in the Public Schools," *School Management,* November

1968, 50–98; Riot Data Clearinghouse information cited in *School Management,* November 1968, "Special Report on Student Unrest in the Public Schools," 50–98; Fred Halstead, *Out Now! A Participant's Account of the American Movement Against the Vietnam War* (New York: Monad Press, 1978), 386; *New York Times,* April 6, 1968, 26:5.

3. Petroni and Hirsch, *Two, Four Six,* 16, 195.

4. Gary Carnog, "To Care and Not to Care," in Kevin Ryan, ed., *Don't Smile Until Christmas: Accounts of the First Year Teaching* (Chicago: University of Chicago Press, 1970), 22; *Guzick v. Drebus,* 305 F. Supp. 472 (1969); Rossner, *Year Without an Autumn,* 10–11, emphasis in original.

5. Donald Reeves, *Notes of a Processed Brother* (New York: Pantheon Books, 1971), 69; John Canfield, "White Teacher, Black School," in Ryan, *Don't Smile Until Christmas,* 46.

6. Susan Lindholm, e-mail to author, May 18, 2000; Jan Weiland, e-mail to author, May 5, 2000.

7. David Watchtel, letter to author, November 12, 1999; Jan Scarbrough, e-mail to author, June 1, 2000.

8. Jan Weiland, e-mail to author, May 4, 2000.

9. Petroni and Hirsch, *Two, Four, Six,* 106; Eleanor Fuke, "Identity or Discipline," in Ryan, *Don't Smile Until Christmas,* 152–53.

10. Gail Richardson, "X is for the Unknown," in Ryan, *Don't Smile Until Christmas,* 74.

11. Canfield, "White Teacher, Black School," 50–51.

12. James Ross Irwin, *A Ghetto Principal Speaks Out: A Decade of Crisis in Urban Public Schools* (Detroit: Wayne State University, 1973), 11–14.

13. J. Anthony Lukas, *Common Ground: A Turbulent Decade in the Lives of Three American Families* (New York: Vintage Books. 1985), 384; Ronald P. Formisano, *Boston Against Busing: Race, Class, and Ethnicity in the 1960s and 1970s* (Chapel Hill: University of North Carolina Press, 1991), 33; Davison M. Douglas, *Reading, Writing, and Race: The Desegregation of the Charlotte Schools* (Chapel Hill: University of North Carolina Press, 1995), 225–26.

14. Lloyd E. Peterman, "A Place of Responsibility: Where it Worked Both Ways," reprinted in Irving G. Hendrick and Reginald L. Jones, eds., *Student Dissent in the Schools* (Boston: Houghton Mifflin, 1972), 232–39; Reeves, *Notes of a Processed Brother,* 112–19; Williams, *Hassling,* 30–35, 120–21.

15. Irwin, *Ghetto Principal,* 215, 216; *New York Times,* March 2, 1969, 58:4.

16. U.S. Commission on Civil Rights, *What Students Want: A National Survey Prepared by the U.S. Commission on Civil Rights* (New York: Emerson Hall, 1971), 43–44; "Special Report on Student Unrest," 50–98.

17. Edna Bonacich and Robert F. Goodman, *Deadlock in School Desegregation: A Case Study of Inglewood, California* (New York: Praeger, 1972), 37; "My Teacher is a Racist," "Susan Snow" interview in Marc Libarle and Tom Seligson, eds., *The High School Revolutionaries* (New York: Random House, 1970), 91.

18. James Brown, "The Black Athlete," interview in Libarle and Seligson, *High School Revolutionaries,* 44–45, 50–51.

19. Libarle and Seligson, *High School Revolutionaries,* xvi, and "Keep On Pushing," interview with Paul Gayton, 83.

20. Connie Brown, letter to author, June 22, 1999.

21. Ibid., 154, 158.

22. Charles E. Billings, "Black Activists and the Schools," *High School Journal* 54, no. 2 (November 1970): 98; Betsy Fancher, *Voices From the South: Black Students Talk about Their Experiences in Desegregated Schools* (Atlanta: Southern Regional Council, 1970), 45.

23. Billings, "Black Activists in the Schools," 98, 102; Simon Wittes, *People and Power: A Study of Crisis in Secondary Schools* (Ann Arbor: Institute for Social Research, University of Michigan, 1970), 70–71.

24. Jan Weiland, e-mail to author, May 5, 2000.

25. Terre Hanson Burkhart, e-mail to author, June 13, 1999; Jacque Switzer, e-mail to author, June 22, 1999.

26. Terre Hanson Burkhart, e-mail to author, June 15, 1999.

27. Roger Rapoport and Laurence J. Kirshbaum, *Is the Library Burning?* (New York: Random House, 1969), 134.

28. *What Students Want,* 18–20, 113–14; Irwin, *Ghetto Principal,* 130.

29. *New York Times,* October 4, 1970, 1:4; Rapoport and Kirshbaum, *Is the Library Burning?* 138.

30. Irwin, *Ghetto Principal,* 116–17.

31. Elnore Grow, e-mail to author, April 22, 2000; Alice Krause Young, e-mail to author, May 24, 2000.

32. Jacque Switzer, e-mail to author, June, 22, 1999; Terre Hanson Burkhart, e-mail to author, June 13, 1999.

33. Petroni and Hirsch, *Two, Four, Six,* 63; Reeves, *Notes of a Processed Brother,* 104–5.

34. *New York Times,* October 4, 1970, 1:4; February 28, 1969, 20:1; Hendrick and Jones, *Student Dissent,* 227; Stephen K. Bailey, *Disruption in Urban Public Secondary Schools* (Washington, D.C.: National Association of Secondary School Principals, 1970), 8–11, 55–66; Beatrice M. Gudridge, *High School Student Unrest* (Washington, D.C., National Public Relations Association, 1969), 1–2.

35. *New York Times,* May 10, 1968, 26:4; September 26, 1968, 34:5; and October 5, 1968, 28:1.

36. Irwin, *Ghetto Principal,* 196.

37. "Strategies for Coping with Student Disruption," *School Management,* June 1969, 47–50.

38. Ibid., 51–55.

39. Irwin, *Ghetto Principal,* 162–65.

40. Kenneth L. Fish, *Conflict and Dissent in the High Schools* (New York: Bruce Publishing 1970), 2, 130; Harold Saltzman, *Race War in the High School: The Ten-Year Destruction of Franklin K. Lane High School in Brooklyn* (New Rochelle, N.Y.: Arlington House, 1972), 14; Senate Select Committee on Equal Educational Opportunity, *Quality and Control of Urban Schools: Hearings before the Select Committee on Equal Educational Opportunity,* 92d Cong., 1st sess., July 27, 29, and August 5, 1971, 6131.

41. Janet Eyler, Valerie S. Cook, and Leslie E. Ward, "Resegregation: Segregation Within Desegregated Schools," in Christine H. Rossell and Willis D. Hawley, eds., *The Consequences of School Desegregation* (Philadelphia: Temple University Press, 1983), 143–45.

42. "Jesus Says I Should," interview with Mary Ann Kennedy in Libarle and Seligson, *High School Revolutionaries,* 129–30; *New York Times,* February 4, 1969, 28:1; Louis R. Negrete, "Culture Clash: The Utility of Mass Protest as a Political Response," in F. Chris García, ed., *La Causa Política: A Chicano Politics Reader* (Notre Dame, Ind.: University of Notre Dame Press, 1974), 353.

43. Susan Worley, e-mails to author, May 23, 2000 and May 29, 2000.

44. Libarle and Seligson, *High School Revolutionaries,* xvii–xviii.

45. *New York Times,* March 22, 1969, 1:4.

46. *New York Times,* December 3, 1967, 139:3; Irwin, *Ghetto Principal,* 109; *New York Times,* November 16, 1968, 27:3.

47. Libarle and Seligson, *High School Revolutionaries,* 215, 220–21.

48. "High School Activists Tell What They Want," *Nation's Schools* 82, no. 6 (December 1968): 30; Fancher, *Voices From the South,* 20.

49. Henry Hampton and Steve Fayer, *Voices of Freedom: An Oral History of the Civil Rights Movement from the 1950s through the 1980s* (New York: Bantam Books, 1990), 485–98; Reeves, *Notes of a Processed Brother,* 73.

50. Rossner, *Year Without an Autumn,* 152–53; Todd Gitlin, "The Liberation of Bronx H.S. of Science," *San Francisco Express Times,* November 13, 1968, reprinted in Mitchell Goodman, comp., *The Movement Toward a New America: The Beginnings of a Long Revolution (A Collage)—A What?* (Philadelphia: Pilgrim Press, 1970), 287–89.

51. Rossner, *Year Without an Autumn,* 15, 149, 164.

52. Jerald E. Podair, *The Strike That Changed New York: Blacks, Whites, and the Ocean Hill-Brownsville Crisis* (New Haven, Conn.: Yale University Press, 2002), 145–49; Rossner, *Year Without an Autumn,* 201–2, 212–16.

53. Joseph Lelyveld, "Negro-White Friction Is Eroding Teacher-Student Relations in City's High Schools," *New York Times,* reprinted in Goodman, *Movement Toward a New America,* 167–68.

54. Lelyveld, "Negro-White Friction," 167–68; transcript of Radio WBAI interviews with three Taft High School seniors, *Leviathan,* June 1968, reprinted in Goodman, *Movement Toward a New America,* 173–75.

55. Diane Divoky, "The Way It's Going to Be," *Saturday Review,* February 15, 1969, 83–85; 89, 101–2; *New York High School Free Press,* no. 8, reprinted in John Birmingham, *Our Time Is Now: Notes from the High School Underground* (New York: Praeger, 1970), 176, 177–81.

56. Sylvia Berry Williams, *Hassling* (Boston: Little, Brown, 1970), 86–92.

57. Ibid., 107–26.

58. Ibid., 187–94, 208–20.

59. Ibid., 179–94.

60. *What Students Want,* 106.

61. L. Ling Chi Wang, "The Chinese-American Student in San Francisco," reprinted in *Chinese-American School and Community Problems* (Chicago: Integrated Education Associates, 1972), 53–57.

62. Edward J. Escobar, "The Dialectics of Repression: The Los Angeles Police Department and the Chicano Movement, 1968–1971, *Journal of American History* 79, no. 4 (March 1993): 1483–1514; Johns [*sic*] Harrington, "L.A.'s Student Blowout," *Phi Delta Kappan* (October 1968), 74–75, 77–78, reprinted in Sol Cohen, ed., *Education in the United States: A Documentary History* (New York: Random House, 1974), 2938.

63. *New York Times,* December 19, 1968, 41:5.

64. Kenneth García, letters to author, September 7, 1999, and October 6, 1999.

65. Ibid.

66. Ibid.

67. Carlos Muñoz, *Youth, Identity, Power: The Chicano Movement* (London: Verso, 1989), 99–103; Ignacio García, *Chicanismo: The Forging of a Militant Ethos Among Mexican-Americans* (Tucson: University of Arizona Press, 1997), 102.

68. Senate Select Committee on Equal Educational Opportunity, *Mexican American Education: Hearings before the Select Committee on Equal Educational Opportunity,* 91st Cong., 2nd sess., August 18, 19, and 21, 1970, 2469.

69. Della Rossa, "Fight for Chicano Control Erupts in L. A. High Schools," *The Militant,* February, 1970, reprinted in Goodman, *Movement Toward a New America,* 271; Escobar, *Dialectics of Repression.*

70. *What Students Want,* 28, 35. Senate hearings on Mexican-American education in 1970 put into the record newspaper articles about the school boycotts in Texas and a copy of student demands. See Senate Select Committee on Equal Educational Opportunity, *Mexican American Education,* 2475, 2483, 2487.

71. For Hearings before the Select Committee on Equal Educational Opportunity, see appended article from the *Uvalde Leader-News,* "Parents Association of Mex-Americans Explains Objectives," 2488–2489; John Staples Shockley, *Chicano Revolt in a Texas Town* (Notre Dame, Ind.: University of Notre Dame Press, 1974), 120, 135–38; Thomas Weyr,

Hispanic U.S.A.: Breaking the Melting Pot (New York: Harper & Row, 1988), 53–70; Durward Long, "Black Protest," 459–82, in Julian Foster and Durward Long, eds., *Protest! Student Activism in America* (New York: William Morrow, 1970).

72. U.S. Commission on Civil Rights, *What Students Want*, 21.

73. Williams, *Hassling*, 267–69.

74. Long, "Black Protest," 467; Rossa, "Fight for Chicano Control."

4—THE HIGH SCHOOL STUDENT RIGHTS MOVEMENT

1. *New York Times*, February 9, 1970.

2. Jack Allen, "The Role of Ninth Grade Civics in Citizenship Education," *High School Journal* 44, no. 3 (December 1960): 110–11.

3. Charles E. Silberman, *Crisis in the Classroom: The Remaking of American Education* (New York: Random House, 1970), 341–42.

4. James Ross Irwin, *A Ghetto Principal Speaks Out: A Decade of Crisis in Urban Public Schools* (Detroit: Wayne State University Press, 1973), 112–14; Silberman, *Crisis in the Classroom*, 341–42.

5. Thomas Hine, *The Rise and Fall of the American Teenager* (New York: Avon, 1999), 196; Gael Graham, "Flaunting the Freak Flag: *Karr v. Schmidt* and the Great Hair Debate in American High Schools, 1965–1975," *Journal of American History* 91, no. 2 (September 2004): 522–43.

6. Quoted in *Livingston v. Swanquist*, 314 F. Supp. 1 (1970).

7. Beverly Gordon, "American Denim: Blue Jeans and Their Multiple Layers of Meaning," in Patricia A. Cunningham and Susan Vaso Lab, eds., *Dress and Popular Culture* (Bowling Green, Ohio: Bowling Green State University Popular Press, 1991), 31–45; UPI photo of billboard, *New York Times*, February 6, 1968, 47:3; John Birmingham, *Our Time Is Now: Notes From the High School Underground* (New York: Praeger, 1970), 74.

8. *Turley v. Adel Community School District* 322 F. Supp. 402 (1971).

9. *Turley v. Adel* (1971); poll cited in Warren L. Steinberg, "Behavioral Standards for Youth," *Journal of Secondary Education* 43, no. 1 (January 1968): 34–38.

10. Geoff Burkman, e-mail to author, June 7, 2000.

11. Telephone conversation with James McNamara, June 23, 1999; *Ferrell v. Dallas Independent School District*, 392 F. 2d 697 (1968).

12. *Ferrell v. Dallas*, 261 F. Supp. 545 (1966); *Ferrell v. Dallas* (1968).

13. *Ferrell v. Dallas* (1966).

14. *Ferrell v. Dallas* (1968).

15. *Corley v. Daunhauer*, 312 F. Supp. 811 (1970); John Pepple to author, June 17, 1999.

16. J. P. and B. Barrett, "Our Patriarch," *Freethinker* 1, no. 2, quoted in Birmingham, *Our Time Is Now*, 66.

17. David Super, e-mail to author, May 17, 2000; John Pepple, letter to author, June 17, 1999.

18. John Canfield, "White Teacher, Black School," in Kevin Ryan, ed., *Don't Smile Until Christmas: Accounts of the First Year Teaching* (Chicago: University of Chicago Press, 1970), 33–35.

19. *Gfell v. Rickelman*, 313 F. Supp. 364 (1970).

20. *Sims v. Colfax Community School*, 307 F. Supp. 485 (1970); *Crossen v. Fatsi*, 309 F. Supp. 114 (1970).

21. David E. Shelton, "The Legal Aspects of Male Students' Hair Grooming Policies in the Public Schools of the United States" (PhD diss., University of North Carolina, 1980).

22. Marsh' Fenstermaker, e-mail to author, June 18, 1999; *Sims v. Colfax* (1970).

23. Brett Harvey, quoted in Ruth Rosen, *The World Split Open: How the Modern Women's Movement Changed America* (New York: Viking, 2000), 14.

24. Kathie Grant, e-mail to author, May 15, 2000.

25. Sharon Breitweiser, letter to author, October 10, 1999; *School Management,* November 1967, 32–37.

26. *New York Times,* November 13, 1965, 31:5.

27. Gail Marsh, e-mail to author, May 23, 2000; Diane Arave, e-mail to author, September 10, 1999; Sharon Rab, e-mail to author, May 25, 2000.

28. Marc Libarle and Tom Seligson, eds., *High School Revolutionaries* (New York: Random House, 1970), xxiv.

29. Sandra Kral, e-mail to author, May 19, 2000.

30. "If the School Board Gets More Money. . ." cartoon by "Waleed S. Al-Fahdly," from *New Improved Tide* (John Marshall High School underground newspaper), reprinted in Irving G. Hendrick and Reginald L. Jones, eds., *Student Dissent in the Schools* (Boston: Houghton Mifflin, 1971), 79; Sharon Bialy-Fox, e-mail to author, May 12, 2000.

31. *New York Times,* February 9, 1970, 1:40; Irwin, *Ghetto Principal,* 116.

32. "What People Think about Their High Schools," *Life,* May 16, 1969, 27; *New York Times,* January 20, 1969, 7:1.

33. *Hatter v. Los Angeles City High School District,* 452 F. 2d 673 (1971); Alice Krause Young, e-mail to author, May 25, 2000.

34. Edgar Z. Friedenberg, "Ceremonies of Humiliation in School," *Education Digest,* November 1966, quoted in the *Phi Delta Kappan* (December 1966), 155; Robert Rossner, *The Year Without an Autumn: Portrait of a School in Crisis* (New York: Richard W. Baron, 1969), 41; Helen Baker, "Growing Up Unheard," in Beatrice Gross and Ronald Gross, eds., *The Children's Rights Movement: Overcoming the Oppression of Young People* (Garden City, N.Y.: Anchor Books, 1977), 197; phone interview with James D. McNamara, June 23, 1999.

35. Kathy Mulherin, "High School Revolt: Greasers Lightning," *Dock of the Bay,* September 9, 1969, reprinted in Mitchell Goodman, comp., *The Movement Toward a New America: The Beginnings of a Long Revolution (A Collage)—A What?* (Philadelphia: Pilgrim Press, 1970), 541; *New Free Press* [Niles Township High School underground newspaper], September 1969, 2, in author's possession, courtesy of Leslie Robbins; interview with Dr. Willard in Alice Duffy Rinehart, *Mortals in the Immortal Profession: An Oral History of Teaching* (New York: Irvington Publishers, 1983), 250; "What People Think about Their High Schools," 27.

36. Canfield, "White Teacher, Black School," in Ryan, *Don't Smile Until Christmas,* 57; Marilyn Hall, e-mail to author, June 6, 2000; Libarle and Seligson, *High School Revolutionaries,* xi–xiii, and in the interview with Tom Lindsay, 241. The story of the confrontation at Wellesley High School was also reported in the *New York Times* and reprinted in Goodman, *Movement Toward a New America,* 24.

37. In *School Management's* "Administrator's Forum," a number of school principals and superintendents debated the matter (September 1967, 25–29, 32, 37, 41, 45).

38. Susan Bowman Prendergast, e-mail to author, June 16, 2000.

39. *New York Times,* May 7, 1971, 41:5.

40. Geoff Burkman, e-mail to author, June 7, 2000.

41. *Scoville v. Board of Education,* 425 F. 2d 10 (1970); *Peterson v. Board of Education,* 370 F. Supp. 1208 (1973); *Koppell v. Levine,* 347 F. Supp. 456 (1972); *Shanley v. Northeastern Independent School District,* 462 F. 2d 960 (1972); *New Free Press* 2, no. 1 (September 1969): 2, courtesy of Leslie Robbins.

42. Birmingham, *Our Time Is Now,* 6–7.

43. Toby Mamis, "The High School Underground Press: A Brief History of the New York Underground High School Press and Why Underground Papers are Necessary," in Libarle and Seligson, *High School Revolutionaries,* 252–53.

44. Diane Divoky, "The Way It's Going to Be," *Saturday Review,* February 5, 1969, 83–84, 89, 101–2. Abe Peck expands Divoky's claim to between five hundred and a

thousand high school undergrounds, but he does not cite a source. Abe Peck, *Uncovering the Sixties: The Life and Times of the Underground Press* (New York: Pantheon Books, 1985), xvii. Robert Glessing cites a study by a UCLA journalism professor of four hundred Southern California high schools. Projecting this finding (fifty-two of four hundred high schools had underground papers) onto the country as a whole, Glessing suggested that the number of high school undergrounds around the country could be higher than three thousand. He did note that small-town and rural high schools were unlikely to have as many undergrounds as the metropolitan areas. Thus, his projection of 3,250 undergrounds is almost certainly too high. Equally, however, Divoky's figure of five hundred is too low. Robert J. Glessing, *The Underground Press in America* (Bloomington: Indiana University Press, 1970), 129. Mamis also discusses some of the turnover in high school undergrounds. See Mamis, "The High School Underground Press," in Libarle and Seligson, *High School Revolutionaries,* 248–51.

45. Libarle and Seligson, *High School Revolutionaries,* xxi; Mamis, "The High School Underground Press," 249, 250; Divoky, "The Way It's Going to Be," 101; Glessing, *The Underground Press,* 75–76.

46. Divoky, "The Way It's Going to Be," 101; letter to John Birmingham, quoted in Birmingham, *Our Time Is Now,* 23; Glessing, *Underground Press,* 76; Youth Liberation of Ann Arbor, "We Do Not Recognize Their Right to Control Us," in Gross and Gross, *The Children's Rights Movement,* 132.

47. Sharon Breitweiser, letters to author, October 10, 1999, and November 4, 1999; *New Free Press* 2, no. 2 (October 1969), courtesy of Leslie Robbins; letter to John Birmingham, quoted in Birmingham, *Our Time Is Now,* 24.

48. Sharon Breitweiser, letters to author, October 10, 1999, and November 4, 1999; Silberman, *Crisis in the Classroom,* 154, 155; Birmingham, *Our Time Is Now,* 31.

49. Quoted in Birmingham, *Our Time Is Now,* 22; Rossner, *Year Without an Autumn,* 104.

50. *New Free Press,* November 1969, 2, courtesy of Leslie Robbins.

51. The *New Free Press* shows the range of topics covered by undergrounds, as do Diane Divoky, "The Way It's Going to Be"; Divoky, *How Old Will You Be in 1984? Expression of Student Outrage from the High School Press* (New York: Avon, 1969); Birmingham, *Our Time Is Now.*

52. "Obscenity: In the Eyes of the Beholder," *New Free Press* 2, no. 2 (October 1969): 2, courtesy of Leslie Robbins.

53. *Shanley v. Northeast* (1972); Divoky, "The Way It's Going to Be," 83.

54. Birmingham, *Our Time Is Now,* 28–30.

55. Mamis, "The High School Underground Press," 255.

56. Ibid., 256.

57. Birmingham, *Our Time Is Now,* 42; "Sticks and Stones May Break My Bones, But Words Only Clarify Our Experiences," *Links,* quoted in Birmingham, *Our Time Is Now,* 40.

58. "Why We Don't Use the Word Shit," *American Revelation* 1, no. 7, quoted in Birmingham, *Our Time Is Now,* 41–42.

59. Joe Harris, "Firebomb," interview in Libarle and Seligson, *High School Revolutionaries,* 64; Nicholas Pileggi, "Revolutionaries Who Have to Be Home by 7:30," *New York Times Magazine,* March 16, 1969, 26–27, 119–23; Birmingham, *Our Time Is Now,* 11–12; Samuel Walker, *In Defense of American Liberties: A History of the ACLU* (New York: Oxford University Press, 1990), 306.

60. *Quarterman v. Bryd,* 453 F. 2d 54 (1971); *Schwartz v. Schuker,* 298 F. Supp. 238 (1969).

61. John W. Johnson, *The Struggle for Student Rights:* Tinker v. Des Moines *and the 1960s* (Lawrence: University Press of Kansas, 1997), 2–7, 26–27, 99, 119, 175–79.

62. *Tinker v. Des Moines, Independent School District,* 393 U.S. 503 (1969).

63. Ibid.

64. Ibid.

65. Quoted in Birmingham, *Our Time Is Now,* 59–61.

66. Donald Reeves, *Notes of a Processed Brother* (New York: Pantheon, 1972), 129, 324.

67. Interview with Chesley Karr, November 26, 2002.

5—STUDENT RIGHTS, STUDENT POWER, AND THE CRITIQUE OF CONTEMPORARY EDUCATION

1. Richard S. Fuller, "Schools versus Education: A Discussion of the Film *High School,*" *Colloquy,* March 1970, reprinted in Mitchell Goodman, comp., *The Movement Toward a New America: The Beginnings of a Long Revolution (A Collage)—A What?* (Philadelphia: Pilgrim Press, 1970), 278–79; "The High School: How Much Change—and How Fast?" *School Management* 13, no. 12 (December 1969): 56–60; Bhob [*sic*] Stewart, All Movie Guide, *New York Times,* movies2nytimes.come/gst/movies /movie.html:v_id=140936 (accessed December 13, 2004).

2. Fuller, "Schools versus Education," 278; "The High School," 56–58; Donald Reeves, *Notes of a Processed Brother* (New York: Pantheon Books, 1971), 381.

3. "What People Think about Their High Schools," *Life,* May 16, 1969, 23–33; "High School Activists Tell What They Want," *Nation's Schools* 82, no. 6 (December 1968): 29–34.

4. "We Do Not Recognize Their Right to Control Us," Youth Liberation of Ann Arbor, reprinted in Beatrice Gross and Ronald Gross, eds., *The Children's Rights Movement: Overcoming the Oppression of Young People* (Garden City, N.Y.: Anchor Press, 1977), 131; *New Free Press,* November 1969, 10, courtesy of Leslie Robbins; John Birmingham, *Our Time Is Now: Notes from the High School Underground* (New York: Praeger, 1970), 12.

5. Swerdloff quotation from Diane Divoky, "The Way It's Going to Be," *Saturday Review,* February 15, 1969, 101; *Common Sense* 2, no. 1, quoted in Birmingham, *Our Time Is Now,* 128; *Minstrel* (Waukegan, Ill.) 2, no. 1, reprinted in Birmingham, *Our Time Is Now,* 128.

6. Rich Shadden, "Interview," *Minstrel* 1, no. 4, reprinted in Birmingham, *Our Time Is Now,* 79–81.

7. "My Teacher is a Racist," "Susan Snow" interview in Marc Libarle and Tom Seligson, eds., *High School Revolutionaries* (New York: Random House, 1970), 93–94.

8. Ward Sybouts and Wayne J. Krepel, *Student Activities in the Secondary Schools: A Handbook and Guide* (Westport, Conn.: Greenwood Press, 1984), 220.

9. Birmingham, *Our Time Is Now,* 55–57, 165; Jerry Farber, "The Student as Nigger," reprinted in Goodman, *Movement Toward a New America,* 303–4.

10. Quoted in Libarle and Seligson, *High School Revolutionaries,* 19.

11. *Weakly Reader,* no. 13, quoted in Birmingham, *Our Time Is Now,* 98.

12. *New Free Press* 2, no. 2 (1969): 5, courtesy of Leslie Robbins.

13. "High Schools Becoming More Political," *Liberation News Service,* September 1969, reprinted in Goodman, *Movement Toward a New America,* 271; Todd Gitlin, *The Sixties: Years of Hope, Days of Rage* (New York: Bantam, 1897), 391; *Weakly Reader,* no. 13, quoted in Birmingham, *Our Time Is Now,* 97.

14. Mike Fox, "Students as Cattle," *Observed* 1, no. 4, reprinted in Birmingham, *Our Time Is Now,* 91.

15. "My Teacher Is a Racist," "Snow" interview in Libarle and Seligson, *High School Revolutionaries,* 88, emphasis in original; Toby Mamis, "The High School Underground Press: A Brief History of the New York Underground High School Press and Why Underground Papers are Necessary," in Libarle and Seligson, *High School Revolutionaries,* 257.

16. Libarle and Seligson, *High School Revolutionaries,* xxvi.

17. Reeves, *Notes of a Processed Brother,* 174.

18. Birmingham, *Our Time Is Now,* 99; Bob Musikantow, letter to the editors, *New Free Press,* February/March 1970, 11, courtesy of Leslie Robbins; *New York Times,* April 5, 1968, 27:4.

19. *Links,* quoted in Birmingham, *Our Time Is Now,* 99–101. Emphasis in original.

20. Homestead Student Bill of Rights, in Dennis Gall, *Kaleidoscope,* February 27, 1969, reprinted in Goodman, *Movement Toward a New America,* 282; Philadelphia High School Bill of Rights, in Elsie Y. Cross and Irving Rosenstein, "Do Teachers Want What Students Need?" in Dwight Allen and Jeffrey Hecht, eds., *Controversies in Education* (Philadelphia: W. B. Saunders, 1974), 385–403; Detroit High School Bill of Rights, in James Ross Irwin, *A Ghetto Principal Speaks Out: A Decade of Crisis in Urban Public Schools* (Detroit: Wayne State University Press, 1973), 144–47; New York City, in Dick Roberts and Derrick Morrison, "High School Rights," *The Great Speckled Bird,* March 23, 1970, reprinted in Goodman, *Movement Toward a New America,* 279; Robert Rossner, *The Year Without an Autumn: Portrait of a School in Crisis* (New York: Richard W. Baron, 1969), 248–51; "Power," *New York Herald-Tribune* (high school underground), no. 5, reprinted in Birmingham, *Our Time Is Now,* 147; Reeves, *Notes of a Processed Brother.*

21. Senate Committee on Appropriations, *Senate Hearings before the Committee on Appropriations, Department of the Interior and Related Agencies Appropriations,* 92nd Cong., 2d sess., April 11, 1972.

22. *Freethinker* 2, no. 1, La Puente, California, reprinted in Birmingham, *Our Time Is Now,* 68.

23. *Sansculotte* 28, Bronx, New York, reprinted in Birmingham, *Our Time Is Now,* 125; Steve Wasserman, "We Will Exercise Our Rights," interview in Libarle and Seligson, *High School Revolutionaries,* 231; Irwin, *Ghetto Principal,* 144–45.

24. Irwin, *Ghetto Principal,* 145–46; *New York High School Free Press,* no. 8, reprinted in Birmingham, *Our Time Is Now,* 178–81.

25. Rossner, *Year Without an Autumn,* 41; Reeves, *Notes of a Processed Brother,* 123. On illegal suspensions, see *New York High School Free Press,* reprinted in Birmingham, *Our Time Is Now,* 108–9, Reeves, *Notes of a Processed Brother,* 188; *New York High School Free Press* 8, reprinted in Birmingham, *Our Time Is Now,* 180–81; Irwin, *Ghetto Principal,* 145; State Education Department memorandum no. 8022, reprinted in *Dissent and Disruption in the Schools: A Handbook for School Administrators* (Dayton, Ohio: Institute for the Development of Educational Activities, 1969), 46.

26. John Koskinen, Richard Shadden, and Stuart Steffan, "Toward a Democratic Student Government," *Minstrel* 2, no. 1, reprinted in Birmingham, *Our Time Is Now,* 128–30.

27. *Goss v. Lopez,* 419 U.S. 565 (1975).

28. *The High School Free Press,* no. 7; *New York Herald-Tribune* (high school underground), no. 5, both quoted in Birmingham, *Our Time Is Now,* 145–49.

29. Bruce Trigg to Diane Fowler, *San Francisco Good Times,* quoted in Robert J. Glessing, *The Underground Press in America* (Bloomington: Indiana University Press, 1970), 132; Reeves, *Notes of a Processed Brother,* 212–13.

30. Reeves, *Notes of a Processed Brother,* 216–18, 301–2.

31. Ibid., 344–49; *New York Times,* April 5, 1970, 51:1.

32. Reeves, *Notes of a Processed Brother,* 338–39, 344–46, 364–67, 376–80.

33. Ibid., 320.

34. Ibid., 329–31, 359.

35. Ibid., 366.

36. *New York Times,* July 8, 1970, 1:6; Seymour P. Lachman and Murray Polner, "How Much Freedom for High School Students?" *New York University Education Quarterly* 1 (Summer 1970): 21–23, reprinted in Irving G. Hendrick and Reginald L. Jones, eds., *Student Dissent in the Schools* (Boston: Houghton Mifflin, 1972), 170–74; Reeves, *Notes of a Processed Brother,* 418–20.

37. Ralph Nader and Donald Ross, with Brent English and Joseph Highland, *Action for a Change: A Student's Manual for Public Interest Organizing* (New York: Grossman Publishers, 1972), 105.

38. Reeves, *Notes of a Processed Brother,* appendix B, 461–62.

39. Ibid., 461.

40. Cross and Rosenstein, "Do Teachers Want?" 385–403.

41. Ibid., 399.

42. Irwin, *Ghetto Principal,* 216.

43. "Brown Power," reprinted in Goodman, *Movement Toward a New America,* 230; Johns [*sic*] Harrington, "L.A.'s Student Blowout," *Phi Delta Kappan* (October 1968), 74–75, 77–78, reprinted in Sol Cohen, ed., *Education in the United States: A Documentary History* (New York: Random House, 1974), 2936.

44. *New Free Press* 2, no. 6 (February/March 1970), and 2, no. 7 (April 1970): 3, courtesy of Leslie Robbins; *Karp v. Becken,* 477 F. 2d 171 (1973) and *Russo v. Central School District No. 1,* 469 F. 2d 623 (1972).

45. *Minstrel* 2, no. 1, quoted in Birmingham, *Our Time Is Now,* 129.

46. *New York High School Free Press,* no. 7, reprinted in Birmingham, *Our Time Is Now,* 142.

47. Corman, "Hangman or Victim," in Kevin Ryan, ed., *Don't Smile Until Christmas: Accounts of the First Year Teaching* (Chicago: University of Chicago Press, 1970), 114.

48. "What People Think about Their High Schools," 24.

49. *New York Times,* April 5, 1968, 28:1; whites seeking court injunction, *New York Times,* March 13, 1969, 41:1. It is not clear whether the white parents prevailed.

50. Miss "Iace Hoc Ad Illi," "We're Number One (Boom), We're Number One!" *T.R.I.P.,* vol. 2, Long Beach, Calif., quoted in Birmingham, *Our Time Is Now,* 78.

51. Gross and Gross, *The Children's Rights Movement,* 129; Reeves, *Notes of a Processed Brother,* 159–60.

52. Joe Harris, "Firebomb," interview in Libarle and Seligson, *High School Revolutionaries,* 59.

53. Birmingham, *Our Time Is Now,* 65; Michael Marquee, "Turn Left at Scarsdale," interview in Libarle and Seligson, *High School Revolutionaries,* 16.

54. "High School Activists," *Nation's Schools,* 30; Paul Steiner, "H. S. Liberation Front," *New York High School Free Press,* no. 6, reprinted in Birmingham, *Our Time Is Now,* 256–59.

55. *New Free Press,* April 1970, 4, courtesy of Leslie Robbins; Goodman, *Movement Toward a New America,* 267, 277.

56. Birmingham, *Our Time Is Now,* 262; *New York Times,* February 13, 1970, 34:1.

57. *New York Times,* February 13, 1970, 34:1.

58. Elizabeth Cleaners Street School, *Starting Your Own High School* (New York: Random House, 1972).

59. *New York Herald-Tribune,* no. 5, reprinted in Birmingham, *Our Time Is Now,* 181–87.

60. "Stuyvesant Open During Strike!" *New York Herald-Tribune* 2, no. 2, reprinted in Birmingham, *Our Time Is Now,* 218–21; Reeves, *Notes of a Processed Brother,* 74, 78; Beatrice M. Gudridge, *High School Student Unrest* (Washington, D.C.: National School Public Relations Association, 1969), 20.

61. Rossner, *Year Without an Autumn,* 111, 129, 159, 191, emphasis in original.

62. Nicholas Pileggi, "Revolutionaries Who Have to Be Home by 7:30," *New York Times Magazine,* March 16, 1969, 123.

63. Deborah Astley, letter to author, June 24, 2000; "Grades, Bah Humbug!" *Open Door,* Milwaukee, Wis., reprinted in Birmingham, *Our Time Is Now,* 210–11; letters to the editor, *New Free Press,* November 1969, 11, courtesy of Leslie Robbins.

64. Irwin, *Ghetto Principal,* 175; David Wachtel, letter to author, November 12, 1999; House Subcommittee on General Education report, summarized in Irwin, *Ghetto Principal,* 112–14.

65. Libarle and Seligson, *High School Revolutionaries,* xxvii; Dennis Gall, "Homestead High Smothers Student Rights," *Kaleidoscope,* February 27, 1969, reprinted in Goodman, *Movement Toward a New America,* 282.

66. Linda Corman, "Hangman or Victim," in Ryan, *Don't Smile Until Christmas,* 115–16.

67. Fuller, "Schools Versus Education," 279.

6—HIGH SCHOOL STUDENTS, THE VIETNAM WAR, AND RADICAL POLITICS

1. *New York Times,* June 28, 1968, 43:1.

2. Marc Libarle and Tom Seligson, eds., *The High School Revolutionaries* (New York: Random House, 1970), xxii, xxiii; Vicki Aldrich, e-mail to author, September 18, 1999; *Vail et. al. v. The Board of Education of the Portsmouth School District,* 354 F. Supp. 592 (1973).

3. *New York Times,* December 16, 1968, 43:3.

4. Mark Kleinman, "High School Reform: Toward a Student Movement," in Massimo Teodori, ed., *The New Left: A Documentary History* (Indianapolis: Bobbs-Merrill, 1969), 318–23.

5. *New York Times,* December 30, 1968, 29:1; James Ross Irwin, *A Ghetto Principal Speaks Out: A Decade of Crisis in Urban Public Schools* (Detroit: Wayne State University Press, 1973), 138; Jerry Rubin, "Do It!" in Judith Clavir Albert and Stewart Edward Albert, eds., *The Sixties Papers: Documents of a Rebellious Decade* (New York: Praeger, 1984), 437–48; Todd Gitlin, *The Sixties: Years of Hope, Days of Rage* (New York: Bantam Books, 1993), 391.

6. Kirkpatrick Sale, *SDS* (New York: Random House, 1973), 400, 481–82, 588–89.

7. Todd Gitlin, *The Whole World is Watching: Mass Media in the Making and Unmaking of the New Left* (Berkeley: University of California Press, 1980), 85–86; House Committee on Internal Security, *SDS Plans for America's High Schools: Report of the Committee on Internal Security,* 91st Cong. 1st sess, reprinted in Irving G. Hendrick and Reginald L. Jones, eds., *Student Dissent in the Schools* (Boston: Houghton Mifflin, 1971), 289–303.

8. Sale, *SDS,* 79, 88,158, 271, 341, 399–400, 409, 416, 479, 485. 523, 529; "High Schools Becoming More Political," *Liberation News Service,* September 1969, reprinted in Mitchell Goodman, comp., *The Movement Toward a New America: The Beginnings of a Long Revolution (A Collage)—A What?* (Philadelphia: Pilgrim Press, 1970), 271; Irwin, *Ghetto Principal,* 142–43; *Iceberg* (high school underground), no. 1, Nashville, Tenn., reprinted in John Birmingham, *Our Time Is Now: Notes From the High School Underground* (New York: Praeger, 1970), 154; *Links* (high school underground), reprinted in Birmingham, *Our Time Is Now,* 100; Irwin, *Ghetto Principal,* 142–43.

9. "High School Activists Tell What They Want," 29–30; Diane Divoky, "The Way It's Going to Be," *Saturday Review,* February 15, 1969, 82; Kenneth L. Fish, *Conflict and Dissent in the High Schools* (New York: Bruce Publishing, 1970), 158–60.

10. Sale, *SDS,* 524.

11. Interview with Robbie Newton and Jaime Friar, *Smuff* 1, no. 2, reprinted in Birmingham, *Our Time Is Now,* 16–18.

12. Dale Gaddy, *Rights and Freedoms of Public High School Students* (Topeka, Kans.: National Organization on Legal Problems of Education, 1971), 19–21.

13. Jan Weiland, e-mails to author, May 5, 2000, and May 11, 2000; Gitlin, *Sixties,* 391; Sale, *SDS,* 582–89, 602, 609: David Burner, *Making Peace with the Sixties* (Princeton, N.J.: Princeton University Press, 1996), 160.

14. Fred Halstead, *Out Now! A Participant's Account of the American Movement against the Vietnam War* (New York: Monad Press, 1978), 293–95, 373; Eve Levin, e-mail to author, June 18, 1999.

15. Dick Roberts and Derrick Morrison, "High School Rights," *The Great Speckled Bird,* March 23, 1970, reprinted in Goodman, *Movement Toward a New America,* 279; Donald Reeves, *Notes of a Processed Brother* (New York: Pantheon Books, 1971), 338, 349, 364, 376–79; Irwin, *Ghetto Principal,* 193.

16. *New York High School Free Press,* no. 8, reprinted in Birmingham, *Our Time Is Now,* 187–88; "Keep On Pushing," interview with Paul Gayton in Libarle and Seligson, *High School Revolutionaries,* 68.

17. James Brown, "The Black Athlete," interview in Libarle and Seligson, *High School Revolutionaries*, 54–57.

18. Susan Jacobson, letter to editor, *New Free Press*, October 1969, 5, courtesy of Leslie Robbins; Underground Newspaper Collection, Roll 12 (1968), *Midpeninsula Observer* 1, no. 12 (January 22–February 5, 1968): 4, "Free Speech Eliminated in Paly High Schools"; *Midpeninsula Observer* 1, no. 13 (February 5–February 9, 1968): 12, "Discrimination against Blacks in New HS Plan?"; *Midpeninsula Observer* 1, no. 19 (May 6–20, 1968): 1, "50 Paly Students Strike for Rights"; Underground Newspaper Collection, Roll 8, *The Guardian* (June 15, 1968): 4, "Model City's High School Erupt"; 5, "Students Shut Down High Schools"; *Guardian* (October 19, 1968): 9, "Chicago Schools Disrupted"; *Guardian* (December 7, 1968): 6, "NY Schools Erupt"; Nicholas Pileggi, "Revolutionaries Who Have to Be Home by 7:30," *New York Times Magazine*, March 14, 1969, 120.

19. Underground Newspaper Collection, Roll 8 (1968), *Helix* (Seattle) 3, no. 9 (n.d.), 17; *Washington v. Oyen*, 480 P. 2d 766 (1971); *Washington Free Community v. State's Attorney of Montgomery City*, 310 F. Supp. 436 (1970); *Mandel v. Alameda County*, 276 Cal. App. 2d 6490 (1969).

20. *Castro v. Los Angeles*, 9 Cal. App. 3d 675 (1970); Edward J. Escobar, "The Dialectics of Repression: The Los Angeles Police Department and the Chicano Movement, 1968–1971," *Journal of American History* 79, no. 4 (March 1993): 1483–1514; Carlos Muñoz, Jr., e-mail to author, July 14, 2000; David Gómez, *Somos Chicanos: Strangers in Our Own Land* (Boston: Beacon Press, 1973).

21. John Staples Shockley, *Revolt in a Texas Town* (Notre Dame, Ind.: University of Notre Dame Press, 1974), 116; Kenneth García, letter to author, August 11, 2000.

22. Samuel Walker, *In Defense of American Liberties: A History of the ACLU* (New York: Oxford University Press, 1990), 306–8; Richie Cohen, "Jewing Down South," interview, in Libarle and Seligson, *High School Revolutionaries*, 146.

23. American Civil Liberties Union, *Academic Freedom in the Secondary Schools* (pamphlet, originally printed September 1968; reprinted December 1969, May 1971).

24. Pilgeggi, "Revolutionaries," 122; David Romano, "I Saw America in the Streets," interview, and Tom Lindsay, "High School Students Unite," interview, both in Libarle and Seligson, *High School Revolutionaries*, 11–12, 245.

25. "Special Report on Student Unrest in the Public Schools," *School Management* 12, no. 11 (November 1968): 50–98.

26. Ibid.

27. Gitlin, *Sixties*, 177–83; Charles DeBenedetti, *An American Ordeal: The Antiwar Movement of the Vietnam Era* (Syracuse, N.Y.: Syracuse University Press, 1990), chap. 5.

28. Gitlin, *Sixties*, 293.

29. "What High School Students Think of Their Schools," *Life*, May 10, 1969, 22–42; Richard Ramy, "Teachers, Students, and the War in Vietnam: A Research Note on Controversial Issues in the Classroom," *High School Journal* 54, no. 2 (November 1970): 137–44; Mark Richards, letter to author, July 17, 2000; Loretta Nunn, e-mail to author, June 17, 1999; Kathleen Casey, *I Answer with My Life: Histories of Women Teachers Working for Social Change* (New York: Routledge, 1993), 97–100. Goodman's *Movement Toward a New America* (p. 302), reprinted an advertisement for a "Vietnam Curriculum," put out by five Boston area teachers; it is not clear if the woman Casey interviewed was one of these five, or whether there was more than one "Vietnam Curriculum" in circulation. For the story about Martha Zimmerman, see Kathy Mulherin, "High School Revolt: Greasers Lightning," *Dock of the Bay*, September 9, 1969, reprinted in Goodman, *Movement Toward a New America*, 541–42.

30. Gary Carnog, "To Care and Not to Care," in Kevin Ryan, ed., *Don't Smile Until Christmas: Accounts of the First Year Teaching* (Chicago: University of Chicago Press, 1970), 11; Frank Petroni and Ernest Hirsch, with C. Lillian Petroni, *Two, Four, Six, Eight, When You Gonna Integrate?* (Morningside Heights, N.Y.: Behavioral Problems, 1970), 98; Robert Rossner, *The Year Without an Autumn: Portrait of a School in Crisis* (New York:

Richard W. Baron, 1969), 15–16; William Kline and Jan L. Tucker, "The 'Cambodian May,'" *High School Journal* 55, no. 4 (January 1972): 165.

31. Mary Ann Kennedy, "Jesus Says I Should," interview in Libarle and Seligson, *High School Revolutionaries,* 128; Eve Levin, e-mail to author, June 18, 1999; Jacqueline Rummel Groll, e-mail to author, September 8, 1999.

32. Catherine Strahm, letter to author, September 7, 1999.

33. Louise Lancaster-Keim, e-mail to author, July 12, 2000; Susan Lindholm, e-mail to author, May 19, 2000.

34. Poll of West Milford Township High School students provided by Bradley Bender, in author's possession; *New York Times,* November 1, 1970, 7:1.

35. Brent Coatney, letter to author, date unclear, 1999; "My Teacher is a Racist," "Susan Snow" interview in Libarle and Seligson, *High School Revolutionaries,* 90.

36. Pete Biscus, letter to author, September 6, 1999.

37. Jean Hartley Davis Sidden, e-mail to author, May 7, 2000.

38. John Pepple, letter to author, June 17, 1999.

39. Brent Coatney, letter to author, date unclear, 1999; Joyce Mitchel, e-mails to author, June 13 and June 16, 1999.

40. Carole Palmer, letter to author, May 21, 2000; Joyce Mitchel, e-mails to author, June 17, 1999, 9:34 a.m. and 11:13 p.m.

41. Mike Ward, letter to author and to the *Denver Post,* September 7, 1999. The *Denver Post* printed my request for memories about high school in the 1960s and featured some of the responses in a newspaper story on November 21, 1999. Ward therefore addressed his letter both to me and to the newspaper.

42. Joyce Mitchel, e-mails to author, June 17, 1999, 9:34 a.m. and 11:13 p.m.

43. Eve Levin, e-mail to author, June 18, 1999.

44. Vicki Aldrich, e-mail to author, September 12, 1999.

45. Elizabeth Harzoff, e-mail to author, August 8, 1999.

46. David Wachtel, letter to author, December 20, 1999.

47. Cohen, "Jewing Down South," interview in Libarle and Seligson, *High School Revolutionaries,* 142.

48. Paula Smith, "Nuns against the Wall," interview in Libarle and Seligson, *High School Revolutionaries,* 215; David Romano, "I Saw America in the Streets," interview in Libarle and Seligson, *High School Revolutionaries,* 7.

49. Jim Gardiner, "Growing Up Radical," interview in Libarle and Seligson, *High School Revolutionaries,* 167.

50. Gretchen Keller Gallucci, e-mail to author, July 3, 1999.

51. Alice Krause Young, e-mails to author, May 24, 2000, and May 25, 2000; Jonathan Wallace, "Kent State, May 4, 1970: America Kills Its Children," *Ethical Spectacle,* May 1995, www.spectacle.org/595/kent.html (accessed January 7, 2005).

52. Halstead, *Out Now!* 558, 561; "About Jonathan Wallace," www.spectacle.org/bio.html (accessed January 7, 2005).

53. "Eric Oakstein," "The Headmaster's Word Is Law," interview in Libarle and Seligson, *High School Revolutionaries,* 207.

54. "High School Students Tell What They Want," *Nation's Schools* 82, no. 6 (December 1968): 30–31.

55. Interview with Joe Pickering of the United Student Movement (Palo Alto, Calif.) in "High School Activists Tell What They Want," *Nation's Schools* 82, no. 6 (December 1968): 30–31.

56. Halstead, *Out Now!* 387; B. Taylor and S. Brucker, "Moratorium," from the West Milford Township High School literary magazine, 1969, typescript copy courtesy of Bradley J. Bender, who edited the magazine in that year; *New Free Press* 2, no. 3 (October 14, 1969), and 2, no. 4 (November 1969), courtesy of Leslie Robbins.

57. Sharon Bialy-Fox, e-mail to author, May 13, 2000; *Zucker v. Panitz,* 299 F. Supp. 102 (1969).

58. Eliot Asinof, *Craig and Joan: Two Lives for Peace* (New York: Viking Press, 1971).

59. *New Free Press* 2, no. 1 (September 1969): 8; and 2, no. 6 (February/March, 1970): 9, courtesy of Leslie Robbins; Pileggi, "Revolutionaries Who Have to Be Home," 122.

60. *New Free Press* 2, no. 3 (October 14, 1969): 2–3, courtesy of Leslie Robbins; Susan Worley, e-mail to author, May 23, 2000.

61. Cynthia Lynn Barnes, e-mail to author, n.d.

62. Durward Long, "Black Protest," in Julian Foster and Durward Long, eds., *Protest! Student Activism in America* (New York: William Morrow, 1970), 459–82; *New York High School Free Press*, no. 7, reprinted in Birmingham, *Our Time Is Now*, 140–47; Petroni and Hirsch, *Two, Four, Six*, 64; Rossner, *Year Without an Autumn*, 19.

63. Sylvia Williams, *Hassling* (Boston: Little, Brown, 1970), 108.

64. Mount, quoted in Ruth Rosen, *The World Split Open: How the Modern Women's Movement Changed America* (New York: Viking, 2000), 287; Skywalker Payne, letter to author, September 24, 1999.

65. Edward K. Spann, *Democracy's Children: The Young Rebels of the 1960s and the Power of Ideals* (Wilmington, Del.: Scholarly Resources, 2003), 136; Gregory L. Schneider, *Cadres for Conservatism: Young Americans for Freedom and the Rise of the Contemporary Right* (New York: New York University Press, 1999), 37, 78; John A. Andrew III, *The Other Side of the Sixties: Young Americans for Freedom and the Rise of Conservative Politics* (New Brunswick, N.J.: Rutgers University Press, 1997).

66. Jeff Schramek, letter to editor, *New Free Press,* April 1970, 7, courtesy of Leslie Robbins.

67. Robert Rossner, *The Year Without an Autumn: Portrait of a School in Crisis* (New York: Richard W. Baron, 1969), 22; Carnog, "To Care and Not to Care," in Ryan, *Don't Smile Until Christmas,* 11; Mark Richards, letter to author, July 17, 2000; Terre Burkhart, e-mail to author, June 13, 1999; John W. Johnson, *The Struggle for Student Rights:* Tinker vs. Des Moines *and the 1960s* (Lawrence: University Press of Kansas, 1997), 7–8; Mike Ward, letter to author, September 7, 1999; *Crews v. Cloncs,* 432 F. 2d 1259 (1970); Fish, *Conflict and Dissent,* 32–33; *Butts v. Dallas Independent School District,* 436 F. 2d 728 (1971); Underground Newspaper Collection, Roll 12 (1968), *The Other Other* (Brooklyn), no. 3 (May 20, 1969): 7.

68. *New York Times,* December 2, 1969, 26:1.

69. Alice Krause Young, e-mails to author, May 24, 2000, and May 25, 2000.

70. Eve Levin, e-mail to author, June 18, 1999; Alice de Rivera, "Jumping the Track," *Leviathan,* June 1969, reprinted in Goodman, *Movement Toward a New America,* 54.

71. De Rivera, "Jumping the Track," 54; Sharon Bialy-Fox, e-mail to author, May 12, 2000; Eve Levin, e-mail to author, June 18, 1999.

72. Deborah Astley, letter to author, June 24, 2000; JoAnne Dickens, e-mail to author, June 15, 1999; Betty Ann Hans, e-mail to author, May 16, 2000.

73. "June Stewart," e-mail to author, October 13, 1999.

74. "June Stewart," e-mail to author, October 13, 1999; Kathy Goecke, letter to author, September 10, 1999.

75. "June Stewart," e-mail to author, October 13, 1999; Kathy Goecke, letter to author, September 10, 1999; anonymous e-mail to author, June 13, 1999.

76. Libarle and Seligson, *High School Revolutionaries,* xxvii; Allen Mott, "Silence Kills," *New Free Press* 2, no. 4 (November 1969): 6, courtesy of Leslie Robbins.

77. U.S. Commission on Civil Rights, *What Students Want: A National Survey Prepared by the U.S. Commission on Civil Rights* (New York: Emerson Hall, 1971), 24; "High School Activists Tell What They Want," 29–31.

7—COPS IN THE HALLS, STUDENTS ON THE SCHOOL BOARD

1. Chuck Lowenhagen, "Anatomy of a Student Demonstration," *NASSP Bulletin* 53, no. 341 (December 1969): 81–86.

2. David Tyack and Elisabeth Hansot, *Managers of Virtue: Public School Leadership in America, 1820–1980* (New York: Basic Books, 1982), 238.

3. Kathleen Casey, *I Answer with My Life: Life Histories of Women Teachers Working for Social Change* (New York: Routledge, 1993); Alice Duffy Rinehart, *Mortals in the Immortal Profession: An Oral History of Teaching* (New York: Irvington Publishers, 1983); *New York Times,* August 20, 1970, 15:1.

4. *Dissent and Disruption in the Schools: A Handbook for Administrators* (Dayton, Ohio: Institute for the Development of Educational Activities, 1969), 19.

5. U.S. Commission on Civil Rights, *What Students Want: A National Survey Prepared by the U.S. Commission on Civil Rights* (New York: Emerson Hall, 1971), 2; J. Edgar Hoover, "The SDS and High Schools: A Study in Student Extremism," *PTA Magazine* 64 (January/February 1970): 2–5, 8–9, reprinted in Irving G. Hendrick and Reginald L. Jones, eds., *Student Dissent in the Schools* (Boston: Houghton Mifflin, 1973), 303–11; House Committee on Internal Security, *SDS Plans for America's High Schools: Report of the Committee on Internal Security,* 91st Cong., 1st sess., reprinted in Hendrick and Jones, *Student Dissent,* 298–303; *New York Times,* April 23, 1969, 23:1; *New York Times,* October 17, 1968, 38:3; Tom Wells, *The War Within: America's Battle over Vietnam* (Berkeley: University of California Press, 1994), 341–44; Toby Moffett, *The Participation Put-On: Reflections of a Disenchanted Washington Youth Expert* (New York: Delacorte Press, 1971).

6. *Blackwell v. Issaquena County Board of Education,* 363 F. 2d 749 (1966); *Burnside v. Byars,* 636 F. 2d 744 (1966); *Tinker v. Des Moines Independent School District,* 393 U. S. 503 (1969); Lawrence Brammer, "The Coming Revolt of High School Students," *Education Digest* 34, no. 3 (November 1968): 18–20; "Student Unrest Will Spread to High Schools, Many Fear," *Nation's Schools* 82, no. 3 (September 1968): 71; Beatrice Gudridge, "Is Student Protest Spreading to the High School?" *Today's Education* 57, no. 7 (October 1968): 30–32.

7. Lloyd E. Peterman, "A Place of Responsibility: Where it Worked Both Ways," *NASSP Bulletin* 53 (September 1969): 1–44, reprinted in Hendrick and Jones, *Student Dissent,* 230–39 (quotation on p. 230); James Enoch, "The Crisis in the Colleges: A Primer for High Schools," *Journal of Secondary Education* 44, no. 6 (October 1969): 280–85; Aaron Cohodes, "Colleges Give High Schools a Cram Course in Dissent," *Nation's Schools* 83, no. 5 (May 1969): 34; Brammer, "Coming Revolt," 19; "Three of Five Principals Reports Protest Activities," *Ohio Schools* 47, no. 5 (March 14, 1969): 31–32; Rafael M. Kudela, "Facing Student Unrest," *Clearing House* 44, no. 9 (May 1970): 547–52; James Irwin, *A Ghetto Principal Speaks Out: A Decade of Crisis in Urban Public Schools* (Detroit: Wayne State University, 1973), 113.

8. See Marc Libarle and Tom Seligson, eds., *The High School Revolutionaries* (New York: Random House, 1970); Kenneth L. Fish, *Conflict and Dissent in the High Schools* (New York: Bruce Publishing, 1970); Irwin, *Ghetto Principal,* 116; Philip Cusick, *Inside High School: The Student's World* (New York: Holt, Rinehart, and Winston, 1973).

9. James M. Jacob, "Student Views on Controversial Issues," *NASSP Bulletin* 53, no. 335 (March 1969): 20–30; Arlene Richards, "What Do Students Really Want?" *Today's Education* 60, no. 4 (April 1971): 57–58.

10. "What People Think about Their High Schools," *Life,* May 16, 1969, 23–33; Jon Schaller, Mark Chesler, and Keith Hefner, *Student and Youth Organizing: A Youth Liberation Pamphlet* (Ann Arbor, Mich.: Youth Liberation Press, n.d.), 49.

11. Moffett, *Participation Put-On,* 151–52; Stephen K. Bailey, *Disruption in Urban Public Secondary Schools* (Washington, D.C.: National Association of Secondary School Principals, 1970), 7–9.

12. Irwin, *Ghetto Principal*, 114; "Violence Hits Schools, Colleges," *U.S. News & World Report*, May 20, 1968, 36–40; Bailey, *Disruption in Urban Public Secondary Schools*, 10, table 2.

13. James E. Allen, "Student Unrest in the High Schools," *School and Society* 98, no. 2323 (February 1970): 75–76.

14. Fred M. Hechinger, "The Imitators: A Look at Why Schoolchildren Rebel," *New York Times*, April 26, 1969, 15:5; "Student Unrest Will Spread," 71; "Now It's High-School Students on a Rampage," *U.S. News & World Report*, March 24, 1969, 8–9; "Worst of Student Disorders May Be Over," *Nation's Schools* 87, no. 2 (February 1971): 17; Rinehart, *Mortals*, 279.

15. Margaret Mead, "Youth Revolt: The Future is Now," *Saturday Review*, January 10, 1970, 23–25, 113; Gordon Cowelti, "Youth Assess the American High School," *PTA Magazine* 62, no. 9 (May 1968): 19. "Student Activism Steers Away from SDS," *Nation's Schools* 84, no. 1 (July 1969): 39–42; Don Parker, *Schooling for What?* (New York: McGraw-Hill, 1970), 41–58; Kenneth L. Fish, "Coping with Activism in the Secondary Schools," *Education Digest* 35, no. 2 (October 1969): 8–11.

16. Fish, *Conflict and Dissent*, 14; U.S. Commission on Civil Rights, *What Students Want*, 8.

17. Irwin, *Ghetto Principal*, 249; Edgar Friedenberg, "The Generation Gap," in Joseph Boskin and Robert Rosenstone, *Protest in the Sixties. Annals of the American Academy of Political and Social Science*, vol. 382 (Philadelphia: American Academy of Political and Social Science, 1969), 32–42.

18. Beverly Gifford, "Students at the Barricades," *Ohio Schools* 47, no. 5 (March 14, 1969): 12–14, 30; Ira Marienhoff, "The Courts and the Schools: A Dissent," *Social Education* 31, no. 8 (December 1967): 719–20; "Three of Five Principals Reports Protest Activities," 32; Dale Baughman, Wendell G. Anderson, Mark Smith, and Earle W. Wiltse, *Administration and Supervision of the Modern Secondary Schools* (West Nyack, N.Y.: Parker Publishing, 1969), 182; "Worst of Student Disorders," 17.

19. Brammer, "Coming Revolt," 20; Fish, "Coping with Activism," 9; Edward T. Ladd, "Teachers as Cause and Cure of Student Unrest," in Dwight W. Allen and Jeffrey C. Hecht, eds., *Controversies in Education* (Philadelphia: W. B. Saunders, 1974), 462–73.

20. Newton W. Fink and Benjamin Cullers, "Student Unrest: Structure of Public Schools a Major Factor?" *Clearing House* 44, no. 7 (March 1970): 415–19.

21. Jane Hunt, "Principals Report on Student Unrest," *Education Digest* 35, no. 4 (December 1969): 51; *Report of the White House Conference on Youth, April 18–22, 1971* (Washington, D.C.: U.S. Government Printing Office, 1971), 8; Joyce Mitchel, e-mail to author, June 17, 1999.

22. Robert L. Ackerly and Ivan B. Gluckman, *The Reasonable Exercise of Authority. II* (Reston, Va.: National Association of Secondary School Principals, 1976); Richard A. Gorton, "Student Activism in the High School: The Underground Newspaper and Student Dress and Appearance," *High School Journal* 53, no. 7 (April 1970): 411–16.

23. Friedenberg, "Generation Gap," 38; Bernard Filcher, "The Courts and the Schools: A Response," *Social Education* 32, no. 5 (May 1968): 451–52; Morris J. Weinberger, "Dress Codes: We Forget Our Own Advice," *Clearing House* 44, no. 8 (April 1970): 471–73; "Oh, Those Troublesome Dress Codes!" *American School Board Journal* 157, no. 4 (October 1969): 6; William McCarter, "Long Hair, Short Skirts . . . and the Courts," *Ohio Schools* 47, no. 5 (March 14, 1969): 15–16; Teresa Blackledge, "Glenn's Haircut," *Education Digest* 33, no. 1 (September 1967): 30–31.

24. "Try This Dress Code on for Size," *American School Board Journal* 157, no. 6 (December 1969): 14.

25. Hoover, "SDS and the High Schools," 310.

26. Robert Sullivan, "Let Them Write—Responsibly," *Education Digest* 43, no. 5 (January 1969): 50–51; Robert Sullivan, "The Overrated Threat," *NASSP Bulletin* 53, no. 338 (September 1969): 36–44; "High School Students Are Rushing into Print—and into Court," *Nation's Schools* 83, no. 1 (January 1969): 30–31, 90.

27. Sullivan, "Overrated Threat," 44; "High Schools Students Are Rushing . . . ," 90; Samuel M. Graves, "A Description of Student Unrest," *NASSP Bulletin* 53, no. 337 (May 1969): 191–97.

28. Gifford, "Students at the Barricades," 30; "New Respectability for Underground Papers," *Nation's Schools* 84, no. 3 (September 1969): 43.

29. Elizabeth Eisiedler, "How Free Should the High School Press Be?" *Today's Education* 58, no. 6 (September 1969): 52–54, 85; Galen Gritts, "Censorship Hinders Student Publications," *Revelation Now: A National Student Journalism Review* 1 (January 1970): 4, reprinted in Hendrick and Jones, *Student Dissent,* 206; *New Free Press,* October 1969, 5, courtesy of Leslie Robbins.

30. "New Respectability for Underground Papers," *Nation's Schools* 84, no. 3 (September 1969): 43.

31. Edwin Schneider, "What Is the Law Concerning Student Demonstrations?" *School Management,* November 1970, 19–21.

32. Diane Divoky, "The Way It's Going To Be," Saturday Review, February 15, 1969, 102; Elise Y. Cross and Irving Resenstein, "Do Teachers Want What Students Need?" in Allen and Hecht, *Controversies in Education,* 385–403.

33. Divoky, "The Way It's Going To Be," 89; Wallace E. Good, "Regulation of Student Conduct." Part 2, *American School Board Journal* 155, no. 2 (August 1967): 9–11; Ira Glasser, "Schools for Scandal: The Bill of Rights and Public Education," *Phi Delta Kappan* 51, no. 4 (December 1969): 190–94, emphasis in original.

34. *Ingraham v. Wright,* 430 U.S. 651 (1977).

35. Johns [sic] Harrington, "L.A.'s Student Blowout," *Phi Delta Kappan* (October 1968), 74–75, 77–78, reprinted in Sol Cohen, ed., *Education in the United States: A Documentary History* (New York: Random House, 1974), 2940; Fink and Cullers, "Student Unrest," 418; David Kukla, "Protest in Black and White: Student Radicals in High Schools," *NASSP Bulletin* 54, no. 342 (January 1970): 72–86.

36. Russell J. Spillman, "Students' Concerns and Protests Merit Educators' Perceptive Response," *Contemporary Education* 40, no. 6 (May 1969): 332–42; Carlos Muñoz, Jr., *Youth, Identity, Power: The Chicano Movement* (London: Verso, 1989), xi, 64–65; Fish, *Conflict and Dissent,* 69–75; Schaller, Chesler, and Hefner, *Student and Youth Organizing,* 31, 78.

37. Eleanor Fuke, "Identity or Discipline," 128–63, in Kevin Ryan, ed., *Don't Smile Until Christmas: Accounts of the First Year Teaching* (Chicago: University of Chicago Press, 1970).

38. Fish, *Conflict and Dissent,* 7, 18–20; Irwin, *Ghetto Principal,* 114; Fish, "Coping with Activism," 9; Adam Fairclough, *Race and Democracy: The Civil Rights Struggle in Louisiana, 1915–1972* (Athens: University of Georgia Press, 1995), 452.

39. Brammer, "Coming Revolt," 20.

40. Thomas McGuire, "Help Your Student Council Justify its Existence," *Journal of Secondary Education* 45, no. 4 (April 1970): 152–54; Brammer, "Coming Revolt," 20; Cohodes, "Colleges Give High Schools," 34; Keith Beavan, "New Office Should Lessen Student Unrest," *Times Educational Supplement* 2838 (October 10, 1969): 12; New York State Board of Education's resolution on "Rights and Responsibilities for Senior High Students," cited in Donald Reeves, *Notes of a Processed Brother* (New York: Pantheon, 1971), 460–62; James Irwin refers to both the New York City and Detroit document on "Student Rights and Responsibilities," the latter being a modification of the Student Mobilization Committee's Student Bill of Rights." Irwin, *Ghetto Principal,* 172–73.

41. Irwin, *Ghetto Principal,* 186–90; *Nitzberg v. Parks,* 525 F. 2d 378 (1975).

42. Fish, "Coping with Activism," 10; Ralph Nader and Donald Ross, with Brent English and Joseph Highland, *Action for a Change: A Student's Manual for Public Interest Organizing* (New York: Grossman Publishers, 1972), 105–21; Harold W. Gentry and Morrill M. Hall, "Organizational Response to Student Militancy in Secondary Schools," *High School Journal* 54, no. 5 (February 1971): 297–311; "Student Involvement: Channeling Activism into Accomplishment," *Nation's Schools* 84, no. 3 (September 1969): 39–50. In its "Special

Report on Student Unrest in the Public Schools, the journal *School Management* (November 1968, 50–98), also highlighted the "channeling" efforts of many administrators.

43. Fish, "Coping with Activism," 11.

44. Irwin, *Ghetto Principal*, 117; *Report of the White House Conference on Youth, April 18–22, 1971* (Washington, D.C.: Government Printing Office, 1971); *Listening to Young Voices: White House Conference on Youth* (Washington, D.C.: Government Printing Office, 1971).

45. *Report on the Follow-Up Activities of the 1971 White House Conference on Youth* (Washington, D.C.: Government Printing Office, 1972), 18–21.

46. Helen Baker, "Growing Up Unheard," in Beatrice Gross and Ronald Gross, eds., *The Children's Rights Movement: Overcoming the Oppression of Young People* (Garden City, N.Y.: Anchor Books, 1977), 187–99; Elizabeth Cleaners Street School, *Starting Your Own High School* (New York: Random House, 1972), vii.

47. Thomas Shannon, "Legal Aspects of Confrontation," *Journal of Secondary Education* 45, no. 5 (May 1970): 195–201.

48. "Student Unrest Will Spread," 71; Leslie H. Browder, Jr., "Bergen County Battle Plans: What to Do *Before* Students Demonstrate," *Nation's Schools* 85, no. 4 (April 1970): 86–87.

49. "Student Unrest Will Spread," 71; Fish, "Coping with Activism," 11; Browder, "Bergen County Battle Plans," 86; Christopher Fearon, "Campus Protest and the Administrator," *NASSP Bulletin* 54, no. 338 (September 1969): 28–35.

50. Joseph Stocker, "Cops in the Schoolhouse," *School Management* 12 (May 1968): 46–50; Fish, *Conflict and Dissent*, 45, 52; George Shepard and Jesse James, "Police: Do They Belong In the Schools?" *American Education* 3, no. 8 (September 1967): 2–4. See also *New Free Press*, November 1969, 11, courtesy of Leslie Robbins.

51. Irwin, *Ghetto Principal*, 184–85; *New York Times*, August 14, 1968, 21:6.

52. House Special Select Subcommittee on the District of Columbia, *Problems in the Public School System of the District of Columbia: Hearings before a Special Subcommittee of the Committee on the District of Columbia*, 91st Cong., 2nd sess., May 12, 22; June 11, 15, 17, 23, 25; July 7, 14, 23, 30; August 4, 11; October 14, 1970, 269–377.

53. "What People Think about Their High Schools," 24, 29; "Nonconformity in Administration: Would You Fire This Principal?" *School Management*, February 1969, 79–85.

54. "How Oakland Stiffened Student Discipline," letter from the Oakland [California] Board of Education and School Administration, *Nation's Schools* 83, no. 1 (January 1969): 31; Lesley H. Browder, Jr., "The New American Success Story Is Called Student Confrontation," *American School Board Journal* 157, no. 12 (June 1970): 23–25.

55. "Confidential: For High School Principals Association Use Only, Communique #3," reprinted in Reeves, *Notes of a Processed Brother*, appendix C, 463–72.

56. Ibid.

57. "Student Involvement: Channeling Activism into Accomplishment," *Nation's Schools* 84, no. 3 (September 1969): 39–50; Irwin, *Ghetto Principal*, 146; Beatrice M. Gudridge, *High School Student Unrest* (Washington, D.C.: National School Public Relations Association, 1969), 27–47.

58. Irwin, *Ghetto Principal*, 114.

59. Gudridge, "Is Student Protest Spreading?" 32; Jacob, "Student Views," 20–21; Fish, "Coping with Activism," 9.

60. *San Francisco Examiner*, September 11, 1969, 1:3; Divoky, "The Way It's Going To Be"; Beavan, "New Office," 12; Browder, "New American Success," 25; *New York Times*, May 16, 1971, 51:1; Schaller, Chesler, and Hefner, *Student and Youth Organizing*, 20; Reeves, *Notes of a Processed Brother*, 324, 327.

61. "Student Involvement," 40–41; Bob Klein, "Given a Chance," *Observed* 1, no. 4, Flushing, New York, reprinted in Birmingham, *Our Time Is Now*, 207.

62. "Student Involvement," 46; Charles E. Silberman, *Crisis in the Classroom: The Remaking of American Education* (New York: Random House, 1970), 349–51.

63. Nicholas Pileggi, "Revolutionaries Who Have to Be Home by 7:30," *New York*

Times Magazine, March 14, 1969, 120; Montgomery County Student Alliance, "Wanted: A Humane Education," reprinted in Gene Stanford, ed., *Generation Rap: An Anthology about Youth and the Establishment* (New York: Dell Publishing, 1971), 47.

64. Allen, "Student Unrest in the High Schools," 76; Divoky, "The Way It's Going To Be," 102.

65. "Student Activism," 47; "Worst of Student Disorders," 17.

66. Moffett, *Participation Put-On,* 215–23.

67. *Tinker v. Des Moines.*

EPILOGUE

1. *Lamp,* October 23, 1968; April 16, 1969; December (no date) 1969, courtesy of Susan Bowman Prendergast.

2. *Lamp,* March 13, 1970; May 28, 1970; September 10, 1971; October 29, 1971; February 4, 1972, courtesy of Susan Bowman Prendergast.

3. *Lamp,* May 8, 1970 April 14, 1972; September 25, 1970.

4. Todd Gitlin, "The Liberation of Bronx H.S. of Science," *San Francisco Express Times,* November 13, 1968, reprinted in Mitchell Goodman, comp., *The Movement Toward a New America: The Beginnings of a Long Revolution (A Collage)—A What?* (Philadelphia: Pilgrim Press, 1970), 289; Cheri Yannuzzi, letter to author, June 2, 2000. She included a photocopy of her school newspaper, *Mountaineer,* from April 1970, which covered the protest. Marilyn Hall, e-mail to author, June 6, 2000; Sandra Kral, e-mail to author, May 19, 2000; *New York Times,* October 29, 1969, 46:3.

5. Samuel Huntington, quoted in Stewart Burns, *Social Movements of the 1960s: Searching for Democracy* (Boston: Twayne Publishers, 1990), 175.

6. Toby Moffett, *The Participation Put-On: Reflections of a Disenchanted Washington Youth Expert* (New York: Delacorte Press, 1971), 142–43, 151–52.

7. Tom Wells, *The War Within: America's Battle over Vietnam* (Berkeley: University of California Press, 1994), 108–9; 374; "Spiro Agnew: The King's Taster," *Time* 94, no. 20 (November 14, 1969): 17–22.

8. Thomas Hine, *The Rise and Fall of the American Teenager* (New York: Avon, 1999), 21, 275.

9. Education Commission of the States, ECS StateNotes, "Uniforms/Dress Codes," www.ecs.org/ecsmain.asp?page=/search/default.asp (accessed November 13, 2003); "Girl Booted From Highschool for Dreadlocks," YRFire: The Hub of the Youth Rights Community, www.yrfire.com/story/2002/9/25/214654/794 (accessed February 5, 2004). The two key cases narrowing *Tinker* here are *Hazelwood School District v. Kuhlmeier,* 484 U.S. 260 (1988); and *Bethel School District v. Fraser,* 478 U.S. 675 (1986).

10. Derrick Bell, *Silent Covenants:* Brown v. Board of Education *and the Unfulfilled Hopes for Racial Reform* (Oxford: Oxford University Press, 2004), 127.

11. nces.ed.gov/pubsearch/pubsinfo.asp?pubid=2001033 (accessed January 29, 2004); www.doa.nc.us/dnpe/hhh201.htm (accessed January 29, 2004); nces.ed.gov/fastfacts/display.asp?id=30 (accessed January 27, 2005).

12. Reho F. Thorum, "The High School Student of the Seventies," *High School Journal* 61, no. 1 (October 1977): 27–30.

13. Doug Rossinow, *The Politics of Authenticity; Liberalism, Christianity, and the New Left in America* (New York: Columbia University Press, 1998), 335.

14. Martin Chancy, "The Teaching of Politics in the Secondary Schools in Middle America in the Era of Watergate Coverup," *High School Journal* 58, no. 4 (January 1975): 131–60; Thorum, "Student of the Seventies," 29.

15. *New York Times,* February 26, 2003; American Civil Liberties Union, www.aclu.org/StudentsRights/StudentsRightslist.cfm?c=156 (accessed November 13, 2003).

16. Jonathan Zimmerman discusses school prayer advocates, but it is not clear if these are high school students or solely adults. Zimmerman, *Whose America? Culture*

Wars in the Public Schools (Cambridge, Mass.: Harvard University Press, 2002), 173–83. The ACLU's "In the Courts" website identifies youthful activists who have used the courts to press their demands, at www.alcu.org/court/clients/dweis.html, www.aclu.org/court/clients/acton.html, and www.aclu.org/court/clients/pyles.html (accessed October 10, 2000); other issues for high school students appear on other ACLU sites. See archive.aclu.org/news/no31998a.html; www.aclu~wa.org/issues/students; www.aclu~wa.org/issues/students/Beidler.5.12.00.html;www.aclunc.org/aclunews/news199/students.html; and www.aclunebraska.org/acluneb/litigate/student_rights.htm (all accessed July 6, 2004).

17. See archive.aclu.org/issues/student/hmes.html, www.aclu.org/StudentsRights/StudentsRightsMain.cfm, and www.studentpress.org/nspa (accessed July 6, 2004).

18. www.Radcheers.tripod.com/RC (accessed November 13, 2003).

19. Christine A. Kelly, *Tangled Up in Red, White, and Blue: New Social Movements in America* (Lanham, Md.: Rowman and Littlefield, 2001), chap. 5; Philip G. Altbach and Robert Cohen, "American Student Activism: The Post-Sixties Transformation," *Journal of Higher Education* 61, no. 1 (January/February 1990): 32–49. Note that all of the "students" discussed in this article are college students. For high school students and the invasion of Iraq, see *Mercury News,* February 21, 2003; *IthacaJournal.com,* March 6, 2003; *Asheville Citizen-Times,* March 6, 2003; and *New York Times,* March 6 and 7, 2003. All but the Asheville paper were on-line.

20. yconservatives.com/; www.teenagerepublicans.org/; www.aclu.org/StudentsRights/StudentsRightslist.cfm?c=162 (accessed January 27, 2005).

21. Jean Hartley Davis Sidden, e-mail to author, May 7, 2000; Elizabeth Harzoff, e-mail to author, July 1, 1999; Susan Worley, e-mail to author, May 23, 2000; Sharon Breitweiser, letter to author, October 10, 1999; Gail Marsh, e-mail to author, May 23, 2000.

22. Deborah Astley, letter to author, June 24, 2000; Susan Bowman Prendergast, e-mail to author, June 16, 2000; Paul E. Kohli, letter to author, June 23, 1999.

23. Kathy Goecke, letter to author, September 19, 1999; Jacqueline Rummel Groll, e-mail to author, September 8, 1999; Jan Weiland, e-mail to author, May 5, 2000; "Claire Johnson," letter to author, September 21, 1999; Saralee Etter, e-mail to author, June 14, 1999.

24. Nicholas Pileggi, "Revolutionaries Who Have to Be Home by 7:30," *New York Times Magazine,* March 16, 1969, 122.

SELECTED BIBLIOGRAPHY

PRIMARY SOURCES

PAMPHLETS

American Civil Liberties Union. *Academic Freedom in the Secondary Schools.* September 1968; reprinted December 1969, May 1971.

Bayer, Alan E., Alexander W. Astin, and Robert F. Boruch. *Social Issues and Protest Activity: Recent Student Trends.* ACE Research Reports, vol. 5, no. 2, February 1970. Washington, D.C.: American Council on Education, Office of Research, 1970.

Chesler, Mark. *In Their Own Words: A Student Appraisal of What Happened after School Desegregation.* Atlanta: Southern Regional Council, 1967.

Chinese-Americans: School and Community Problems. Chicago: Integrated Education Associates, 1972.

Dissent and Disruption in the Schools: A Handbooks for School Administrators. Dayton, Ohio: Institute for the Development of Educational Activities, 1969.

Fancher, Betsy. *Voices From the South: Black Students Talks about Their Experiences in Desegregated Schools.* Atlanta: Southern Regional Council, 1970.

Schaller, Jon, Mark Chesler, and Keith Hefner. *Student and Youth Organizing: A Youth Liberation Pamphlet.* Ann Arbor, Mich.: Youth Liberation Press, n.d.

GOVERNMENT DOCUMENTS

Listening to Young Voices: White House Conference on Youth. Washington, D.C.: Government Printing Office, 1971.

Report of the White House Conference on Youth, April 18–22, 1971. Washington, D.C.: U.S. Government Printing Office, 1971.

Report on the Follow-Up Activities of the 1971 White House Conference on Youth. Washington, D.C.: Government Printing Office, 1972.

U.S. Commission on Civil Rights. *A Generation Deprived: Los Angeles School Desegregation: A Report of the U.S. Commission on Civil Rights.* Washington, D.C.: U.S. Commission on Civil Rights, 1977.

U.S. Commission on Civil Rights. *What Students Want: A National Survey Prepared by the U.S. Commission on Civil Rights.* New York: Emerson Hall, 1971.

U.S. Congress. House. Special Select Subcommittee on the District of Columbia. *Problems in the Public School System of the District of Columbia: Hearings before the Special Select Subcommittee of the Committee on the District of Columbia.* 91st Cong., 2d sess., May 12, 22; June 11, 15, 17, 23; July 7, 14, 23, 30; and October 11, 14, 1970.

U.S. Congress. Senate. Committee on Appropriations. *Senate Hearings before the Committee on Appropriations, Department of the Interior and Related Agencies Appropriations.* 92d Cong., 2d sess., April 11, 1972.

U.S. Congress. Senate. Select Committee on Equal Educational Opportunity. *Mexican American Education: Hearings before the Select Committee on Equal Educational Opportunity.* 91st Cong., 2d sess., August 18, 19, 20, 21, 1970.

U.S. Congress. Senate. Select Committee on Equal Educational Opportunity. *Quality and Control of Urban Schools: Hearings before the Select Committee on Equal Educational Opportunity.* 92d Cong., 1st sess., July 27, 29; and August 5, 1971.

JOURNALS

American School Board Journal, 1960–1975
American Education, 1965–1975
Clearing House, 1965–1975
Education Digest, 1965–1975
High School Journal, 1955–1975
Journal of Secondary Education, 1965–1971
National Association of Secondary School Principals [NASSP] Bulletin, 1960–1975
Nation's Schools, 1965–1975
Ohio Schools, 1965–1975
Phi Delta Kappan, 1965–1975
PTA Magazine, 1965–1975
Saturday Review, 1965–1975
School and Society, 1965–1975
School Management, 1960–1975
School Review, 1965–1975
Social Education, 1965–1975
Today's Education, 1965–1975

UNDERGROUND NEWSPAPERS

Underground Newspaper Collection. Underground Press Syndicate and the Photo Division of Bell and Howell, rolls 8, 12, 23, 65, and 86. Wisconsin Historical Society, University of Wisconsin, Madison.

BOOKS

Ackerly, Robert L., and Ivan B. Gluckman. *The Reasonable Exercise of Authority. II.* Reston, Va.: National Association of Secondary School Principals, 1976.

Adams, Julianne Lewis, and Thomas A. DeBlack. *Civil Obedience: An Oral History of School Desegregation in Fayetteville, Arkansas, 1954–1965.* Fayetteville: University of Arkansas Press, 1994.

Albert, Judith Clavir, and Stewart Edward Albert, eds. *The Sixties Papers: Documents of a Rebellious Decade.* New York: Praeger, 1984.

Allen, Dwight W., and Jeffrey C. Hecht, eds. *Controversies in Education.* Philadelphia: W. B. Saunders, 1974.

Bailey, Stephen K. *Disruption in Urban Public Secondary Schools.* Washington, D.C.: National Association of Secondary School Principals, 1970.

Baughman, M. Dale, Wendell G. Anderson, Mark Smith, and Earle W. Wiltse, eds. *Administration and Supervision of the Modern Secondary School.* West Nyack, N.Y.: Parker Publishing, 1969.

Birmingham, John. *Our Time is Now: Notes From the High School Underground.* New York: Praeger, 1970.

Bonacich, Edna, and Robert Goodman. *Deadlock in School Desegregation: A Case Study of Inglewood, California.* New York: Praeger, 1972.

Boskin, Joseph, and Robert Rosenstone. *Protest in the Sixties. Annals of the American Academy of Political and Social Science,* vol. 382. Philadelphia: American Academy of Political and Social Science, 1969.

Brickman, William W., and Stanley Lehrer, eds. *Conflict and Change on the Campus: The Response to Student Hyperactivism.* Cambridge, Mass.: Harvard University Press, 1974.

Cohen, Sol, ed. *Education in the United States: A Documentary History.* New York: Random House, 1974.

Cusick, Philip A. *Inside High School: The Student's World.* New York: Holt, Rinehart, and Winston, 1973.

Divoky, Diane, ed. *How Old Will You Be in 1984? Expressions of Student Outrage From the High School Free Press*. New York: Avon Books, 1969.

Eden, Lynn. *Crisis in Watertown: The Polarization of an American Community*. Ann Arbor: University of Michigan Press, 1972.

Elizabeth Cleaners Street School. *Starting Your Own High School*. New York: Random House, 1972.

Fish, Kenneth L. *Conflict and Dissent in the High Schools*. New York: Bruce Publishing, 1970.

Foster, Julian, and Durand Long, eds. *Protest! Student Activism in America*. New York: William and Morrow, 1970.

Gaddy, Dale. *Rights and Freedoms of Public School Students: Directions from the 1960s*. Topeka, Kans.: National Organization on Legal Problems of Education, 1971.

Golloaday, Mary A., and Jay Noell, eds. *The Condition of Education, Statistical Report*. National Center for Education Statistics, U.S. Department of Health, Education, and Welfare, 1978.

Goodman, Mitchell, comp. *The Movement Toward A New America: The Beginnings of a Long Revolution (A Collage)—A What?* Philadelphia: Pilgrim Press, 1970.

Greene, Bob. *Be True to Your School: A Diary of 1964*. New York: Atheneum, 1987.

Gudridge, Beatrice M. *High School Student Unrest*. Washington, D.C.: National School Public Relations Association, 1969.

Halstead, Fred. *Out Now! A Participant's Account of the American Movement against the Vietnam War*. New York: Monad Press, 1978.

Hampton, Henry, and Steve Fayer. *Voices of Freedom: An Oral History of the Civil Rights Movement from the 1950s through the 1980s*. New York: Bantam Books, 1990.

Hendrick, Irving G., and Reginald L. Jones, eds. *Student Dissent in the Schools*. Boston: Houghton Mifflin, 1971.

Irwin, James Ross. *A Ghetto Principal Speaks Out: A Decade of Crisis in Urban Public Schools*. Detroit: Wayne State University Press, 1973.

Libarle, Marc, and Tom Seligson, eds. *The High School Revolutionaries*. New York: Random House, 1970.

Lipset, Seymour Martin, and Philip G. Altbach, eds. *Students in Revolt*. Boston: Beacon Press, 1970.

Moffett, Toby. *The Participation Put-On: Reflections of a Disenchanted Washington Youth Expert*. New York: Delacorte Press, 1971.

Morrison, Joan, and Robert K. Morrison. *From Camelot to Kent State: The Sixties Experience in the Words of Those Who Lived It*. New York: Oxford University Press, 1987.

Nader, Ralph, and Donald Ross, with Brent English and Joseph Highland. *Action for a Change: A Student's Manual for Public Interest Organizing*. New York: Grossman Publishers, 1972.

Ornstein, Allan C. *Urban Education: Student Unrest, Teacher Behaviors, and Black Power*. Columbus, Ohio: Charles E. Merrill, 1972.

Parker, Don. *Schooling for What?* New York: McGraw-Hill, 1970.

Petroni, Frank A., and Ernest A. Hirsch, with C. Lillian Petroni. *Two, Four, Six, Eight, When You Gonna Integrate?* Morningside Heights, N.Y.: Behavioral Problems, 1970.

Rapoport, Roger, and Laurence J. Kirshbaum. *Is the Library Burning?* New York: Random House, 1969.

Reeves, Donald. *Notes of a Processed Brother*. New York: Pantheon, 1972.

Rinehart, Alice Duffy. *Mortals in the Immortal Profession: An Oral History of Teaching*. New York: Irvington Publishers, 1983.

Rossner, Robert. *The Year Without an Autumn: Portrait of a School in Crisis*. New York: Richard W. Baron, 1969.

Ryan, Kevin, ed. *Don't Smile Until Christmas: Accounts of the First Year Teaching*. Chicago: University of Chicago Press, 1970.

Saltzman, Harold. *Race War in High School: The Ten-Year Destruction of Franklin K. Lane High School in Brooklyn*. New Rochelle, N.Y.: Arlington House, 1972.

Sampson, Edward E., and Harold A. Korn. *Student Activism and Protest: Alternatives for Social Change.* San Francisco: Jossey-Bass, 1970.

Silberman, Charles E. *Crisis in the Classroom: The Remaking of American Education.* New York: Random House, 1970.

Stanford, Gene, ed. *Generation Rap: An Anthology of Youth and the Establishment.* New York: Dell Publishing, 1971.

Teodori, Massimo, ed. *The New Left: A Documentary History.* Indianapolis: Bobbs-Merrill, 1969.

Williams, Sylvia. *Hassling.* Boston: Little, Brown, 1970.

Wittes, Simon. *People and Power: A Study of Crisis in the Secondary Schools.* Ann Arbor: Institute for Social Research, University of Michigan, 1970.

SECONDARY SOURCES

BOOKS

Adair, Alvis V. *Desegregation: The Illusion of Black Progress.* Lanham, Md.: University Press of America, 1984.

Andrew, John A., III. *The Other Side of the Sixties: Young Americans for Freedom and the Rise of Conservative Politics.* New Brunswick, N.J.: Rutgers University Press, 1997.

Asinof, Eliot. *Craig and Joan: Two Lives for Peace.* New York: Viking Press, 1971.

Atkinson, Pansye. *Brown vs. Topeka: An African American's View: Desegregation and Miseducation.* Chicago: African American Images, 1993.

Bell, Derrick. *Silent Covenants: Brown vs. Board of Education and the Unfulfilled Hopes for Racial Reform.* Oxford: Oxford University Press, 2004.

Braunstein, Peter, and Michael William Doyle, eds. *Imagine Nation: The American Counterculture of the 1960s and '70s.* New York: Routledge, 2002.

Burner, David. *Making Peace with the Sixties.* Princeton, N.J.: Princeton University Press, 1996.

Burns, Stewart. *Social Movements of the 1960s: Searching for Democracy.* Boston: Twayne Publishers, 1990.

Casey, Kathleen. *I Answer with My Life: Life Histories of Women Teachers Working for Social Change.* New York: Routledge, 1993.

Cavallo, Dominick. *A Fiction of the Past: The Sixties in American History.* New York: St. Martin's Press, 1999.

Cecelski, David S. *Along Freedom Road: Hyde County, North Carolina, and the Fate of Black Schools in the South.* Chapel Hill: University of North Carolina Press, 1994.

Cunningham, Patricia A., and Susan Vaso Lab, eds. *Dress and Popular Culture.* Bowling Green, Ohio: Bowling Green State University Popular Press, 1991.

DeBenedetti, Charles. *An American Ordeal: The Antiwar Movement of the Vietnam Era.* Syracuse, N.Y.: Syracuse University Press, 1990.

Dittmer, John. *Local People: The Struggle for Civil Rights in Mississippi.* Urbana: University of Illinois Press, 1994.

Douglas, Davison M. *Reading, Writing, and Race: The Desegregation of the Charlotte Schools.* Chapel Hill: University of North Carolina Press, 1995.

Egerton, John. *Speak Now against the Day: The Generation before the Civil Rights Movement in the South.* Chapel Hill: University of North Carolina Press, 1995.

Escobar, Edward J. "The Dialectics of Repression: The Los Angeles Police Department and the Chicano Movement, 1968–1971." *Journal of American History* 79, no. 4 (March 1993): 1483–514.

Fairclough, Adam. *Race and Democracy: The Civil Rights Struggle in Louisiana, 1915–1972.* Athens: University of Georgia Press, 1995.

Formisano, Ronald P. *Boston Against Busing: Race, Class, and Ethicity in the 1960s and 1970s.* Chapel Hill: University of North Carolina Press, 1991.

García, F. Chris, ed. *La Causa Política: A Chicano Politics Reader*. Notre Dame, Ind.: University of Notre Dame, 1974.

García, Ignacio M. *Chicanismo: The Forging of a Militant Ethos among Mexican Americans*. Tucson: University of Arizona Press, 1997.

Gilbert, James. *A Cycle of Outrage: America's Reaction to the Juvenile Delinquent in the 1950s*. New York: Oxford University Press, 1986.

Gitlin, Todd. *The Sixties: Years of Hope, Days of Rage*. New York: Bantam Books, 1993.

———. *The Whole World is Watching: Mass Media in the Making and Unmaking of the New Left*. Berkeley: University of California Press, 1980.

Glessing, Robert J. *The Underground Press in America*. Bloomington: Indiana University Press, 1970.

Gómez, David. *Somos Chicanos: Strangers in Our Own Land*. Boston: Beacon Press, 1973.

Graebner, William. *Coming of Age in Buffalo: Youth and Authority in the Post-War Era*. Philadelphia: Temple University Press, 1990.

Graham, Gael. "Flaunting the Freak Flag: *Karr v. Schmidt* and the Great Hair Debate in American High Schools, 1965–1975," *Journal of American History* 91, no. 2 (September 2004): 522–43.

Gross, Beatrice, and Ronald Gross, eds. *The Children's Rights Movement: Overcoming the Oppression of Young People*. Garden City, N.Y.: Anchor Press, 1977.

Gutek, Gerald. *American Education, 1945–2000: A History and Commentary*. Prospect Heights, Ill.: Waveland Press, 2000.

Henriksen, Margot A. *Dr. Strangelove's America: Society and Culture in the Atomic Age*. Berkeley: University of California Press, 1997.

Hine, Thomas. *The Rise and Fall of the American Teenager*. New York: Bard, 1999.

Isserman, Maurice. *If I Had a Hammer: The Death of the Old Left and the Birth of the New Left*. Urbana: University of Illinois Press, 1993.

Johnson, John W. *The Struggle for Student Rights: Tinker v. Des Moines and the 1960s*. Lawrence: University Press of Kansas, 1997.

Kelly, Christine A. *Tangled Up in Red, White, and Blue: New Social Movements in America*. Lanham, Md.: Rowman and Littlefield, 2001.

Lukas, J. Anthony. *Common Ground: A Turbulent Decade in the Lives of Three American Families*. New York: Vintage Books, 1985.

Margolis, Maxine. *True to Her Nature: Changing Advice to American Women*. Prospect Heights, Ill: Waveland Press, 2000.

Meyerowitz, Joanne, ed. *Not June Cleaver: Women and Gender in Postwar America, 1945–1960*. Philadelphia: Temple University Press, 1994,

Muñoz, Carlos, Jr. *Youth, Identity, Power: The Chicano Movement*. London: Verso, 1989.

Oakley, Ronald. *God's Country: America in the Fifties*. New York: Bembner Books, 1986.

Owram, Doug. *Born at the Right Time: A History of the Baby-Boom Generation*. Toronto: University of Toronto Press, 1996.

Palladino, Grace. *Teenagers: An American History*. New York: Basic Books, 1996.

Patterson, James T. *Grand Expectations: The United States, 1945–1974*. New York: Oxford University Press, 1996.

Payne, Charles M. *I've Got the Light of Freedom: The Organizing Tradition and the Mississippi Freedom Struggle*. Berkeley: University of California Press, 1995.

Peck, Abe. *Uncovering the Sixties: The Life and Times of the Underground Press*. New York: Pantheon Books, 1985.

Podair, Jerald E. *The Strike That Changed New York: Blacks, Whites, and the Ocean Hill-Brownsville Crisis*. New Haven, Conn.: Yale University Press, 2002.

Ravitch, Diane. *The Great School Wars: A History of the New York City Public Schools*. New York: Basic Books, 1988.

———. *The Troubled Crusade: American Education, 1945–1980*. New York: Basic Books, 1983.

Reams, Bernard D., Jr., and Paul E. Wilson, eds. *Segregation and the Fourteenth Amendment in the States: A Survey of State Segregation Laws, 1865–1953: Prepared for the United States Supreme Court in re,* Brown v. Board of Education of Topeka. Buffalo: W. S. Hein, 1975.

Rosen, Ruth. *The World Split Open: How the Modern Women's Movement Changed America.* New York: Viking, 2000.

Rossell, Christine H., and Hawley, Willis D., eds. *The Consequences of School Desegregation.* Philadelphia: Temple University Press, 1983.

Rossinow, Douglas C. *The Politics of Authenticity: Liberalism, Christianity, and the New Left in America.* New York: Columbia University Press, 1998.

Sale, Kirkpatrick. *SDS.* New York: Random House, 1973.

San Miguel, Guadalupe, Jr. *"Let All of Them Take Heed": Mexican Americans and the Campaign for Educational Equality in Texas, 1910–1981.* Austin: University of Texas Press, 1987.

Schneider, Gregory L. *Cadres for Conservatism: Young Americans for Freedom and the Rise of the Contemporary Right.* New York: New York University Press, 1999.

Shelton, David E. "The Legal Aspects of Male Students' Hair Grooming Policies in the Public Schools of the United States." PhD diss., University of North Carolina, 1980.

Shockley, John Staples. *Chicano Revolt in a Texas Town.* Notre Dame, Ind.: University of Notre Dame Press, 1974.

Shujaa, Mwalimu J., ed. *Beyond Desegregation: The Politics of Quality in African American Schools.* Thousand Oaks, Calif.: Corwin Press, 1996.

Simon, Diane. *Hair: Public, Political, and Extremely Personal.* New York: St. Martin's Press, 2000.

Skolnick, Arlene. *Embattled Paradise: The American Family in an Age of Uncertainty.* New York: Basic Books, 1991.

Small, Melvin. *Antiwarriors: The Vietnam War and the Battle for America's Hearts and Minds.* Wilmington, Del.: Scholarly Resources, 2000.

Spann, Edward K. *Democracy's Children: The Young Rebels of the 1960s and the Power of Ideals.* Wilmington, Del.: Scholarly Resources, 2003.

Stephens, Julie. *Anti-Disciplinary Protest: Sixties Radicalism and Postmodernism.* Cambridge: Cambridge University Press, 1998.

Sybouts, Ward, and Wayne Krepel. *Student Activities in the Secondary Schools: A Handbook and Guide.* Westport, Conn.: Greenwood Press, 1984.

Tashakkori, Abbas, and Salvador Hector Ochoa, eds. *Education of Hispanics in the United States.* Vol. 16 of *Readings on Equal Education.* New York: AMS Press, 1999.

Thompson, Kathleen, and Hilary MacAustin, eds. *Children of the Depression.* Bloomington: University of Indiana Press, 2001.

Tyack, David. *The One Best System: A History of American Urban Education.* Cambridge, Mass.: Harvard University Press, 1974.

Tyack, David, and Elizabeth Hansot. *Managers of Virtue: Public School Leadership in America, 1820–1980.* New York: Basic Books, 1982.

Varon, Jeremy. *Bringing the War Home: The Weather Underground, the Red Army Faction, and Revolutionary Violence in the Sixties and Seventies.* Berkeley: University of California Press, 2004.

Vigil, Ernesto B. *The Crusade for Justice: Chicano Militancy and the Government's War on Dissent.* Madison: University of Wisconsin Press, 1999.

Walker, Samuel. *In Defense of American Liberties: A History of the ACLU.* New York: Oxford University Press, 1990.

Walker, Vanessa Siddle. *Their Highest Potential: An African American School Community in the Segregated South.* Chapel Hill: University of North Carolina Press, 1996.

Watkins, T. H. *The Hungry Years: A Narrative History of the Great Depression.* New York: Henry Holt, 1999.

Wells, Tom. *The War Within: America's Battle over Vietnam.* Berkeley: University of California Press, 1994.

Weyr, Thomas. *Hispanic U.S.A.: Breaking the Melting Pot.* New York: Harper & Row, 1988.

Wilkinson, J. Harvie. *From* Brown *to* Bakke: *The Supreme Court and School Integration, 1954–1978.* New York: Oxford University Press, 1979.

Zimmerman, Jonathan. *Whose America? Culture Wars in the Public Schools.* Cambridge, Mass.: Harvard University Press, 2002.

WEBSITES

"About Jonathan Wallace," www.spectacle.org/bio.html, accessed January 7, 2005.

American Civil Liberties Union,

> www.aclu.org/StudentsRights/StudentsRightslist.cfm?c=156, accessed November 13, 2003.

> www.aclu.org/court/clients/dweis.html, accessed October 10, 2000.

> www.aclu.org/court/clients/acton.html, accessed October 10, 2000.

> www.aclu.org/court/clients/pyles, accessed Octover 10, 2000.

> archive.aclu.org/issues/student/hmes.html, accessed July 6, 2004.

> www.aclu.org/StudentsRights/StudentsRightsMain.cfm, accessed July 6, 2004.

> www.aclu.org/StudentsRights/StudentsRightslist.cfm?c=162, accessed January 27, 2005.

www.doa.nc.us/dnpe/hhh201.htm, accessed January 29, 2004.

Education Commission of the States, ECS StateNotes, "Uniforms/Dress Codes," www.ecs.org/ecsmain.asp?page=search/default.asp, accessed November 13, 2003.

"Girl Booted From Highschool [*sic*] for Dreadlocks," YRFire: The Hub of the Youth Rights Community, www.yrfire.com/story/2002/9/25/214654/794, accessed February 5, 2004.

"Kent State, May 4, 1970: America Kills its Children," *Ethical Spectacle,* May 1995, www.spectacle.org/595/kent.html, accessed January 7, 2005.

www.nces.ed.gov/pubsearch/pubsinfo.asp?pubid=2001033, accessed January 29, 2004.

www.nces.ed.gov/fastfacts/display.asp?id=30, accessed January 27, 2005.

www.Radcheers.tripod.com/RC, accessed November 13, 2003.

Stewart, Bhob [*sic*], All Movie Guide, *New York Times.* movies2nytimes.com/gst/movies/movie.html.vid=140936, accessed December, 13, 2004.

www.studentpress.org/nspa, accessed July 6, 2004.

www.teenagerepublicans.org, accessed January 27, 2005.

www.yconservatives.com, accessed January 27, 2005.

INDEX